Reflections on Liszt

Alan Walker

Reflections on Liszt

CORNELL UNIVERSITY PRESS
ITHACA AND LONDON

First published 2005 by Cornell University Press
First printing, Cornell Paperbacks, 2011

Printed in the United States of America

Library of Congress Cataloging-in-Publication Data

Walker, Alan, 1930–
    Reflections on Liszt / Alan Walker.
        p. cm.
Includes bibliographical references (p.   ) and index.
    ISBN 978-0-8014-4363-3 (cloth : alk. paper)
    ISBN 978-0-8014-7758-4 (pbk. : alk. paper)
    1. Liszt, Franz, 1811–1886—Criticism and interpretation. 2. Music—19th
century—History and criticism. I. Title.
    ML410.L7W296 2005
    780'.92—dc22   2004030467

Cornell University Press strives to use environmentally responsible suppliers
and materials to the fullest extent possible in the publishing of its books.
Such materials include vegetable-based, low-VOC inks and acid-free papers
that are recycled, totally chlorine-free, or partly composed of nonwood
fibers. For further information, visit our website at
www.cornellpress.cornell.edu.

Cloth printing   10 9 8 7 6 5 4 3 2 1
Paperback printing   10 9 8 7 6 5 4 3 2 1

For Valerie Tryon,
whose peerless interpretations of the music of Franz Liszt
have spoiled many another pianist for me

Contents

List of Illustrations   ix

Acknowledgments   xi

Prologue   xiii

1. Beethoven's *Weihekuss* Revisited   1

2. Liszt and the Beethoven Symphonies   11

3. Liszt and the Schubert Song Transcriptions   27

4. Schumann, Liszt, and the C Major Fantasie, op. 17:
   A Study in Declining Relationships   40

5. Liszt and His Pupils: Three Character Sketches   51

   Carl Tausig: A Polish Wunderkind   60

   Hans von Bülow: Heir and Successor   79

   Walter Bache: An English Disciple of Liszt   106

6. Liszt's Sonata in B Minor   128

7. Liszt and the Lied   150

8. Liszt as Editor   175

9. Liszt's *Technical Studies:* Some Thoughts and Afterthoughts   202

10. Liszt the Writer: On Music and Musicians   217

Epilogue: An Open Letter to Franz Liszt   239

Sources   257

Index   263

Illustrations

1. Beethoven embraces the eleven-year-old Liszt at the boy's "farewell" concert in Vienna, April 13, 1823. A fictional scene depicted in an 1873 lithograph by István Halász. 2

2. An 1873 lithograph by István Halász. Top left: Beethoven's imaginary embrace of Liszt. Bottom left: Liszt's birthplace metamorphosed. Bottom right: an imaginary statue of Liszt. 10

3. The original title page of Liszt's piano transcriptions of the Beethoven symphonies (1865), bearing the dedication to Hans von Bülow. 18

4. The manuscript title page of Schumann's C Major Fantasie, op. 17, with its dedication to Franz Liszt. 43

5. The manuscript first page of Schumann's C Major Fantasie, op. 17, with its original title "Ruinen" crossed out by the composer. 44

6. The manuscript last page of Schumann's C Major Fantasie, op. 17, with its original ending crossed out and replaced with the "official" ending. 45

7. The Altenburg. A nineteenth-century woodcut, based on a drawing by Carl Jordan. 52

8. Liszt in the Hofgärtnerei, 1882, surrounded by his pupils and colleagues. An oil painting by Hans W. Schmidt. Front row, right, the Grand Duke of Weimar Carl Alexander, with his wife, Grand Duchess Sophie, listens attentively to Liszt's playing. 54

9. Carl Tausig. An engraving by A. Weger. 73

10. Hans von Bülow at the piano, 1884. A photograph. 96

11. Hans von Bülow on his deathbed, 1894. A photograph. 104

12. Walter Bache, ca. 1887. A photograph. 110

13. Program of an all-Liszt recital by Walter Bache, St. James's Hall, London, October 22, 1883. 120

14. Liszt plays in the concert hall of the old Royal Academy of Music, Tenterden Street, London, April 6, 1886. An illustration by Batt, based on eyewitness accounts. 121

15. The title page of Franz Liszt's edition of the Beethoven sonatas, 1857. 180

16. The title page of Franz Liszt's edition of Schubert's impromptus, op. 90, 1870. 187

17. Cast of Liszt's left hand. A photograph. 212

Acknowledgments

I would like to express my thanks to Mária Eckhardt and the staff of the library of the Liszt Research Centre, Budapest, for their scholarly support on all my visits to Hungary; to the Manuscript Department of the National Széchényi Library, Hungary, for the loan of photographic materials; to Dr. Jane Gottlieb and the staff of the Lila Acheson Library of the Juilliard School, New York; to John Sheppard and the staff of the Lincoln Center Library for the Performing Arts, New York; to the staff of the Music and Rare Books Division of the British Library, London; to Dr. Horst Förster, who provided some important background information for my essays on Tausig and Bülow; to Janet Snowman, librarian of the Royal Academy of Music, London, for making available documents related to Walter Bache; to Gregor Benko, for drawing my attention to some unpublished Bülow correspondence; to William Wright for directing me to the first performance of Liszt's Sonata in B Minor in England; to Dr. William Renwick, who prepared the music examples; and to Pauline Pocknell, who read the entire book in typescript, and, by spotting a number of errors, rescued me from ineptitude.

ALAN WALKER

Prologue

I

The impulse to write the present book arose from a desire to pursue certain topics that had to be glossed over in the course of publishing my three-volume life of Franz Liszt.[1] Voltaire once reminded us, "If you would be dull, tell all." My Liszt biography spanned more than 1,600 pages; even so, in consequence of Voltaire's injunction, it remained highly compressed. Such was the variety of Liszt's life and work, in fact, that there were some things that could be mentioned only in passing, and others not at all. These included his activities as a writer and critic; his important contributions to the Lied; his attachment to the memory of Beethoven; his work as an editor of Schubert, Chopin, Weber, and others; his unusual approach to piano technique; and, above all, the powerful influence he exerted on the lives of his most important pupils, which continued long after they had ceased to study with him. I promised myself that I would one day return to these topics in order to elaborate on them, and it is a pleasure to do so now.

II

Toward the end of his life Liszt was asked why he never wrote his autobiography. "It is enough to have lived such a life as mine," he replied. The remark was entirely typical of his self-irony. It was indeed a life filled with color and with incidents so graphic that the whole of Europe was riveted by them. Marked by triumph and marred by tragedy, Liszt was the first to acknowledge the strange paradox that he was so busy living his life that he had no time to write it. That was a great loss to history. Other composers, after all, had written notable autobiographies, including his great contemporaries Richard Wagner and Hector Berlioz. Liszt could have left them both standing at the post, for he had an amazing tale to tell. Alas, he left it to others to do so, and much mischief was created along the way.

1. WFL, vols. 1–3.

There is surely no other composer in history whose daily existence was filled with such kaleidoscopic variety. As a boy, Liszt met Beethoven; as an elderly man he was introduced to Debussy. Between times he got to know practically every musician of importance and was on nodding terms with many of the crowned heads of Europe. His career unfolded in at least five directions simultaneously: pianist, conductor, composer, teacher, and tireless administrator. And in each of these fields he created something new. In the 1830s and 1840s, for example, he evolved a new style of piano playing and introduced the solo "recital"—a word he appropriated in June 1840 and which all pianists since then have used. In the 1850s he invented the symphonic poem, his reply to the classical symphony, and introduced to the podium new techniques of conducting. He also administered some great international festivals at Weimar, featuring the music of Wagner, Berlioz, and Schumann. In teaching he introduced the concept of the masterclass and mentored pianists of the caliber of Carl Tausig, Hans von Bülow, Moriz Rosenthal, and Eugène d'Albert. Then there was his private life, which brought him much notoriety and included several widely publicized liaisons with interesting women (one of whom, Countess Marie d'Agoult, bore him three children, and another of whom, Olga Janina, planned to kill him and then commit suicide, failing in both endeavors). The fact that Liszt attempted to find solace from the storms of life by entering the lower orders of the Catholic Church when he was fifty-three years old simply added to the fascination. Merely to report the facts is to run the risk of being accused of writing fiction.

In the end it was left to Lina Ramann to take on the role of his official biographer. Her work has been much maligned, but she made the best of difficult circumstances, and Liszt willingly gave her personal interviews, supplementing them with more than 150 handwritten replies to various questionnaires she mailed out to him in the 1870s as he crisscrossed his way through Europe on those endless journeys of his. Liszt's responses reveal him to have been a truth teller of the first order, the Doubting Thomases of Liszt scholarship notwithstanding, who staked their reputations on his lack of integrity, and lost.[2]

III

There was one source of biographical material to which Ramann was obviously denied access: Liszt's personal correspondence. Liszt is known to have written more than 10,000 letters to about 1,000 correspondents across the world.[3] By the year 1875, when Liszt was in his midsixties, we find him complaining that he was re-

2. Ernest Newman's character assassination of Liszt in his *The Man Liszt* (London, 1934) and Emile Haraszti's *Liszt* (Paris, 1967) are prime examples of books written in that spirit of perversity that was fashionable in Liszt scholarship fifty or more years ago. The Ramann questionnaires were always available for scrutiny in the Goethe-Schiller Archive at Weimar, although they were not published until 1983, under the title *Lisztiana: Erinnerungen an Franz Liszt*. They are still underappreciated by scholars.

3. This, at any rate, is the conservative estimate provided by Charles Suttoni in his authoritative *Liszt Correspondence in Print: An Expanded, Annotated Bibliography*, 2nd ed., *Journal of the American Liszt Society* 25 (1989), with a supplement published ten years later by the same journal: 46 (1999).

ceiving upward of 50 letters a week, "not counting shipments of manuscripts, pamphlets, books, dedications, and all kinds of music." It amounted to 200 letters a month, or 2,500 a year. "Some ask for concerts, for advice, for recommendations; others for money, for jobs, for decorations, etc.," he wrote.[4] He was the first to recognize that the time taken to deal with this correspondence would have been far better spent in creating new music. Yet deal with it he did. He wrote from his homes in Weimar, Rome, and Budapest; from hotels, from private residences where he stayed as a guest; and even from the trains transporting him (often at night) from one city to another. Perhaps the most astonishing thing of all is that many of the letters went through preliminary drafts, their final texts being revised before they were dispatched. These "Konzeptbriefe" are often more revealing than the letters themselves, because they confess true sentiments Liszt later thought it better not to disclose. In sheer bulk, then, Liszt's epistolary legacy is astounding. His letters are the autobiography that he claimed he never had the time to write.

That is why his correspondence is proving to be by far the most valuable resource that we have in writing about Liszt's life and music. His letters teem with details about his daily activities. He talks to friends and colleagues about his work-in-progress; he delivers opinions on music and musicians, both past and present; he outlines his theoretical picture of music; he replies to his critics; he gives advice on musical interpretation; and on occasion he even enters the arena of music analysis and offers tantalizing clues as to the internal structure of certain of his compositions. Time and again, the letters provide solutions to those perennial puzzles of musicology, the what, where, how, and when of the matter. Not surprisingly, they are also the source to which the narrative of these *Reflections* most frequently turns.

IV

Liszt's creative process sets him apart from other composers, as a few comparisons will make clear. Unlike Beethoven, he wrote with extreme rapidity, and he would often work on three or four scores simultaneously, editing for good measure the music of others while preparing articles for the press as he did so. Unlike Wagner, for whom the slightest commotion was anathema, Liszt seemed to be able to compose in any environment. Whether he was enjoying the tranquillity of his cell in Rome's Madonna del Rosario, or enduring the hurly-burly of life in a post chaise transporting him along bumpy roads from one town to another during his years as a vagabond virtuoso, the music continued to flow from his pen. His pupil, Berthold Kellermann, once visited Liszt in his hotel room in Marienbad and found the master at his desk, engrossed in the composition of a new work. After bidding Kellermann welcome, he went on composing, chatting to him in the friendliest manner, all the while covering the manuscript paper with notes.[5] That sets him apart from

---

4. WLLM, p. 213.
5. KE, pp. 31–32.

Chopin, who was almost incapable of composing without a piano in the room. Liszt was indifferent to the absence of a keyboard while he put pen to paper, although he certainly liked to try out his compositions at the piano when they were finished. Then there was his unusual ability to compose straight into full orchestral score, and not leave for a later time the instrumentation or coloring of the music. That is how the "Gretchen" movement from the *Faust* Symphony was composed, and much of the oratorio *Christus* as well. Neither Schumann nor Brahms possessed this ability to any degree; at any rate, they are not known to have practiced it. As for Liszt's revisions, they put him into a class by himself. Many of his compositions, especially the early ones, underwent radical transformations. Some of them exist in three or more versions. On occasion the changes are so extreme as to constitute a new work. His students collected ample evidence, in their personal copies of his scores, of his ceaseless interest in changing the surface details of his music—be it adding new measures; subtracting old ones; changing the harmony here and there; providing variants, *ossias,* and optional cadenzas; or even composing two different endings to the same work, while leaving the choice to the performer. Throughout his life he returned obsessively to music once thought finished, driven by discontent, even after it had been published. Liszt destroyed neither his sketches nor those early versions of works he replaced by later ones. He saved everything, although as a result of his itinerant lifestyle some worthy items were lost. Unlike Brahms, he would never knowingly have made a bonfire of his earlier manuscripts. The result is a fascinating glimpse into the composer's workshop. As we compare one version with another, the old conundrum returns to haunt us: "Where does music's true identity lie?" With Liszt the answer is, "Not necessarily in the most recent version"; surprisingly, there is little evidence that he regarded a revision in the usual way, as an improvement. Often it was simply a variation on what had gone before. Liszt might well have agreed with W. H. Auden, who used to say of poetry that it was never finished, simply abandoned. And there is one other thing worth noting. Liszt's activity as a composer spanned more than sixty-five years, which makes him almost unique among the Romantics. His first compositions date from his childhood, his last from just a few weeks before his death. That is a very long time, and what makes it more noteworthy still is that with but two short interruptions[6] the flow of music was continuous. The complete catalog of Liszt's works tells it all. It presently stands at more than 1,400 individual compositions. That is more than the outputs of Chopin, Schumann, and Brahms combined.

Finally, there is Liszt's theoretical picture of music. For Liszt, art was God given; it followed that something had to be given back. It became an ethical imperative for him, well expressed in his device "Génie oblige!"—"Genius has obligations!" He adapted it from the French aristocracy, which used to proclaim, "Noblesse oblige!" Those born to title and wealth have a duty to help those not so fortunately en-

---

6. The first followed the death of his father, Adam Liszt, in the summer of 1827. After composing a brief "Marche funèbre" on August 30, the day after the funeral, Liszt appears to have stopped composing for a period of two years. The second occurred in the 1870s, when he suffered a series of mental depressions that temporarily paralyzed his pen.

dowed. How much greater, Liszt argued, are the obligations of genius! He went on to draw a profound conclusion: Music functions best when placed in the service of some ethical or humanitarian cause. For the first time in history, musicians were being told to give something back. That was a noble ideal, and the fact that Liszt was the first to articulate it secures for him a special place in the minds of musicians. A river of gold may have poured in, especially during his halcyon years as a performer, but a river of gold also poured out. Victims of flood and fire, charitable causes, hospitals, cathedral building funds, schools and academies—whatever the appeal, Liszt responded to them all. There has been nothing like it in the history of music.

These themes informed Liszt's daily life, and they emerge with wonderful clarity in the ten *Reflections* that follow. However diverse the topic—Liszt as a teacher, as a champion of Beethoven, as a transcriber of Schubert, as a pianist, editor, or author—this idea of music as an ethical force illuminated whatever he touched. His Scottish pupil, Frederic Lamond, once called Liszt "the good Samaritan of music."[7] It is a fitting epithet with which we are unable to disagree.

7. LML, p. 74.

Reflections on Liszt

Beethoven's Weihekuss *Revisited*

The report of a Kiss from Beethoven after the concert cannot be true.
WALTHER NOHL[1]

"But you received it."
"Naturally I received it!"
LISZT IN CONVERSATION WITH LINA RAMANN[2]

I

On October 30, 1873, Liszt boarded a train in Rome and crossed the border into Hungary. The train was halted at least twice, first at Esztergom and again at Vác, where local dignitaries waited on the platform to extend their greetings to Liszt. As it drew into Budapest's main terminus, a group of prominent Hungarians stepped forward to meet the composer as he alighted from his carriage, including his old friend Baron Antal Augusz, the composer Henrik Gobbi, and the sculptor Pál Kugler. What was the purpose of Liszt's trip? And why was he the object of such a special outpouring of affection on this occasion?

His visit to Hungary had been carefully planned for months. It was a double celebration. First, it marked an important milestone in the history of the nation: the merging of the twin cities of Pest and Buda into the modern capital of Budapest. Some important ceremonies had been arranged to commemorate the event, and it was natural that Hungary's leading expatriates, among whom Liszt was pre-eminent, should return home for the celebrations. But in Liszt's case a second, more personal reason prevailed. This homecoming was also intended to celebrate the fiftieth anniversary of his public career, which was generally regarded as having begun in Vienna's Redoutensaal, on April 13, 1823, when he was a boy of eleven, and when, so rumor had it, he had received a *Weihekuss,* or public "kiss of consecration," from Beethoven.

Baron Augusz and the others drove Liszt directly to his new apartments at no. 4, Fischplatz, a building that had recently been acquired by the Hungarian government for the purpose of housing the first Royal Hungarian Academy of Music, with

1. NLB, p. 309.
2. NZfM, November 1891, no. 47, p. 503.

Beethoven embraces the eleven-year-old Liszt at the boy's "farewell" concert in Vienna, April 13, 1823. (A fictional scene depicted in an 1873 lithograph by István Halász.)

Liszt as its president. Four days (November 8 to 11) had been set aside for the Jubilee concerts in Budapest, but other celebrations were planned in nearby Esztergom and Pressburg as well. By far the most important event was the first, uncut performance of Liszt's oratorio *Christus,* on November 9, conducted by Hans Richter.[3] On November 23 there would also be a performance of the *Gran* Mass in Pressburg. Between times, Liszt was expected to attend a grueling round of concerts, recitals, and banquets, many held in his honor.

    Amid the clamor surrounding this visit, and the festivities within the city generally, an event took place which passed almost unnoticed. A commemorative lithograph was circulated by the publishing house of István Halász; it consisted of a series of tableaux symbolizing events in Liszt's life. One of these pictures depicted Beethoven embracing the young Liszt at that public concert in Vienna fifty years earlier; Beethoven has advanced toward the piano to place a "kiss of consecration" on the child's brow. Few people bothered to question the truthfulness of this scene; after all, the legend of the *Weihekuss* had been in circulation for half a century and Liszt had done nothing to deny it; in fact, he had actively encouraged it. But we can say with certainty that Beethoven never attended this concert. To explain why, we have to go back to the event itself.

   3. The first performance had taken place in Weimar a few months earlier, on May 29, under Liszt's direction, and it had been heavily abridged. On that occasion Liszt had authorized cuts totaling 806 measures (WFL, vol. 2, p. 323, n. 39).

II

By April 1823, the Liszt family had been in Vienna for about fourteen months, during which time the boy had received piano lessons almost daily from Carl Czerny. Adam Liszt, the father, was now anxious to present his talented son to the world, and decided to mount a "farewell" concert designed to attract the maximum amount of publicity in the Austrian capital, before he and his son set out for Paris in pursuit of further success abroad. The small Redoutensaal was booked and the concert announced for Sunday, April 13. Adam knew that there was no better way to guarantee a success than inviting Beethoven to attend the concert, and perhaps persuading him to provide a theme on which his son might improvise. The contacts that might make such a plan possible were already in place. Carl Czerny had been a pupil of Beethoven, and through him the necessary approach could be made to Beethoven's amanuensis Anton Schindler with a request to arrange a meeting with Beethoven. The deaf composer's *Conversation Books* do, in fact, contain an authentic record of this visit. It is well known that Schindler tampered with the *Conversation Books* after they fell into his possession at Beethoven's death in 1827; this argument is sometimes raised in an attempt to cast doubt on the entire set of entries concerning Liszt, and even on the fact that Liszt and Beethoven met at all. A glance at the entries in question does, in fact, show that Schindler later modified some that concern Liszt. (We have set them in square brackets to indicate that their removal has no bearing on the question of the *Weihekuss*.)

The following entry was written in the first part of April 1823, a few days before the concert, either in the hand of the young Franz or more likely that of his father:

> "I have often expressed the wish to Herr von Schindler to make your high acquaintance, and I rejoice, now, to be able to do so. As I shall give a concert on Sunday the 13th, I most humbly beg you to give me your high presence."

The days passed, and Adam Liszt must have found the delay frustrating. It is clear that he approached Schindler again. On April 12, the day before the concert, the following series of entries appeared in the *Conversation Books,* written in Schindler's hand. Beethoven's replies were spoken, of course; but by reading between the lines we can infer that his earlier reception of the young Liszt had been less than friendly.

> "Little Liszt has urgently requested me humbly to beg you for a theme on which he wishes to improvise at his concert tomorrow. *Ergo rogo humilime dominationem Vestram, si placeat scribere unum Thema.*"[4]

---

4. "Therefore I humbly beseech your lordship, if it pleases, to write a theme." Why did Schindler break into Latin at this point? Presumably to make his request obscure to other eyes. The mock formal, ecclesiastical style of the language, with its tongue-in-cheek reference to "your Lordship," may also have been meant to improve Beethoven's demeanor. The composer did not want to provide a theme, nor did he.

"He will not break the seal till the time comes."

———

["The little fellow's improvisations do not amount to much."]

———

"The lad is a fine pianist, but, so far as improvisation is concerned, it is far from the truth to say that he really improvises."

Beethoven did not provide a theme for this concert. We know from a report in the *Wiener Allgemeine Musikzeitung* (April 26, 1823) that Liszt improvised on twenty-four measures from a ponderous (unidentified) Rondo instead, and that it did not make a particularly favorable impression. The *Conversation Books* go on:

"Carl Czerny [is his teacher]."

———

"[Just] eleven years old."

———

"Do come; it will certainly please Karl to hear how the little fellow plays."

This reference to "Karl" is to Beethoven's young nephew. Schindler's inference is that although Beethoven might take no pleasure in a concert he could not hear, at least Karl himself might enjoy it. As we shall see, later entries in the *Conversation Books* imply that neither Karl nor Beethoven attended the concert. The entries continue:

["It is unfortunate that the lad is in Czerny's hands."]

———

["You will make good the rather unfriendly reception of recent date by coming to the little Liszt's concert."]

———

["It will encourage the boy. Promise me to come."][5]

Why did Schindler introduce these changes? They were made for self-serving ends, as a result of his ongoing work on Beethoven's official biography. He wanted this irreplaceable source to "confirm" his own recollection of events, especially where those events, with some suitable adjustments, might present Schindler himself in a more favorable light. As his memories were stirred, he may even have convinced himself that his revisions created a truer historical record. His modifications have been called "forgeries," but they are not that, because not one of them is in a disguised hand. Nevertheless, Schindler's work as Beethoven's biographer is tainted. Where does that leave his comments about Liszt? Not surprisingly, his well-known assertion in his biography (1860, 3rd edition) that Beethoven was *not* present at Liszt's concert has been challenged by Liszt scholars, who, generally suspicious of

———

5. BK, vol. 3, pp. 186–88.

Schindler's other mistakes, have been anxious to prove that he was. Yet the *Conversation Books* themselves confirm Beethoven's absence in an unmistakable way, which has nothing to do with Schindler's meddling with the historical record. They contain two entries of importance in the second half of April 1823—that is, several days after the concert had taken place.[6] In the first, Beethoven's nephew Karl tells his uncle that the hall was "not full." In the second, he again tells Beethoven that someone from the Blöchlinger Institute, a private school in Vienna which Karl was attending, had reported that "the young List [*sic*] made many mistakes."[7] It is clear that Karl is referring to an event that neither he nor Beethoven had witnessed— else why would Beethoven need to be told that the hall was "not full"? He may have been deaf, but he was not blind. And although the Vienna press carried reports of the concert, there is not a single mention of Beethoven's presence, which, in his capacity as Europe's leading composer, would surely have been headline news.[8]

The story that Beethoven was present at Liszt's "farewell" concert and had placed a public kiss of consecration on the boy's brow had first appeared in print in Joseph d'Ortigue's early biography of Liszt (1835)[9] and had acquired some colorful embellishments along the way. Schilling (1837) even had Beethoven mounting the platform, grasping the boy's hand, and proclaiming him "Artist!" The Halász lithograph, then, was only pictorializing what the printed word had been telling people for years. In 1881, not long after that lithograph appeared, the first volume of Lina Ramann's authorized biography was published. Ramann's text not only had Beethoven attending the concert but described him as fixing the boy with his "earnest eye," a remarkable observation from one who was not even born at the time of the event in question. Later biographers now not only had a picture but an "official" text to go with it (they knew that Liszt had granted Ramann personal interviews to help her with her work, and they therefore assumed that her account of the story of the *Weihekuss* must have had Liszt's sanction). Secure in the knowledge that no one was looking, Frederick Corder, in a twentieth-century update of the story, even moved

6. It is important to remember that the *Conversation Books* remained unpublished for more than a century after Beethoven's death. Liszt scholars simply did not have access to any of this material at the time that the official outlines of his life were being drawn—especially by his "authorized" biographer Lina Ramann. Immediately after Beethoven's death the *Conversation Books*, having been appropriated by Schindler, became the object of negotiations with the Royal Prussian State Library in Berlin; some (but not all) of this material was ultimately transferred to the library, in 1843. The first publication of the *Conversation Books*, in an incomplete run of three volumes, made its belated appearance in 1941 (Georg Schunemann, *Beethovens Konversationshefte*, Berlin, 1941–43). A complete edition is still in progress (see BK). It is only in the past decade or so that the *Conversation Books* have figured in Liszt research at all.

7. BK, vol. 3, p. 199.

8. The *Conversation Books* contain a further entry in the hand of Beethoven's nephew Karl. Responding to a question from Beethoven, Karl writes: "Schwarze Haare," that is, black hair. That entry has recently been used to assert that Beethoven never even set eyes on Liszt, otherwise the composer would never have asked about the color of Liszt's hair. We have to jettison that conclusion, however, because we have no direct proof that it was Liszt of whom Beethoven was asking the question. Moreover, Liszt's hair was not black, but light brown.

9. "Franz Liszt: Etude biographique," *Revue et Gazette musicale*, June 14, 1835. Much of the information used by d'Ortigue had been provided by Marie d'Agoult, Liszt's first mistress.

Beethoven to the front row of the concert, presumably out of consideration for the great man's deafness.[10]

From all the available evidence it seems that scholars have muddled two quite separate incidents: the kiss itself and Beethoven's attendance at the farewell concert. In the last edition of his Beethoven biography (1860), Anton Schindler categorically denied that Beethoven was present and wrote that, because of his deafness, "Beethoven did not attend this concert or any other private concert after the year 1816." We quote this part of his text in full:

> The author knows of only one occasion on which Beethoven's reception of a young artist could not be called friendly. The incident has to do with Franz Liszt whom, in the company of his father, I introduced to the master. Beethoven's lack of cordiality sprang in part from the exaggerated idolatry accorded the lad, whose talent was indeed remarkable; but mainly from the request addressed to the master for a theme on which the twelve-year-old boy might base a free improvisation at his forthcoming farewell concert. It was a request as thoughtless as it was unreasonable. In any case, the excessive enthusiasm for this boy exceeded the bounds of all reason. It was so extreme that, after Beethoven had refused the request with obvious impatience, Emperor Franz, or at least Archduke Rudolph, was approached for a theme upon which the little virtuoso might improvise. The idolatry displayed over this child prodigy prompted the master, who had been trained in the school of hard experience, to expound at length on the obstacles and limitations placed in the way of a quiet ripening of true talent once that talent has been discovered and seized upon by an adoring public. Biographical sketches of Liszt have claimed that Beethoven was present at the farewell concert of 1823. Schilling's *Encyclopedia* even adds that Beethoven took the hand of little Liszt after the concert and pronounced him worthy of the name 'artist.' Beethoven did not attend this concert or any other private concert after the year 1816.[11]

Which leaves the kiss itself. We have direct information from Liszt that he received the *Weihekuss* from Beethoven (he never claimed that Beethoven came to his concert, however), and there is no cause to disbelieve him. In fact, this part of the question was settled once and for all in a little-known article by Lina Ramann. During one of her many interviews with Liszt, Ramann and the composer discussed his Paris concerts of 1841, which had been devoted to raising funds for the erection of a Beethoven monument in Bonn. The conversation naturally turned to Beethoven himself, which triggered in Liszt an explosive response to Schindler's Beethoven biography, the first edition of which had been published in 1840, just one year before

10. CFL, p. 13. It is an interesting commentary on the haste with which biographers generally do their work that Corder later told Carl Lachmund that he wrote his biography "very badly," in a single year (1922/23), and that he was "deeply ashamed" (letter dated February 20, 1927 [LL, pp. 350–51]).

11. SB, p. 376.

Liszt's fund-raising concerts. Suddenly, Ramann reports, Liszt broke out indignantly, "And this fellow wanted to deny me my Kiss." "But you received it," responded Ramann. "Naturally I received it," replied Liszt.[12]

If Beethoven was not present in the Redoutensaal, where did the *Weihekuss* take place? It must surely have been when the boy and his father were taken to Beethoven's lodgings, the only documented occasion when they were in one another's company.[13]

The most famous description of that private encounter was provided by Liszt to his Hungarian follower, Ilka Horowitz-Barnay. Although this account did not appear in print until twelve years after Liszt's death (it was published in the *Neue Freie Presse* on July 7, 1898), Horowitz-Barnay claimed to have received it orally from Liszt as early as 1875, during their first meeting in Budapest.[14]

> "I was about eleven years of age when my venerated teacher Czerny brought me to Beethoven. He had told the latter about me a long time before, and had begged him to listen to me play sometime. Yet Beethoven had such a repugnance to infant prodigies that he had always strongly objected to receiving me. Finally, however, he allowed himself to be persuaded by the indefatigable Czerny, and in the end cried impatiently: 'In God's name, then, bring me the young Turk!'
>
> It was ten o'clock in the morning when we entered the two small rooms of the Schwarzspanier house where Beethoven lived, I somewhat shyly, Czerny amiably encouraging me. Beethoven was working at a long, narrow table by the window. He looked gloomily at us for a time, said a few brief words to Czerny, and remained silent when my kind teacher beckoned me to the piano. I first played a short piece by Ries. When I had finished, Beethoven asked me whether I could play a Bach fugue. I chose the C-minor Fugue from the Well-Tempered Clavier. 'And could you also transpose the fugue at once into another key?' Beethoven asked me. Fortunately I was able to do so.
>
> After my closing chord I glanced up. The great master's darkly glowing gaze lay piercingly upon me. Yet suddenly a gentle smile passed over his gloomy features, and Beethoven came quite close to me, stooped down, put his hand on my head, and stroked my hair several times. 'A devil of a fellow,' he whispered, 'a regular young Turk!' Suddenly I felt quite brave. 'May I play something of yours now?' I boldly asked. Beethoven smiled and nodded. I played the first movement of the C major Concerto. When I had concluded Beethoven caught hold of me with both hands, kissed me on the forehead, and said gently: 'Go! You are one of the fortunate ones!

---

12. See KFLB and Ramann's response in NZfM, November 1891, no. 47, p. 503.

13. BK, vol. 3, p. 168.

14. Liszt was in Hungary from February 11 to April 1 of that year, the only period during which this conversation with Horowitz-Barnay could have taken place. She later republished her account in her book *Berühmte Musiker: Erinnerungen,* Berlin, 1900, pp. 31–32.

For you will give joy and happiness to many other people! There is nothing better or finer!'"

Liszt told the preceding in a tone of deepest emotion, with tears in his eyes, and a warm note of happiness sounded in the simple tale. The polished man of the world, the adulated artist, had vanished—the great moment that he had experienced in his youth was reverberating again in rich, solemn harmonies in his soul. For a brief space he was silent, and then he said:"This event in my life has remained my greatest pride—the palladium of my whole career as an artist. I tell it but very seldom and—only to good friends.

Felix Raabe declared this memoir to be "unbelievable," a view shared by many other scholars.[15] It does indeed contain one or two obvious errors. In April 1823 Beethoven was still living in an apartment on Kothgasse and Pfarrgasse; he did not move to the Schwarzspanier house until 1825, by which time Liszt was no longer in Vienna. Moreover, he was by that time totally deaf, and would have been unable to hear anything the young Liszt played. True, he might have been able to form an impression of the boy's physical dexterity by observing him manipulate the keyboard, but would have been unable to appreciate the finer points of the playing, on which much of the anecdote's value rests. Finally, Horowitz-Barnay has Liszt asking Beethoven a question and getting an immediate response. It was well known, however, that all questions to Beethoven had to be put in writing, and the *Conversation Books* contain no such interrogation. Moreover, and more seriously, they contain no mention of Liszt having played anything for Beethoven.[16] As for the rest, the memoir stands in vigorous opposition to the many other reminiscences of this event, by having the *Weihekuss* take place in private, not in public.

Before joining the general rush to accuse Horowitz-Barnay of writing fiction, we would do well to recall that the story as she recounts it had first appeared nearly forty years earlier—as poetry. Liszt had just stepped down from his post as Kapellmeister to the Grand Duke of Weimar, and on December 17, 1858 (Beethoven's birthday), he had conducted an all-Beethoven concert to mark both the composer's anniversary and his own farewell to the city. Liszt's disciple Peter Cornelius captured the occasion in his poem "Zu Beethoven's Geburtsfeier," which was read aloud from the stage by the singer Feodor von Milde. In the last stanza Cornelius seized on the happy idea of Liszt's childhood link with Beethoven, and put into poetry what Horowitz-Barnay was later to put into prose. After describing the scene in which the young Liszt plays for the deaf Beethoven, who follows the playing with his eyes, Cornelius has the Master "drawing the child-artist to him with a kiss."[17] The existence of the poem is proof that the story of a personal meeting between Beethoven and the young

15. RLS, vol. 1, p. 230, fn. 12.

16. Having said that, let us remember that of the 400 *Conversation Books* Schindler claimed to have acquired at the time of Beethoven's death, only 136 were handed over to the Royal Prussian State Library. The rest were either lost or, more probably, destroyed by Schindler.

17. NZfM, February 1859, no. 50. The poem later appeared in CLW, vol. 4, pp. 249–51.

Liszt was already well established in the Weimar of the 1850s. And the details could have come only from Liszt himself. Cornelius here provides unwitting corroboration of the essential points of the Horowitz-Barnay narrative.

By the turn of the century, the controversy over the *Weihekuss* had reached a level of invective that had become troubling. Liszt's credibility was now questioned. Some thought his memory might be at fault; others considered the story a fabrication. Theodor von Frimmel[18], Ludwig Nohl,[19] Hugo Riemann, and Beethoven's biographer Alexander Thayer[20] had all meanwhile come along and fashioned their own particular variations of the anecdote. It was at this point that the greatest living Liszt authority of that time felt constrained to enter the fray and address a problem that seemed to be getting out of hand. La Mara had devoted a lifetime to editing and publishing Liszt's correspondence, in thirteen volumes. She knew that there was one piece of evidence from Liszt himself that had not yet been considered. "It pleases me," she wrote in her little-known article on Beethoven's *Weihekuss*, "to give Liszt's own testimony in black and white."[21] She then pointed out that in November 1862 Liszt had written a letter to the grand duke of Weimar, in which he himself makes a direct reference to the kiss (others had merely reported him on the topic). In this letter Liszt tells the grand duke about the composition of his new work, the *Evocation à la Chapelle Sixtine,* and a mystical experience surrounding it. He had often visited the Sistine Chapel, he says, and had many times stood on the exact spot where one of the most famous events in the annals of musical history had taken place. It was there that the fourteen-year-old Mozart had heard a performance of Allegri's "Miserere" and had then gone back to his lodgings in Rome and written it out from memory. On this particular occasion, Liszt continues, "it seemed to me as if I saw him [Mozart], and as if he looked back at me with gentle encouragement. Allegri was standing by his side, basking in the fame which his 'Miserere' now enjoyed." Liszt then adds the revealing comment: "Then there emerged from the background, next to Michelangelo's *Judgement Day,* slowly, unutterably great, another shadow. Full of emotion, I recognized it at once; for while he was still bound to this earth, *he had consecrated my brow with a kiss* [my italics]."[22] Liszt then directs the grand duke to listen to the Funeral March of Beethoven's *Eroica* Symphony, to the Andante of the Seventh Symphony, and to the Adagio of the *Moonlight* Sonata— all works whose main motives, he maintained, had been strikingly anticipated by Allegri in his "Miserere."[23]

We regard this letter as conclusive proof of the *Weihekuss.* But it is also vital to note that Liszt provides no testimony, on this or any other occasion, regarding Beethoven's presence in the small Redoutensaal on April 13, 1823, and neither does

18. FBLM.
19. NL.
20. TBL.
21. See LBW.
22. LBLCA, p. 116.
23. It was perceptive of Liszt to observe these musical connections. All three compositions are indeed linked through the use of the same musical motif—which binds them in turn to Allegri's "Miserere."

An 1873 lithograph by István Halász. Top left: Beethoven's imaginary embrace of Liszt. Bottom left: Liszt's birthplace metamorphosed. Bottom right: an imaginary statue of Liszt.

anyone else. From the evidence at our disposal, then, three things emerge: (1) Liszt received his kiss of consecration, (2) the Liszt-Beethoven encounter took place in private, and (3) Beethoven did not attend Liszt's concert or fulfill Liszt's request to provide a theme on which he might improvise.

Incidentally, two other pictures shown in the Halász lithograph are also false. The humble cottage where Liszt was born in the village of Raiding has been metamorphosed into an imposing manor worthy of an aristocrat; and the "memorial statue" to Liszt, standing on a large outdoor plinth surrounded by groups of admirers, did not exist at all (see above). Surprisingly, no public statues to Liszt had been erected at that point in his career. These exercises in fantasy should have alerted his biographers to the fact that the depiction of Beethoven's *Weihekuss* at a public concert might also be false.

III

Liszt finally left Budapest on May 17, 1874, almost seven months after his arrival. Although he did not know it at that time, the "Beethoven question" would return to complicate the story of his life the following year, when he probably gave the aforementioned interview to Horowitz-Barnay. Two years after that interview, in December 1877, the fiftieth anniversary of Beethoven's death was commemorated all over Europe. Once again Liszt was to play a major role in the Hungarian celebrations, and once again the Halász lithograph would serve as "proof" of an event that had only ever existed in the imagination of his biographers.

Liszt and the Beethoven Symphonies

For us musicians, Beethoven's work is like the pillar of cloud and fire
that guided the Israelites through the desert—a pillar of cloud to guide us by day,
a pillar of fire to guide us by night—"so that we may progress both day and night."
FRANZ LISZT[1]

I

In April 1865 Liszt brought to completion his great series of piano transcriptions of the Beethoven symphonies. The task had occupied him, off and on, for nearly thirty years. As a young man of twenty-five he had embarked on an arrangement of the Fifth Symphony, probably with little thought that he might one day tackle the entire set. But as his skill as a transcriber grew, and as his involvement with Beethoven became more complete, the work assumed all the characteristics of a lifelong crusade, until the task of laying Beethoven's orchestral textures across the keyboard had been solved—once and for all, it would seem. Nothing could be further from the truth than to assume that Liszt took these transcriptions lightly, or that he threw them off with the same nonchalant ease that characterized much of his other output. On the contrary, they cost him a great deal of labor. They are the result of a profound study of the scores, of the keyboard, of the limitations of two hands, and of the art of transcription itself. Sir Donald Tovey said of them that they "prove conclusively . . . that Liszt was by far the most wonderful interpreter of orchestral scores on the pianoforte the world is ever likely to see,"[2] a judgment with which Liszt's greatest successor in this field, Ferruccio Busoni, readily concurred.

What fascination did these symphonies hold for Liszt? His transcriptions served no practical purpose. By 1865 the symphonies were universally known and recognized as masterpieces. Dozens of piano reductions were already on the market, and publishing houses across Europe vied with one another to bring out "hack" arrangements of these works. Kalkbrenner had completed a version of the entire set as early as 1840; Hummel's set had appeared even earlier;[3] and what may well have been the

---

1. LLB, vol. 1, pp. 123–24.

2. *Essays in Musical Analysis,* vol. 1 (London, 1925), p. 193.

3. Although the publishers (Chappell & Co.) announced them as "arranged for the Piano Forte with accompaniments of Flute, Violin and Violoncello," the piano part is self-contained, the "accompaniments" amounting to no more than discreet doublings.

first attempt to compress Beethoven's orchestral ideas into ten fingers was made by
Carl Czerny, Beethoven's pupil and Liszt's own teacher, and had appeared between
1827 and 1829, that is, immediately after Beethoven's death. Liszt found them all unsatisfactory and made no bones about it. In his preface to the transcriptions he declared: "I confess that I should have to consider it a rather useless employment of
my time if I had added yet another version of the symphonies in a manner up to
now routine."[4]

Liszt was not content, then, to produce something that was "up to now routine."
The thing that gripped his imagination was the challenge these symphonies pre-
sented in defying ten fingers to reproduce them *without harming Beethoven's thought*.
It was a challenge no other arrangement had successfully met.

By training and temperament Liszt was ideally equipped to succeed where others had failed. Lina Ramann relates that when Liszt visited her in 1876 she happened
to mention that Ludwig Böhner had played fugues on the organ, in spite of two
lame fingers. Liszt pondered this problem for several minutes, then, "with a certain
tension of the muscles of the face, he seated himself at the piano and began to play
a difficult fugue by Bach, with *three fingers* of each hand."[5] The result evidently
pleased him, and Ramann concluded that he found this kind of physical challenge
irresistible. Shortly afterward, he was obliged to demonstrate these powers in public. He had been invited to play Beethoven's *Emperor* Concerto in Vienna, on the
fiftieth anniversary of the composer's death. Just before the performance he damaged the second finger of his left hand. Rather than cancel the concert, he played
the concerto without using that particular finger, redistributing the notes among
the remaining ones in such a way that no one was aware of the injury he had sustained.[6] Grieg witnessed a similar feat when he visited Liszt in Rome in early 1870,
at the Santa Francesca Romana, carrying with him his recently published Sonata for
Violin and Piano in G Major. He was too shy to play it for Liszt, so the latter sat
down and played the piece at sight, incorporating the violin part as he went along.
A few weeks later Grieg returned with the manuscript of his unpublished Concerto
in A Minor. Liszt glanced briefly at the manuscript and then played through the
concerto at sight, singing the orchestral parts as he went along and holding a running conversation with the astonished composer at the same time.[7]

These incidents would hardly rise above the level of anecdote if they did not
show us where Liszt's talents as a transcriber lay. He could take in a full score as the
average person takes in a newspaper, and he possessed the technique to reproduce
it instantly on the keyboard. But we must look elsewhere to account for the loving

---

4. Preface to Liszt's transcriptions of the Beethoven Symphonies. See pp. 16–17 for the complete text.

5. RLKM, vol. 1, p. 166, n. 1.

6. This was in March 1877. By a curious coincidence the ten-year-old Busoni was in the audience.
It was the only occasion on which he ever heard Liszt (who by this time rarely performed in public),
and he was somewhat disappointed in his idol (DFB, p. 24). He had no idea that Liszt was playing under
a handicap.

7. Grieg himself left detailed descriptions of both visits. They are reproduced in M-JEG, pp. 137–
42.

care, the meticulous attention to detail, that shines out of every page of his Beethoven transcriptions.

II

Liszt was first presented to Beethoven by his teacher Carl Czerny, as a boy of eleven. In later life he often spoke of this meeting, the memory of which was a powerful stimulus to the further study and performance of Beethoven's music.[8] He was already playing some of the Beethoven sonatas, even at this early stage in his career, and we gather from his later correspondence that he had even embarked on a study of the *Hammerklavier* Sonata, a work he was to make very much his own.

Liszt's next encounter with Beethoven was a posthumous one, so to speak. It occurred in 1839. Liszt was staying in Pisa, Italy. One morning he opened his newspaper and read that the Beethoven Committee in Bonn had failed to raise enough money to erect a statue of Beethoven, despite an international appeal. The French section of the fund had discredited itself by donating a paltry 424 francs, 90 centimes. Liszt was dismayed at this insult, and he promptly wrote to the Beethoven Committee from Pisa (October 3, 1839) offering to relieve them of all further responsibility.

> Gentlemen:
>
> As the subscription for the Beethoven monument is only getting on slowly, and as the carrying out of this undertaking seems to be rather far distant, I venture to make a proposal to you, the acceptance of which would make me very happy.
>
> I myself offer to make up, from my own means, the sum still wanting for the erection of the monument, and ask no other privilege than that of naming the artist who shall execute the work. That artist is Bartolini of Florence, who is universally considered the first sculptor in Italy.
>
> I have spoken to him provisionally about the matter, and he assures me that a monument in marble (which would cost about fifty to sixty thousand francs) could be finished in two years, and he is ready to begin the work at once.
>
> I have the honor to be, etc.
>
> FRANZ LISZT[9]

The letter indicates an emotional attachment of an unusual order to Beethoven's memory. The only way that Liszt could raise such a large sum of money was to or-

---

8. See the essay "Beethoven's *Weihekuss* Revisited" in the present volume.
9. LLB, vol. 1, pp. 30–31.

ganize a series of benefit concerts, which was announced without delay. One month later, in November 1839, his "Beethoven tour" opened in Vienna with a series of matinee concerts. Tobias Haslinger acted as his impresario. Between November 19 and December 14 Liszt gave six recitals in aid of the Beethoven Fund. The opening concert was a gala affair attended by the dowager empress, at which Liszt played the last three movements of the *Pastorale* Symphony for the first time. (By now he had already transcribed three of Beethoven's symphonies: the Fifth, the Sixth (*Pastorale*) and the Seventh; the slow movement of the *Eroica* Symphony followed in 1843.) At subsequent concerts he played the *Appassionata* and the *Pastorale* Sonatas. He also accepted an invitation to play Beethoven's Concerto in C Minor, a work he did not at that time know, but which he learned in twenty-four hours and played with an improvised cadenza.[10] A newspaper article proclaimed him "Protector of Bee-thoven," a mantle of authority he wore throughout his Beethoven crusade.

Within months Liszt accomplished what the fumbling and ineffective Beethoven Committee had been trying to bring about for years. The sum of 10,000 francs was credited to the Fund, solely as a result of Liszt's generosity.[11] But because Liszt also underwrote the cost of the specially constructed *Festhalle* in Bonn, in which the memorial concerts took place during the week of the unveiling of the statue (in August 1845), his total contribution was much greater than that and was the largest sum received from a single source. The bronze statue that stands today in Bonn's Domplatz was sculpted by Ernst-Julius Hähnel. Bartolini, Liszt's first choice of sculptor, was disadvantaged because he worked with marble, a material that was considered unable to withstand the elements of a north German city, so Liszt went along with the committee in its desire to look for a more durable monument.

The unveiling ceremony took place in Bonn on August 12, 1845, during the sev-enty-fifth anniversary of the composer's birth. Queen Victoria and her cousin King Wilhelm IV of Prussia were present, together with their retinues. Among the lead-ing musicians who converged on the small town were Ignaz Moscheles, Hector Berlioz, Giocomo Meyerbeer, Ludwig Spohr, Charles Hallé, and George Smart. Liszt was the chief guest of honor. The day should have crowned his years of en-deavor for Beethoven. In the event, what happened calls for a suspension of dis-belief. At the banquet that followed the unveiling ceremony Liszt was asked to make a speech. Because the assembled guests represented many different countries, Liszt thought that it would be appropriate to take as his theme the universality of Beethoven's music. He got to his feet and began, "Here all nations are met to pay honor to the master. May they live and prosper who have made a pilgrimage here—the Dutch, the English, the Viennese." There was a moment's pause. Then the French representative Hippolyte Chélard leapt to his feet in a rage and shouted at Liszt: "Vous avez oublié les Français." Immediately there was an uproar. Some guests tried to calm the Frenchman down. Others applauded him. Dr. Wolff, a member of

---

10. On December 5, 1839 in a "concert spirituel" (ACLA, vol. 1, p. 311).

11. This was the sum that Liszt disclosed to Lina Ramann in his reply to one of her questionnaires on the topic (RL, p. 400).

the Committee, valiantly mounted the table and tried to restore order. He was howled down. A climax of sorts was reached when a somewhat intoxicated Lola Montez, the dancer whose infatuation with Liszt had led her to pursue him to Bonn, jumped on the table, executed a pirouette, and exclaimed, "Speak up, Mr. Wolff, pray speak up!" She in turn was howled down. Beneath the din, Liszt vainly tried to extricate himself from the consequence of his gaffe; he explained that he had lived in France for fifteen years and would not deliberately insult his adopted country. Nobody listened. The banquet finally broke up in disarray and the guests re-formed themselves into tight little knots of partisans, all arguing simultaneously about the shortcomings of the committee. It later transpired that the members of the French delegation were sensitive about their poor contribution to the fund, as well they might have been, and they had mistaken Liszt's omission of France from his speech for a rebuff.[12]

III

During the years 1847 to 1859 Liszt lived in Weimar where, as Kapellmeister-in-Extraordinary, he was in charge of the court theater and orchestra. The experience was of inestimable value to him. It taught him to conduct; it taught him to orchestrate; it taught him above all a fuller appreciation of the Beethoven symphonies. Weimar heard a number of them under his baton, especially the Ninth, a work he promoted with uncommon zeal across Germany at a time when few people understood it. Traditions of performance were established there that have persisted down to modern times. It is not always remembered that Felix Weingartner and Hans von Bülow, great Beethoven interpreters both, were pupils of Liszt. Liszt's own career as a conductor is hardly acknowledged today, since the petty jealousies and court intrigues brought it to an untimely end. After 1859 his appearances on the rostrum were rare. Cut off as he was from the world of orchestral music, it seemed that Liszt's intimate association with the Beethoven symphonies might be about to end. In fact, it was about to intensify.

The period that followed his leaving Weimar was a time of personal stress for Liszt. Apart from a succession of family blows, which hardly concern us here,[13] he experienced a religious crisis which eventually led him, in 1865, to enter the lower orders of the Roman Catholic Church. He moved into the oratory of the Madonna del Rosario, a semideserted monastery just outside Rome, where from June 1863 he lived in relative seclusion from the world, meditating, studying, and composing.

---

12. The best eyewitness accounts of this scene were left by the historian Karl von Schorn (SLE, vol. 1, pp. 193–216) and Ignaz Moscheles (MAML, vol. 2, pp. 142–44).

13. He lost children. First Daniel, his youngest, died when he was only twenty years old. Then Blandine, his eldest, died of postnatal complications at the age of twenty-seven. And hanging like a dark cloud over his life was his thwarted desire to enter into matrimony with his lifelong companion Princess Carolyne von Sayn-Wittgenstein; the long-standing plans for the marriage, after a series of wrangles within the Church hierarchy, now lay in ruins.

He was given a cell containing a bed, a writing desk, and a small upright piano—with a missing D-natural. It was in this unlikely setting, and on this unlikely instrument, that Liszt returned with renewed vigor to his transcriptions of the Beethoven symphonies. It seems that the first ears to hear the strains of these emerging arrangements were those of the three Dominican brothers with whom he shared the oratory. Within eighteen months the task was finished. Liszt received the tonsure of the Roman Catholic Church on April 25, 1865, not long after sending off the manuscript of his transcriptions to Breitkopf and Härtel. Because he moved into a suite of rooms in the Vatican immediately after the ceremony, and because the transcriptions were already published by July of that year, it seems that the Vatican was where Liszt actually checked his proofs. When the volumes appeared, Liszt included a preface, which he had penned in the late 1830s but had not used until now. It is a remarkable tribute to Beethoven and his nine symphonies.

> The name of Beethoven is sacred in art. His symphonies are nowadays universally recognized to be masterpieces. No one who seriously desires to extend his knowledge, or create something new himself, can ever devote sufficient thought to them, or ever study them enough. That is why every way of making them widely known and popular has some merit (not that the rather numerous arrangements published so far are without a certain merit, though for the most part deeper study readily reduces their value). The poorest lithograph, the faultiest translation, always gives an idea, however vague, of the genius of a Michelangelo and of a Shakespeare; and even the most imperfect piano arrangement will now and then reveal traces, a little obliterated perhaps, of a master's inspiration. But the advances the piano has gained of late, in both the technique of performance and in mechanical improvement, make it possible to produce more and better arrangements than ever before. As a result of the vast development of its harmonic power, the piano is trying more and more to take possession of all orchestral compositions. Within the compass of its seven octaves it is capable, with but a few exceptions, of reproducing all the features, all the combinations, and all the configurations of the deepest musical creations. And it leaves to the orchestra no other advantages than those of contrasting tone colors and mass effects—immense advantages, to be sure.
>
> Such has been my aim in the work I lay before the public today. I confess that I should have to regard it as a rather useless employment of my time if I had produced just another version of the Symphonies in a manner up to now routine. But I shall think my time well spent if I have succeeded in transferring to the piano not only the grand outlines of Beethoven's compositions, but also that multitude of details and finer points that make such a significant contribution to the perfection of the whole. I will be satisfied if I stand on the level of the intelligent engraver, or the conscientious translator, who grasps the spirit of a work and thus

contributes to our insight into the great masters and to our sense of the beautiful.

Rome, 1865[14]

IV

The incentive to return to the Beethoven symphonies, after a lapse of more than a quarter of a century, had come from the publishers Breitkopf and Härtel, who had sent Liszt a set of their newly engraved Beethoven symphony scores in March 1863, inviting him to complete the work he had abandoned.[15] Liszt accepted the commission, on condition that he be allowed not merely to republish but to revise his earlier efforts. In his reply he drew Breitkopf's attention to the limitations of the piano:

> Nothing shall be wanting on my part, by way of goodwill and industry, to fulfill your commission. A pianoforte arrangement of these creations must . . . expect to remain a very poor and distant approximation. How to instill into the futile hammers of the piano the breath and soul, the resonance and power, the fullness and inspiration, the color and accent of such music? However, I will at least endeavor to overcome the worst difficulties and to furnish the piano-playing world with as faithful an illustration as possible of Beethoven's genius.[16]

The first part of the work proceeded quickly, despite his relocation from the Via Felice in the heart of Rome to the Madonna del Rosario on the Monte Mario, outside the city. By August 28, 1863, Liszt was able to tell Breitkopf that the transcriptions of the first eight symphonies were "almost finished." He went on:

> By using the title "Partition de Piano" [see page 18] I wish to indicate my intention of associating the spirit of the performer with the effects of the orchestra, and to make evident, in the narrow limits of the piano, the different sonorities and *nuances*. To this end I have frequently noted the names of the instruments: oboe, clarinet, kettledrums, etc. as well as the contrasts of string and wind instruments. It would certainly be highly ridiculous to pretend that these designations suffice to transplant the magic of the orchestra to the piano; nevertheless I do not consider them superfluous.[17]

14. The symphony transcriptions were dedicated to Liszt's pupil Hans von Bülow. When, a few years later, Bülow published his famous edition of the Beethoven sonatas, he dedicated them in turn to "My Master Franz Liszt, as the fruits of his teaching" (J. G. Cotta, 1871; 2nd ed. 1881).

15. Breitkopf and Härtel had recently begun to bring out its *Complete Edition* of Beethoven's music, a task which required more than 13,400 engraved plates, and which took the firm just over three years to finish (1862–65).

16. LLB, vol. 2, p. 35.

17. LLB, vol. 2, pp. 47–48.

The original title page of Liszt's piano transcriptions of the Beethoven symphonies (1865), bearing the dedication to Hans von Bülow.

"Highly ridiculous" or not, anyone who has played from Liszt's scores knows how useful his instrumental cues are. They encourage the player to draw more color from the keyboard, and to produce distinct levels of sound from what would otherwise remain anonymous, black-and-white textures.

V

Liszt's transcriptions differ from the usual "hack" arrangements of the Beethoven symphonies in two important respects, both of which represent the twin ideals toward which he constantly strives. First, they remain unsurpassed in the amount of fine orchestral detail incorporated into their texture. Second, the seemingly impossible technical problems posed by such an ideal are solved, in a masterly fashion, in the most pianistic way. In his preface, Liszt mentions the piano's lack of color. Not the least useful feature of his transcriptions, in fact, is that he cues in many of the orchestral instruments, so that the pianist always has some idea of the idealized sound that he must approximate. And as a bonus Liszt provides the player with a set of fingerings, which are indispensable for a better rendering of these works.

A simple illustration occurs at the beginning of the Fifth Symphony. A respectable, and respected, arrangement by Otto Singer, with which Liszt was undoubtedly acquainted, gives this:

Compare that with Liszt's solution. There is not a note to choose between the two arrangements (except for Liszt's octaves in bar 4, which are in Beethoven's score anyway). But how much simpler is Liszt's to play:

The fingering, a crucial aspect of each solution, is reproduced exactly as the arrangers left it.[18]

18. Incidentally, in their *Collected Edition* of Liszt's works, Breitkopf and Härtel engraved bar 169 of the first movement of the C Minor Symphony twice, by mistake.

Equally revealing is the slow movement of the Fifth. All the arrangements I have seen produce the obvious solution; that is to say, they give the famous cello tune to the right hand and its pizzicato accompaniment to the left—all, that is, except Liszt's.

At first sight this seems perverse. Why cross the hands to do something that can be done perfectly well without? Nevertheless, it is Liszt's arrangement that shows the deepest insight. The others see a cello *tune:* Liszt sees a *cello* tune. What could be more natural to a pianist than to have his left hand "play the cello"? By disposing of the melody in this way, its phrasing and articulation, and its relationship to the accompaniment, are naturally assured.

As for those "finer points" mentioned in Liszt's preface, he will sometimes go to enormous trouble to incorporate Beethoven's original phrasing, even where this conflicts with the pianist's best interests. Consider Kalkbrenner's phrasing of this figure from the first movement of the *Eroica:*

It is marvelous to play, but it is not what Beethoven wrote. Liszt does not compromise on such matters. He leaves Beethoven's phrasing unharmed, knowing that the result will take care of itself, and that no amount of fussing over the exact notation will make any difference:

Even professional pianists cannot achieve the unattainable. As Tovey pointed out in this same connection, some things that violins can do are impossible on the pianoforte.[19] Of course, at this high level of exactitude, impossibilities fall thick and fast on the transcriber. The most innocent-looking orchestral figure, this type of thing from the Eighth Symphony, for instance,

---

19. See his informative preface to *Beethoven's Complete Pianoforte Sonatas,* London, 1931 in BCPS.

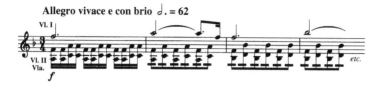

simply cannot be transcribed without modification. Liszt had already learned about such things to his cost. Years earlier, in his heyday as a traveling virtuoso, he had met Mendelssohn, who jokingly inquired whether it was true that he could play any orchestral score at sight on the piano. Liszt was obliged to admit that it was, whereupon Mendelssohn thrust a copy of Mozart's G Minor Symphony on the music desk. Liszt looked at the score. Then he looked at Mendelssohn. Then he got up. He was unable even to start the symphony. Kalkbrenner might have benefited from Mendelssohn's joke. Instead, when he came to transcribe the above passage, he contented himself with "making omelets," as Liszt witheringly called this kind of piano texture:

Liszt's solution is the best that can be managed under the circumstances. Because Beethoven's original is impossible to reproduce, Liszt does not attempt to reproduce it. Instead, he brings some creative thought to bear on the problem, finally settling for this:

The first movement of the *Eroica* Symphony contains a passage that sets a special challenge. It occurs during the leadback, where Beethoven has the first subject playing in canon against itself. Otto Singer dutifully transcribes what Beethoven actually wrote. The texture, though accurate, is deadly dull:

What is required to enliven this passage is the very thing denied to the piano transcriber: orchestral color. Liszt understands this and acts accordingly. Instead of reproducing Beethoven's notes unchanged, he attempts to capture Beethoven's orchestral *effect*. The result is startling. We hear a continuous, ever-growing surge of sound, with Beethoven's canon actually suggested by Liszt's shimmering keyboard texture:

This is more than transcription; it is translation. Liszt may have forsaken the letter of Beethoven's notation, but, paradoxically, this brings him closer to its spirit. We are reminded of one of Liszt's telling aphorisms: "In matters of translation there are some exactitudes that are the equivalent of infidelities."[20]

The *Eroica*'s slow movement illustrates how completely Liszt was able to re-create a pseudo-orchestral sound at the piano and thereby do justice to one of the grand peaks of classical music. There can be few more instructive experiments than to play Hummel's arrangement of the great climax to the Funeral March,[21]

and then to play Liszt's:

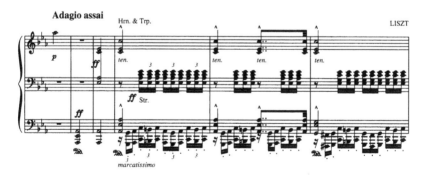

20. PWC, p. 114.

21. Kalkbrenner's solution to the same passage is, curiously enough, identical to Hummel's. Perhaps he was familiar with the Hummel arrangements. It is not the only place where the two composers find themselves in mysterious agreement.

Liszt's arrangement is by no means as difficult as it looks, and its layout is ideal for the release of a tremendous volume of sound.

VI

It was in the chorale finale of the Ninth Symphony, however, that even Franz Liszt went down to defeat. His work ground to a halt at the very point where Schiller's verses address mankind in transfixing language: "Seid umschlungen Millionen!" (Be embraced, ye millions!). Far from embracing the millions, Liszt's attempts to telescope both chorus and orchestra into two hands did not get beyond his cell in the Madonna del Rosario. One look at the score will tell us why. He wrote to Breitkopf, who had naturally expected to publish all nine symphonies complete, asking to be excused from the task of transcribing the finale: "After various endeavors one way and another, I became inevitably and distinctly convinced of the impossibility of making any pianoforte arrangement of the fourth movement *for two hands,* that could in any way be even approximately effective or satisfactory."[22] He went on to ask Breitkopf to consider his work of transcription finished with the conclusion of the third movement of the Ninth. Breitkopf refused to be brushed aside, however, doubtless haunted by the specter of certain financial ruin if, instead of the nine "complete" symphonies, he were to publish eight and three-quarters of them. So Liszt reluctantly returned to the task. In his letter of compliance, he characteristically fell back on a proverb to express the dilemma facing him: "Tant va la cruche à l'eau qu'à la fin . . . *elle s'emplit.*"[23] It never was quite filled, however. Liszt openly acknowledges his difficulty by printing the choral parts on separate staves above the transcribed orchestral score. Although the music is at such times strictly unplayable, deployed as it is across four staves, it has the great advantage of not obscuring Beethoven's thought—as it surely would have done if Liszt had attempted to squeeze everything into two hands:

---

22. LLB, vol. 2, p. 76.

23. LLB, vol. 2, p. 77. "The pitcher goes so often to the water that at last . . . *it is filled.*" Liszt has modified the original proverb to his advantage. It says, "The pitcher goes to the well so often that it breaks." This image he wanted to contradict, hence his italics.

Admirers of this otherwise flawless transcription might draw solace from the East-ern philosophy that considers anything perfect an affront to the gods, a notion that is rooted in the belief that imperfection will ward off retribution. Kalkbrenner, like Liszt, escapes the retribution of the gods by falling back on the expedient of print-ing the choral parts on separate staves. But in every other respect his version falls lamentably short of the high standards adopted by Liszt. The opening of the finale, in Kalkbrenner's arrangement, surely aroused the contempt of whatever deity was within earshot by obliterating all traces of the boldness and grandeur of Beethoven's original:

Beethoven's famous "dominant thirteenth" chord is, apparently, so offensive to Kalk-brenner that he emasculates it. Liszt, as we would expect, transcribes the grinding, glorious dissonance in full.

Note Liszt's pedal marking, which carries the dissonance forward for four measures.

One of the constraints that Liszt surely faced in his work of transcribing the Ninth Symphony for two hands must have been the nagging reminder that much earlier in his career, in 1851, he had transcribed this same work for two pianos. It was the only Beethoven symphony he ever tackled in this vastly simpler medium—simpler, that is to say, from the sole standpoint of having twice the number of places to put the notes, and twice as many fingers to help him put them there. An inspection of his two-piano score shows that Liszt makes the obvious choice: he puts the choral parts on one piano and the orchestral parts on the other.

There is a revealing postscript to Liszt's Beethoven symphony transcriptions. Two years after they were published, Breitkopf invited Liszt to tackle the string quartets. On October 4, 1866, Liszt wrote to the publisher, after having wrestled with the pieces for several months:

> It is very mortifying to me to have to confess that I have most awkwardly come to a standstill with the transcription of the Beethoven Quartets. After several attempts the result was either absolutely *unplayable*—or *insipid* stuff. Nevertheless, I shall not give up my project, and shall make another attempt to solve this problem of pianoforte arrangement. If I succeed I will at once inform you of my "Eureka."[24]

He never did succeed. The reason was his unwillingness to publish anything unplayable—a word he italicized in his letter. As for the playable, that was merely pointless to him where the result simply obscured Beethoven's intentions. Time and again, these were the principles on which Liszt refused to yield. They raise his transcriptions above the humdrum level of mere "piano reduction" to that of great art.

---

24. LLB, vol. 2, pp. 94–95. One wonders what Liszt would have made of the piano transcriptions of "Six Movements from Beethoven's String Quartets," by his pupil Carl Tausig, which were published by Peters (Leipzig) in 1872. The movements are: Adagio, op. 59, no. 1; Scherzo, op. 59, no. 2; Andante, op. 59, no. 3; Cavatina, op. 130; Presto, op. 131; and Scherzo, op. 135.

Liszt and the Schubert Song Transcriptions

O never-resting, ever-welling genius, full of tenderness!
O my cherished Hero of the Heaven of Youth!
FRANZ LISZT[1]

I

In March 1838, after an unusually severe winter, the frozen Danube melted and over-flowed its banks. The massive tidal wave that rolled across western Hungary was un-stoppable. Entire villages were swept away and the crops of the Hungarian peasants were ruined. Pest, the low-lying city of the Magyars, which stood in the path of the oncoming waters, was completely inundated. Nearly 3,000 houses collapsed in the water. More than 150 people drowned and thousands more faced disease and famine.[2] It was the greatest natural disaster to strike Hungary in modern times. The Hungarian government, sitting in its ancient capital of Pozsony, launched an inter-national appeal for aid. Liszt, who was in Venice when he heard about the catastro-phe, hurried to Vienna and gave eight charity concerts for the victims. These historic recitals, widely reported in the foreign press, raised the colossal sum of 24,000 *gulden*—the largest figure received by the Hungarians from a private source. Liszt had not been in Vienna since his childhood. And his return to the city of Schubert and Beethoven had a marked effect on him, for some of his earliest memories were enshrined there. He was reunited with his teacher Carl Czerny, the tenor Benedict Randhartinger (they had both studied theory under Antonio Salieri), and Count Thadé Amadé, one of his early benefactors. Liszt's life was always reflected in his work. It was no accident that in this dramatic year of 1838 he rediscovered Schu-bert. Almost as soon as he entered Vienna, the Schubert song transcriptions started to pour from his pen.[3]

---

1. LLB, vol. 2, p. 133.
2. The statistical details of the 1838 flood, from which these facts are drawn, are preserved in the Record Office of the Hungarian Legislature, Budapest.
3. Liszt was already familiar with some of the Schubert songs before arriving in Vienna. In 1837, while they were on a visit to George Sand's country home at Nohant, his companion Countess Marie d'Agoult had translated a selection of Schubert's German texts into French for him, in order to help him toward a fuller understanding of the nuances of the words. He was always more at home in French than in German. By July 29, 1837, according to his own testimony, he had already transcribed seven of the

Liszt's first attempts included "Auf dem Wasser zu singen," "Erlkönig," "Hörch, hörch, die Lerch!" and "Ave Maria"—twenty-eight songs altogether. He played groups of them in at least four of his charity concerts, and they became overnight successes.[4] Some of them were immediately published by Diabelli; others were brought out by Haslinger, who sold them so quickly that he at once commissioned more. The next year, 1839, Liszt obliged him by transcribing twelve songs from *Winterreise* and the whole of *Schwanengesang*. In 1840 Diabelli brought out the four *Geistliche Lieder*, and in 1846 groups from *Müllerlieder* and *Sechs Melodien,* including "Die Forelle." Within eight years Liszt had produced fifty-six Schubert song transcriptions, which are models of their kind. They remain faithful to the originals, are effective to play, and are enjoyable to listen to. With three or four solitary exceptions, however, these arrangements remain undervalued by pianists and public alike, and have not yet entered the repertoire. Have the arrangements of the *Winterreise* and *Schwanengesang* cycles ever been played in public? If so, they have left no trace of a visitation.

II

In 1907, Breitkopf and Härtel launched its great *Collected Edition* of Liszt's music, published in thirty-four volumes, under the distinguished editorship of Busoni, Bartók, d'Albert, Peter Raabe, Philip Wolfrum, Emil von Sauer, and others. This massive enterprise was finally abandoned nearly thirty years later, in 1936, the fiftieth anniversary of Liszt's death, by which time several of the editors were dead themselves. The Schubert song transcriptions were excluded, along with much else, for which no official explanation was ever given. We surmise that the money ran out; that is, the subscription list on which Breitkopf depended to keep the *Collected Edition* growing was not large enough to cover the costs, and the volumes simply stopped appearing. It was by now difficult for the average pianist to find copies of the transcriptions, many of which were available only in research collections, in the original edition. In any case, between the two world wars the musical climate shifted away from Liszt in general and from arrangements in particular, and pianists tended to abandon them. The rise of the early music movement, with its insistence on the urtext, did the rest: that is, arrangements came to be regarded as second-class music (by definition they modify the urtext) and purists frowned on them. The conspiracy of silence spread to the record companies, a policy they pursued for many years until the "Romantic revival" of the 1960s and 1970s forced them into a change of heart.

Broadly speaking, Liszt's arrangements fall into two categories: paraphrases and transcriptions. The *paraphrase,* as its name implies, is a free variation on the original.

---

songs (VFL, p. 30). There is a solitary Schubert song, "Die Rose," which Liszt had transcribed no later than 1835. Nonetheless it was Vienna that opened the floodgates.

4. See the diary of Theresa Walter in WLCC. The eight concerts Liszt gave in Vienna between April 18 and May 25 are recorded there in detail.

Its purpose is metamorphosis. It can concentrate exclusively on one theme, decking it out with ever more complex ornamentation, or it can embrace the entire act of an opera, mixing and mingling the material en route, giving us (so to speak) an aerial view of the original composition. Liszt's paraphrases of Verdi, Meyerbeer, and Mozart provide good examples of this process. The *transcription*, on the other hand, is quite different. It is strict, literal, objective. It seeks to unfold the original work as accurately as possible, down to the smallest details. We are probably correct to call the Schubert song arrangements transcriptions, although one or two of them do stray over the border and behave, albeit fleetingly, like paraphrases.[5]

These transcriptions served a triple purpose: (1) they promoted the name of Schubert, little known outside Vienna; (2) they advanced the field of piano technique, posing special problems of spacing and timbre which had never before been solved; and (3) they widened Liszt's own repertory. A few of these arrangements, "Erlkönig" and "Ave Maria," for example, are effective showpieces which he played on numerous occasions in public.

Let us look at these three points in turn, because they take us to the heart of the Schubert-Liszt connection.

III

Liszt's commitment to the music of Schubert was lifelong and profound. He first heard about Schubert as a boy in Vienna. Surprisingly, the two musicians never met,[6] although Liszt lived in Vienna for fourteen months, during the years 1822–23. However, his theory teacher Salieri often talked to his young pupil about the phenomenal ability of that other Franz who had been his student ten years earlier. At this time, too, Liszt's and Schubert's names were linked musically. In 1822 the publisher Diabelli had invited fifty-one prominent composers living in Austria each to compose a variation on a waltz theme he himself had written. Czerny, Moscheles, Cramer, and Schubert all participated in this unique exercise; so did the eleven-year-old Liszt, the youngest member of the group. Liszt's variation is his first published composition. He no doubt played through this unusual collaborative work and came across Schubert's particularly beautiful transformation of Diabelli's theme; he must have been struck by its fresh harmonization. By 1828, the year of Schubert's death, Liszt was living in Paris. He was seventeen years old and had fallen under the spell of the violinist and composer Chrétien Urhan, who led the Paris Opera Orchestra. Urhan was a strange, somewhat mystical personality, much older than Liszt, and historians have had a field day with him. His moral precepts were said to have been so

---

5. Liszt laid claim to the terms *transcription* and *paraphrase*, together with the term *reminiscence*, in a marginal note found in his personal copy of the first volume of Lina Ramann's biography of him. It is preserved in the Goethe-Schiller Archive (GSA 59/352. 2).

6. We have Liszt's own testimony for that. He told his pupil August Göllerich, "Schubert . . . habe ich nicht persönlich gekannt" (I did not know Schubert personally [GLK, p. 20]). The point is worth noting because the rumor of a meeting with Schubert has haunted the Liszt literature for years.

strict that during the ballet he played his violin with gaze averted so as not to expose himself to the temptations of the dancers on the stage. It was widely believed in Paris that, during all the years Urhan led the orchestra, he had not seen a single ballet.[7]

However, he was an enthusiastic champion of Schubert and within months of Schubert's death had brought this neglected master to the attention of the Parisians. Two of Urhan's string quintets are actually based on themes of Schubert, and he also composed a set of highly individual piano studies based on Schubert songs. Who plays a note of Urhan nowadays? Yet it was this shadowy figure who confirmed the young Liszt in his love of Schubert's songs and helped make of him a Schubertian for life. Liszt transcribed Schubert's *Wanderer* Fantasie for piano and orchestra; he conducted the first performance of Schubert's *Alfonso und Estrella* in Weimar; he edited several volumes of Schubert's piano compositions,[8] and he recommended Schubert to his students. In the 1850s, after he had settled in Weimar, he even contemplated writing a biography of Schubert. He asked Anselm Hüttenbrenner to provide some basic materials for this project (Hüttenbrenner and Schubert had been boyhood friends and had taken lessons contemporaneously from Salieri in Vienna). Hüttenbrenner certainly sent a short biographical sketch to Liszt in Weimar but, much to his dismay, Liszt never acknowledged it. This is so uncharacteristic of Liszt that we assume the manuscript went astray. In any event, Liszt's projected biography remained unwritten.[9] This, then, was the primary purpose of these transcriptions: to celebrate the name of Schubert.

Their second purpose was to advance piano technique, and it is important to recall Liszt's historic mission in this regard. More than any of his contemporaries—Chopin, Schumann, Mendelssohn—Liszt had an unshakable belief in the future of the piano. During the early stages of his career, especially, he was convinced that there was an almost unlimited potential locked up inside the instrument simply waiting to be released, and that it was his task to find the key.[10] He had, by this very year of 1838, already transcribed five of Paganini's unaccompanied violin caprices and three of the Beethoven symphonies, discovering some new technical resources in the process.[11] Transcription, then, was the means par excellence of conquering new musical territory for the keyboard, and the Schubert songs formed a part of that wider vision.

7. Ernest Legouvé devotes a whole, pioneering chapter to Urhan in his memoirs. It is from his eyewitness accounts of Urhan's mournful character that all our later impressions ultimately derive (LSS, vol. 3, pp. 168–77).

8. See the essay "Liszt as Editor" in the present volume.

9. See DSM, pp. 65ff. and 178ff.

10. In this regard see his "Credo" on piano playing (RGS, vol. 2, p. 151), written when he was only twenty-six years old, and reproduced in the essay "Liszt the Writer" of this volume (pp. 226–27). There Liszt observes, "My resolution would be firm not to abandon the study and development of piano playing, until I had accomplished whatever is practicable, whatever it is possible to attain nowadays."

11. The symphonies, as we have already seen, were no. 5 in C minor, no. 6 in F major (the *Pastorale*), and no. 7 in A major. The five Paganini caprices, plus a free arrangement of "La campanella" which also appeared in 1838, later formed the six *Etudes d'éxécution transcendante d'après Paganini*.

The technical problem facing Liszt was obvious: how to telescope the vocal line of the songs into Schubert's accompaniment, thus creating a self-contained piano piece, with no loss of musical substance and no distortion of musical sense. Some of Schubert's accompaniments are difficult and demand a virtuoso technique. To reproduce the vocal line as well compounds the problem, but Liszt invariably succeeds in finding a solution. One of the very best, and most literal, of the Schubert song transcriptions is "Auf dem Wasser zu singen," in which Liszt incorporates all the fine detail of the original song.

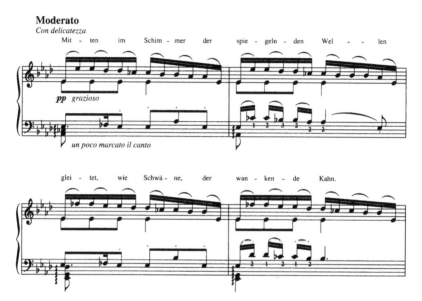

Perhaps the stiffest challenge Liszt faced was in transcribing "Erlkönig," which remains the most daunting of all the transcriptions to play, taxing muscle and sinew to their limits. To compare Schubert's original with Liszt's arrangement can be highly revealing. The first line of the song poses a seemingly insoluble problem.

The texture is strictly impossible for two hands to play. Yet Liszt sees to the heart of the difficulty and reproduces the same passage in a totally pianistic way, one that feels absolutely secure to play and exerts minimum harm on Schubert's thought.

Liszt's version of the song does not contain a single measure that Schubert himself did not write. Only the occasional octave doubling has been added to the left hand in such passages as the following:

Liszt's octaves actually serve to enhance the drama, as the father (in Goethe's poem), riding swiftly through the night, his horse's hooves pounding beneath him, draws his terrified son ever closer to him with the sinister Erlkönig in relentless pursuit. Liszt even contrives to bring out the four characters who play a role in this unique song—father, son, Erlkönig, and narrator—through skillful changes in the melodic register, a technique obviously not available to Schubert:

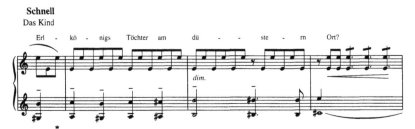

There is one giddy moment in the headlong rush of this song where Liszt expects the pianist to play the following passage with a repeating fifth finger. Goethe's lines run: "I will play beautiful games with you." The bouncing hand discloses a wonderful sense of humor on Liszt's part. But only the Erlkings of the keyboard can afford to smile.

Liszt himself played "Erlkönig" many times. One of his Weimar students, Anton Strelezki, has provided an eyewitness account of one such performance which throws light on Liszt's general approach to the piano.

> I was surprised to note that as he left the piano, not a trace of fatigue was noticeable on his face or hands. Only a few weeks after this I heard the same piece played by Rubinstein. From his outward appearance, at the close, you would imagine that he had just walked out of a shower-bath, taken with all his clothes on. And yet Liszt's rendering was just as vivid as Rubinstein's, and his fortissimo was as tremendously powerful.[12]

This brings us to the third purpose of these transcriptions: that of extending Liszt's own repertory. They were immensely popular with the general public, and Liszt played them in Pest, Leipzig, Berlin, St. Petersburg, and London, as a perusal of his programs shows. It must be stressed, however, that Liszt rarely regarded these pieces as display works with which to dazzle the audience. Their difficulties are mostly of a private, not a public, nature. They embody the "art that conceals art." Many of their finger-twisting solutions are known only to the pianist, who gets no public ovation whatever for them.

Liszt's hands were long and narrow and could encompass a tenth. His fingers had

12. SPRL, p. 7.

little or no webbing between them (which prompted Edward Dannreuther to describe them as "the opposite of webbed feet"), and this allowed unusual internal
stretches—especially between the fourth and fifth fingers. His fingertips were square
and blunted, not tapered, which afforded greater traction on the surface of the keys.
Such physical characteristics are decided advantages for the virtuoso pianist.

IV

All these thoughts come to mind when considering the transcription of "Ave Maria."
It sounds easy, but is in fact very difficult. Where should the melody be placed? Schubert put his accompaniment in the very register occupied by the voice—the one
overlaps with the other—thus posing a problem for the transcriber. Liszt resolves the
difficulty by distributing the individual notes of Schubert's melody between alternating hands. This actually has the effect of creating more physical space on the keyboard than would otherwise be the case; that is, the hand not presently engaged in
"holding the line" is now safely out of the way of the one that is.

According to the contemporary journals, Liszt often accompanied famous singers in performances of these songs. On August 3, 1837, for example, he accompanied Adolphe Nourrit singing Schubert at a concert in Lyon.[13] The tenor Benedict Randhartinger also performed Schubert several times with Liszt at the keyboard in Vienna during April and May 1838.[14] Liszt also played for Mme Schröder-Devrient when she sang a group of these songs, including "Erlkönig," at a concert in Dresden in March 1840.[15] While depicting Liszt in an unusual light, all this activity as an "accompanist" must have given him an insider's knowledge of these songs. It certainly gave him a healthy respect for the originals. He took pains always to find the solution that best met the demands of the music, the keyboard, and the limitations of ten fingers. He was quite meticulous over such matters as fingering, phrasing, and pedaling. And due to his judicious deployment of notation (up and down stems to indicate the separate hands, for example, or the use of three staves where the texture is crowded), we are never in doubt as to Liszt's intentions. Much more than the operatic paraphrases or even the *Transcendental Studies,* these Schubert transcriptions reveal Liszt's total command of the keyboard. This judgment may sound perverse, but it can be substantiated. Transcription is more difficult than paraphrase. In a paraphrase, the arranger is free to vary the original, to weave his own fantasies around it, to go where he wills. This is not so in a transcription. The transcription must be obedient, a true copy of the original; it binds the transcriber to it, making him its slave. And there is the paradox. Only the greatest master is capable of becoming the perfect slave.

V

Another of the transcriptions Liszt played in Vienna during his 1838 charity concerts was "Gretchen am Spinnrade." He appears to have retained a lifelong affection for this piece. His pupils often brought it to his masterclasses.[16] Liszt was deeply familiar with Goethe's *Faust,* from which the poem is drawn, and given his well-known susceptibility to this literary masterpiece it is hardly surprising that he lavished all his skill on the piece. The scene Goethe depicts is familiar to all. Gretchen is sitting at her spinning wheel, dreaming about her lover. We hear the spinning wheel whirling quietly in the background, wonderfully evoked by Schubert's accompaniment. Lost in reverie, she recalls her lover's touch, his smile, his kiss. And at that magical moment the music is suspended, the spinning wheel stops. Haltingly, Gretchen sets the wheel spinning again and continues with her song. Liszt has absorbed every detail of this work into his transcription—and has even discovered

---

13. *Courrier de Lyon,* August 6, 1837.
14. WLCC, p. 48.
15. NZfM (1840), no. 12, pp. 102–3.
16. See, for example, GLK, p. 56, and LL, pp. 13–14. Liszt himself usually selected the repertory to be played in the masterclasses, after rummaging through the music scores the pupils brought with them.

how to make Schubert's melody emerge from its own "spinning wheel" accompaniment.

Only toward the end, as the music surges to its climax, does Liszt double the melody in octaves and thicken the texture, an apotheosis that he could well claim was justified by the words ("and kiss him, just as I liked").

The extent to which Liszt steeped himself in the verbal imagery of these songs has already been remarked. Nowhere does it stand more clearly revealed than in "Ständchen"—a lover's serenade. Liszt here perceives a possibility not pursued by Schubert: he presents the melody of the first verse as if sung by a soprano, that of the second as if sung by a baritone. He then brings the two lovers together in canon—one voice trailing the other like an echo at a measure's distance. The effect is peculiarly apt, and, though it does not occur in Schubert's original, it is not out of keeping with the spirit of the song.

VI

Liszt's arrangement of the song cycle *Schwanengesang* shows him at his thoughtful best. Schubert had composed these fourteen songs mainly in the summer of 1828, just a few months before his death. They are not a cycle in the deepest sense of that term (unlike *Winterreise* or the *Müllerlieder*), but rather consist of random settings of seven poems by Ludwig Rellstab, six by Heinrich Heine and one by Johann Seidl, all of which remained unpublished at Schubert's death. Schubert's brother Ferdinand offered this miscellany of manuscripts to Haslinger shortly after the composer's funeral. Haslinger not only selected the running order of the songs but also published them (in the spring of 1829) under the topical title *Swan Song*. In the 170 years that have elapsed, history has entangled these songs in romantic associations (including a retrospective "foretaste" of death) which they could not possibly have had at the time. Such information helps us to understand what might otherwise be a puzzling decision on Liszt's part. Unencumbered by a historical legacy, he changes the published order of the songs, producing a new sequence that is (in my opinion) better than Haslinger's. By reshuffling the numbers and bringing six of them into new relationships with their neighbors, and by joining two separate Schubert songs ("Ihr Bild" and "Frühlingssehnsucht") to make one large binary structure, Liszt creates a musically satisfying cycle of contrasting pieces, which begins and ends in the key of C minor. Liszt's cycle also unfolds a series of interior key-relationships of falling and rising thirds—C minor—A-flat major—E minor—C major—E-flat major—and so on, relationships that are absent in Haslinger's random sequence and come to us as an unexpected musical bonus, made all the more gratifying because Liszt remains true to Schubert's original keys.[17] Haslinger's numberings are given here in parentheses:

17. We know of only one case among the fifty-six Schubert song transcriptions in which Liszt transposed the song into a new key: the second version of his transcription of "Ungeduld."

"Die Stadt"	(11)	C minor
"Das Fischermädchen"	(10)	A-flat major
"Aufenthalt"	(5)	E minor
"Am Meer"	(12)	C major
"Abschied"	(7)	E-flat major
"In der Ferne"	(6)	B minor
"Ständchen" ("Leise flehen")	(4)	D minor
"Ihr Bild"	(9)	B-flat minor
"Frühlingssehnsucht"	(3)	B-flat major
"Liebesbotschaft"	(1)	G major
"Der Atlas"	(8)	G minor
"Der Doppelgänger"	(13)	B minor
"Die Taubenpost"	(14)	G major
"Kriegers Ahnung"	(2)	C minor

Though purists will always object to such license, they have in this case no final authority on which to fall back. Schubert himself left no instructions in the matter.

VII

The years 1839–47 are sometimes called by Lisztians his "years of transcendental execution," when he unfolded a concert career unmatched in the history of performance. Not even Paganini, with whose career Liszt's own has often been compared, enjoyed such phenomenal success. He played in Austria, Germany, Italy, France, Britain, Hungary, Spain, Portugal, Turkey, and Russia, among other countries. His crushing itinerary during March and April 1840 is typical. After giving six concerts in eight days in Prague, he moved to Dresden where he gave three more the following week. He then journeyed to Leipzig, and another four concerts followed—thirteen concerts in just over three weeks. In Berlin, during the winter of 1841, he gave twenty-one concerts in ten weeks, during which he played eighty works—fifty of them from memory. Liszt gave more than a thousand recitals during this grueling eight-year period; no wonder we find him complaining that he was exhausted. He had hardly begun this long odyssey when we find him exclaiming, "The good Haslinger overwhelms me with Schubert. I've just sent him another twenty-four new Lieder ('Schwanengesang' and 'Winterreise'), and for the moment I am rather tired of this drudgery."[18] In the midst of so much activity, why did Liszt bother about his Schubert transcriptions at all?

Liszt saw himself and his piano as vessels through which the whole of music might pass. His lifelong motto was "Génie oblige!" If nature endows you with genius, Liszt maintained, it puts you under a moral obligation to repay the debt and serve the rest of humanity not so fortunately endowed. In all his musical works and

18. LLB, vol. 1, p. 29.

deeds Liszt lived out this remarkable precept. His arrangements amount to a kind of self-effacement. When we survey them complete, it is rather like walking around a gallery peopled by many of the great personalities of the past—Bach, Beethoven, Berlioz, Wagner, Schumann, Mendelssohn, Verdi, Mozart—the roll call seems endless. It is as if Liszt were trying to place music itself under his benevolent protection. In his day, there were no gramophone records, no radio, no real interest in preserving the music of the past. Liszt's answer was to enshrine it in the piano (or as much of it as ten fingers and one lifetime enabled him to do). It is some measure of his achievement that, while our entire musical heritage is now available to us literally at the push of a button, many of Liszt's arrangements have transcended both their time and their utilitarian origins. They continue to give the modern listener pleasure and enlightenment.

Schumann, Liszt, and the C Major Fantasie, op. 17

A Study in Declining Relationships[1]

The first movement [of my Fantasie] is a deep lament about you.
ROBERT SCHUMANN TO CLARA SCHUMANN, MARCH 17, 1838[2]

I am really proud of the honor you have done me in dedicating to me so grand a composition.
LISZT TO ROBERT SCHUMANN, JUNE 5, 1839[3]

I

The sale at Sotheby's in November 1977 of the autograph of the original version of Schumann's Fantasie in C Major, op. 17, aroused widespread interest. Not only is the Fantasie one of the masterworks of the nineteenth-century piano repertoire, but as a patently autobiographical work it also throws light on Schumann himself. Originally composed in 1836, it reflects the twenty-seven-year-old Schumann's deepest despair over his thwarted love affair with Clara Wieck and contains symbolic references to Clara which have occupied Schumann scholars for years.[4] At the same time, the Fantasie was supposed to represent the life of Beethoven. A Beethoven Committee had been established in the 1830s, and musicians from across Europe were invited to contribute to the erection of a monument.[5] Schumann thought that the best gesture he could make was to donate the proceeds from the sales of one of his own compositions, and he accordingly began work on a "Grand Sonata" in three

---

1. This is a greatly expanded version of an article originally published in *Music and Letters* 60, no. 2 (April 1979): pp. 156–65.

2. *Jugendbriefe*, p. 278.

3. LLB, vol. 1, p. 26.

4. See Hermann Abert, *Robert Schumann*, Berlin, 1920, p. 69; Robert Schauffler, *Florestan*, New York, 1945, pp. 297ff.; Eric Sams, "Did Schumann use ciphers?" *Musical Times* 106 (1965): pp. 584–91, and "The Schumann ciphers," ibid. 107 (1966): pp. 392–400.

5. As we have seen in connection with Liszt's own involvement in the Beethoven cause (pp. 14–15), the monument was eventually unveiled at Bonn in August 1845, in celebration of the forthcoming seventy-fifth anniversary of Beethoven's birth.

movements. The title was soon abandoned as the work began to assume its programmatic character, and the three movements were later called "Ruins," "Triumphal Arch," and "Starry Crown," in pictorial allusion to Beethoven's heroic career. The musical quotations from Beethoven's song cycle *An die ferne Geliebte* [To the Distant Beloved] woven into the work strengthen its symbolic links both with Beethoven and with Clara.

The words say, "Accept, then, these melodies that I sang for you, my love." They make it plain that the "distant beloved" was Clara, and her melody shimmers behind much of the first movement, as a comparison with the following example shows:

The Sotheby sale prompted a question which at that time no one could answer. It is well known that Schumann revised this masterpiece before finally publishing it under the title "Fantasie," with a dedication to Liszt, in April 1839. What became of the manuscript of this final version? Where, in other words, is the musicological evidence for these revisions? Georg Eismann, in his authoritative Schumann catalogue, implies that the manuscript is missing.[6] It can now be said with some certainty that this is no longer the case.

II

The National Széchényi Library in Budapest possesses a fair manuscript copy of the Fantasie signed and dated December 19, 1838, by Schumann himself and containing corrections and comments in the composer's own hand.[7] A careful perusal of this thirty-page manuscript and a line-by-line comparison with the printed version of the Fantasie leave no doubt that this is the copy Schumann prepared for the printers just a few weeks before the work went to press. He appears to have been in a hurry. Instead of copying out the entire Fantasie afresh, he took a beautifully prepared professional copy of the first version and pasted his revisions over the original manuscript. He also wrote in a number of marginal comments in his charac-

---

6. *Sammelbände der Robert-Schumann-Gesellschaft,* vol. 2, Leipzig, 1966, p. 11.
7. The manuscript, shelf mark Ms. Mus. 37, was purchased by the Széchényi Library in 1906.

teristic handwriting and added expression marks and phrasing throughout. The result is a document of far greater musical interest than an autograph; from it one can see at a glance precisely what Schumann's revisions were. The most prominent additions and emendations are as follows:

1. To the title page has been added the famous inscription to Liszt:

Dichtungen
für das Pianoforte
H[er]rn. Franz Liszt
zugeeignet
von
Robert Schumann
Op. 16

The word "*Dichtungen*" (poems)[8] has been struck out to make way for the new title "Fantasie." The designation "op. 16" has likewise been changed to "op. 17" (Schumann's opus numbers were subjected to constant revision during this period). (See page 43.)

2. Each movement of the Széchényi manuscript is headed by a title, now vigorously crossed out: I "Ruinen"; II "Siegesbogen"; III "Sternbild." At the foot of the first page of music Schumann instructs the printer: "Please place three stars at the head of each of the three individual movements" (see page 44).

3. Schlegel's well-known motto has been added to the reverse side of the title page:

Durch alle Töne tönet
Im bunten Erdentraum
Ein leiser Ton gezogen
Für den, der heimlich lauschet.[9]

4. The last page of the manuscript contains a major musical surprise. The quotation from Beethoven's *An die ferne Geliebte* that rounds off the first movement was originally recapitulated in full at the end of the third movement, but with some changed harmonies (see page 45).

---

8. That Schumann nearly let the work go to press under the title *Dichtungen* will interest all those who have always insisted on the close connection between his music and his verbal ideas. And this first choice of title is confirmed in his correspondence. As early as April 13, 1838, he had told Clara, "It was a long time before I could think of that last word [*Dichtungen*]. It strikes me as being a very refined and most characteristic title for a piece of music" (*Jugendbriefe*, p. 281).

9. "Through all the tones in Earth's many-colored dream there sounds one soft long-drawn note for the secret listener." See Schumann's letter to Clara of June 9, 1839, in which he asks her, "Are you not the 'note' in the motto? I almost believe you are" (*Jugendbriefe*, p. 303).

The manuscript title page of Schumann's C Major Fantasie, op. 17, with its dedication to Franz Liszt.

This musical reminiscence (fifteen bars of it altogether) works beautifully within the context of the composition as a whole. A comparison of the final bars of the first movement with the final bars of the third movement as they were originally conceived by Schumann (see pp. 44–45) makes the connection clear:

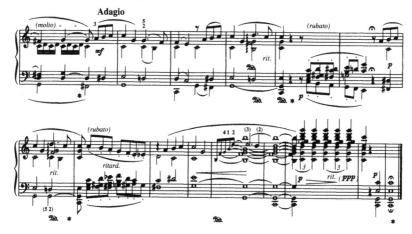

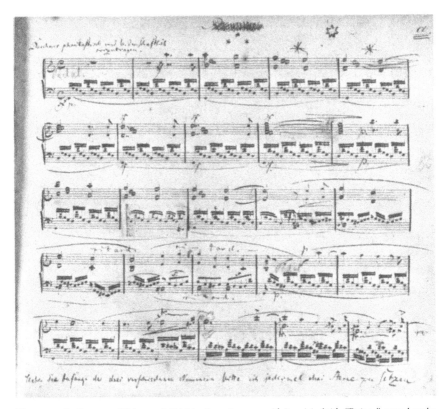

The manuscript first page of Schumann's C Major Fantasie, op. 17, with its original title "Ruinen" crossed out by the composer.

The manuscript last page of Schumann's C Major Fantasie, op. 17, with its original ending crossed out and replaced with the "official" ending.

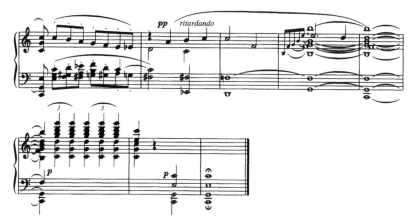

This ending was originally destined to begin four measures before the end of the work. Schumann, however, has struck it out and has continued the arpeggios with which the Fantasie now closes. On purely musical grounds it is possible to regard the suppressed coda as an alternative ending to the Fantasie. It is certainly worth a hearing.[10]

III

In view of its autobiographical origins, why did Schumann dedicate the Fantasie to Liszt? This question, puzzling at first, is easy to answer once we understand the historical background. In 1837, before the two composers had even met, Liszt published a long and highly favorable article about Schumann's keyboard works in *La Revue et Gazette musicale*.[11] Schumann, who was still struggling for recognition, was deeply appreciative (he was still far better known in Germany as the editor of the *Neue Zeitschrift für Musik* than as a composer). He sent Liszt more of his compositions and the pair struck up a friendly correspondence. Then, in April 1838, Clara visited Vienna and heard Liszt for the first time. On April 12 she wrote in her diary: "We have heard Liszt. He can be compared to no other player. . . . He arouses fright and astonishment. . . . His appearance at the piano is indescribable. He is an original . . . he is absorbed by the piano."[12] Such descriptions must have aroused Schumann's curiosity. And when a few weeks later Liszt dedicated to Clara his newly composed "Paganini" Studies, thus cementing that early acquaintance, it was clear that some kind of reciprocal gesture was called for. Schumann invited Liszt to Leipzig, but Liszt was unable at first to accept.[13] Throughout 1838, Liszt's total commitment to the idea of a Beethoven memorial statue was actually keeping alive this flagging international effort, the organizers of which were incompetent, and this increased Schumann's admiration still further.[14] Schumann had in manuscript at this time a number of compositions (including *Kreisleriana, Kinderszenen,* and the great *Humoreske*), any one of which could have been dedicated to Liszt. His choice fell, however, on the Fantasie, the one work that was itself intended to raise funds for the Beethoven monument, that was "about" Beethoven, and that quoted from his music. At the time, no gesture could have seemed more appropriate. The dedication

---

10. When I first penned those lines, in 1977, I had no idea that they would arouse any particular interest. Among the many letters I received was one from my friend the American pianist Jeffrey Siegel who asked to see my copy of the manuscript, and later gave a performance of the Fantasie with its "alternative" ending at his Carnegie Hall recital, on November 22, 1981; he now prefers to play the work in that form. Meanwhile, Charles Rosen also read my article and sent to Budapest for a copy of the manuscript. He too gave a public performance of the work with its original ending (incorporating as well throughout his rendering of the Fantasie a few other minor differences found only in Schumann's unrevised manuscript). Rosen made generous mention of my article in his interview with David Dubal (in DRK, p. 305). That is more than can be said for the editors of Henle's so-called Urtext Edition of this Fantasie, who, having been alerted to the discovery of the manuscript, hastened to bring out their edition, without any of the usual scholarly courtesies.

11. RGS, vol. 2, pp. 99–107.

12. LCS, vol. 1, p. 199.

13. LLB, vol. 1, p. 20.

14. Liszt eventually offered to donate the whole of the outstanding balance needed to erect a monument. See his letter of October 3, 1839, to the Beethoven Memorial Committee in Bonn, reproduced on p. 13 of the present volume.

arose from purely idealistic motives. The work was printed in the spring of 1839. Liszt and Schumann had still not met.

No one could have foreseen that Liszt's relations with Schumann would deteriorate so sharply. The two composers were united in Dresden, on or about March 11, 1840. Schumann had traveled there from Leipzig in order to cover Liszt's concerts for the *Neue Zeitschrift für Musik*. He wrote to Clara that it was as if he and Liszt had already known one another for twenty years.[15] They journeyed back to Leipzig together and spent a whole fortnight in one another's company. Schumann wrote two glowing reviews of Liszt's historic concerts in the Leipzig Gewandhaus,[16] the musical highlight of which was Liszt's public sight-reading of Mendelssohn's Piano Concerto in D Minor. Then occurred an extraordinary sequence of events. Schumann was at that time in the middle of a lawsuit against Friedrich Wieck, the object of which was to force Wieck to show cause why his twenty-year-old daughter Clara should not marry Schumann. Liszt took Schumann's side, snubbed Wieck, and refused to send him complimentary tickets for his Dresden concerts. The litigious Wieck, already fighting a rearguard action against Schumann, was outraged; he started to slander Liszt and his brilliant young pupil Hermann Cohen in the Leipzig papers. Liszt shrugged off the episode. Cohen, however, took Wieck to court and won his case.[17] Clara now sprang to her father's defense, turned against Liszt, and wrote to Schumann, "This has cost me bitter tears and it is not right of you at all."[18] As for Wieck, he came out with his classic remark: "I told Liszt that he could have been the finest pianist in the world—if only he had had a proper teacher."

Liszt now continued on those historic European tours of his, a series of magisterial journeys which his biographers still call his "years of transcendental execution." In some places he was treated like royalty. At his Berlin concerts, in 1842, "Lisztomania" swept the city and he was mobbed. Admiring women collected his cigar butts, and his recitals became a heady combination of revivalist meeting and séance. When he left the Prussian capital, it was at the head of a procession with his carriage drawn by a team of white horses. The Schumanns looked on appalled. It seemed to them that Liszt had betrayed his genius for cheap successes, that he was dazzled by his own myth. They came to agree with Mendelssohn's diagnosis of his character as "a continual alternation between scandal and apotheosis." Schumann concluded that there was "too much tinsel" about Liszt's art; Clara added, somewhat smugly, that Liszt's paraphrases could not give "lasting pleasure." Later she made her position clearer and described Liszt as "a smasher of pianos."

The outcome was a dreadful scene which took place in Schumann's home in Dresden, in June 1848. Liszt, who was once more passing through the city, paid the Schumanns a surprise visit. Clara went to considerable pains to arrange a musical dinner in his honor. A time was set, the musicians assembled, but Liszt failed to appear.

---

15. LCS, vol. 1, p. 413. Liszt had just arrived in Dresden from Prague, where he had given six concerts in eight days.
16. NZfM, xii (1840), pp. 102, 118–20.
17. LLB, vol. 1, pp. 256–07.
18. LCS, vol. 1, p. 418.

The exasperated players had almost finished a performance of Beethoven's D major Trio, in the guest of honor's absence, when Liszt, in Clara's words, "burst in at the door,"[19] two hours late, in the company of Richard Wagner. A performance of Schumann's Piano Quintet followed, which Liszt tactlessly described as "Leipziger-isch." The atmosphere was tense throughout dinner. Schumann was ready to boil over; Liszt obliged him by providing more heat. He started to praise Meyerbeer at Mendelssohn's expense. At this, Schumann broke into a violent rage. He sprang up, rushed toward Liszt, seized him by both shoulders, and shouted angrily, "Who are you that you dare to speak in such a way of a musician like Mendelssohn?" He then stalked out of the room, leaving the other dinner guests staring angrily at Liszt. Liszt rose to the occasion superbly, turned to Clara, and said, "Tell your husband that he is the only man in the world from whom I would take so calmly the words just offered to me."[20] Liszt then left the house. Clara declared, "I have done with him forever."[21]

The Schumanns' open hostility toward Liszt contrasted sharply with his own generosity to them. In 1849, shortly after Liszt had settled in Weimar, and less than a year after Schumann's assault on him, he conducted Part II of Schumann's *Scenes from 'Faust.'*[22] Three years later he gave the first performance of the incidental music to Schumann's *Manfred*. All he got for his trouble on that occasion was a note from Clara asking him to return the autograph score of *Manfred*, which he had hoped to keep as a token of friendship.[23] Liszt's response was to dedicate to Schumann, in 1853, his B Minor Piano Sonata.[24] And he followed this gesture, in 1855, with a full-scale production of Schumann's opera *Genoveva* in Weimar's opera house.[25]

---

19. LCS, vol. 2, p. 121.

20. JSB, p. 523. Clara's diary gives a milder version of the story, but Gustav Jansen declared in 1879 that he had shown his account to Clara, who had confirmed "everything." In considering Schumann's extraordinary outburst, it has to be remembered that Mendelssohn, who was revered by the Leipzig-Dresden circle, had died only a few months previously. More important, Schumann was now irreversibly ill and was already presenting symptoms of tertiary syphilis, which was affecting both his physical and his mental behavior (see E. Slater and A. Meyer, "Contributions to a Pathography of the Musicians: I. Robert Schumann," *Confinia Psychiatrica* 2 (1959): p. 87). The essential correctness of the story was confirmed around the same time by Liszt himself in the course of responding to one of Lina Ramann's biographical questionnaires. After telling her about his first encounters with Wagner in the early 1840s, he went on, "A few years later we met again in Dresden, where we suffered a very agitated evening at Robert Schumann's house, for which I was blamed" (RL, p. 399).

21. LCS, vol. 2, p. 122.

22. On April 14, 1849.

23. LLB, vol. 1, p. 113.

24. By the time the sonata was published, in 1854, Schumann was already a mental patient at Endenich, in the private clinic run by Dr. Franz Richarz, having attempted to commit suicide by throwing himself into the Rhine. The parcel containing Liszt's music was received by Clara on May 25. Her diary entry for that particular day describes her reaction to the piece: "merely a blind noise—no healthy ideas any more, everything confused, one cannot find a single, clear harmonic progression—and yet I must thank him for it [i.e., the dedication to Robert]. It really is too awful" (LCS, vol. 2, p. 317). When the sonata arrived, Brahms was staying with Clara as her houseguest, and her diary reveals that it was Brahms, not Clara, who actually played through the sonata—Brahms, who had apparently fallen asleep when Liszt had played the work in his presence the previous year (MMML, pp. 129–31). See also p. 145 of the present volume.

25. On April 9, 1855.

In 1856 Schumann died. Liszt was now approached by Wilhelm Wasielewski, Schumann's first biographer, for help in sketching in some of the details of their relationship. He left his sickbed in order to write to Wasielewski an extremely long letter[26] covering their twenty-year relationship in affectionate terms, even comparing *Carnaval* with Beethoven's "Diabelli" Variations and making no mention of their personal quarrel.

IV

What has this to do with the Fantasie? After Schumann's death, Clara returned to her career as a concert pianist, which she had abandoned at the time of her marriage to Robert in 1840, and she became known as the principal interpreter of his music. In 1887 she published her own edition of his piano music, changing a number of things (including Schumann's metronome markings) in accordance with her "memory" of how Robert had liked his music to be interpreted.[27] When preparing the Fantasie for republication, she had no hesitation in striking out the dedication to Liszt.[28] The Fantasie had always been hers symbolically, she may have argued, and never Liszt's. These dismal proceedings had a direct bearing on the fate of the Fantasie. The work fell into a kind of limbo. Neither Clara nor Liszt seemed particularly anxious to play it in public; it symbolized too acutely the rift that now separated them. It was Clara who finally broke the stalemate when she performed the Fantasie in Leipzig, in 1866, almost thirty years after it had been composed.[29] Having settled the question of "ownership," Clara then appears to have dropped the Fantasie from her repertoire.

26. LLB, vol. 1, pp. 253–59. Liszt was confined to his bed for several weeks with abscesses on his feet, which made it nearly impossible for him to walk. He asked Wasielewski to have patience with the length of his letter, which, he added charmingly, "I do not have time to make shorter."

27. This led to widespread speculation that Schumann's metronome was faulty. But Schumann himself had already confirmed that this was not so. On February 8, 1853, he wrote to the composer Ferdinand Böhme: "Have you a correct metronome? . . . Mine is accurate. It always gives as many beats to the minute as the number on which the weight is placed. . . . As far as I know, this is the test of correctness" (JSB, p. 365). Jansen claimed that Schumann erred in making this remark, but the only evidence he adduced was that the metronome markings themselves were questionable! Clara's "personal tradition" sometimes increases, sometimes decreases Schumann's metronome markings. We might well ask what kind of metronome sometimes runs fast and sometimes runs slow. A faulty metronome, like a faulty watch, might run slow and might run fast. But it cannot run both slow *and* fast.

28. Clara's so-called Instructive Edition of Schumann's piano music, with the dedication of the Fantasie omitted, was published less than one year after Liszt died. The timing was unfortunate and caused much indignation within the circle of Liszt's pupils. Both Carl Lachmund and August Göllerich mention Clara's snub in their reminiscences (see LL, p. 24, and GLK, p. 47). So, too, does Berthold Kellermann, who appends to his observation an earlier conversation with Liszt in which the composer talked of "ex-friends" who took things away from him: "I cannot repay them for that, for I must above all else value them as artists" (KE, p. 29). For the text of Clara's edition see *Klavier-Werke von Robert Schumann. Erste mit Fingersatz und Vortragsbezeichnung versehene Instructive Ausgabe. Nach den Handschriften und persönlicher Ueberlieferung herausgegeben von Clara Schumann*, vol. 3, Leipzig, 1887.

29. Nancy Reich, *Clara Schumann* (1985), p. 268. This performance is often regarded as the first one ever given in public. Ironically, that honor falls to Hans von Bülow, Liszt's leading pupil and Clara's nemesis, who had already introduced the Fantasie at a recital he gave in Stettin in January, 1858.

And what of Liszt? He never played the Fantasie in public at all. Shortly after he got to know it, in 1839, he told Schumann that the work was too difficult for the general public and he therefore wished to postpone putting it into his programs until a later date.[30] He never did so, and we have some evidence to suggest that he may have regretted that fact.[31] He played the Fantasie in private, however, and Schumann himself was once treated to a performance. Liszt described the occasion to a visitor in 1869:

> I remember the first time I played it to the great composer; he remained perfectly silent in his chair at the close of the first movement, which rather disappointed me. So I asked him what impression my rendering of the work had made on him, and what improvements he could suggest, being naturally anxious to hear the composer's ideas as to the reading of so noble a composition. He asked me to proceed with the "March," after which he would give me his criticism. I played the second movement, and with such effect that Schumann jumped out of his chair, flung his arms around me, and with tears in his eyes, cried: *Göttlich!* Our ideas are absolutely identical as regards the rendering of these movements, only you with your magic fingers have carried my ideas to a realization that I had never dreamed of![32]

It is an irony of history that when, at last, the Fantasie was taken up in a big way, it was by Liszt's own pupils. Most of the pianists who dominated the international scene between 1880 and 1910, with the notable exception of Busoni, had studied with Liszt. Some of them used to bring the Fantasie along to Liszt's masterclasses in Weimar, Budapest, and Rome.[33]

Today the Fantasie stands before us as perhaps Schumann's very greatest keyboard work. The discovery of the Széchényi manuscript adds an extra dimension to its colorful historical background and will ensure that this masterpiece remains perennially fascinating to scholars and performers alike. As for the autograph of the original version of the Fantasie, mentioned at the beginning of this essay, it surfaced once more at Sotheby's in November 1984, the last time it was seen in public. It is today in private hands.[34]

---

30. LLB, vol. 1, p. 27.

31. LLB, vol. 1, p. 257.

32. SPRL, pp. 4–5. It is difficult to date this particular encounter of Liszt and Schumann, but from collateral evidence we assume that it must have been during Liszt's visit to Leipzig, in March 1840.

33. The diaries of Carl Lachmund (LL) and August Göllerich (GLK) present some detailed records of the repertory played on these occasions, together with Liszt's own commentary. On May 27, 1882, for example, Emma Grosskurth played the Fantasie for Liszt. Pointing to the infamous last page of the March, with its wide leaps for both hands in opposite directions, Liszt remarked, "That is a dangerous place," and then sat down and played the passage to perfection, and without effort (LL, p. 59).

34. See MST-B, p. 76, for the chequered history of this manuscript.

Liszt and His Pupils

Three Character Sketches: Carl Tausig, Hans von Bülow, and Walter Bache

I

The three character sketches that follow—on Carl Tausig, Hans von Bülow, and Walter Bache—were selected for a reason. Each one of these pupils of Liszt had a personal relationship with him that runs so deep that we have to place them in a different category from most of the others. The golden thread that connects them to him also connects them to one another. Liszt emerges at crucial moments in their lives and even changes the course of their destiny. They are attached to him at a hundred different points; an account of their careers throws almost as much light on him as it does on them. Moreover, not one of them has yet succeeded in finding a satisfactory biographer; that is reason enough to bring them forward here. In the cases of Bülow and Tausig, the absence of full-scale biographies is lamentable, given their obvious importance to the history of nineteenth-century piano playing. Walter Bache is not so well known, even to the aficionado, although his name will usually be found as a footnote to the story of Liszt's final years. The mantle of silence that Bache wanted to fall on his acts of philanthropy, especially those in behalf of Liszt and his music, has fallen on him as well. It is time that it was lifted, so that Bache can take his proper place in the Lisztian scheme of things.

All three pupils were also unusual in that they had many private lessons from Liszt, a privilege he rarely offered to others. Bülow and Tausig belonged to his first generation of pupils, sometimes referred to as the "Altenburg Eagles," while Bache belonged to a later generation that gathered around Liszt during his Hofgärtnerei years. Some background will make the distinction clear.

II

Most of Liszt's teaching during the Weimar years (1848–61) was done in the Altenburg, the old house on the hill overlooking the river Ilm. The dwelling had been set aside for Liszt's use by Maria Pawlowna, who was then the reigning grand duchess of Weimar. It contained more than forty rooms and became a shrine to Liszt's memory even during his tenure there, housing many of the treasures he had accumulated

The Altenburg. (A nineteenth-century woodcut, based on a drawing by Carl Jordan.)

during his years as a touring virtuoso. Some of the gifts from kings and potentates were exhibited for visitors to admire. Here could be seen the jewel-encrusted Hungarian sword of honor (presented to him by a grateful nation in 1840); the silver breakfast service from the Philharmonic Society in London; the decorations and gold medallions from such far-flung places as Madrid, Lisbon, Berlin, and Constantinople; and the solid silver music desk inscribed with the names of more than a hundred eminent musicians. Beethoven's old Broadwood piano was also housed there, together with his priceless death mask, both of which had been presented to Liszt ten years earlier.[1]

Liszt did most of his teaching in the small reception room on the ground floor, which was dominated by an Erard grand piano. The music room proper was located on the second floor. It was here that Liszt held his Sunday afternoon "matinees," where singers and instrumentalists from the court theater would gather to perform lieder and chamber music, often with Liszt himself taking part. These Altenburg matinees had begun almost by accident in the early 1850s, and they soon became regular fixtures in which Liszt's students were also expected to participate. The room contained two Viennese grand pianos (by Streicher and Bösendorfer) and a spinet that had once belonged to Mozart. Liszt's so-called piano-organ, which was installed there in the summer of 1854, commanded a lot of attention. Designed by the Parisian

1. For a comprehensive history of the Altenburg, and an accurate description of its interior at the time of Liszt's tenure, see HAG.

firm of Alexandre et fils, to specifications provided by Liszt himself, the "monster instrument," as he called it, boasted three keyboards, a pedalboard, eight registers, and a set of pipes that could reproduce the sounds of all the wind instruments. (Liszt worked out much of the orchestration of his *Faust* Symphony on this contraption.)[2] The walls were lined with books from Liszt's large library, collected since his days as a young man in Paris, together with precious autograph scores by Chopin, Schumann, Beethoven, Wagner, and other composers whom Liszt had encountered on his European travels.

Visitors to the Altenburg during the 1850s included Wagner, Berlioz, Brahms, Joseph Joachim, Joachim Raff, Peter Cornelius, George Eliot, and Hans Christian Andersen. By the mid 1850s the old house had become a mecca of modern music, to which the faithful trekked across Europe in search of help and support from Liszt, who was already acknowledged as the leader of the avant-garde in music. Aside from Bülow and Tausig, Liszt's pupils from this earlier period included Karl Klindworth, Robert Pflughaupt, Dionys Pruckner, Hans von Bronsart, and the American William Mason, whose memoir on this *goldene Zeit,* as he called it, remains one of the best.[3]

Liszt's second generation of Weimar pupils worked with him in the much smaller Hofgärtnerei—or court gardener's house—a residence set aside for his use after his return to the city in 1869, following an absence of eight years in Rome. This small two-story villa lay at the end of Marienstrasse, near Belvedere Allee, and backed onto the Goethe Park. A large music room occupied much of the first floor, with tall windows overlooking the gardens. A Bechstein grand piano stood in the center of the room, and Liszt also installed a small upright piano on which to accompany his students whenever they played a concerto.[4] This room was to become the scene of the most famous piano classes in history. For seventeen summers Liszt taught there, and a steady stream of gifted pupils passed through his hands. They included Arthur Friedheim, Alfred Reisenauer, Moriz Rosenthal, Emil von Sauer, Alexander Siloti, Eugène d'Albert, Sophie Menter, and Frederic Lamond. These young men and women helped to lay the foundations of modern piano playing. A number of them lived well into the twentieth century and made gramophone records, which helped to carry Liszt's reputation into modern times.

Three afternoons a week a dozen or more students would gather in the music room of the Hofgärtnerei, shortly before Liszt himself entered, having first deposited the music they wished to play in a growing pile on top of the piano. Liszt would then enter. Someone at the back would whisper, "Der Meister kommt!" Everyone would stand respectfully, and Liszt would advance toward the piano in order to leaf through the music that had been left for his scrutiny. When he found something he wanted to hear, he would hold it up and ask, "Who plays this?" The owner would

---

2. The instrument is today exhibited in the Kunsthistorisches Museum, Vienna, although it is no longer in working order.

3. See MMML, especially pp. 88–182.

4. The Bechstein was provided courtesy of Carl Bechstein; it was put into storage whenever Liszt left town for extended periods. The upright piano was provided by G. Höhne, a local Weimar manufacturer. In 1885 it was replaced by the better-known Ibach upright.

Liszt in the Hofgärtnerei, 1882, surrounded by his pupils and colleagues. Front row, right, the Grand Duke of Weimar Carl Alexander, with his wife, Grand Duchess Sophie, listens attentively to Liszt's playing. (An oil painting by Hans W. Schmidt.)

then come forward and play before an audience of his peers. These were the first masterclasses in musical history. Liszt believed that they fostered the competitive spirit, and that by hearing one another play his students would be encouraged to excel. The results bore him out. It was a nerve-racking experience for the students, but it was one of the finest possible training grounds. If these young artists could survive such a baptism of fire, nothing they were likely to encounter in the years ahead need bother them. Those attending included not only pianists but also composers who wanted to show him their work, as well as violinists, cellists, and singers. The group was often joined by painters, poets, and scientists from Weimar's intelligentsia. Even the grand duke and duchess of Weimar would make an occasional appearance and listen with interest to Liszt's comments on music and musicians.

Did Liszt have any general principles of teaching? Two of them can be mentioned here, although they have nothing to do with pedagogy, a subject he regarded with suspicion. He often spoke of the "Pontius Pilate offense," by which he referred to those artists who ritually washed their hands in public of the music that they played, in a mistaken attempt to achieve objectivity. He argued that the "cult of personality" was less harmful to music than the "cult of anonymity," an intriguing idea that is still debated today. The other idea is equally stimulating. When Liszt became the first president of the newly formed Royal Academy of Music in Hungary, he was able to influence its curriculum. He insisted that all piano students study composition and that all composition students study the piano. He wanted to stress the indivisibility of music. And by way of extending this idea, he felt that students must be able to improvise freely, to transpose, and to read from full orchestral score, and not to be rendered immobile when faced with such tasks. He even made them basic requirements for admission to the Academy. In Liszt's day the music conservatories were already dividing the discipline into small compartments, headed by specialists in history, theory, pedagogy, and performance, and he regarded this as a dangerous development. The twentieth-century suffered the lamentable consequences. These subtopics have penetrated the very fabric of the institutions that have come to dominate music education. They have even developed their own bureaucracies, which express themselves in insulated departments, often housed in separate buildings and offering separate degrees. The age of specialization came to invade every aspect of our musical lives, but it did not make us more musical. We should heed Liszt's best aphorism on the topic: "For the formation of the artist, the first prerequisite is the improvement of the human being."[5] It is light-years away from the position in which we nowadays find ourselves, and the typical instructor at the typical conservatory probably does not even know what it means.

Liszt's masterclasses never lost the social atmosphere that marked their origins in Weimar. They were not lessons in the ordinary sense of the word. It was the "improvement of the human being" that he attempted to foster. It was as if Liszt were presiding over a large party. Music would be played, Liszt would make some observations about the performance and even about the composition itself, anecdotes would be exchanged, and at suitable intervals Liszt's housekeeper, Pauline Apel, would serve refreshments. If the mood was particularly elevated, the party would wend its way to the local Erbprinz Hotel and might not break up until well after dark. Sometimes Liszt would take his young charges for day-long outings to nearby Jena, Erfurt, or Tiefurt, to hear a concert followed by a picnic. Jena's "sausage parties," put on by his friend Carl Gille, were annual events that produced a special camaraderie among the pupils. Liszt's Hungarian student Etelka Willheim expressed it well when she said, "His pupils were somewhat in the position of a student of philosophy sitting at the feet of a wise man. The student must needs know a good deal about philosophy to have gained the wise man's confidence to the extent that he was allowed his friendship. So it was with Liszt."[6]

Felix Weingartner, who was Liszt's pupil in the 1880s, reinforces this view of Liszt as a philosopher-teacher:

> "When he was feeling well and in good spirits he was full of the most wonderful ideas which he distributed with the lavishness of a king dealing out gold from a bottomless purse. Often he was sarcastic. His praise had to be sifted carefully, as it was no rare thing for it to conceal an envenomed point. True, only the finer intelligences among his hearers appreciated this side of his nature. Delicate irony such as he employed is rare, and a delightful and most refreshing gift, as it pierces the matter in hand unhampered and without effort.[7]

5. RGS, vol. 5, p. 195.
6. CLC, series 1, folder no. 169.
7. WBR, pp. 98–99.

Examples of the irony to which Weingartner refers abound in the written accounts of the masterclasses. To a pupil who played Liszt's own "La campanella," and hesitated before taking those notoriously high D-sharps after that famous leap across the void, he remarked drily, "Do not look for the house number." To another, who had not got beyond the first page of the *Waldstein* Sonata before Liszt stopped him, he observed, "Do not chop beefsteak for us." A work that his students often brought to the masterclass was his concert study "Gnomenreigen," a piece that was nearly always played too fast for him. "There you go, mixing salad again," was his response to a young performer who had once more got those interlocking hands into a tangle. These comments were for insiders, of course. Anyone familiar with the music in question would know at once what the performances were like, and why Liszt was objecting to them. To a student whose tremolandos contained surplus movement, he made the witty observation: "Do not make omelets." Liszt liked both trills and tremolandos fast. "Such economy of notes!" he would declare mordantly, if they moved too slowly. If he heard a performance about which he felt there was little good to say, but not much bad either, he would declare, "Let it go—at discount!" or worse, "I consider it my duty to reject nothing."[8]

Frederic Lamond, who studied with Liszt during the period 1885–86, noticed that Liszt liked to teach by parable and analogy. Lamond recalled a student who played Chopin's Polonaise in A-flat Major, op. 53, with great gusto. When he came to the celebrated octave passage for the left hand, Liszt interrupted him with the observation, "I don't want to hear how fast you can play octaves. What I wish to hear is the canter of the horses of the Polish cavalry before they gather force and destroy the enemy!"[9] These few words were characteristic of Liszt, Lamond continued. "The poetical vision always arose before his mental eye, whether it was a Beethoven sonata, a Chopin nocturne, or a work of his own. It was not merely interpreting a work, but real reproduction." Arthur Friedheim adds to the store of anecdotes. He once sat down to play Liszt's transcendental study "Harmonies du soir" for Liszt in the master's apartments at the Villa d'Este, near Rome. Before he could even begin, Liszt drew Friedheim to the window. It was late autumn and the sun was about to set over the Italian *campàgna*. "Play that," he said. "There are your evening harmonies."[10]

III

Even during Liszt's lifetime there were growing debates in the field of piano pedagogy. The conservatories of Berlin, Leipzig, and Frankfurt had laid down strict curricula for the training of pianists, and these institutions were gaining ascendancy. Notable pedagogues had also emerged, including Theodor Kullak, Theodor Leschetitzky, and Ludwig Deppe, and some of them had written textbooks to pro-

8. GLK, p. 142.
9. LML, p. 68.
10. FLL, p. 52.

mote the Royal Road to Parnassus. Methodology was the order of the day. To sit high or low? To play from the knuckle or the wrist? To play with bent or flat fingers? How best to achieve digital independence?[11] And so forth. Kalkbrenner's "handrail" was still a popular device. It ran the whole length of the keyboard; when the pianist inserted the wrists beneath it, the arms were forcibly restrained. It was often used at the conservatories. Another contrivance was the "finger tormenter," a kind of sling designed to keep one finger out of the way while the others were being exercised. It had ended Robert Schumann's career as a pianist twenty years earlier when, in a mistaken attempt to achieve finger independence, he had used the device and had suffered irreversible motor damage.[12] Most remarkable of all was Johann Logier's "Chiroplast" (bearing the sinister subtitle "hand director"), a complex invention of sliding rings into which the player fitted the hand and fingers, which were then "directed" back and forth across the keyboard. Logier was an empty vessel which others filled with their expectations. He was invited to Berlin in 1822 by the Prussian government, where his method had already spread across Germany and into neighboring countries. It was still being promoted in England as late as 1877. Technical exercises of a more orthodox kind were also dispensed by the conservatories, in quantities usually out of all proportion to the results obtained, and 'prentice assistants were appointed to oversee the daily grind. Hands and fingers were developed to Olympic standards, and were sometimes damaged in the process, but the musician within rarely emerged.

Contrast that with Weimar and Liszt. In teaching he was a crusader against all crusades. "I am no piano professor!" he would often declare, as if he held the profession itself in contempt. As he surveyed the conservatories, Liszt must often have thought of Rousseau's dictum, "Man was born free, but everywhere he is in chains." That was literally true for pianists. Liszt had no method, no system, no technical advice of any kind to offer his students. "I possess no talent for the pedantic discussion

---

11. Then, as now, great emphasis was placed on finger independence, but the lengths to which pianists were prepared to go in order to achieve this goal still surprise the modern reader. Liszt once heard that one of his students, Johanna Wenzel, was about to submit to a hand operation, probably to have the webbing of her fingers cut in order to increase her stretch. It was a common enough procedure in the nineteenth century, and shows the desperate measures that students would take in order to overcome technical problems. Liszt's reply (in a letter from Weimar on June 10, 1872) is a beacon of common sense: "My dear young lady: I beg you to think no more of having the barbarous finger-operation. Better to play every octave and chord wrong throughout your life than to commit such a mad attack upon your hands. With best thanks, I sign myself yours respectfully, F. Liszt" (LLB, vol. 2, p. 174).

For details of a similar hand operation offered to young hopefuls by the medical profession, see p. 209, fn. 7.

12. In his *Biographisches Notizen* (1831) Schumann writes, "Overdone technical exercises. Laming of my right hand"(BRS, p. 224). Years later Schumann's teacher Friedrich Wieck wrote in his book *Clavier und Gesang* (Leipzig, 1853) that the "sling" was used by "a famous pupil of mine, contrary to my wish and used behind my back to the righteous outrage of his third and fourth fingers." The homeopathic remedies that Schumann is known to have used in an attempt to deal with the syphilis he contracted in 1831 remain contributing factors to his finger injury. Much new light has been shed on this problem, which has always fascinated Schumann scholars, by the recent publication of the casebook of Dr. Franz Richarz, Schumann's attending physician at the asylum in Endenich where the composer spent the last two years of his life (see DRS, p. 484).

of the rules of playing, of interpretation, and of expression," he once observed.[13] But to this should be added a shrewd comment by the grand duchess of Weimar, one of his admirers: "Liszt has the gift of doubling the talents of others while he is talking to them."[14] Liszt was a guru figure, an enormously attractive personality, and while you were in his magnetic presence, as more than one student testified, you played the piano better than you dreamed possible. He offered his pupils direct contact with music and the most wonderful model to follow in his own interpretations. He would sometimes take apart a Beethoven sonata, phrase by phrase, in an effort to reveal the music behind the music. Of course, by observing Liszt himself play— watching the lie of his hands on the keyboard, noting his unique way of fingering certain passages, and listening to his pedal effects—the students learned far more than they would have by reading a textbook on these matters. And there was something else as well. All of Liszt's students were different, as their gramophone records show. He had no interest in producing copies of himself. He had too much respect for human individuality. He knew that the teacher's first duty was to make himself unnecessary. The second was to teach his students to teach themselves, a precept which flowed from the first. He well understood the original meaning of the word *education,* which comes from the Latin *educare,* "to lead forth." Liszt did indeed lead his students forth toward a rich and exciting world of music they might never have known without his inspiring example.

The question is often asked, how can anyone acquire technique without being taught it? It is a mysterious topic, and the answer does not lie readily to hand. But there is no doubt that it happens. We are all familiar with brilliant teachers who produce inept pupils, and brilliant pupils who are produced by inept teachers. How can such a disconnection occur? It is one of the great paradoxes of education, and it produces a quiet panic in the minds of pedagogues, whose very existence is threatened by the notion of a casual rather than a causal connection between teaching and learning. We begin to see what the pessimistic Schopenhauer meant when he declared, "If teaching were of any avail, how could Nero be Seneca's pupil?" Hans von Bülow even turned the matter into cruel humor by declaring, "There are no great teachers, only great pupils!" One vital element usually goes unspoken, and it may explain everything else: the presence of admiration, empathy, and even love between teacher and pupil, without which the pupil will never accept anything the master has to say. But with empathy present, the student will begin mysteriously to absorb whatever it is he feels that his model has to offer. The pupil, in brief, must find his guru. It is the most important quest he will ever have to face in his professional development.

"Go to a conservatory!" It was the one sentence that Liszt's students dreaded hearing. They knew they must have incurred his wrath to warrant such a condemnation. And if Liszt was confronted by obvious technical defects which he thought the student had not worked hard enough to remedy, he would come out with his

13. RL, p. 39.
14. LLB, vol. 6, p. 248.

celebrated injunction, "I do not take in washing here. Wash your dirty linen at home." When pressed about his own superlative technique and how he had acquired it, Liszt came back with his famous dictum, "Technique should create itself from spirit, not from mechanics."[15] The meaning runs deep and offers much food for thought.

Liszt charged nothing for his lessons. All were welcome to attend. Weimar was crowded with students during the months that Liszt was in residence. The sound of practicing filled the air. Eventually the city council was forced to pass a bylaw forbidding practicing with open windows. Offenders were fined three marks and given an official receipt.

This, then, is the background against which the following character sketches should be read. The students' lives are inspiring, their accomplishments unique. But it is doubtful that they could have gone so far, and achieved so much, had they been deprived of the golden years they spent in Liszt's stimulating company. By admitting them into the fellowship of his inner circle, he enriched their lives beyond measure. Today the Altenburg and the Hofgärtnerei resonate with history, much of which they helped to create. And behind it all lies the charismatic figure of Franz Liszt himself.

15. RL-P, p. 6.

Carl Tausig

A Polish Wunderkind

*The intellectual claws and pinions were already giving signs of mighty power
in the youth who was scarcely fourteen years of age.*
FRANZ LISZT[1]

I

Among Liszt's many students, one name passed into legend even while the others
were struggling for recognition. When Liszt first heard him he declared that he did
not really need a teacher, and accepted him with reluctance. He appeared to have arrived at the keyboard fully armed. The feats of pianism attributed to him cannot be
proved conclusively; he died young, still on the threshold of his career. But those
within the inner circle who were privileged to hear him on a daily basi, came away
with stories that are now enshrined in the literature. They talked of the peculiar pen-
etration of his tone, of the diamond brilliance of his passagework, of the deadly accuracy of his leaps, of the cascades of notes rolling effortlessly up and down the
keyboard, and of abundant reserves of energy left over to deal with any emergency.
And all this was achieved without the slightest movement of the head or body. Whatever the struggle in executing the music, he remained immobile. Like the Zen Bud-
dhist, he exhibited inner calm in the face of outer turmoil. And his leading principle
was the same: the greater the technical difficulty the greater the physical repose. When
he died, Liszt mourned and Wagner prepared an inscription for his tombstone.

Carl Tausig was born in 1841, in Warsaw. He was the son of Aloys Tausig, a respected piano teacher and composer of some virtuoso piano pieces. Aloys had been
a pupil of Sigismond Thalberg, and from him he had acquired something of Thalberg's aristocratic bearing at the keyboard, a quality he was to transmit to his son.
In 1855, when Carl was thirteen years old, Aloys brought the boy to Weimar to play
for Liszt. It was well known that Liszt disliked infant prodigies. He usually turned
them away with the contemptuous phrase, "Artists who *are* to be!" Aloys was not be
treated so lightly, however. When father and son arrived at the Altenburg, Liszt was

1. LLB, vol. 2, p. 166.

socializing with friends, enjoying a glass of wine and a good cigar. Knowing that the odds were stacked against him, Aloys is said to have smuggled young Carl to a piano in an adjoining room, and, at a pre-arranged signal, he had the boy launch into an energetic performance of Chopin's great A-flat Major Polonaise. Peter Cornelius was present and later wrote, "He knocked us clean over with the octaves."[2] Bülow was also there and recalled the "astonishment, almost mixed with awe, which the play of the wonderful boy created in us. . . . We were all absolutely electrified."[3] After Liszt had inquired who the pianist was, Tausig senior emerged and confessed to the deception. Far from being annoyed at this stratagem, Liszt was delighted. Nonetheless, he informed the father that the boy had such a natural talent that he did not need a teacher and should be left to develop on his own. Carl begged to remain with Liszt, however, and Liszt finally relented. Years later Liszt summed it up like this:

> I remember how greatly astonished I was at his extraordinary talent when I first heard him play. The intellectual claws and pinions were already giving signs of mighty power in the youth who was scarcely 14 years old, and rather delicate in appearance. I felt some compunction in undertaking to give him further instruction, decided not to undertake the task, and therefore informed the father that in the case of such a stupendous organization the wisest plan would be to allow it free, unfettered development, without a teacher. However, Tausig insisted on remaining with me. He studied immoderately, generally keeping very much to himself while in Weimar, and getting into various little scrapes as a result of his sharp, ironical sense of humour. I was accused of being overindulgent with him, and of therefore *spoiling* him. But I really could not have acted otherwise and loved him with all my heart.[4]

Carl moved into the Altenburg and lived as one of the family, while Tausig senior traveled back to Warsaw, his mission accomplished. Because Liszt was out of town for several weeks during much of 1855 and 1856, the lessons were at first irregular. The fact that Liszt had taken the boy into his protection, however, allowed his talent to develop without exploitation. Aside from Bülow and Cornelius, Liszt's wide circle of musicians at that time included Joachim, Raff, Hans von Bronsart, Klindworth, and Pruckner. Tausig had the opportunity to hear all these musicians perform at the Sunday afternoon matinees held each week at the Altenburg, to hear a lot of new music, to visit the Weimar opera, and, above all, to observe Liszt himself play the piano on an almost daily basis. In brief, Tausig enjoyed one of the finest and most privileged musical educations for which any student could ask, because he was able to form himself on the best models. In this stimulating environment he embarked on an ambitious program of work, and on his own initiative the fourteen-year-old started to learn Liszt's *Transcendental Studies*. In the summer of 1856, Princess

2. BFA, p. 131. See also FMG, p. 251.
3. *Dwight's Journal,* October 21, 1871. Translated from the Leipzig *Signale,* August 22, 1871.
4. LLB, vol. 2, pp. 166–67.

Carolyne von Sayn-Wittgenstein, Liszt's companion during the Weimar years, wrote to Liszt, "Yesterday Tausig dined with us and played your two studies *Eroica* and *Mazeppa*. . . . He is not yet the master of *Mazeppa,* but he played the admirable *Eroica* with fire."[5] In this same letter she informed us that Tausig also played his own arrangement of Liszt's newly published symphonic poem *Prometheus* "quite passably." It was an augury of things to come. Tausig's later arrangements of Bach, Beethoven, Schubert, and above all Wagner are among the more polished examples of the genre to emerge from the nineteenth century.[6]

II

During his two-year sojourn in Weimar, the rambunctious young teenager proved difficult to control. He indulged to the full his love of pranks and practical jokes, and he often taxed the patience of both Liszt and Princess Carolyne. Shortly after his son had taken up residence in the Altenburg, Tausig senior purchased a new grand piano from Leipzig and sent it to Weimar. The boy proceeded to saw off the corners of the keys in order to make them more difficult to strike, and the father was faced with a hefty repair bill before the instrument was even paid for. It was an early manifestation of Tausig's lifelong interest in the physical problems connected to piano playing: making them yet harder to overcome. His most famous exploit caused Liszt anguish. Because he was often short of pocket money, Carl sold for five talers a pile of music to a wastepaper man who had called at the door. It happened to include the manuscript of Liszt's *Faust* Symphony. The precious composition might have been lost to the world had not Liszt's disciple Alexander Gottschalg, whose suspicions had been aroused, gone off in pursuit of the man, bought back the stack of music from him, and returned with it to the Altenburg. By the time he got back the household was in turmoil. Quite by chance, the publisher had asked Liszt for the *Faust* Symphony that very day, and Gottschalg found Liszt and Carolyne in the middle of a frantic search for the missing symphony. "A whole year's labor lost!" Liszt cried. When Gottschalg produced the manuscript, there was an outbreak of joy. Liszt rushed to the foot of the stairs shouting: "Carolyne! Carolyne! We're saved."[7] It is unlikely that any chastisement was carried out. Liszt could never remain angry with his young charge for long; such episodes were dismissed with humor. "Cärlchen," Liszt used to say, "You will either become a great blockhead or a great master!" There

---

5. Unpublished letter dated September 18, 1856 (GSA, Kasten 35).

6. During his 'prentice years Tausig also transcribed for solo piano at least five other symphonic poems of Liszt, including *Ce qu'on entend sur la Montagne, Les Préludes, Tasso, Hamlet,* and *Orpheus.* He completed as well transcriptions of both the *Dante* and the *Faust* symphonies. With the exception of *Tasso* and *Les Préludes,* all these scores remain unpublished, their precise dates of composition unknown. Bülow, the severest of critics, greatly admired Tausig's piano transcription of Wagner's *Die Meistersinger,* in which things "seemingly untranscribable come together" (NZfM, October 21, 1871). The compliment is all the more generous if we bear in mind that Bülow himself had conducted the world premiere of the work and had also arranged the Overture for solo piano.

7. FMG, pp. 250 and 278–79.

was never any doubt which it would be. On the very day that Liszt had first accepted Tausig as his pupil, he had made a witty pun on Tausig's name, "Das ist ein ganz *tausiger* Kerl" (He is a phenomenal fellow),[8] an opinion from which he never wavered.

Tausig worked with Liszt for sixteen months, during which time Liszt observed of him that he was "a real iron-eater"—a phrase that Hummel had used years earlier to describe Liszt himself at a similar age.[9] We have some idea of the iron that Tausig could eat when we learn that the fourteen-year-old was already learning *Mazeppa* by Liszt, one of the most difficult works in the repertory.[10] By January 1858 Liszt felt that Tausig was ready to make his debut in Berlin, appearing in Bülow's newly founded series of orchestral and chamber concerts, with Bülow himself conducting. The reviews were mixed, a state of affairs which infuriated the irascible Bülow, who was at that time having some running battles of his own with the gentlemen of the press. Everyone admired Tausig's physical dexterity, but there was talk of "noise and rant," and some critics thought that they observed some "Lisztian eccentricities." The more perceptive ones predicted that he would play much better once his period of Sturm und Drang was behind him. He was still only sixteen years old.

Immediately following his Berlin debut, Tausig gave a solo recital in the city on January 28, 1858, including the following works:

Chromatic Fantasy and Fugue	Bach
Ballade, op. 11	Bülow
Hungarian Rhapsody	Liszt
Sonata in E Major, op. 109	Beethoven
Don Juan Fantasy	Liszt

It should be added that this demanding program began with a performance of his own arrangement for two pianos of Liszt's symphonic poem *Les Préludes,* in which he was partnered by Bülow.

A few weeks later Tausig also made his Vienna debut. In the spring of 1858 he journeyed to the imperial capital and appeared as a solo pianist. It was a repeat of the Berlin experience. The critics found his playing brilliant but chaotic. The youth was thrown into despair by the hostility of his reviews, retreated to his hotel room, and refused to meet anybody. Liszt appears to have had no advance knowledge of this Viennese adventure, because he observed that "Tausig made a little mistake by making his debut in [Ferdinand] Laub's concert in Vienna. I have advised him to remain absolutely quiet for the time being."[11] Privately, however, he was angered at the reception of his protégé, and he continued to do much good by stealth in the promotion of Tausig's career.

8. LLB, vol. 3, p. 36.
9. LLB, vol. 1, p. 287.
10. WFL, vol. 2, pp. 180–81.
11. LLB, vol. 4, p. 425.

III

In the summer of 1858 Liszt arranged for Tausig to travel to Zurich in order to meet Wagner, who was still in the middle of a Swiss exile for his part in the Dresden uprising of 1849, unable to return to Germany and pick up the threads of his abandoned career. "I am sending you today a wonderful fellow, dearest Richard," wrote Liszt engagingly. "Receive him kindly. Tausig is to work your Erard thoroughly and to play all manner of things for you."[12] Unlike Liszt, Wagner did not like houseguests because they disturbed his routine, so he found some quarters for Tausig a stone's throw away from his own, which guaranteed that the young man had constant access to him and his Erard. Almost at once he regretted the decision. Tausig's pranks frustrated him. The youth devoured all his cheese and biscuits, and Wagner was gradually driven to distraction by Tausig's strong cigars, smoked as an accompaniment to his incessant piano playing. Wagner was not wrong when he described it as "putting on the airs of a Liszt." In an attempt to bring back some order into his disrupted life, Wagner arranged for the young "iron-eater" to practice on an old piano in a nearby tavern. In his *Mein Leben* he is unstinting in his praise of Tausig, however. "As a musician he is enormously gifted," he wrote to Liszt, "and his furious piano playing makes me tremble."[13] Tausig, for his part, acknowledged that this encounter with Wagner proved to be a turning point. He became one of the composer's staunchest supporters, and in later years he would raise money through recitals in benefit of the first Bayreuth Festival while it was still in the planning stage. He would also throw himself wholeheartedly into the formation of a Wagner-Verein in Berlin, and into the creation of a special orchestra, to be conducted by Tausig himself, whose immediate purpose would be to make Wagner's works better known to the Berlin public. By 1870 Wagner had appointed Tausig chairman of the so-called Patron's Voucher Committee, an organization specially created to supervise the sale and distribution of vouchers to aid the Bayreuth Festival. Tausig's premature death brought everything to a standstill. For the present, however, as a youth of seventeen, he determined to embark on a serious study of Wagner's scores, and began to contemplate the herculean task of paraphrasing some of them for the piano keyboard.[14]

After undertaking a tour of various German towns in 1859–60 Tausig made Dresden his temporary home. In 1862, however, he moved to Vienna where he attempted to copy the example of Bülow by putting on a series of orchestral concerts featuring modern music, including Liszt's, with himself as conductor. These concerts featured some of his own symphonic poems, works which were never published and

---

12. KWL, vol. 2, p. 200. This reference to "your Erard" was a veiled allusion to the fact that a new grand piano now graced Wagner's quarters, which had been delivered from Paris at Liszt's special request, and possible expense. Wagner had at once fallen in love with the instrument, on which he had already begun to compose *Tristan,* and he grew alarmed at the prospect of having Tausig hammering away at it for several hours a day.

13. KWL, vol. 2, p. 204.

14. His paraphrase of the "Liebestod" from *Tristan* can stand comparison with Liszt's; while his wonderful transfer of "The Ride of the Valkyrie" still represents a challenge for today's heroes of the keyboard.

whose manuscripts appear to be lost. Artistically the concerts were only moderately successful; financially they were failures and Tausig lost money. At this time, too, the twenty-one-year-old attempted once more to promote himself as a pianist in Vienna. The critic Eduard Hanslick heard him, and delivered some unfavorable opinions of the young lion. He likened Tausig's piano playing to "chopping frozen notes out of ice," and took offense at his "jabbing at the keys."[15] Tausig withdrew from the concert platform for a time in order to re-assess the direction his piano playing was taking. He devoted himself to the acquisition of foreign languages, and took up the study of philosophy at the University of Vienna, reading Kant, Hegel, and Schopenhauer. During this period of self-imposed exile his piano playing became transformed and took on all those defining characteristics for which he became famous. He eventually won over the grudging Hanslick, who revised his early opinion, observing that Tausig's youthful impetuosity had subsided and had made way for more tenderness and warmth.

It was during this early Viennese period that Tausig met Brahms, who was then about thirty years of age, and with whom he struck up an important friendship. Anyone who has studied Tausig's inventive piano textures will not be surprised to learn that they helped to stimulate Brahms in the composition of his virtuoso "Paganini" Studies. It was well known that Brahms liked to banter his friends, and having heard that Tausig "knew all about piano playing" made a good-humored attempt to cut the young pianist down to size by showing him some keyboard configurations that, he felt sure, would be unfamiliar to him. Somewhat crestfallen, Tausig had to admit that he found them to be quite new, but he quietly resolved to get his revenge by creating some unusual technical combinations of his own and then challenging Brahms. The next time the pair met, Tausig played them for Brahms and was gratified to see the composer nettled. This to-ing and fro-ing went on for some time, until Brahms went to work with a will; which is why we have two books of "Studies on a Theme of Paganini," op. 35. In March 1865 Brahms gave their first performance in Vienna; a fortnight later Tausig introduced them to Berlin.[16] Although no dedication appears on the title page, Brahms's biographer Max Kalbeck tells us that the composition was "a monument to the friendship between the pair of artists" Brahms and Tausig.[17]

---

15. HGC, vol. 2, p. 263.

16. These were almost certainly private performances. The "official" ones took place later. Brahms gave the first public performance from manuscript on November 25, 1865, in Zurich. Tausig gave the second public performance in Berlin, on March 25, 1867. Let us note in passing that although this work is a set of variations on Paganini's well-known theme, and the term *Variations* is commonly used to identify it, Brahms himself chose the designation *Studies*. That is rather important when we recall the Tausig connection.

For the rest, it is well known that there are some striking similarities between Brahms's "Paganini" Studies and those of Liszt on the same theme, composed much earlier and titled "Grande Etude de Paganini, no. 6, in A Minor." The resemblance between the two works is at times uncanny, and it was close enough to prompt Liszt himself to remark, somewhat drily, "I am glad that my variations were of service to Brahms when he composed his; it gives me great pleasure!" (GLK, p. 53.) For more information on this connection see pp. 70–71.

17. KJB, vol. 2, p. 40.

That friendship extended to a joint appearance on the concert platform—a rarely reported aspect of the collegiality that existed between the two men. On April 17, 1864, Tausig was the chief guest in a "Brahms evening," on which occasion the two musicians performed Brahms's Sonata for Two Pianos—better known as the first version of the Piano Quintet in F Minor.

It was in Vienna, too, that Tausig renewed his acquaintance with Wagner, who had arrived in the city to supervise rehearsals for the world premier of *Tristan,* which was scheduled to take place in the Vienna Opera House some time during the 1862/63 season.[18] Bülow had recently published a much-admired piano reduction of the massive score, so Tausig transported a Bösendorfer grand piano into Wagner's hotel room, where, in Wagner's words, a "musical orgy was soon in full swing." In order to arouse the interest of the Viennese public in his music, Wagner hit upon the expedient of presenting selections from his other operas adapted for concert performance, and he enlisted the help of friends in copying the parts. The main share of this drudgery was undertaken by Tausig and by Liszt's pupil Cornelius, who had also recently arrived in Vienna. Wendelin Weissheimer, a Wagner acolyte, was also placed on the production line. Tausig then remembered Brahms, whom he recommended to Wagner as "a very good fellow." He assured Wagner that Brahms, despite his growing fame, would gladly roll up his sleeves, so to speak, and help in the all-important task of copying Wagner's scores. Accordingly, a part of *Meistersinger* was allotted to Brahms, who good-naturedly joined the team and applied himself conscientiously to this routine work. To think of Brahms serving the Wagner cause is a chimerical notion. It is one of those encounters about which posterity ought to be better informed, in light of the violent partisanship that was soon to surround the two composers. All Wagner has to say about the matter in his *Mein Leben* is that Brahms "showed little vivacity and was often hardly noticed at our gatherings."[19] It is safe to say that Wagner would have "showed little vivacity" either, had he been invited to copy out the scores of Brahms.

During his failed attempt to establish himself in Vienna, and with it the collapse of his plans to mount *Tristan* there, Wagner built up large debts. Unfortunately Tausig had endorsed some of the credit notes issued to Wagner, and the young pianist now found himself responsible for these liabilities. The matter was eventually sorted out by Eduard Liszt, Franz Liszt's lawyer-uncle, but not without difficulty, and not without Eduard having to supervise the sale of some of Wagner's furniture during one of the composer's absences from the city to help liquidate the debt, much to Wagner's dismay. Some of the details of the complex position into which Wagner had manipulated himself may be found in a letter that he wrote to Eduard on March 25, 1864.[20]

The first signs of Tausig's ill-health manifested themselves in the early 1860s. Al-

18. It was finally abandoned after seventy-seven rehearsals—and a series of intrigues. Vienna was not to hear *Tristan* until after Wagner's death.

19. WML, p. 847.

20. SLRW, pp. 574–78. Eduard Liszt (1817–79) was a brilliant criminal lawyer who rose to become the royal imperial public prosecutor in Vienna, the most powerful legal position in the Austro-Hungarian Empire. He looked after the financial affairs of both Liszt and Princess Carolyne.

ways of a weak and delicate constitution, Tausig started to suffer from excessive fatigue, the cause of which was never disclosed. He refused to modify his work schedule, however, and close observers began to worry that he was driving himself too
hard. Cornelius reports that Tausig underwent some serious surgery in the spring of
1863, but the nature of that, too, remained undisclosed.[21] The *Neue Zeitschrift für
Musik,* in its issue of July 27, 1863, reported that Tausig had been ill for several
months and was now recuperating at the resort of Bad Ischl in Austria.

In the summer of 1864, Tausig went on a short trip to Pressburg, accompanied
by Brahms and Cornelius. There he fell in love with Szerafina von Vrabély, one of
the daughters of a Jewish postmaster. The young woman was an exact contemporary of Tausig, and together with her sister Stephanie she was a talented pianist, well
known in local musical circles. After a whirlwind courtship, Tausig and Szerafina
were married in November 1864. In the months following, Tausig appeared in a
number of concerts with his bride, and in November 1865 he gave a concert in Vienna in which both his wife and his sister-in-law participated.[22] The marriage did
not last, and within a few years after moving back to Berlin the couple separated.[23]

It was in the Prussian capital that Tausig resumed his concert career in earnest
and emerged as the most polished pianist of his generation. Liszt heard him at this
time and remarked on his "fingers of steel" and his "infallible technique." Edward
Dannreuther summed it up by saying that "The Sturm and Drang was finished. . . .
[Tausig] had achieved self-possession, breadth and dignity of style."[24] Tausig featured
every composer of value in his recitals, but was particularly associated with the music of Chopin, devoting entire recitals to his music, all of which he played from memory. His interpretations of the Polish master were marked by fidelity to the text,
clarity of texture, a singing line, and an aristocratic bearing at the keyboard behind
which burned fire and emotion. The English man of letters William Beatty-Kingston
heard him in Berlin at this time, and observed

> that he produced a broader tone than any other Berlin pianist of his day—
> that his lightness of touch in rendering the fanciful and elaborate orna-
> mentations of Chopin and Liszt was simply exquisite, and that he was es-
> pecially remarkable for the *verve* and *ton* with which he executed those
> amazing *tours de force* invented by himself as well as by the mighty Hungar-

---

21. CLW, vol. 1, p. 708. "Du hast eine schlimme Operation überstanden? Wäre ich bei Dir, wären wir
doch zusammen!" [So, you have undergone a serious operation? If only I were with you, if only we were
together!]

22. According to the NZfM (1865, p. 440) these concerts attracted only small audiences.

23. Szerafina von Vrabély (1841–1931) lived to the advanced age of ninety. Tausig, too, was born Jewish, but was not observant. There are some gratuitous remarks in the diaries of Cosima Wagner to the
effect that Tausig was "conscious of the curse of his Jewishness . . . the marriage to a Jewess ended almost
at once" (WT, July 20, 1871).

24. Entry on Tausig. *Grove,* 1st ed., vol. 4, London, 1899. It is an indication of the general lack of scholarly interest in Tausig that Dannreuther's article has been reprinted, with scarcely any modifications, in
every subsequent edition of Grove, including the seventh (2001). That is a life span of more than one
hundred years.

ian ecclesiastic [Liszt], which are the terror of ninety-nine expert pianists in every hundred. No one who ever listened to his feats in this direction will be likely to forget what a wealth of sound and complexity of combinations his deft fingers extracted from the keyboard. In him were combined the more salient excellences of the old and new schools of pianism.[25]

Because of Tausig's growing fame, both at home and abroad, the Prussian court nominated him royal court pianist, a title that was his for life. Among the Berliners he had a reputation for aloofness and haughtiness, often mistaken for arrogance. He was once invited to give a private recital for a family of wealthy Berlin Jews, the Epsteins, for a very large fee. He despatched a terse, hand-delivered reply, which was not calculated to win friends and influence people. "I only play on three occasions. (1) When the King of Prussia commands it, (2) in public, and (3) in the homes of people I know well."[26] Behind the public facade, however, was a somewhat shy and withdrawn personality. In her useful memoir of Tausig, Bettina Walker tells us that she met Tausig in the winter of 1870. She was let into his rooms before he himself arrived there, and she recalls the confusion that appeared to reign in his inner sanctum. There were unbound volumes of French philosophy scattered on the broad windowsills, several editions of Bach lying on chairs near the piano, and no look of comfort anywhere in the room. Nonetheless, she concluded, that small chamber represented in a subtle and mysterious way the life of the mind, a life centered exclusively on art, which was now the most important thing in Tausig's world.[27]

IV

In the autumn of 1866, after his move back to Berlin, Tausig opened his School for Advanced Piano Playing, which he ran together with his colleague Ludwig Ehlert. To help develop the curriculum he engaged some well-known musicians, including the theorist C. F. Weitzmann, the composer Adolf Jensen, and the pianist Franz Bendel.[28] According to Bülow, Tausig was a reluctant teacher, confining himself to the best three or four students who, thankful for the privilege of having him as their mentor, clung to him with doglike devotion.[29] He preferred to leave to others the daily grind of teaching beginners. Inclined to be short-tempered even with his better students, he frequently stopped their performances and fussed over details to such an extent that they played even worse from sheer nervousness. Amy Fay confirmed these observations. She studied at the school during 1869–70 and witnessed several

25. B-KMCE, p. 208.

26. LLM-K, p. 213.

27. WMME, p. 45.

28. See the advertisement for Tausig's school, which appeared in no fewer than four issues of the NZfM (September/October 1867, vol. 63, nos. 38—42).

29. Two of his best students were Rafael Joseffy, who went on to study with Liszt, and Oscar Beringer, who later opened his own School for Advanced Pianists in London, modeled on that of his teacher.

"scenes" in which Tausig lost his temper when confronted with piano playing he considered less than satisfactory, uttering insults at the students, and even flinging the printed music down on the piano in frustration. He never taught technique. After telling a pupil that "it was awful," he would sit down, play the offending bars to perfection, and say, "Play like that." As Fay put it, "It was as if someone wished me to copy a streak of forked lightning with the end of a wetted match."[30] The female students frequently ended their lessons in tears. Even one of his best pupils, the fifteen-year-old prodigy Vera Timanova from Russia (who later studied with Liszt) was not immune from his sharp tongue. On one occasion she brought the great Chopin Etude in A Minor (*Winter Wind*) to the class and created a minor sensation with her powerful delivery. That one so young could perform this difficult piece in such a commanding manner stunned the other pupils. All that Tausig could say to her was, "So! Have you practiced the *next* Etude as well?" At that Amy Fay privately dubbed him "Rhadamanthus."[31] It was as if Tausig found it difficult to praise anyone. The worst sin was to create what he called a *Spektakel,* to play to the gallery with false emotion, heart on sleeve. Was there perhaps a guilty recollection of his own past, when, at the same age, he had received a drubbing from the critics for his "Lisztian eccentricities"? Timanova also played the Schubert Sonata in A Major for the class, and although she had studied the work for many weeks, and played it very well, Tausig came down on her and started to fret over the details of expression, stopping her many times. "Child, there's a soul in this piece," he declared. "Don't you know there is a *soul* in it?" The young girl usually kept her composure in the face of his barbed words, but on this occasion she flushed to the tips of her ears. In Fay's memorable words, "From an apple-blossom she changed to a carnation."[32]

Tausig nonetheless created a lasting monument to piano pedagogy in his *Tägliche Studien,* a set of difficult daily exercises which help the advanced player keep in shape. Edward Dannreuther shrewdly remarked that of the many sets of studies routinely described as "indispensable," Tausig's *Studies* really are indispensable. In them a supreme piano technician stands revealed. They represent the golden doors through which those with ambition are invited to pass en route to Parnassus. They appear to have evolved slowly in the mid- to late 1860s, in response to pedagogical requirements, and were left in manuscript at the time of Tausig's death. The task of assembling and editing them fell to his colleague Heinrich Ehrlich, who published them in two volumes in 1872, a year after Tausig's death, together with a useful introduction. Ehrlich himself tells us that Tausig had earlier shown him these studies in manuscript, a number of them in sketch form, and that before his demise he had entrusted to Ehrlich the task of arranging, sifting, and classifying them. Appropriately, they are dedicated to Franz Liszt.

Here are just two examples taken at random from the collection: the first for double thirds, the second for trills.

30. FMG, p. 103.

31. In Greek mythology Rhadamanthus was the son of Zeus and Europa. Because of his inflexible integrity he was made one of the judges of the dead.

32. FMG, pp. 40–41.

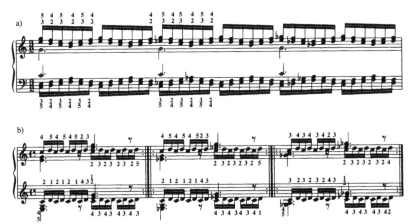

Nor should we overlook the *Ten Preludes* that Ehrlich obligingly provided as a supplement to the *Studies*. They are brief compositions which, though they embody
many of the technical drills presented in the exercises, are nonetheless intended for
the musical enjoyment of listener and player alike. Some of these preludes are by
Tausig, while others are by Ehrlich. One or two of them would make intriguing encore pieces with which to conclude a recital today.

Tausig had small hands, but he compensated for this handicap through their extreme flexibility. Evidently he could just span an octave, yet his listeners were bowled
over by his rendering of such pieces as Liszt's Hungarian Rhapsody no. 6 in D-flat
Major, whose famously repeated octaves in the Friska, first in the right and then in
the left hand, have been the downfall of many a pianist with a far larger span. In
concert Tausig's powerful delivery of this passage appeared all the more spectacular
because these great waves of sound came from a man possessed of such a small frame
which barely moved.

In light of the earlier connection between Brahms and Tausig, and the origins of
the "Paganini" Studies, it is intriguing to read Tausig's disclosure that one of his *Daily
Studies* was given to him by Brahms. It is "Study no. 7," which involves this difficult
pattern through all the major and minor keys:[33]

33. Brahms produced his own set of *Fifty-one Exercises* for advanced piano students about the same

Ehrlich was not wrong to warn the pianist, "Only a skillful and experienced player will be able to carry it through more than three or four keys."

It was during this period, too, that Tausig brought out his own selections from Clementi's *Gradus ad Parnassum* and from the *Preludes and Fugues* by Bach, which he chose for teaching purposes.[34] His concert versions of Scarlatti, Schubert, Carl Maria von Weber, and Johann Strauss all date from the same time and continue to carry his reputation as a brilliant arranger. There are more of these arrangements than are generally supposed; for example, the transcriptions of six movements from various Beethoven string quartets remain unknown even to the aficionado.[35] His original compositions include two concert studies, ten preludes, and various character pieces bearing such titles as *Rêverie, L'Espérance, Le Ruisseau,* and above all the better-known *Das Geisterschiff,* which occasionally graces the concert platform today.

Das Geisterschiff (The Ghost Ship) Tausig subtitles "A Symphonic Ballade." The piece is based on a poem by Moritz Strachwitz, from a collection called *Out of the Northlands.* The setting is a huge storm in the North Sea.

> A ghostly night, a horrible hour,
> A night for water spirits and elves,
> The vessel moans as with mortal wounds
> The helmsman groans "God help us!"

---

time as Tausig's, although they were not published until 1893. Confirmation of this early date may be found in the unpublished memoirs of the Hungarian pianist Róbert Freund, who was a pupil of Tausig before he studied with Liszt, and who later became a close colleague of Brahms. Freund tells us that in the summer of 1893, during a visit to Brahms who was staying at the Austrian resort of Bad Ischl, Brahms handed him the manuscript copy of the "Fifty-one Exercises" and asked him to comment on their suitability for piano teaching. Freund took the manuscript back to Budapest and recommended the omission of one of the "chromatic jests," as he put it, because something similar had already appeared in Tausig's collection. In his reply, Brahms makes clear that the manuscript he had given to Freund actually dated from Tausig's time, almost thirty years earlier, and that Tausig had borrowed a number of exercises from him. The letter, headed "Ischl, 31 July, 1893," runs:

> Esteemed and dear friend:
> I have to thank you heartily for having looked at the exercises so kindly and thoroughly. If they actually appear in print this autumn, it will be in no small way due to your kind encouragement.
> I cannot decide against leaving out the chromatic jest, because it is mine, and Tausig took it from me together with many other jests. Indeed, the copy of the volume which you held in your hand is from that time, by a long-gone copyist.
> Once again, my best thanks and heartiest greetings,
> Your devoted
> J. Brahms.(FMML, p. 17)

34. His edition of Clementi's *Gradus* was warmly recommended by Heinrich Neuhaus, the teacher of Sviatislav Richter, Emil Gilels, and other Russian virtuosos of modern times.

35. They, like the *Tägliche Studien,* were published posthumously, in 1872. They are: Adagio from op. 50, no. 1; Scherzo from op. 59, no. 2; Andante from op. 59, no. 3; Cavatina from op. 130; Presto from op. 131; and Scherzo from op. 135. These intricate transcriptions show that Tausig ventured where angels feared to tread. As we have seen, Liszt had earlier turned down an invitation from Breitkopf to transcribe the Beethoven quartets on the grounds that the task was too complicated (see page 26, fn. 24).

The poet then observes:

> An enormous ship, big as a mountain,
> The flood has ruptured it,
> The sails are black, black as the mast
> And black is spar and hull.

A particularly effective passage depicts the heaving of the ocean, the last two measures of which could have come straight out of the "Liebestod," from Wagner's *Tristan*.

At the climax of the piece there is a dazzling technical effect where Tausig calls for a chromatic glissando. The device is strictly impossible on a piano, but the will becomes the deed; the illusion is complete:

* The nail of the right hand's 3rd finger slides over the white keys, while the 2nd finger of the left hand slides over the black keys– producing a chromatic glissando.

Liszt himself was taken aback by this passage. It appears to have been the very first time in the complex history of music notation that the device was written out.

V

As Tausig's fame increased, his tours took him further afield. In March 1870 he set out for St. Petersburg, where he gave three recitals in the vast Hall of the Nobles, which held three thousand people. Wilhelm von Lenz was present and he reports that every seat was taken. Even the balcony opposite the emperor's box, usually re-

Carl Tausig. (An engraving by A. Weger.)

served for the diplomatic corps, was given up to the public. In the entrances to the hall, and in the spaces between the pillars and the windows, stood row upon row of densely packed people. Tausig played on a piano he had brought with him from Berlin. The year 1870 also happened to be the centenary of Beethoven's birth, and to mark the event Tausig played the *Emperor* Concerto at one of these concerts. Von Lenz described his initial entries (after each one of the powerful opening orchestral chords of E-flat, A-flat, and B-flat major) as fearful "club strokes" which resounded through the hall. And he likened Tausig to "a rhapsodist, drunk with the passion of the immortal poet."[36] While Tausig was on this extended tour of Russian and Eastern Europe he had a serious rift with his academic colleague Ludwig Ehlert, who had been left in sole charge of the school in Berlin since early March and had started to chafe at Tausig's long absences. Ehlert, in fact, tendered his resignation that April. Much to everyone's surprise, Tausig then announced that his school was to close later that year. There was consternation among both pupils and faculty at what appeared to them to be a fit of pique, but Tausig kept his word and gave his last lessons in October 1870.[37]

In the summer of that same year, Tausig was reunited with Liszt. Although there were many Beethoven centennial celebrations taking place across Europe, Liszt wanted the one that he was planning for Weimar to attract national attention. What

36. LGPZ, p. 79.
37. FMG, pp. 44 and 83.

better way than to have his young prodigy return to the city of Goethe and Schiller, fresh from his conquests in Russia, and demonstrate his transcendental powers? At the beginning of May he wrote:

> Dear Tausig:
>
> . . . I long to chat with you again here. Can you come from the 25th to the 29th of this month? Will you grant all of us, but especially me, the great plea-sure of hearing you at one of the concerts of the Tonkünstler-Versammlung? I have taken it upon myself to urge you [to come], and your pupil M. We-ber, who will hand you these lines, will tell you in greater detail how much I want you to celebrate with me the Beethoven festival in Weimar. If you will be content with a somewhat cramped lodging, I invite you to share mine. Try not to refuse me—and believe in all my constant affection.
>
> F. Liszt[38]

Tausig appears to have been unable at first to accept his old master's invitation, and Liszt was hurt by his refusal "which prevents me from re-issuing the invitation." Tausig was doubtless burdened with a very heavy schedule of concerts, and he must also have known that there was no question of Liszt's paying him a fee. But his re-fusal still comes as a surprise, directed as it was against a man and a city that had launched his career without ever submitting a bill. But Liszt persisted, pointing out that everybody in Weimar would be more than content if Tausig could simply find time to come for the final concert of the festival and deliver the *Emperor* Concerto for the greater glory of Beethoven. That diplomatic phrase "for the greater glory of Beethoven" worked, and the concert took place on Sunday, May 29, with Liszt him-self conducting.

Liszt had assembled a large body of more than one hundred players for this con-cert (which included Beethoven's Ninth Symphony) by combining the orchestras of Weimar and nearby Jena. The chorus was provided by the Riedel Verein from Leipzig. Liszt also brought in no fewer than six distinguished orchestral leaders to strengthen the rank and file, which reads like a Who's Who of violin playing. The names included Karl Uhlrich (Sondershausen), Leopold Damrosch (Breslau), Fer-dinand David (Leipzig), Joseph Hellmesberger (Vienna), Friedhold Fleischhauer (Meiningen), and August Kömpel (Weimar).[39] La Mara was present and described Tausig's performance as "great and mighty."[40] It was the last known occasion on which Liszt and Tausig were together.

---

38. LLB, vol. 8, pp. 216–17.

39. This festival, which has been consistently underreported by Liszt scholars, ran for ten days. It be-gan on May 19 with a performance of Beethoven's *Missa Solemnis* and closed on May 29 with Beethoven's Ninth Symphony. Among the galaxy of musicians appearing in the festival were Anton Rubinstein, Saint-Saëns, and Pauline Viardot.

40. LDML, vol. 1, p. 116.

By now Tausig was at the height of his powers. It was not uncommon for commentators openly to compare him with Liszt. Tausig dismissed such talk with his famous reply, "No mortal can measure himself with Liszt. He dwells upon a solitary height."[41] Liszt, of course, had long since ceased to play the piano in public, but he was still the gold standard by which others were measured. Wagner was sufficiently intrigued by such comparisons already to have made one in his *Mein Leben*. He tells us that once, in his company, Tausig had filled up a spare hour by playing Liszt's Fantasie and Fugue on the name B.A.C.H. The very next day Liszt himself chanced to play the same piece, and Tausig "literally collapsed with amazement before this wonderful prodigy of a man."[42]

VI

During the early days of July 1871, Tausig traveled to Leipzig to give more concerts. He appears to have brought the seeds of death with him. Quite unexpectedly he fell ill, developed a high fever, and was admitted to the St. Jacob Hospital. Typhus was diagnosed, and the end came quickly. His compatriot and admirer Countess Marie Mouchanoff-Kalergis, a devoted follower of his career, was at his bedside when he died. Assisting in the final ministrations was another Polish devotee, the Countess Elisabeth Krockow.[43] Marie Mouchanoff-Kalergis later wrote scathingly of the incompetence of Tausig's doctors, whom she accused of administering useless remedies while uttering bland messages of reassurance. "I proposed some radically different ones," she observed, "but they laughed in my face." Tausig expired at 3:30 a.m. on Monday, July 17, 1871, "between the two people who knew and loved him best." There were death throes of about a quarter of an hour. Just before the end a look of deep sorrow passed across his face, then everything was over.[44] The body was transported to Berlin, and the funeral service was held at 11:00 a.m. on the morning of July 21, at the Belle Alliance Cemetery.[45] During the ceremony a spectacular thunderstorm broke out, and the performance of the Funeral March from Beethoven's *Eroica* Symphony was punctuated with thunder and lightning—a moment of high drama reminiscent of those that the pianist had achieved on the concert platform during his brief lifetime. It marked the passing of a hero.

This theme of a dead hero was pursued by Otto Lessmann, an acolyte of Liszt, in the fine obituary notice he wrote for the *Neue Berliner Musikzeitung*.[46] It began

41. HMML, p. 646.

42. WML, p. 780.

43. Countess Elisabeth Krockow (1820–82), née Atcherley. Years earlier, in the 1860s, and before Tausig's marriage to Vrabély, Wagner had suspected the young man of conducting a secret love affair in Vienna with Countess Elisabeth, despite the twenty-one year difference in their ages. After his marriage collapsed, Tausig continued to maintain a close connection with this Polish aristocrat.

44. LLM-K, pp. 270–71.

45. The Belle Alliance Cemetery is today called the Third Jerusalem-Friedhof, situated at the Mehringdamm.

46. July 26, 1871, vol. 25, pp. 234–35.

with the arresting sentence, "Once again, one whom Apollo loved has passed away." Already the gods were being invoked. Doubtless mindful of the qualifications about Tausig's piano playing put into general circulation by Hanslick in Vienna, qualifications which still resonated in Berlin, Lessmann went on to place before the public an idea that has become part and parcel of the Tausig legend. "Tausig's meaning as a pianist lay in his infallible technical accomplishment, placed in the service of the ennoblement of art." That last part of the sentence was almost certainly addressed to Vienna, and was meant as a reply to those who saw in Tausig only a supreme technician. And lest the point be lost, Lessmann went on to re-assert it: "With him technique was never a goal—no; as a worthy follower of art he strove to interpret the masterworks of all periods and styles for his audiences."

Whatever the dispute among Tausig's contemporaries, he was at the time of his death universally regarded as the greatest interpreter of Chopin. Anton Rubinstein's telling description of the last movement of the *Funeral March* Sonata as "night winds sweeping over churchyard graves" assumes an almost uncanny prescience when we recall that it was one of the last pieces to have come from Tausig's fingers.

Shortly after the funeral, Tausig's effects were put up for public auction, which was held in his elegant apartments in Berlin. Everything was liquidated. His beautiful carved-oak furniture, his wardrobe of clothes including the patent leather shoes he wore on the concert platform, his paintings, his music library, and his piano—all went under the hammer. The dispersal of such an estate in such a manner was a final indignity not lost on his friends and colleagues.

Liszt was in Weimar as these mournful events were unfolding. He, like many other people, thought that the burial service would be held in Leipzig, about an hour away by train, and he made preparations for the journey. Word then reached him that Tausig's body was being moved for burial to Berlin. A five-hour trip to the Prussian capital was not possible for him. So he and a few friends gathered in the home of Adelheid von Schorn, in Weimar, to honor the memory of the great pianist. They were joined by Marie Mouchanoff-Kalergis, who had journeyed down to Weimar immediately after the funeral in order to give Liszt a firsthand account of Tausig's last days. Among the other mourners was the Weimar singer Emilie Genast, who later wrote about this emotional evening to Eduard Lassen, the conductor who had taken over Liszt's old job in Weimar. As they reminisced about Tausig, they all became sad and silent.

> In the evening, as I sat together with Liszt and Frau von Mouchanoff, serious and silent, [Liszt] suddenly opened the piano and played [his arrangement of] your lied "Das Leben draussen" [The Life Beyond]. I would like you to have been able to participate in the experience which we received. I think it must make you happy that on that evening this was the only music he could bear.[47]

47. SNW, vol. 2, p. 295.

News of Tausig's passing was brought to Hans von Bülow in Ponte à Seraglio, near Lucca in Italy. In a lengthy eulogy which he wrote a month later for the Leipzig *Signale,*[48] he recollected that he had last met Tausig in Berlin a year earlier and had enjoyed the rare privilege of hearing the Polish pianist play for him in private, including the Schumann Toccata, Bach's newly published Suite in E-flat Major, and some études by Chopin. Bülow was overwhelmed by what he heard. He concluded that although in former days Tausig had been a volcano, he was now transformed into a beneficent sun, spreading warmth and light. "Hail, young Apollo!" he had proclaimed impulsively.[49] As he rejoiced in the talent of his younger colleague, Bülow could never have imagined that Tausig's days were numbered. "*Le lame a usé le fourreau,*"[50] he later declared. It was a fitting epitaph, but it is not the one that we find on Tausig's tombstone. That was provided by Wagner.[51]

> "Ripe for Death's harvest,
> too early to pluck
> the shyly sprouting fruits of life
> in the fleeting bloom of spring—
> was it thy fate, was it thy bourn—
> thy fate and thy daring both we must mourn."

At the moment of Tausig's death, Wagner was at Triebschen, in Switzerland. In Switzerland, too, there had been a terrible storm. Cosima recorded in her diary that she did not sleep a wink; in retrospect it appeared to her that the thunderclouds gathering over Triebschen that night contained a premonition, because the next morning, she tells us, she received a letter from Countess Krockow informing her and Wagner of Tausig's passing. "In Tausig we have certainly lost a great pillar of our enterprise," Cosima wrote; while Wagner shrugged his shoulders "at the stupidity of Fate, snatching Tausig away at the moment when a great new activity would have brought inner joy and satisfaction."[52]

---

48. August 22, 1871.

49. This second reference to "young Apollo" was self-evidently influenced by Lessmann's earlier use of the same image. Clearly, within days of his death, Tausig was being elevated to the pantheon. Bülow's article was translated into English and published by installment in *Dwight's Journal of Music,* in the issues of October 21 and November 18, 1871, pp. 116–17, 125, and 129. The detailed obituary notice published in the *Monthly Music Record* (August 1871, p. 118) is also worth noting.

50. "The blade has worn out the scabbard."

51. "Grabschrift für Karl Tausig" in RWGS, vol. 9, p. 324. "Reif sein zum Sterben, / Des Lebens zögernd spriessende Frucht, / Früh reif sie erwerben, / In Lenzes jäh eblühender Flucht, / War es dein Loos, war es dein Wagen / Wir müssen dein Loos wie dein Wagen beklagen."

52. WT, vol. 1, July 20, 1871. The "great new activity" to which Wagner refers had nothing whatever to do with Tausig's shining career as a pianist, now so abruptly terminated. Rather it was a reference to the loss that Tausig's sudden death meant for the Bayreuth enterprise. As chairman of the Patron's Voucher Committee, Tausig's demise left a vacancy. The job eventually went to Baron August von Loën, intendant of the Weimar Court Theater. Wagner genuinely mourned Tausig's passing, of course; but it should surprise no student of the composer to learn that this comment reflected his total absorption in his own plans.

VII

It is difficult to assess with certainty Tausig's proper place in the history of piano playing. His life was short, and he died more than a decade before the earliest sound recordings were made. The testimony of Liszt, Wagner, and Hans von Bülow, however, carries great weight. Next to Liszt, Tausig may well have been the greatest pianist of the nineteenth century. Scores of other musicians, too, claimed that he was one of a kind, the sort of phenomenon who appears but once in a generation. All agreed that his playing was magisterial, his execution crystalline. And his approach to whatever score he was interpreting was always the same: to play it to perfection. His rubato was subtle, his tone unique. He was a master of the nuance, and he used the sustaining pedal for color, not for volume. His interpretations were marked by refinement, by delicacy, and by a constant search for the inner flame. That is why he was the supreme Chopin player of his time. And that *Spektakel* of which we have already spoken he held in contempt. Here a comparison with his older contemporary Anton Rubinstein is revealing. Rubinstein lumbered onto the concert platform like a bear, and dwarfed the piano. The wrong notes fell in abundance across the stage, and nobody noticed. The perspiration ran off him during the prodigious efforts he put into the manipulation of the keyboard, particularly at the climaxes, and the great public loved to watch the struggle. By contrast, Tausig was small and refined, and it was a matter of pride with him that he barely moved while playing the most strenuous passages. Wrong notes were so rare that on the solitary occasions they were struck people flinched, because it reminded them of the perfection with which they were surrounded. With him everything was easy. He was the pianist's pianist. Tausig's repertory was enormous, and his abilities to sight-read and transpose at the keyboard were legendary. We could even call him the intellectual among nineteenth-century pianists were it not for the fact that posterity has already bestowed this title on Bülow, above all for his Beethoven playing. Yet Tausig played Beethoven's music too, a lot of it, and had he been allowed to live out his three score years and ten, he would have been alive during the years leading up to World War I, and would have overlapped with Mahler, Debussy, and the young Richard Strauss. He would certainly have influenced a later generation of pianists, including such diverse figures as Rachmaninoff (who admired and played a number of his transcriptions), Leopold Godowsky, Ignaz Friedman, and even the classically severe Artur Schnabel, with all of whom Tausig appears to have had certain qualities in common. He would undoubtedly have made gramophone records. But it was not to be.

A life, somewhat like history, is full of might-have-beens, about which it is usually better not to speculate. But for piano aficionados Tausig is the tempting exception. Had he lived longer, he would not only have changed the times, but perhaps the checkered history of Liszt interpretation itself.

Hans von Bülow

Heir and Successor

I do not consider him my pupil but rather my heir and successor.
FRANZ LISZT[1]

I

Bülow's childhood was marred by chronic illness. From his earliest years he was under the continuous care of doctors. He frequently succumbed to violent headaches and bouts of what his mother called "brain fever," which no amount of medical attention could cure. He himself tells us that until he was nine years old he had neither much talent for nor interest in music. This changed in a dramatic way after a serious illness. Propped up in bed, he began to grapple with the scores of Beethoven and Bach, and as an amusement he started to engrave each note on his brain. What began as a pastime soon turned into an obsession. Bülow discovered that he possessed a photographic memory, which in later life allowed him to play at the piano whole pages of music he had seen but once, and which eventually extended to the total recall of full orchestral scores. He also became a master of the art of transposing at sight. Moreover, he came to expect similar skills in others. In his preface to his edition of Cramer's *Studies,* he wrote, "A modern virtuoso of the right sort must be able to play Beethoven's Sonata, op. 57 (the "Appassionata"), with the same ease in the key of F-sharp minor as in the one of F minor."

Born in Dresden, in 1830, Bülow began his first real music lessons when he was nine years old. He soon outgrew this early instruction—his teacher was a local cellist named Henselt—and became a student at the Leipzig Conservatory of Music, under the well-known pedagogue Louis Plaidy, who laid the foundations of his technique. He also sought instruction in Dresden from Friedrich Wieck, the father and teacher of Clara Schumann, whose pupil he briefly became in 1845. This encounter is scarcely remembered today, so we do well to recall the tribute that Bülow made years later to his old master. "You were the one who first . . . taught my ear to hear, who impressed upon my hand the rules of correct formation, and who

1. CLBA, p. 42.

led my talent from the twilight of the unconscious toward the bright light of the conscious."[2]

As a self-conscious youth Bülow suffered from the knowledge that his head was slightly too large for his short body, and that his eyes had a tendency to bulge, giving the impression that he glared at everyone. Throughout his life he was also ravaged by headaches which often laid him low, especially when he was confronting a personal crisis. He eventually learned to retaliate against the slings and arrows of the world, both real and imagined, by fighting back with sarcasm and wit. His critics feared his banter because he did not hesitate to bring his formidable vocabulary to bear on their shortcomings. With the gentlemen of the press his legendary skirmishes were almost suicidal, and may have held back the proper recognition of his talents for several years.

The turbulent marriage of his parents, which ended in an acrimonious divorce when he was nineteen years old, cast a shadow over Bülow's adolescence. His mother Franziska was, in the words of Du Moulin Eckart, "a hard woman" who exercised a tyrannical domination over her gifted son, even after he had come to world prominence and she herself had entered old age.[3] Franziska could never reconcile herself to the fact that Bülow had chosen a career in music, a profession she held in low esteem, and she placed many obstacles in his path. His father Eduard had a softer nature, and a more sympathetic attitude toward his son's profession. A classical scholar by training, Eduard spent most of his life working on a huge biographical lexicon containing entries on all the great personalities of antiquity, a project he never lived to complete. Bülow inherited leading qualities from both parents: an acerbic tongue from his mother, and a love of intellectual pursuits from his father.

His first encounter with Liszt occurred under unlikely circumstances, while he was still a boy. Liszt was giving concerts in Dresden, and since he was already casually acquainted with Franziska and Eduard von Bülow, he was invited into their home. The conversation turned on the pianistic talents of their twelve-year-old son. Liszt must have remembered that conversation because on his next visit to Dresden, a few weeks later, he invited Hans to attend a concert he was about to give in the neighborhood. Despite the late hour—Hans was in bed—the youngster was roused from his slumbers and taken to hear Liszt. He never forgot the occasion, or his first glimpse of a man whom he came to venerate.

In an effort to placate his parents, Bülow reluctantly agreed to study jurisprudence, and in 1848 he enrolled as a law student at Leipzig University. He chafed beneath its restrictions, however, and within a year he had resolved to transfer to Berlin University. This was a fateful decision because it was while he was en route to Berlin that he stopped off at Weimar in order to make the further acquaintance of Liszt, who not only heard Bülow play the piano but also arranged for his young visitor's newly composed string quartet to be performed a day or two later at one of the Altenburg matinees. During this same visit, Liszt played for Bülow his paraphrase of

---

2. BB, vol. 3, p. 554.
3. BNB, p. xxviii.

Wagner's *Tannhäuser* Overture and made an overwhelming impression on the young man.[4]

The following year, in August 1850, Bülow and his mother visited Weimar in order to attend the Herder Festival. There Bülow witnessed Liszt conducting the world premier of Wagner's *Lohengrin* and experienced an epiphany. He decided to abandon the law for music. After the usual confrontations with his parents, they reluctantly agreed to allow Bülow to move to Weimar and place himself under Liszt's care. A letter from Liszt to Franziska, assuring her that her son's natural talent would guarantee his success, did much to assuage her initial hostility to this idea.

II

When Bülow arrived in Weimar, in June 1851, he found that Liszt had left town for several weeks and was staying at Bad Eilsen, because of an illness of his companion Princess Carolyne von Sayn-Wittgenstein who was taking the waters there. Having heard that the young man now awaited him in Weimar, and was meanwhile encamped at the Altenburg (see picture reproduced on page 52), Liszt wrote to Bülow from Eilsen on June 21, "I was delighted to hear of your safe arrival in Weimar, and since I must renounce the pleasure of receiving you there for several more weeks, let me at least bid you welcome there."[5]

Bülow was allotted his own rooms in the Altenburg and the use of a piano. He himself tells us that he practiced from eight to ten hours a day. He rose at 6:00 a.m., went straight to the keyboard in his dressing gown, "and set to work at my hammering with a calm and peaceful soul." Liszt's valet cleaned his shoes and pressed his clothes, while the cook prepared his breakfast. At 1:30 p.m. he went into town and had his midday meal at the Erbprinz Hotel. Then he walked for a couple of hours. By 4:00 p.m. he was back in his "hole," as he put it, and practiced until 9:00 p.m. His evening meal he would take at one of the local taverns. Back at the Altenburg he would "improvise by moonlight, or in the dark—it makes no difference."[6] As there was no spare door key, he would, if he got back late, often clamber over the wall and get into the house through a window that he had discovered how to open from the outside, in order to avoid disturbing the servants. This simple routine suited Bülow's monklike devotion to art. Within a few short days he had mastered a difficult piano trio by Raff ("one with which even Liszt had to take no end of trouble") and was able to play it with two of Weimar's best string players, both of whom had recently been brought to Weimar by Liszt—the cellist Bernhard Cossmann and the violinist Joseph Joachim, who now led the court orchestra.[7]

Bülow must have complained to someone about the poor condition of the piano that Liszt had placed at his disposal, for Liszt told him:

4. BB, vol. 1, pp. 178–79.
5. LBLB, p. 1.
6. BB, vol. 1, p. 332.
7. BB, vol. 1, p. 330.

I am sorry that you found such a bad piano in the rooms I beg you to consider yours at the Altenburg. If, as I would like, you prolong your stay in
Weimar, it would be necessary for you to have a better instrument sent to
you from Leipzig or elsewhere, for keyboards like Mr. Hippe's [a local man-
ufacturer] ruin the fingers. For the first weeks, the damage will not
be great, but in the long run it could happen that your performance might
be affected unfavorably.[8]

Liszt got back to Weimar on Sunday, October 12, and the lessons began the next
day. They worked on the last sonatas of Beethoven, the more significant compositions of Chopin and Schumann, and the newer works of Liszt himself. Liszt promised to help Bülow build a repertoire "that no other pianist could show."[9] Since Liszt
never taught technique, Bülow was left very much to his own devices in this area,
and he chose to work at Czerny's *School of Velocity* and the studies of Henselt, on
which "I crucify, like a good Christ, the flesh of my fingers, in order to make them
obedient, submissive machines to the mind."[10] To make the "crucifixion" yet more
severe, Bülow installed in his rooms a piano with a particularly stiff keyboard, and
he drilled his fingers on this instrument for four or five hours a day.

Within eighteen months Liszt felt that Bülow was ready to make his public debut, and he encouraged his twenty-three-year-old protégé to undertake a short concert tour, first to Vienna and then to Pest, Dresden, and Leipzig. Liszt had solid
contacts in all these cities, and as "a pupil of Liszt" many doors were opened for the
young man that might otherwise have remained closed. Liszt nonetheless followed
Bülow's journey with some trepidation, for he knew that much hinged on the outcome. At first the news from Vienna was bad. The hall was not full and Bülow had
to make good the deficit out of his own pocket. Worse, the Viennese critics found
his playing frigid. Part of the trouble was that he was billed as a "Pianist aus Weimar."
To the conservative Viennese this would have been a provocation. The "war of the
Romantics" was already in full swing, with progressive Weimar in opposition to re-
actionary Vienna, Leipzig, and Dresden, cities where the music of Liszt was now
much criticized. After reading the reviews Bülow fell into a depression, developed
one of his famous headaches, and retired to his hotel bedroom. Franziska von Bülow
foresaw a disaster-in-the-making for her son, and worked herself into a hysteria.
"God forgive those who led him to it" she told Liszt, doubtless lacking the courage
to blame him directly for her son's misfortune.[11] Liszt was magnanimity itself. He
told Franziska to be patient and reminded her of Hans's boundless talent, which was
certain to guarantee for him "a good and fine career." He then wrote to Bülow himself, advising him to remain in the imperial city for a while in order to strengthen
his contacts there. He also got in touch with his uncle Eduard Liszt, the prominent
Viennese lawyer who looked after Liszt's investments, and instructed him to advance

8. LBLB, p. 1.
9. BB, vol. 1, 343.
10. BB, vol. 1, p. 381.
11. BB, vol. 2, pp. 9–10.

Bülow one hundred florins for ongoing expenses and keep another hundred in reserve for him. Bülow's first real success came in Hungary, as Liszt hoped that it would. To ensure that the young man's first appearance in Pest went smoothly, Liszt had written ahead of time to a number of his powerful friends. On June 1, 1853, Bülow walked onto the stage of the Hungarian National Theater and played Liszt's Fantasia on themes from Beethoven's *Ruins of Athens* for piano and orchestra, with Ferenc Erkel conducting, and received a standing ovation. Bülow later wrote to his mother that the occasion was "an unparalleled triumph."

Having established himself as a pianist, Bülow moved to Berlin, where he succeeded Theodor Kullak as head of the Piano Department at the Stern Conservatory, a position he held until 1864. In Berlin he performed much modern music, and he also wrote a number of polemical articles for the German press, gaining for himself a reputation as a musical provocateur.

A major turning point occurred in Bülow's career when Liszt entrusted him to give the premier performance of his Sonata in B Minor, which took place in Berlin, on January 27, 1857. Bülow elected to play on the recently introduced Bechstein grand piano, which was at that time virtually unknown, and thereafter he was identified primarily as a Bechstein pianist. His friendship with Carl Bechstein was one of the closest he ever enjoyed with anyone, as their correspondence proves, although it was marred by various disagreements along the way. Bülow had such a high regard for the Bechstein grand piano that he called Bechstein his *Beflügler*—that is, the person who gave him his wings.[12]

III

On August 18, 1857, Bülow married Cosima Liszt, the nineteen-year-old daughter of Franz Liszt. The wedding took place in Berlin's Hedwigskirche. The young couple had known one another for two years, ever since Cosima and her elder sister Blandine had been uprooted from Paris by Liszt, as a result of his quarrel with their mother Countess Marie d'Agoult, and placed in the care of Bülow's own mother at her house on Wilhelmsstrasse.[13] In these domestic surroundings Bülow and Cosima had seen one another on a daily basis, Bülow even taking charge of Cosima's piano lessons, about which he sent regular reports to Liszt. When Bülow first declared himself, Cosima was only seventeen, and Liszt asked him to wait for one year, after which he would give his blessing. The match was doomed from the start, however, Bülow's constant irascibility proving to be a grave handicap. Moreover, Franziska von Bülow had come to dislike Cosima and was disliked by her in turn. There were two children of the union, Daniela and Blandine, named in memory of Cosima's brother and sister respectively, who had died just a year or two earlier, before Cosima's first

---

12. In German the term *Flügel* means both "wing" and "grand piano." See also p. 147, fn. 32.

13. The complications in Liszt's family life were now mixed with those of Bülow. It was an explosive combination, and it would take us far afield to discuss it here. I have dealt with the matter in great detail in the second and third volumes of my biography of Franz Liszt (WFL, vols. 2 and 3).

two children were born. A third child, Isolde, born to Cosima while she was still married to Bülow, was the daughter of Richard Wagner.

Wagner was the catalyst that rent the Bülows' marriage asunder and led in 1865 to their painful separation and in 1870 to their widely publicized divorce. It has long been a matter of speculation among scholars whether Bülow himself knew that Wagner was Isolde's father. The daughter always bore Bülow's name, and he recognized her as his legitimate offspring in the property settlement he later drew up with Cosima. In his letters to Cosima he constantly refers to "our three daughters."[14] Wagner and Cosima had fallen in love while Wagner was on a visit to the Bülows in Berlin, in 1861. Wagner later procured for Bülow the conductorship of the Royal Court Opera in Munich, in part because Bülow was emerging as the greatest Wagnerian of his generation, and Wagner trusted him with his scores; and in part because this appointment brought Cosima into daily proximity to Wagner.

In Munich Bülow continued to conduct Wagner's music even as he was being dragged through the public mire as a result of having been cuckolded by him. In this he showed true nobility, and history has come to admire him for it. During his tenure he gave the world premieres of both *Tristan* (1865) and *Die Meistersinger* (1868), making a meticulous piano reduction of the first opera, a time-consuming activity for which he garnered much praise from his peers. Unable to endure his situation in Munich and the pain of knowing that his wife was Wagner's lover, he suffered a nervous breakdown, and in 1869 he resigned his position. By then Cosima had eloped with Wagner to Switzerland and had meanwhile borne the composer two more children: Eva in 1867 and Siegfried in 1869. Because Cosima was a Catholic, a divorce was not available to her. Bülow therefore procured a Protestant divorce on July 18, 1870. Cosima and Wagner were married on August 25, 1870, in a Protestant ceremony. Eventually, Cosima abandoned her Roman Catholic faith, an act that undermined her relations with Liszt, now an abbé in the Catholic church. Despite the fact that Bülow was the injured party he paid all the legal costs himself.

Liszt suspended his relationship with Cosima and Wagner for five years (1867–72) in a show of support for Bülow, whom he felt had been cruelly wronged. It was not until 1872 that the parties put aside their differences when Wagner invited Liszt to attend the ceremonies connected to the laying of the foundation stone of the Bayreuth Theater. Despite the turmoil that the Cosima-Bülow-Wagner triangle had created in all their lives, both Liszt and Bülow went on to give a number of fundraising recitals in Germany in aid of the fledgling Bayreuth enterprise.

During the tumult and turmoil of his separation and divorce, Bülow entered a period of severe depression and contemplated suicide. His letters to Carl Bechstein tell the story. In July 1869 he wrote despairingly, "Ah, my dear Bechstein, everything

14. Both Cosima and Isolde knew better, however. In June 1914 Isolde brought a petition before the Bayreuth Landesgericht to have them declare her an offspring of Wagner. The Wagner succession was now at stake, and Isolde did not want her son, born in 1901, excluded from the possibility of directing future Wagner festivals. Cosima submitted a deposition in which she declared that at the time of Isolde's conception she was having sexual relations only with Wagner. But the court was not entirely convinced, since Wagner's old housekeeper Anna Mrazeck testified that Cosima and Hans shared the same bedroom.

within me is crashing! And it had to be!"[15] The following month he reached a point where living is more difficult than dying. "My situation is so incredibly and uniquely horrible, that any other way out than an exit from the world altogether requires superhuman pluck." And later in that same letter he actually raises the specter of suicide. "The best would be for some sympathetic soul to give me the necessary dose of Prussic acid! Is there no accommodating chemist in Berlin?"[16] These last words were to prove chillingly prophetic. By September 1869, after a number of meetings with his divorce attorney Herr Simson in Berlin, something of the old cynicism reemerged when he wrote, "It is really terrible that the second half of one's life should have no other object than to repair the follies of the first."[17]

In order to bring back some sanity into his troubled life, Bülow spent the two years following his divorce in Florence. He began a serious study of the Italian language, enlarged his keyboard repertoire, and brought back his concert fingers to a point where he was ready to embark on those world tours which gained for him a lasting place in the history of piano playing.

IV

Bülow came to be regarded as the greatest classical pianist of his time. He was renowned for his fidelity to the score, with each note in its proper place. His creed was never in doubt. The role of the performer was to be the servant of the composer, not the master. Bach and Beethoven dominated his repertoire, but he also played a lot of music by Chopin, Schumann, and Liszt, and, in later years much Brahms.[18] When Bülow confronted a musical masterpiece he believed that he was in the presence of greatness. And he expected his listeners to share his sense of reverence. When they did not, he berated them. Like the prophets of old, the interpreter was a chosen one, there to be ushered into the presence of God in order to take back the Word. Nor is the biblical analogy inappropriate, for Bülow himself was always making them. His aphorism "In the beginning was rhythm" is an obvious modification of the opening verse of the book of Genesis, and it has been widely quoted. He once described Bach's forty-eight preludes and fugues as the Old Testament of Music, while Beethoven's thirty-two piano sonatas were the New. To which observation he added, "We must believe in both." And in an interview that he gave to *The Etude,* he observed, "I believe in Bach the father, Beethoven the son, and in Brahms the holy ghost of music."[19] The abandon and excess that sometimes characterized the playing of his great contemporary Anton Rubinstein, with its self-indulgent departures from the text, was for him a form of blasphemy—as if the Bible

15. BNB, p. 95.
16. BNB, p. 96.
17. BNB, p. 99.
18. The full extent of Bülow's vast repertoire, both as a pianist and as a conductor, may be seen in HMI, pp. 458–515.
19. Issue of May 1889, p. 73.

itself was being used to justify a personal opinion. It was a part of his creed that no performance could be as perfect as the work it interpreted. For Bülow perfection, by definition, was always placed beyond reach. At particularly expressive moments, he would half turn toward the audience with a meaningful expression, as if to "reveal one of Beethoven's secrets in confidence," as the *New York World* would later put it.[20] This was a mannerism he had almost certainly acquired from Liszt, who also liked to look at his audience while he played. At such hushed moments everybody was on trial, and the slightest disturbance from the audience would occasionally provoke Bülow into a paroxysm of rage. One observer tells us that

> [Bülow] had played as usual with half-closed eyes gazing over the audience, as much to say, "Now, just listen to this! Isn't it something quite too exquisite?" But I suppose someone whispered or coughed; for when a sweet young girl, in all the purity of white muslin and blue ribbons, presented him with the customary laurel wreath, he stamped upon it with both feet, and the poor child ran down the hall weeping pure little tears and crying out: *"Er ist wüthend! Er ist wüthend!"* And indeed "raging" would hardly have translated his fury.[21]

Edward Dannreuther used the words "passionate intellectuality" to describe Bülow's playing, and they have often been quoted. Other critics found it cold and devoid of imagination. Clara Schumann called it "wearisome." During his American tour of 1875–76, the critic of *The Musical Trade Review* longed for a false note, such as Rubinstein and even Liszt were known to strike. But Bülow rarely obliged them with such symptoms of vulnerability.

These and other descriptions of Bülow's playing have misled many into supposing that he was a mere automaton, incapable of departing from the notes on the printed page. But a glance at his many reviews is enough to correct that impression. He would sometimes provide short, improvised preludes and interludes, before and between works, leading his listeners gently from one piece to the next. He liked to pave the way for a performance of Beethoven's A-flat Major Sonata, op. 110, with the four introductory bars of the Sonata in F-sharp Major, op. 78, transposed into A-flat major. Even more striking was his penchant for introducing the *Moonlight* Sonata with an improvised prelude based on the Adagio of the Ninth Symphony. He was also fond of playing the *Tempest* Sonata, having first extemporized a passage based on the opening of its sister Sonata in G Major, op. 31, no. 2. One of his more graphic aphorisms runs: "The interpreter should be the opposite of a grave-digger: he should draw the departed back into daylight."[22] These were hardly the habits of someone who had taken an oath to present "the text, the whole text, and nothing

---

20. Issue of November 15, 1875.
21. NCC, p. 66.
22. BB, vol. 3, part 2, p. 274.

but the text." They belong to an earlier generation, and exhibit an old-world charm almost forgotten today.[23]

On the concert platform his posture was restrained. He was once memorably described as "marble from the wrists up." According to Richard Strauss (a great admirer) Bülow had small hands, and could barely stretch an octave—providing yet another instructive example to pianists that nimbleness and dexterity may yet compensate for a small grasp.

Bülow was one of the first pianists to devote an entire evening to one composer—Bach, Chopin, Schumann, and above all Beethoven, whose last five sonatas were regularly presented by him in complete cycles. He was the thinking man's pianist who came to prominence at a time when the concert platform stood in danger of being taken over by a generation of "light entertainers"—Leopold de Mayer, Louis Gottschalk, and (later) Vladimir de Pachmann among them—who laced their programs with paraphrases of popular operas and potpourris of favorite melodies. With this sort of program Bülow would have nothing to do, and once said so from the concert platform.

V

During the difficult days of Bülow's divorce and his dark depressions, it was Liszt who helped his former son-in-law to face the world and who did much to rehabilitate him. Although it takes us somewhat ahead of our narrative, this is the place to point out that when Liszt accepted the position of president of the newly formed Royal Academy of Music in Budapest, in 1875, he stipulated that the post of head of the Piano Department should go to Bülow. Bülow refused to accept this position, however, and gave Liszt the reason that he was about to begin a long and much-postponed tour of America. That was literally true, as we shall discover. But in a deeply personal letter to Cosima, which Liszt probably never saw, he disclosed his underlying reasons, which we summarize here:

1. "[I] look upon official duties in a Conservatorium as slavery of the most annihilating kind. I can speak of it as one who knows, as a victim."

2. "I find myself morally and intellectually unable to justify the highly valued confidence [placed in me by] the Abbé Liszt."

3. "I am not in a position to fulfil the task of an—apostolate (pardon the

---

23. Nonetheless, these practices were still alive in the first half of the twentieth century, especially in the concerts of Mark Hambourg, Vladimir de Pachmann, and Ignaz Friedman. I myself heard Louis Kentner "preluding" before and between pieces in a public recital in Maryland given as late as the 1970s. In Bülow's case, the practice of "linking" Beethoven's works in the manner described may well have sprung from deeper considerations: namely, his conviction that Beethoven's music, especially the pianos sonatas, represented a unity that he wanted his listeners to share.

presumptuous expression), for which I no longer have the faith and the enthusiasm."

4. "The eternal gratitude which I owe him will make me ever and everywhere alive to and eager to seize any opportunity to testifying my loyal affection, but I am much more likely to meet such opportunities elsewhere than in a very dubious temple among people who are half barbarians and half Jews or Judaized."[24]

Bülow's arguments reveal a deep and newly developed ambivalence toward his former father-in-law. On the one hand he owed to Liszt so many of his greatest successes that he could not deny the debt. But for how long was he supposed to go on expressing his thanks to Liszt for opening doors that might otherwise have remained closed? On the other hand, Bülow's very public divorce in which he had been dragged through the mire, his subsequent breakdown, and his slow but heroic recovery as he pulled back from the abyss had given him an independence of mind and a new faith in himself and his talent that he did not want to lose. The other thing to emerge from this letter is Bülow's anti-Semitism. Interestingly, he has never been brought to the bar of history to answer for his many racial slurs, which in their way were more pointed than those of Richard Wagner.

Liszt's warm support of Bülow never wavered. His appreciation of Bülow's gifts reached its most public expression in his famous open letter to the editor of the *Gazette de Hongrie,* a French-language newspaper in Budapest:

> You wish to know what impression yesterday's Bülow concert made upon me. He belongs to you, he belongs to us all, to the entire intelligent public of Europe. Stated in two words: it was admiration, enthusiasm. Twenty-five years ago Bülow was my pupil in music, just as twenty-five years previously I was the pupil of my highly honored and dearly loved master, Czerny. But it has been given to Bülow to strive better and more perseveringly than to me. His edition of Beethoven, which is worthy of all admiration, is dedicated to me as the "Fruit of my teaching."[25] But here the teacher had to learn from his pupil, and Bülow continues to instruct—as much by his astonishing virtuosity as a pianist as by his extraordinary musical knowledge, and now also by his incomparable direction of the Meiningen Orchestra. There you have an example of the musical progress of our times.
> Heartily yours,
> Franz Liszt[26]

---

24. BNB, p. 268.

25. First published in 1871 by J. W. Cotta (Stuttgart). The edition was revised and republished in 1881, the year of Liszt's letter.

26. Issue of February 18, 1881.

Even though their paths had often taken them in different directions, Bülow remained in sporadic contact with his old master. From time to time, he even took over the Weimar masterclasses when Liszt was indisposed. Bülow had long looked askance at the relaxed social atmosphere that characterized Liszt's classes, peopled as they were with students whom he considered little better than hangers-on who took advantage of the master's generosity. In June 1880, he answered the call, traveled to Weimar, and used the opportunity to "clean out the Augean stable," as he put it. Bülow assembled the class and delivered a speech: "Ladies and gentlemen! Do not forget that the Master was born as long ago as 1811, or that he is the essence of goodness and gentleness; and do not misuse him in this revolting way. You ladies in particular: most of you, I assure you, are destined for the myrtle rather than the laurel."[27]

Some of the pupils left. Dori Petersen elected to stay. Evidently she was a rather rough, unwieldy player. She hammered out Liszt's transcendental study *Mazeppa* (which depicts a Cossack chieftain bound naked by his enemies to a wild horse, streaking across the Ukrainian steppes), a performance Bülow found to be so execrable he rounded on her, "You have but *one* qualification for playing this piece—the nature of a horse."[28] There was another confrontation with the Weimar masterclass the following year. Liszt was unwell, and quite by chance Bülow happened to be in Weimar visiting. Bülow insisted that Liszt go to bed, while he would take over the class. The door to the music room suddenly opened and in walked Bülow, to the consternation of the students. "It was as if a great hawk had swept down among us," remarked Liszt's pupil Emma Grosskurth, and she described how the "sparrows," Liszt's pupils, fluttered away in all directions in an effort to escape Bülow's orbit. Lina Schmalhausen, a somewhat inferior pianist who had been playing when Bülow entered the room, tried to gather up her music and flee, but Bülow barked at her, "No, it is you I wish to hear first." Schmalhausen was famously unreliable in matters of tempo and Bülow proceeded to humiliate her before the class. "I have heard it said that there are people who cannot count three; but you cannot count *two*."[29] Schmalhausen picked up her music and fled. The luckless Dori Petersen once more found herself at the receiving end of Bülow's sharp tongue. He listened to her with growing impatience and remarked, "I hope never to see you here again. You should be swept out of here—not with the broom but with the handle."[30] He later informed Adelheid von Schorn (a Liszt disciple), that he was merely providing the same service for Liszt as he did for his own dog in ridding him of his fleas. Nevertheless, such was Liszt's goodness of heart that the moment Bülow left Weimar the "fleas" were back, and the classes resumed their social atmosphere.

27. BBLW, p. 273.
28. BBLW, p. 273.
29. LL, p. 20.
30. LL, p. 20.

VI

As part of his divorce agreement with Cosima, Bülow had undertaken to settle 15,000 francs on each of his three daughters—a total of 45,000 francs—in order to pay for their education. The only way he could discharge this heavy obligation was to undertake a series of concert tours—which eventually took him to Russia, Britain, and the United States. Bülow made the first of several visits to England in the spring of 1873. His debut took place on April 28 when he played the *Emperor* Concerto at a Philharmonic Society concert in St. James's Hall, London, with William Cusins conducting. A second appearance at a Philharmonic Concert followed on May 26, when he played Rubinstein's Piano Concerto no. 3, in G major. These two appearances did more than anything else to prepare the way for what would become a long and fruitful relationship with the British public. At an ad hoc meeting of the Directors of the Philharmonic Society, held during the intermission of the second concert, a decision was taken to bestow on Bülow the Gold Medal of the Society.[31] That same month he conducted a memorable performance of the "Liebestod" from Wagner's *Tristan* for the Wagner Society. Bülow then found himself in demand as a conductor, and directed an all-Liszt concert in St. James's Hall, London, on November 27, 1873, at the invitation of Walter Bache, an English pupil of Liszt, whose acquaintance we shall make in the next essay. Thereafter, Bülow frequently appeared in the dual capacity of conductor and pianist, not only in London but also in such provincial cities as Manchester, Sheffield, Liverpool, and even as far north as Glasgow. His habit of playing and conducting from memory aroused universal admiration, for the English were still not used to a practice that had been introduced by Liszt a generation earlier.[32]

In January 1875, while he was on a second tour of Britain, Bülow suffered a stroke that temporarily paralyzed his right arm. This potentially fatal occurrence laid him low for several weeks. His "completely ignorant" English doctors misdiagnosed the symptoms as gout, but on his return to Munich the medical specialists there confirmed that he had been affected by an apoplectic stroke, albeit a mild one. He later told Cosima that "a blood vessel broke in the brain." Though he had to stop practicing for a time, it does not appear to have done any long-term damage to his piano playing, and he gradually recovered.[33]

Meanwhile, he built up resentment among the English because of his sharp tongue and abrasive personality. Of musical life in England he was generally contemptuous. He derided the amateur status that music was given within the social fabric of the country, and he held forth in a series of "Travelogues" which were published in the Leipzig *Signale,* and were almost immediately translated into English and reprinted in the London papers. Nothing and no one was spared. Sir Julius

31. Bülow's letter of thanks is dated "June 4, 1873" and is preserved in the archives of the Society, BL, RPS MS 337, ff. 155–56.

32. The *Musical Times* (June 1873) went out of its way to inform its readers that "since his arrival in England he has never had a note of music before him at his public performances."

33. BNB, pp. 159 and 264.

Benedict, August Manns, Sir Sterndale Bennett—all fell victim to his rapier comments. One of the few musicians to elicit his praise was Charles Hallé, the founder and conductor of the Manchester Orchestra (which would later bear his name) but since Hallé was German born and trained, the praise that Bülow heaped on him made the indigenous English musicians even more irate.

It goes to the heart of Bülow's complex personality that he was incapable of observing the conflict of interest in which he so frequently placed himself. Here he was, a distinguished guest in a foreign country that was treating him well, and he repaid them by lampooning their provincial ways for the amusement of his German readers. His comments eventually drew the ire of the *Musical Times:*

> Dr. von Bülow has been writing to a German paper from England some things about England, which display his usual good taste and amiability. As far as we know, nobody invited this virtuoso to come amongst us; but he did come, and, having constituted himself a guest, proceeded to sneer at his hosts. A few examples of his politeness will suffice. Finding himself at Sheffield under a canopy of smoke, he bethought him of Sterndale Bennett, and wrote, "It is said that the English Toledo or Solingen can boast of knowing the sun only from hearsay. In this report I always believed I could find an explanation of the style of composition affected [*sic*] by the late Sir W. S. Bennett, who first beheld the darkness of the world amid the ocean of smoke-clouds at Sheffield, and whose want of colour is as remarkable as his correct drawing, which latter obtained for him, as we know, the surname of the miniature Mendelssohn." This was graceful about a dead artist in the place of his birth, but Dr. von Bülow is above all ordinary considerations. Engaged to play at the Liverpool Philharmonic, he sent a transcript of the programme to Germany, with the sneer, "The ostrich-like stomach of the English public is worthy of all respect, is it not?" Next he girded at Sir Julius Benedict's "urbanity," laughed at the orchestra as containing "tolerably heterogeneous elements" and a "disturbing contingent of Falstaffian recruits;" while the rehearsals, he declared, were conducted in a "liquoring-up kind of way." Whether all this and much like it be true or untrue is beside the question. It is hardly for Dr. von Bülow, who comes here to pick up English money, to say it. This is not the first time he has lampooned us, nor probably will it be the last. He will no doubt perform another journey "in a fog," as he calls it, and write more letters to his friend Herr Senff [the publisher of the Leipzig *Signale*]. Contemplating this, he need not be afraid of popular retribution. Englishmen are used to ridicule, and they know that he laughs best who laughs last."[34]

It might have cheered the anonymous writer of this piece to know that Bülow's criticisms of his fellow Germans were yet more damning than the ones he was

34. MT 20 (March 1879): p. 140.

presently leveling against the English. He talked of "the beery complacency with which Herr Richter conducted *Meistersinger.*" And he damned with faint praise two of his German contemporaries when he described Max Bruch as "a Hiller who has turned out well."[35] Nor did he fear locking horns with the Berlin Hochschüle für Musik, whose director was Joseph Joachim. In an article in the Leipzig *Signale* in November 1877, Bülow attacked this famous institution because of its official policy of banning the music of Liszt, and for punishing those students who ignored the ban. Bülow went straight for the two people responsible for this practice. Ernst Rudorff, the head of the piano department, he castigated for "the incredible fact of forbidding the pupils of the institution, to their most serious detriment, not only from studying, but even from rendering themselves acquainted with Franz Liszt's works for the piano."[36] And Bülow also issued a challenge to Joseph Joachim himself, "Will the Director kindly point out to me a piece by Herr Rudorff which contains such *good,* specific music as, to take just one example, the 3rd of the grand master's Twelve [Transcendental] Studies?"[37] It is surprising to find Bülow holding up the relatively simple "Paysage" Study as an example of Liszt at his best, when he must have known that there were many other keyboard pieces of Liszt that were far more effective. But perhaps the choice was deliberate. Knowing how Bülow's mind worked, he may well have been saying that even inferior Liszt was preferable to superior Rudorff.

VII

After declining several invitations to tour America, Bülow finally agreed to travel to the New World. This undertaking was urged on him by his manager Bernard Ullman, who had recently taken Bülow under his wing, and whose vast experience of the American music scene (he had earlier arranged tours of America for both Henri Herz and Anton Rubinstein) virtually guaranteed a success. Moreover, Bülow needed money for the continuing education of his children. The statistics speak for themselves. During the season 1875/76 he undertook no fewer than 139 American concerts—that is, 4 or 5 recitals a week, including matinees, performing a repertoire of nearly one thousand pieces, and traveling across vast distances of thousands of miles. It was an artistic triumph over impossible logistics. His American travels have entered the record books.

The tour began in Boston, on Monday, October 18, 1875, after a very rough transatlantic crossing on the steamer *Parthia,* during which Bülow was seasick.[38] Im-

---

35. From the Leipzig *Signale,* November 1877, later republished in *Dwight's Journal of Music,* February 2, 1878.

36. We shall meet Rudorff again, in connection with his displacement of Liszt as the editor of the Chopin *Studies,* in Breitkopf's famous *Complete Edition* of the Polish master's works (see page 195).

37. Reprinted in *Dwight's Journal of Music,* February 2, 1878, from the Leipzig *Signale,* November 1877.

38. BB, vol. 5, pp. 291–92. To add to this indignity, Bülow had evidently been berthed in a cabin opposite one containing four German babies "crying in Saxon."

mediately after his arrival in Boston, Bülow locked himself away in his private quarters at 23 Beacon Street. The local newspapers reported that he practiced for eight or nine hours a day—as well he might in view of the workload before him. And the memory of the stroke that he had suffered in England a few months earlier must have haunted him. Having given up on the medical experts, Bülow, with Prussian doggedness, had simply practiced his way back to normality. The city's large Music Hall was packed for his premier concert, not only with listeners from Boston itself but also from the outlying towns. Even the New York newspapers sent reporters. We are told that Bülow walked onto the platform, a short, dapper figure, carrying a hat. This disconcerting appendage he proceeded to place on the piano. He also wore gloves which he ceremoniously removed before surveying the audience with his usual aristocratic disdain (he called it "exploring the local physiognomy"). After these preliminaries were over, he launched into a performance of Beethoven's *Emperor* Concerto. The program also contained a group of Chopin pieces and concluded with a performance of Liszt's *Fantasy on Hungarian Folk Themes*—a work dedicated to him, and whose premier performance he had given in Budapest as early as 1853 when he was only twenty-three years old. This opening concert was hugely successful, and Bülow could not have been happier with the press notices, although his relationship with the newspapers was to change as the tour unfolded. On the strength of this first concert the *New York Times* had already accorded him a position of pre-eminence among the pianists who had visited America during the past fifteen years, including Anton Rubinstein. He wrote to Ullman to thank him for having "morally forced me to cross the ocean."[39] During that first week in Boston Bülow gave four more concerts. And during the following week he made more history when he gave the world premier of Tchaikovsky's Piano Concerto in B-flat Minor, a work that Tchaikovsky had dedicated to him in gratitude, after it had been unceremoniously rejected as "unplayable" by its intended dedicatee Nicholas Rubinstein. So popular was the concerto that Bülow was obliged to repeat the Finale, a fact that Tchaikovsky found astonishing.[40] These Boston concerts were marred only by the fact that they were given with a scratch orchestra of a mere thirty-five players. That would not have been so bad had it not been for the incompetence of the conductor, the German-born Carl Bergmann, who missed several rehearsals and put Bülow in the position of having to fire him.[41]

VIII

By the time Bülow got to New York, word of his problems with Bergmann had reached the press. The large German population in Manhattan knew all about Bülow's idiosyncrasies, especially his habit of making negative comments about his

---

39. BB, vol. 5, p. 292.
40. See Tchaikovsky's letter of thanks to Bülow (BB, vol. 5, pp. 297–98).
41. A stimulating account of Bülow's American tours has been provided by R. Allen Lott, in LFP.

fellow countrymen when he was abroad, and they were waiting for him. His troubles started when he gave an interview to the *New York Sun,* which was eager to learn why he had fired Bergmann so soon after his opening concerts.[42] Bülow obliged the *Sun* and its readers by denouncing Bergmann as incompetent. He went on to berate him for "showing more interest in drinking beer" than in pursuing his duties as a conductor. He explained that he had now hired as a replacement Leopold Damrosch, his trusted friend and colleague from the Weimar years. The interview was so outspoken that it created what *Harper's Weekly* called a "hulla*bülow.*"[43] The German press gored him, calling him a great artist but a small man. That only made matters worse. Bülow went on to criticize the Germans in general as a beer-swilling crowd who drank until their brains were stupid, rendering them incapable of appreciating great music because they listened to everything through an alcoholic haze. This led to a further outcry, and Bülow received hostile letters, including some death threats.

The *New York Herald* infuriated Bülow when it described him as "Liszt's son-in-law." This was a particularly sensitive issue with him because he had invested a lot of psychological capital in breaking away from the Liszt-Cosima-Wagner triangle and was now his own man. He had put up a fierce resistance after learning that Ullmann had initially wanted to bill him in America as "the pupil and son-in-law of Liszt." On December 28, 1875, Bülow wrote to the *Herald:* "Allow me most humbly to decline the honour given me this morning by the musical critic of the *New York Herald* in calling me the son-in-law of Abbé Liszt, this honour belonging since 1870 *exclusively* to the composer of *Lohengrin,* Rich. Wagner Esq."[44]

Even before he had set foot in the New World, Bülow had been involved in discussions about the make of piano he would use for his concerts. Bechstein was unable to provide them, so Bernard Ullman entered into protracted negotiations with both Steinway and Chickering to provide the quality instruments that Bülow demanded. The approach to Steinway fell through, but Frank Chickering stepped in with necessary guarantees. Bülow was at first delighted with the Chickering pianos ("On other pianos, I have to play as the piano permits; on the Chickering I play just as I wish") but later started to quibble over their tone and their action. Nonetheless, this special relationship with Chickering laid the groundwork for Bülow's much publicized concert in New York on November 15, 1875. This concert inaugurated the newly built Chickering Hall, which stood on Fifth Avenue and 18th Street, and represented Chickering's answer to Steinway Hall, home of the firm's chief rival.[45]

Bülow appears to have been unprepared for the vigorous trade wars that were being pursued between Steinway and Chickering. Both companies insisted on dis-

---

42. *New York Sun,* November 17, 1875.

43. *Harper's Weekly,* 4 December, 1875.

44. BB, vol. 5, p. 316.

45. Built in six months at a cost of $175,000, Chickering Hall seated fifteen hundred people and was widely praised for its acoustics. When Bülow gave his inaugural recital, the interior decorations were still unfinished.

playing large proprietary signs next to their pianos, visible to all parts of the auditorium. In America it was a normal way of doing business. Bülow objected to being used as a traveling salesman, and he declared war on the signs. On one occasion he walked onto the platform and kicked the large advertisement off its stand and stamped on it. That was at his Baltimore concert, on December 6. On another occasion his audience was astonished to see him pause in midconcert, take out a jackknife and scrape the name "Chickering" off the instrument itself.

Bülow also felt constrained to give his audiences lessons in concert decorum whenever he felt that their crass behavior warranted it. This was especially true in the Midwest, which had little or no experience of classical piano recitals. He once berated a group of men in Steubenville, Ohio, who had kept their hats on during a performance of Wagner's "Spinning Song" in Liszt's transcription. The hats were hastily removed; respect for great music restored. On another occasion he stopped in midperformance, put on his glasses, and glared at a party of latecomers walking across the hall in squeaky shoes. Not until their perambulations had ceased did he resume playing. Nothing and no one was spared. On one occasion in St. Louis he had the misfortune to follow a soprano onto the stage who had screeched her way through some songs preceding his piano solos. He sat down at the piano, and as a little prelude to the beginning of his piece, he played the recitative from Beethoven's *Chorale* Symphony, "O Freunde, nicht diese Töne," ("Friends, not these sounds"). This was subtle, but there were those in the audience who grasped it.[46]

All this extracurricular activity gained for Bülow yet more notoriety, and there is no doubt that a sizeable portion of his audience came not so much to hear the music as to observe the spectacle. Nonetheless it was the music that lingered, and it was Bülow's integrity as an artist that won the day. America had never before witnessed such faithful renderings of the classics.

IX

Bülow's brief dalliance with the Baroness Romaine von Overbeck in the American capital is a subject about which there is more to be learned than the official record reveals. The encounter shows him to have been completely incapable of handling his emotional life after it had been shattered by Cosima's betrayal a few years earlier. Bülow was introduced to Romaine on December 9, 1875, by the German ambassador to the United States, Kurd von Schlözer, during a postconcert reception at the German embassy. Schlözer had been a close personal friend of Franz Liszt during an earlier posting to Rome, in the mid-1860s, during the period when Liszt had taken holy orders in the Catholic Church. Schlözer had long followed the career of Liszt's most prominent pupil, and he now wanted to open the doors of Washington's wealthy and famous to the Prussian pianist. Five years earlier, Romaine had married an Austrian baron, Gustav von Overbeck, and there were already two young

46. GLL, p. 223.

Hans von Bülow at the piano, 1884. (A photograph.)

sons of the union. Because the baron, who was a naval officer, spent long periods abroad in pursuit of a mercantile career (he was eventually given command of the steamship *America*), Romaine must have given every appearance of living an independent life. She was a talented amateur pianist and Schlözer thought that her playing was polished enough for her to have become a professional. Bülow was at first doubtless pleased to find a ravishing woman who could talk about the piano and its repertoire with intelligence. But as their conversations unfolded he was quickly swept away by her charms, and he appears to have built up some false hopes of a permanent liaison.

The barest review of the facts of Romaine's life ought to have been sufficient to convince Bülow that his dreams stood no chance of becoming reality. Romaine came from one of the most distinguished families in the nation's capital. Her grandfather was Samuel F. Vinton, a well-known former congressman from Ohio; her mother was Madeleine Vinton, who had honed her social skills by arranging her politician-father's dinner parties and official engagements. Romaine's father, Daniel Goddard, had died while she was still young. This was an important turning point in her own life because her mother then went on to contract a distinguished marriage to Rear Admiral John A. Dahlgren, a naval hero of the Civil War. It was the rear admiral who led Romaine to the altar for her wedding to Baron Gustav von Overbeck in 1870, one of the social events of the season. Among the guests were

President and Mrs. Grant, members of the Cabinet and Congress, and the chief justice of the United States. Bülow's letters to Romaine reveal his agitation at the
thought of parting from her. Five days after their first meeting, and just before leaving Washington, he wrote, "If I don't see you again in two weeks in New York, I'll
kill myself."[47] Romaine evidently made two trips to New York during his sojourn
there. He confided to Kurd von Schlözer, who had brought them together, that his
dearest wish was to change her name from O[verbeck] to B[ülow], but he lacked
any sensible plan to detach her from the baron. By January 7, 1876, he told Romaine, who had meanwhile returned to Washington, "I adore you so much that I
turn not only crazy, but what is worse, dumb like a simpleton."[48] Although she may
have been flattered by Bülow's attentions, Romaine evidently kept both her head
and her heart intact, knowing that she had much more to lose than Bülow himself
if their infatuation ever become public. We do not have her replies to his messages,
but it is not hard to read between the lines of a letter written by Bülow (whose tour
had once more taken him back to Boston) dated January 12, 1876, reproaching her
with the words, "I imagine that as a child you amused yourself by tormenting flies
and butterflies, considering that you excel with virtuosity in making me suffer, me
who loves you, me who adores you so—superlatively."[49]

Bülow's infatuation with Romaine ended, as it was bound to end, when he
learned that she was planning to join her husband in Europe. By then he was in
Cleveland, and he could only write helplessly that he was ready to abandon his career as an artist and follow her from the New World back to the Old. What he proposed to do once he had caught up with her he had no clear idea. Of lawyers and
divorces he had already had his fill. Romaine promised to meet him in Baltimore a
few weeks later in order to hear a program of his orchestral works at the Peabody
Institute. When she failed to turn up, Bülow knew that he had been abandoned.
There was a marked change in the tone of his letters to her. He abruptly dropped
the intimate "*tu*" for the formal "*vous*," and from "*Chère Adorée*," she was relegated
to "*Madame*." Bülow had been deeply wounded, was once more in despair, and was
still only halfway through his American tour.

X

It all ended on May 9, 1876, with a concert in St. Louis, from where Bülow embarked on the fifty-hour train journey back to New York in a state of utter exhaustion. Arrived in New York, he sought medical help. The New York doctors gave
him a series of treatments that they labeled "experimental," because they had little
idea of what was wrong with him. His condition was described as "nervous pros-
tration." According to the *New York World*, Bülow fell to the floor in a fainting fit

47. BB, vol. 5, p. 326.
48. BB, vol. 5, p. 332.
49. BB, vol. 5, p. 333.

while practicing, and he suffered a memory lapse of such severity that when Bernard Ullman entered the room Bülow failed to recognize his old manager, and he wept when Ullman's identity was revealed. It appears that Bülow had suffered another stroke, a diagnosis made all the more plausible by the findings of the autopsy carried out on his body many years later, which pointed to chronic hemorrhaging of the brain, among other things.[50] Even a man of normal health might have buckled under the strain to which Bülow had subjected himself. His American journeys had taken him to more than thirty towns and cities across the continent, involving thousands of miles of travel, and his health was devastated. He was obliged to cancel the remaining 33 concerts of the 172 that Ullman had planned for him, some of which were already being announced at the very moment that Bülow himself lay prostrate in his hotel room. He had to forfeit one quarter of his fee of 100,000 francs for breaking his contract. But at least one of his objectives had been reached: he had raised 75,000 francs for his young family, an uncommonly large sum of money, and had dutifully made much of it available to Cosima for the education of their children. As he approached the end of his American tour, filled as it was with stress and deprivation, he privately described it as "nauseating slavery, which I have entered because of vile mammon."[51] As for the hope that his grueling workload would clear his mind of depression, that remained unfulfilled. By the time he got back to Germany, in May 1876, his gloom had deepened. His friend and fellow Liszt-pupil Hans von Bronsart, with whom he was reunited at this time, procured for him the position of director of music at the court of Hanover. The slough of despond into which Bülow had descended is revealed in his correspondence with Carl Bechstein. Alarmed by one of Bülow's letters, Bechstein tells us that he traveled to Hanover and walked into Bülow's garden just in time to prevent him from shooting himself.[52] The immediate cause of the crisis was a serious quarrel with Bronsart himself. Anyone else would have shrugged off the incident. But the altercation had penetrated Bülow's soul and gave him no peace.

Liszt was well informed of his former son-in-law's uncertain mental state and of the rumors swirling around Bülow after his return from America, one of which had him incarcerated in Endenich undergoing treatment for insanity. In a letter to Princess Carolyne, dated September 26, 1876, Liszt wrote:

When someone told you that Bülow had taken refuge in a lunatic asylum with a very high reputation, near Bonn, where Robert Schumann ended his days, they were mistaken. No trace of insanity with Bülow—but great exhaustion as a result of excessive work and of labors beyond measure. He disregarded a slight stroke which took him unawares in London last year. The doctors then advised him to take care of himself—whereupon he left

50. BB, vol. 7, pp. 490–92.
51. LFP, p. 285.
52. BNB, p. xxii.

as rapidly as possible for America, and there, in a period of 6 or 8 months, played more than a thousand pieces of music at 140 public concerts! On returning to London, he finally followed the doctors' orders, by betaking himself to Godesberg, near Bonn, there to undergo a *Stahlbadkur* [chalybeate bath cure] under the direction of the celebrated Dr. Finkelburg.[53]

XI

With Liszt's encouragement, Bülow had always spent time on the podium. Once Liszt had discovered his pupil's penchant for conducting, in fact, he had done much good by stealth and procured a number of important engagements for his young protégé. Bülow had first picked up the baton years earlier, before he had even met Liszt. With Wagner's encouragement, first in Zurich and then in the small opera house in St. Gallen, he had sharpened his skills on modest orchestras and indifferent singers with such works as Donizetti's *La fille du regiment* and Weber's *Der Freischütz*. Then came Liszt and higher piano studies, but the podium was never far from his thoughts. In 1861 Liszt entrusted Bülow with the performance of his *Faust* Symphony, in its fully revised form, a work that Bülow rehearsed and then conducted entirely from memory. It was Bülow's appointment as Hofkapellmeister in Munich, in 1864, that brought him to national prominence. While there he conducted the world premiers of *Tristan* (1865) and *Die Meistersinger* (1868). As we have seen, he resigned his position because of his inability to cope with the breakup of his marriage to Cosima and her elopement with Richard Wagner. Only then did he begin his long odyssey as a concert pianist which marked much of his subsequent career.

The two years that Bülow spent in Hanover, after his return from America, re-established him as Germany's leading conductor. Once more his biting tongue got him into trouble and he resigned after a quarrel with the tenor Anton Schott, whom he described as a "Knight of the Swine," rather than as a "Knight of the Swan," a barbed reference to his role in Wagner's *Lohengrin*. From Hanover, Bülow moved in 1880 to Meiningen where he was appointed conductor of the Meiningen Court Orchestra, and it became clear that he had reached his definitive position. This forty-eight-piece orchestra he formed in his own image, insisting that the members play from memory, and that they play standing up. Such discipline had never before been imposed on an orchestra. Bülow would doubtless have justified such radical demands by observing that he was not asking the players to accept anything that he himself was unwilling to do. The five years that Bülow spent at Meiningen gained for him a reputation as the finest orchestral trainer of his generation. His success was due in part to his insistence on sectional rehearsals. At this time, too, he began to champion the music of Brahms, becoming the composer's chief exponent. As his interest in Brahms waxed, his regard for Liszt waned—to the extent that he later described Liszt's *Faust*

53. LLB, vol. 7, pp. 156–57.

Symphony (a work he had conducted with distinction in earlier years and from which he had in the meantime distanced himself) as "Unmusik, Aftermusik, Antimusik."[54]

During his term at Meiningen, Bülow made the twenty-year-old Richard Strauss his assistant conductor, taught him the rudiments of the profession, and conducted the young composer's Serenade for Thirteen Wind Instruments in Berlin to great acclaim, helping to launch his career. He also made room on his own concert programs for Strauss to conduct his early orchestral works, including the youthful Symphony in F Minor and the tone poem *Macbeth*. Strauss's debt to Bülow was incalculable, a fact made evident in the touching memoir that Strauss wrote about his old mentor many years later, when he himself was at the height of his fame.[55]

After stepping down from his Meiningen post in 1885, Bülow became in turn the chief conductor of the Hamburg Philharmonic and the Berlin Philharmonic orchestras, bringing both ensembles to a state of perfection hitherto unrealized. This was not achieved without effort. The rehearsals were often filled with dramatic outbursts as Bülow screamed at the players for their incompetence, insulting them both individually and collectively. He referred to himself as "a swineherd," a sufficient commentary on those he bent to his will. On the podium Bülow was a figure of enormous authority, bouncing with energy. His arm gestures were wide, and his baton swished the air with military precision. His body would sway back and forth as he attempted to capture that elusive quality called *tempo rubato* (elusive, that is, to orchestras). He darted here and there, attending to the shape of every phrase, piercing the players with his gaze and drawing from them music of unimaginable intensity. And of course everything was performed, and even rehearsed, from memory. Felix Weingartner was overwhelmed when he first witnessed Bülow conducting in Hamburg. Later he became one of Bülow's severest critics, accusing him of self-aggrandizement and of having done damage by creating "a lot of little Bülows," those aspiring conductors who aped the choreography of their hero while not possessing a sliver of his talent. "Sensation-mongering in music began with Bülow," Weingartner wrote in his famous treatise *On Conducting*.[56] A very different opinion was recorded by Liszt's pupil Frederic Lamond, who had studied with Bülow and was intimately acquainted with the European scene from the 1880s up to World War II. "He was the greatest conductor who ever lived—not even Toscanini approaching him," Lamond wrote. "I have seen and heard them all. No one, Nikisch, Richter, Mahler, Weingartner, could compare with him in true warmth of expression, which is the soul and substance of music and of all art."[57]

Closely allied to Bülow's conducting activities was his work as a composer. From the beginning he had naturally associated himself with the New German school of Liszt and Wagner, and his musical language tended to copy their style. His compositions include music for solo piano, lieder, chamber music, and orchestral works.

---

54. "Un-music, pseudo-music, anti-music" (BBLW, p. 169).
55. SRR.
56. WMC, p. 22–23; and WBR, p. 163.
57. LML, p. 43.

Unfortunately it did not outlast its time, although two of his orchestral pieces—
Nirvana, op. 20, and *Julius Caesar,* op. 10—were well enough known and frequently
played during his lifetime. Doubtless he would have preferred posterity to remember him as a composer, but he was too intelligent not to understand that his musical
destiny was that of an executant, serving the music of others. He once summed
up his fate in the following symbol, showing that his own name was simply there
to be supported by those of his three great contemporaries—Liszt, Wagner, and
Berlioz.[58]

```
B  ü  L  o  W
   e     i     a
   r     s     g
   l     z     n
   i     t     e
   o           r
   z
```

On July 29, 1882, Bülow married the Meiningen court actress Marie Schanzer, a
young woman twenty-seven years his junior. In this union Bülow found much
contentment. Richard Hoffman, the Anglo-American pianist, described her as "a
woman of unusual culture, charm, and intelligence."[59] Posterity owes Mme Schanzer
a great debt, because she made it her life's work to promote Bülow's legacy, eventually publishing his letters and articles in eight volumes and writing a useful memoir
of him.

Two further trips to the USA, in 1889 and 1890, brought Bülow more success
as a pianist. He played in New York's Broadway Theater, and during the five-day
period April 1 to 6, 1889, treated the American public to no fewer than eighteen Beethoven sonatas, all of them performed from memory. At one concert he
played the last three sonatas, opp. 109, 110, and 111. At another he played the
fugue from the *Hammerklavier* Sonata as an encore. Later that month he arrived
in Boston and made history by cutting a wax cylinder for Edison. The recording
engineer was Edison's colleague Theodore Wangemann. Bülow recorded what he
called "Chopin's last nocturne"—presumably the one in E major, op. 62, no. 2.
"Five minutes later," he wrote, "it was replayed to me—so clearly and faithfully
that one cried out in astonishment." Wangemann also played other cylinders for
Bülow, including parts of a Schumann symphony that had been recorded by the
Theodore Thomas Orchestra, and also the entrance of Lilli Lehmann as Brynhilde
in *Die Walküre.* Bülow went into raptures and described Edison's invention as "an
acoustical marvel." He was not satisfied with his own recording, however, claiming
that the presence of the machine had made him nervous.[60]

58. BB, vol. 3, p. 439.
59. HMR, p. 151.
60. Unpublished letter to Bülow's friend Cécile Gorissen-Mutzenbecher, dated "Boston, April 15,
1889." Copy in AWC, box 29.

XII

In 1887 Bülow was appointed the principal conductor of the recently formed Berlin
Philharmonic Orchestra. This was an epoch-making event, both for the orchestra
and for Bülow himself. When the Philharmonic approached him, it was little better than a ragtag group of players who had broken away from the popular Benjamin
Bilse Orchestra and were no longer willing to accept the stringent salaries that this
profit-driven maestro was imposing on them. They remembered the musical sensation that had been created when Bülow brought his Meiningen players to Berlin a
few years earlier, and they knew that he was the only conductor under whom they
might achieve greatness. In his letter of acceptance to his new manager Hermann
Wolff, Bülow wrote, "I can only justify my existence [there] by making reforms."
And make reforms he did. He drilled the orchestra ceaselessly and within two sea-
sons turned it into the finest musical machine in Europe. His concerts in the old
Philharmonic Hall created a sensation, and set a new standard for the interpretation
of the classics—Beethoven especially. The young Bruno Walter attended one of
those concerts. From his seat behind the kettledrums he had a direct line of vision
to the conductor's podium, and he experienced a revelation. He later recalled:

> I saw in Bülow's face the glow of inspiration and the concentration of en-
> ergy. I felt the compelling force of his gestures, noticed the attention and
> devotion of the players, and was conscious of the expressiveness and pre-
> cision of their playing. It became at once clear to me that it was that one
> man who was producing the music, that he had transformed those hun-
> dred performers into his instrument, and that he was playing it as a pianist
> played the piano. That evening decided my future. Now I knew what I was
> meant for. No musical activity but that of an orchestral conductor could

---

There is a detailed account of Bülow's Boston encounter with Theodore Wangemann and the Edison
phonograph in the *American Art Journal* of April 27, 1889. Wangemann went to Boston for the express
purpose of recording Bülow's recitals—not only taking them in, as the *Journal* put it, but taking them
down as well. It seems entirely possible, then, that Bülow recorded far more than the Chopin nocturne
about which he went into raptures with Gorissen-Mutzenbecher. According to this same journal's music critic, "behind the screen there was a big-mouthed phonograph taking in the afternoon's music, and
taking it down also." Because each cylinder was unique, and could not at that time be replicated, we learn
that it had been Edison's intention to buy them up. What became of them? In one of the great under-
statements of nineteenth-century music criticism the *Journal* added that "a great future is before the
Phonograph."
   Reports of Bülow's nervousness during the recording, and of his "cry of astonishment" as he listened
to the playback, crossed the Atlantic, and led to this colorful depiction in the *Musical Times*:

> After playing upon the pianoforte, from which issued sounds compared to the soft and dreamy
> gurgle of a brook, the far-off sighing of the night wind and the roar of the cataract, [Bülow]
> is described as placing the phonograph tubes to his ears: now a look of surprise creeps over
> his features, his face becomes ashy pale, he staggers back from the machine exclaiming, "Mein
> Gott! Mein Gott! It is bewitched." Recovering from what was almost a faint, he begs to be
> sent home at once, saying that his nerves are completely unstrung, and he must have rest.
> (MT, August 1, 1889)

any longer be considered by me, no music could ever make me truly happy but symphonic music. Before the evening was over I told Father that I would be glad zealously to continue my piano studies and be publicly active as a pianist later, just as Bülow was, but today the die had been cast, today I had recognized what I had been born for. I had decided to become a conductor.[61]

Bülow also put the Berlin Philharmonic on a sound financial footing and organized a pension plan for the players. He cut a lot of dross out of the repertoire, which gave the orchestra more time to rehearse only the best music, and he also shortened the concerts. He refused to conduct the three-hour marathons that were popular in his time, consisting as they did of a smorgasbord of pieces to satisfy all tastes, even the lowest. Program building was of the utmost importance to him, and one of the conditions he laid down with Wolff was that it must remain within his total control. He adopted a formula which has survived, with modifications, down to our own time— an overture followed by a concerto, and after the intermission a major symphony.

Bülow conducted more than fifty concerts with the Berlin Philharmonic, and when he finally stepped down in 1893, gravely ill, it had become an ensemble of international distinction. It was taken over in turn by Arthur Nikisch and Wilhelm Furtwängler, both of whom were quick to acknowledge their debt to him.

XIII

Bülow was now at the pinnacle of his fame, but his artistic triumphs were bought as great physical cost to himself, and his headaches increased. Aside from the conductorship of the Berlin Philharmonic, he had continued to commute to Hamburg in order to direct the Hamburg Subscription Concerts as well, and the workload was crushing. In April 1893 he entered a private hospital for nervous diseases in Pankow, Berlin. He also received medical treatment from Dr. Wilhelm Fliess (a former colleague of Sigmund Freud), whose modish theory of "nasal reflex neurosis" had just become popular among Berlin's intelligentsia. Fliess subjected Bülow to several operations on the inner cavity of the nose, but without alleviating any of the symptoms.[62]

---

61. WTV, p. 39. Bruno Walter, who was about seventeen years old at that time, tells us that he attended every one of Bülow's Berlin concerts toward the end of Bülow's tenure with the orchestra.

62. Wilhelm Fliess (1858–1928) had recently come to prominence after publishing his *Neue Beitrage und Therapie der nasaelen Reflexneurose* in Vienna, in 1892. The fact that Bülow consulted him at all suggests that the patient thought that his troubles may have been psychosomatic in origin. (The autopsy carried out on Bülow's corpse would prove otherwise. Besides the chronic hemorrhaging of the brain, the findings included a growth on the back of the neck pressing on an artery—a probable cause of Bülow's devastating headaches—and calcification of the brain's major blood vessels [BB, vol. 7, pp. 490–92]). The hypothetical link that Fliess had established between the nose and a variety of neurological symptoms, and the operation that he had devised to sever that link, would today be dismissed as quackery of the first rank. Fliess was convinced that the membranes of the nose held the key to neurotic symptoms aris-

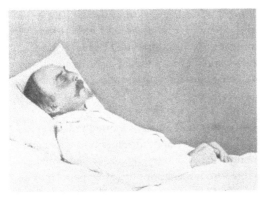

Hans von Bülow on his deathbed, 1894. (A photograph.)

At the suggestion of Richard Strauss, who visited him in Hamburg at the beginning of 1894, Bülow journeyed to Egypt in order to enjoy the benefits of the dry climate and undergo a course of treatment at a sanatorium near Cairo. He and his wife took the train to Vienna and then to Trieste, crossed the Mediterranean Sea, and finally arrived in Cairo on February 7, 1894. The next day Bülow was examined by a German physician, Dr. Wild, who then left to make arrangements for Bülow to receive a course of treatment at the sanatorium. Bülow meanwhile went out onto the terrace of his hotel room to enjoy the warm sunshine, while his wife went to fetch some linen from an adjoining room. Suddenly she heard a heavy fall and a rattling in the throat. Bülow had suffered a major stroke and had collapsed to the floor. The next day, February 12, he was admitted to a German hospital run by Protestant sisters, where he expired at 7:30 p.m. The embalmed body was taken back to Germany on the passenger ship *Reichstag,* and was disembarked at Hamburg on March 22. From there Bülow was taken to Hamburg's imposing Michaeliskirche and for the next seven days thousands of admirers came to view the body and pay their last respects. The coffin was placed before the altar on a raised catafalque, buried beneath beds of flowers. On March 29 the funeral procession set out for Hamburg's Ohlsdorf Crematorium. It paused outside the opera house, where the thirty-three-year-old Gustav Mahler, who stood in awe of Bülow, had assembled the orchestra on the terrace to perform the "Funeral Music" from Wagner's *Götterdämmerung.*[63] It was a fitting farewell. Bülow's remains lay overnight at Ohlsdorf and the next day they were cremated. A memorial stone by the sculptor Adolf Hildebrand marks his final resting place.[64]

---

ing from sexual repression. The operation itself involved the application of cocaine to the interior of the nose. Fliess was later to carry out a similar operation on Freud himself. See JSF, vol. 1, pp. 318–19 and 339.

63. Mahler had been appointed first conductor of the Hamburg Opera in 1891, and Bülow had followed his rising star with interest. He was the only conductor for whom Bülow had any praise. Mahler, for his part, regularly occupied a seat in the front row at all the Bülow concerts. Even before his death, Mahler had taken over some of the Hamburg Philharmonic subscription concerts from which Bülow's ill health had obliged him to resign.

64. BBLW, pp. 189–90; and BB, vol. 7, pp. 459–60.

Shortly after Bülow's death an appeal was launched "in the name of the German nation" for a permanent monument to be erected in Hamburg, the city that he had come to regard as his home. "As the leading champion of German art he won new glory for the German name," the citation read. "It is the solemn duty of the German people to erect a monument to him." The document was signed by many prominent people from the arts and the sciences, including the physicist Hermann von Helmholz; the poets Klaus Groth and Friedrich Spielhagen; the painters Adolf Menzel and Franz von Lenbach. Among the musicians were Johannes Brahms, Joseph Joachim, Gustav Mahler, Felix Mottl, Richard Strauss, and Felix Weingartner. This monument was never built.

As for Bülow, he would surely have preferred the wisdom of Cato the Elder (234–149 BC): "I would rather have men ask why I have no statue, than why I have one."

Walter Bache

An English Disciple of Liszt

I am always thanking you; it comes from the heart, and will ever be so.
FRANZ LISZT[1]

I

Walter Bache was Liszt's most prominent English pupil. He first met Liszt in Rome in 1862. After studying with the master in the Eternal City for three years he returned to England, determined to promote Liszt's cause. He remained a pupil of Liszt and regularly attended the Weimar masterclasses until Liszt's death in 1886—a period of twenty-four years. That is an exceptionally long time, unmatched by any other pupil of Liszt, English or otherwise, and it led to a particularly close bond between master and disciple.

Bache's promotion of Liszt's music in Victorian England, which he mounted in the face of unremitting opposition, was little short of epic. It cost him a small fortune, and may well have cost him his career as well. For Liszt scholars, Bache is one of the unsung heroes of the nineteenth century. The loneliness of his position is dramatically illustrated when we examine the programs of England's premier concert-giving organization, the Philharmonic Society. Between 1840 and 1867, a period of twenty-seven years, not a single work by Liszt was performed. In that latter year the staid directors admitted a solitary piano piece, "La campanella." That was enough to shut the doors again, and five more years elapsed before another note of Liszt was sounded. In the 1870s, the floodgates burst open, so to speak, with the performance of five works in ten years; and in the decade following there were actually twelve. After such undue abandon, the 1890s saw the number of performances dwindle to four. The stranglehold on London's concert life exercised by the Philharmonic Society, with its emphasis on the First Viennese school and such "safe" composers as Mendelssohn (eleven works) and Ludwig Spohr (nine works) killed enterprise and denied both Liszt and Wagner a hearing. Modern music was represented in the London of the 1870s and 1880s by Arthur Sullivan, Sterndale Bennett,

---

1. LLB, vol. 2, p. 264.

and George Macfarren. It was left to Bache to remedy matters, and this he did, carrying the torch for Liszt year after difficult year, almost driving himself into bankruptcy in the process.

II

Born in Birmingham in 1842, Walter Bache was one of seven children sired by a Unitarian minister, the Rev. Samuel Bache, who ran a private school in collaboration with his wife Emily Higginson.[2] Nine years separated Bache from his gifted elder brother, Francis Edward, whose promise as a composer (he had been a pupil of Sterndale Bennett in London and then of Moritz Hauptmann in Leipzig) was abruptly terminated by death from consumption when he was only twenty-four years old. It was said of Edward, whose compositions showed skill, albeit in a traditional style, that had he lived he might well have become his country's leading composer, an English Mendelssohn.[3]

Determined to follow in his brother's footsteps, Walter took organ lessons from the Birmingham organist James Stimpson; and then in August 1858, at age sixteen, he set out for Leipzig in pursuit of higher musical studies at the conservatory. His father had intended to accompany him, but was detained at the bedside of the dying Edward, so young Walter undertook this arduous journey by himself—an early symptom of the resolve and independence that he would exhibit for the rest of his life.

By his own admission Bache wasted much time in Leipzig. His chief teachers were Moscheles for piano and Hauptmann for theory, but there was little supervised study at the conservatory and he lacked direction. On sudden impulse he went to Italy in September 1861, settling in Milan for a few months, thinking that whatever contacts he made there might prove useful to him later on. Finding little to do, the twenty-year-old Bache drifted to Florence, where he was befriended by Jessie Laussot, who had founded a flourishing musical society in the city (the Società Cherubini) and was intimately acquainted with Liszt, Wagner, Hans von Bülow, and other leading musicians.[4] After getting Bache to play at several local concerts and shrewdly observing his native talent, she recommended that he go to Rome in order to make the acquaintance of Franz Liszt.

Bache himself has told us that when he arrived in Rome and first approached

---

2. The Rev. Samuel Bache was also among the first Unitarian ministers to establish Sunday Schools in Birmingham. In 1844 he was directed by the Unitarians there to establish the first "Ministry to the Poor," which served the most squalid areas of the city.

3. The unpublished letters of Edward Bache to his parents give many details of his social and musical life in Leipzig—a pattern that Walter was to follow four or five years later. Brit. Lib. add. ms. 54193.

4. Born Jessie Taylor (1827–1905), this English musician had made the acquaintance of Liszt as early as September 1854, when she and her mother had journeyed to Weimar and attended one of the musical matinees at the Altenburg. She later married Eugène Laussot, who became mentally unstable and from whom she separated. After his death she married (in 1879) her longtime friend and companion, the German historian Karl Hillebrand. Florence was presently her adopted home, and she lived there for many years.

Liszt, on June 4, 1862, he was nervous and became tongue-tied. Liszt observed the untidily dressed youth before him, and assumed from his painful silence that Bache was searching for words to beg for money. Years later his sister Constance Bache wrote, "What an insight it gives into Liszt's life that this should be his first thought when a young stranger came to him."[5] Bache was dreadfully hurt, but once the initial confusion had been sorted out Liszt made him welcome. There followed one or two impromptu lessons and, thanks to Liszt's recommendations, some appearances at the newly formed Ramacciotti[6] chamber concerts and the German Club. Liszt eventually advised Bache that if the young man were prepared to move to Rome the following year, he would work with him on a regular basis.

III

This meeting with Liszt gave Bache's life a new purpose. Liszt expected him to work, and Bache applied himself to the keyboard with a missionary zeal worthy of the son of a Unitarian minister. Like many a student before him, Bache quickly fell under Liszt's magnetic spell, and his letters to his family are filled with detailed accounts of his various encounters with the master. In keeping with Liszt's usual practice, he did not charge Bache a penny for the lessons. Among the solo works the young man studied with Liszt during these first months were Bach's Chromatic Fantasy and Fugue, Mendelssohn's F-sharp Minor Fantasie, Chopin's C-sharp Minor Polonaise, and Liszt's own "Les Patineurs"—a work he felt certain was beyond him but which he mastered with Liszt's encouragement. Bache also had the enormous advantage of hearing Liszt himself play often in private homes, including that of the Ritter family, where the great pianist performed several numbers from the Swiss volume of the *Years of Pilgrimage*. Throughout this early period Bache could not help observing the immense sadness that engulfed Liszt, who was still grieving over the recent loss of his daughter Blandine, and that seemed to affect everything he did. It was in an attempt to seek solitude from the hurly-burly of life that Liszt moved at this time into the peaceful surroundings of the Madonna del Rosario, a monastery on the Monte Mario, with unsurpassed views of the city and the dome of St. Peter's, which lay about three miles distant.

In June 1863 Bache returned to Birmingham to help his family obtain funds for the erection of a memorial window to his brother Edward, in the Church of the Messiah, his father's old church. These efforts culminated in a performance of Mendelssohn's oratorio *St. Paul,* on October 1, in which Bache attracted attention by presiding at the organ. Attention of a somewhat different kind was attracted when he gave a solo piano recital in benefit of the same cause, playing a number of pieces by Liszt. The conservative critics of Birmingham did not much like them, and Bache

5. BBM, p. 154. Although this was Bache's first direct encounter with Liszt, the young man had already seen and heard Liszt play for the students of the Leipzig Conservatory in May 1859.

6. The violinist Tullio Ramacciotti (1819–1910) had begun his long series of chamber concerts in Rome, in December 1862. They were held in a small auditorium on the Via della Frezza.

was piously advised to follow in the footsteps of his Mendelssohnian brother. It was a harbinger of things to come.

Bache returned to Rome in mid-October, and was re-united with Liszt. He spent an entire day in Liszt's company at the Madonna del Rosario, and enthused to his father:

> He has removed to this place on purpose, to get away from people and live quietly. It is a magnificent country, with a splendid view of Rome, and no houses for miles. But this will make no difference to my visiting him, he said. He is writing a great deal: but he put it aside and took me [for] a beautiful walk, and played me several things (amongst others a Prelude and Fugue of his own for organ—on the name B.A.C.H.,[7] which I will show Alfred[8] when he has finished what he has already), and ordered dinner on purpose for me; and so I stopped all day, and have just had the most magnificent walk home—but descriptions of scenery are always stupid and fall so far short of the reality—I wish you could have seen it. He accompanied me part way home, and promised to come and see me tomorrow evening. Liszt desired me to give you his "compliments or kind regards."[9]

Meanwhile, Bache had secured a position as organist at the English Church in Rome, which guaranteed him a modest income. His growing reputation as a performer attracted students, and he was soon financially secure. He also became acquainted with a group of gifted young musicians, including Liszt's pupil Giovanni Sgambati and the violinist Ettore Pinelli. In those days Rome was starved for good music. The oppressive hand of the Vatican was everywhere to be felt. Public concerts and operas were considered to be "worldly" and hardly ever took place. The Eternal City could boast of neither a symphony orchestra nor an opera house. The best music-making went on inside the private homes of the aristocracy and the upper clergy. It gives one an insight into the power of the church that when Sgambati and Pinelli advertised that they were going to include Tartini's *Devil's Trill* Sonata in one of their programs, the Vatican censors insisted that the word *Devil* be dropped from the title. So the work was billed as "Le Trille du Follet" instead.[10]

7. The organist in Bache would have been stirred by this work, which had been published as early as 1855. It had been given its first performance by Liszt's pupil Alexander Winterberger when he inaugurated the new five-manual organ at Merseburg Cathedral, on September 26, 1855. Although the catalogs of Liszt's music inform us that the piano transcription of this work (known as the Fantasie and Fugue on "B.A.C.H.") dates from 1870–71, it is interesting to find that Liszt already had a solo piano version in his fingers, which he played to Bache as early as October 1863. In fact, Moscheles had already heard Liszt play a still earlier version of the transcription in May 1859, when he was Liszt's guest in Weimar (MAML, vol. 2, p. 292). Bache put the work into his own repertory and played it at one of his London concerts on October 22, 1879 (Liszt's sixty-eighth birthday), perhaps the first time that it had been heard in England.

8. Alfred Bache, a brother who was studying the organ in Birmingham at that time.

9. BBM, p. 169. Bache's "magnificent walk home" was his euphemistic way of describing the three-mile stretch that separated the Madonna del Rosario from his lodgings in central Rome.

10. BBM, p. 174.

Walter Bache, ca. 1887. (A photograph.)

Bache might well have stayed longer in the Eternal City, but in April 1865 Liszt received the tonsure, and in July of that year he entered the lower orders of the Catholic Church. Liszt moved into the Vatican, in order to prepare himself for this most solemn undertaking, which necessitated a number of practical changes in his daily life. So Bache gave a "farewell" recital in Rome in March 1865 which was attended by Liszt, took his leave of his master, and began a new life in London, a city that was to remain his home for the rest of his days.

IV

Bache's reputation as a pupil of Liszt had preceded him. Almost from the moment he settled in London he was regarded as "dangerous." This was brought home to him in a particularly vivid manner. In order to establish himself in London, Bache called upon the most powerful music critic in England, J. W. Davison of the *Times*. This was a logical first step, especially since Davison had been well acquainted with Edward Bache, whose musical conservatism chimed with his own. Bache himself relates that when he called on Davison and handed in his card, the maid returned with the message, "Please, sir, Mr. Davison says that he is not at home." It was an early indication of the uphill struggle that was to become a central fact of Bache's career. As Constance Bache remarked, the critics as a body were never "at home" to Bache. Perhaps he had forgotten to bring with him a suitable gift. When many years later Davison was succeeded at the *Times* by Francis Hueffer, the latter had to hire a taxicab to return all the "presents" from various musicians which were customarily delivered to Davison's front door and were now diverted to his.[11]

Bache's annual concerts, created to support the Liszt cause in Britain, began in a modest way in 1865, in Collard's Rooms, Grosvenor Street, W.1.[12] As their popularity grew they were moved to the more spacious Beethoven Rooms in Cavendish Square. Later still they were transferred to the Queen's Concert Rooms in Hanover Square, and finally ended up in the prestigious St. James's Hall in Regent Street. They also grew in stature from their humble beginnings as chamber recitals to full-sized choral and orchestral concerts. Bache lists thirty-eight programs in his diary, a

11. RMM, p. 77. J. W. Davison (1813–85) served as the music critic of the *Times* from 1846 to 1879, an exceptionally long period of thirty-three years. His conservative views, expressed anonymously (as was the practice in those days), wielded great influence and helped to stifle experiment and resist change. Davison was married to the pianist Arabella Goddard (she had earlier been his pupil, studying the classical composers with him), and when Davison started to promote her, the conflict of interest raised eyebrows. A French magazine pilloried the pair by saying that whenever a pianist approached the shores of England, you could be certain to see Davison standing on the cliffs of Dover shouting, "No pianists wanted here!"

12. Collard & Collard was a distinguished firm of English piano manufacturers (second only to Broadwood), one of whose earlier partners had been Muzio Clementi, who had met the young Liszt in London in the 1820s. That point would hardly be worth reporting here, were it not for the fact that the company was eventually taken over by Chappell & Co. in 1929, a prospective misfortune for Collard's, which lost all its records in the fire that destroyed much of the Chappell building in 1964, and with it many traces of the Bache and Liszt connections.

number that includes his solo recitals as well as chamber and orchestral concerts. Each one of them was mounted at his personal expense. The full-scale symphony concerts, which eventually became known to the London public as the "Walter Bache Annual Concerts," and for which he often engaged upward of a hundred players, began in 1871 and continued without interruption to the year of his death.[13] They represented an enormous financial outlay for him and invariably incurred a loss. These novel events nonetheless became fixtures on the London scene, attracting the attention of the press, and Bache often found himself at the center of controversy. He frequently appeared as a soloist, accompanist, or (more rarely) as a conductor, but he also engaged other artists in an attempt to show the public and the critics that it was not his intention to push himself forward. Hans von Bülow conducted two of the concerts (on November 27, 1873, and February 25, 1875), performing at the first of them what may well have been the premier performances in Britain of Liszt's symphonic poems *Tasso* and *Orpheus*.[14] And on November 1, 1875, one of the guest artists was the distinguished violinist August Wilhelmj, who played the Bach Chaconne in D Minor. Bache also brought in that staunch Lisztian, August Manns, the conductor of the popular Crystal Palace concerts.

As we scan Bache's concert programs we are reminded of his artistic isolation. It is astonishing to find him promoting the first British performances of such works as the symphonic poem *Festklänge* (March 21, 1872), the Thirteenth Psalm (February 28, 1873), and the *Faust* Symphony (March 11, 1880). For the Thirteenth Psalm he engaged an orchestra of eighty players and a chorus of two hundred singers. As he himself noted at the time: "I lost 170 (pounds) by my last concert. . . . I am up to my ears in debt, and have to teach from morning to night."[15] Many people assumed that Bache must have had a private income to be able to sustain losses of this magnitude, but his letters prove otherwise. The concert on February 25, 1875 (in which Hans von Bülow conducted a repeat performance of the Thirteenth Psalm, with Liszt's A Major Piano Concerto played by Bache himself) was a financial disaster. Bache noted that he incurred expenses of two hundred and fifty pounds—more than a third of his annual income; Bülow was so concerned that he not only waived his fee but insisted on contributing fifty pounds out of his own pocket.[16] Bache's continuing financial plight emerges from his letters: "I must teach all the young women I can possibly collar, so as to turn their guineas into fiddles and singers."[17] By 1873, when he was already thirty-one years old and time was no

---

13. Since the concerts did not begin until 1871, and Bache died in 1888, his own numbering of thirty-eight "Annual Orchestral Concerts" is somewhat confusing. But it can be reconciled once we take his earlier solo Liszt recitals into account. The entire run of concert programs may be consulted in the Bodleian Library, shelf-mark 7897.e.39.

14. To have the distinguished support of Hans von Bülow was a great advantage for Bache. Whatever the poor standing of Liszt in England might have been, that of Bülow was beyond reproach, and this association gave Bache's concerts a good deal of credibility. The two musicians were well connected through Liszt himself, who remained well informed about the activities of his former son-in-law.

15. BBM, pp. 214–15.

16. BBM, p. 240.

17. BBM, p. 209.

longer on his side, he was confronting what was by now the crucial decision of his professional career. "I must decide whether I shall sacrifice myself entirely to the production of Liszt's orchestral and choral works (which after all can never be immortal as Bach, Beethoven and Wagner: here I feel that Bülow is right). Or shall I make my own improvement the object of my life, and not spend a third of my income in one evening?"[18]

It is instructive to dwell on what, exactly, Bache spent "a third of his income in one evening." The eleventh Annual Concert, conducted by Bülow on February 25, 1875, to which reference has already been made, provides an answer.

ST. JAMES'S HALL
Mr.
WALTER BACHE'S
Eleventh
ANNUAL CONCERT

Thursday Evening, February 25, 1875
Orchestra of sixty-eight performers.
Choir of one hundred and sixty voices.

Conductor
Dr. Hans von Bülow

Liszt	Symphonic Poem: "Festklänge"
Schubert	"Gott in der Natur"—Hymn for female voices, op. 133 (orchestrated from Schubert's piano accompaniment by Hans von Bülow) 1st perf. in England
Liszt	Oh! quand je dors soloist: Mr. Henry Guy (tenor)[19]
Liszt	Piano Concerto no. 2 in A Major soloist: Walter Bache

INTERVAL

Liszt	Psalm Thirteen for Tenor solo, Chorus and Orchestra

---

18. BBM, p. 215. Bache was not yet affiliated with the Royal Academy of Music, the institution with which he became mainly associated, and as yet he enjoyed no regular salary. He was appointed to the piano faculty of the Academy on November 2, 1881, and was paid the princely sum of ten shillings and sixpence per hour. (See the RAM Committee minutes of that date, p. 247, housed in the Academy library).

19. The soloist was originally to have been the better-known W. H. Cummings who, according to an insert in the program, was incapacitated by "a severe Cold, which prevents him singing this Evening."

Weber–Liszt   Polonaise Brillante, op. 72
               soloist: Walter Bache

Liszt   "Soldatenlied," from Goethe's "Faust"

Liszt   "Chorus of Reapers," from Herder's "Prometheus"

[THERE WILL BE AN INTERVAL OF THREE MINUTES, DURING WHICH ALL WHO DO
    NOT WISH TO HEAR THE LAST PIECE ARE REQUESTED TO LEAVE THE HALL]

Wagner: Overture: "Tannhäuser"

NB. THE DOORS WILL BE CLOSED DURING THE PERFORMANCE OF EACH PIECE.

By any standards this represents a marathon event. It contains about two-and-a-half
hours of music, demanding great endurance on the part of the listener. Since the
concert did not start until 8:30 p.m., and contained two intermissions, the audience
would have been streaming out of the hall and into the London fog at an uncommonly late hour—well past the optimistic prophecy in the program that it would
be all over "by half-past 10 o'clock."

Equally praiseworthy were Bache's annual solo piano recitals, which were usually given on October 22, Liszt's birthday. They may well have caused him even
more work than his orchestral concerts, since they placed him squarely in the lime-
light. The recital he gave on Wednesday, October 22, 1879, was of Olympian pro-
portions, consisting entirely of Liszt's own compositions, and suggesting that Bache
was a pianist of considerable skill.

ST. JAMES'S HALL
Wednesday, 22nd October, 1879

Prelude and Fugue on the name "B.A.C.H."
Ballade no. 1, in D-flat Major
Au bord d'une source
Polonaise no. 1, in C Minor
Concert Study in F Minor ("La leggierezza")
Two Transcendental Studies
    no. 3. "Paysage"
    no. 8. "Wilde Jagd"
Three Songs (soloist Mr. Charles Santley)
    Es muss ein Wunderbares sein
    Du bist wie eine Blume
    In Liebeslust
Eglogue (*Années de pèlerinage,* Suisse)
Legend no. 1, "St. Francis of Assisi Preaching to the Birds"
Hungarian Rhapsody no. 4, in E-flat Major

Needless to say, it was Bache who provided the piano accompaniment in the three songs as well.

The high quality of Bache's program notes calls for comment. His missionary zeal led him to expend much time and money on the production of learned essays, which were so thoughtful in their content, and so detailed in their exposition, that they were clearly intended to serve as source material long after the concert itself was over. To help in this task Bache sometimes brought in prominent foreign theorists such as Carl Weitzman from Berlin, and Friedrich Niecks from Düsseldorf (who had settled in Scotland and later became Reid Professor of Music at Edinburgh University); Edward Dannreuther and Ebenezer Prout from London were also recruited as annotators. On other occasions Bache would write the notes himself—page after page of them. Invariably they are filled with insights that were both new and original for their time, and they are lavishly illustrated with music examples—a sure sign that they were aimed at a sophisticated public and were intended to have a potential life after the concert was over.[20]

V

Even while Bache was exhausting himself with the planning and execution of his Liszt concerts, he somehow found time to participate in an activity of a somewhat different kind. In the summer of 1867, about two years after he had returned to London, Bache had formed, with Karl Klindworth, Edward Dannreuther and Frits Hartvigson, a private club devoted to the cause of modern music. They called themselves the Working Men's Society, and they were soon joined by A. J. Hipkins, who kept a journal of the proceedings.[21] These young men met on a regular basis in one another's homes for the discussion and performance of music that was still unknown in England—particularly the music of Liszt and Wagner, and certain works of Schumann. The first "study session" took place on December 6, 1867, and consisted of the "Spinning Song" from Wagner's *The Flying Dutchman* (an opera not yet heard in England), albeit in Liszt's piano transcription, played by Dannreuther. At the next meeting (January 18, 1868) the intrepid group tackled the first two scenes from Wag-

---

20. These program annotations are preserved in the Bodleian Library (shelf-mark 7897.e.39), together with all the other material related to Bache's annual concerts. Bache eventually began issuing these notes under the somewhat grand title "The Book of Words." They still repay scrutiny because it is evident that many of the ideas they contain must have come from Liszt himself, albeit transmitted through members of his inner circle.

21. Bache's fighting spirit comes out in a letter to Hipkins, dated July 3, 1867, in which he writes, "Tannhäuser Overture a regular success! and well played—no wonder Davison and Co. gnash their wretched teeth: but their day is over now, and by Jove, we will go in and *smash them* in about ten years" (British Library add. ms. 41636–9). We are not wrong to suppose that the Working Men's Society was modeled on Schumann's Davidsbündler, the "Band of David" created to fight the philistines in music, some thirty years earlier. Even more striking is the similarity to Liszt's Society of Murls, formed in Weimar just ten years earlier for the purpose of promoting the new and original in art. Karl Klindworth had actually been a member of the Murls at the time of its formation, a Working Mens' Society by any other name.

ner's *Rheingold,* with Klindworth at the piano and the others singing. That was followed at yet another meeting by a reading of *Die Walküre.* These last two operas had
not yet been performed anywhere; their landmark premiere performances at the
Munich Royal Court Opera were still two years away. Klindworth's special relationship with Wagner, however, ensured that the scores were available to the group.
(At Wagner's request Klindworth eventually transcribed the whole of the *Ring* cycle for piano, and his *partitur* was used when the cycle went into rehearsal at the
Bayreuth Opera House, which, at the time the Working Men's Society was grap-
pling with the score, was not yet built.) Liszt was not neglected at these gatherings,
of course, and at the meeting of July 3, 1869, Anna Mehlig, a Liszt pupil who was
on a visit to London, played her master's E-flat Major Piano Concerto to the group.

Liszt had long been aware of Bache's pioneering activities in England and had
often expressed his appreciation. "For years," Liszt wrote, "he has sacrificed money
for the performance of my works in London. Several times I advised him against it,
but he answered imperturbably: 'That is my business!'"[22] Bache used to disarm
those who questioned him by telling them that his concerts were "a just recom-
pense," adding that if Liszt had charged him only at the rate demanded by any village teacher, he would still be deeply in his debt.[23] One of the nicest letters ever to
come Bache's way (from Weimar, October 18, 1884) returns yet again to the gratitude Liszt felt he owed to his distinguished English pupil:

> Very Honored Friend,
>
> For some twenty years past you have been employing your beautiful tal-
> ent as a pianist, your care as a professor and as a conductor to make my
> works known and to spread them in England. The task seemed an un-
> grateful one, and its want of success menacing, but you are doing it nobly,
> with the most honorable and firm conviction of an artist. I renew my
> grateful thanks to you on the occasion of the present edition of the *Leg-
> end of Saint Elisabeth,* published by the well accredited house of Novello.
>
> This work, which was performed for the first time in 1865 at Budapest,
> has been reproduced successively in several countries and languages. Let us
> hope that it will also meet with some sympathy in England.
> Your much attached
>
> F. Liszt.[24]

Bache's evangelical work in behalf of Liszt soon got him into difficulties with the
musical establishment. Nor did it help matters when Bache fought back. In his program booklet for the concert on February 25, 1875, in which he had featured him-

---

22. LLB, vol. 7, p. 438.

23. Bache's obituary notice, MT, April 1888.

24. LLB, vol. 2, p. 370. This letter was first published in the preface to the English edition of *Saint Elisabeth.*

self as the soloist in Liszt's arrangement of Weber's *Polonaise Brillante,* op. 72, for piano and orchestra, he actually reprinted a particularly obtuse criticism from the *Daily Telegraph* (which had attacked this same work when Bache had played it at the Crystal Palace Saturday Concert of November 14, 1874, under the direction of August Manns) so that the audience could judge matters afresh for themselves while listening to the work. In brief, the critic was being publicly served with a second helping of a dish that he abhorred, now flavored with words of his own that he probably no longer wished to recall:

> The personal ascendancy of Liszt over individuals is notorious, and no surprise need be expressed, therefore, when one, who was once the great man's pupil, not only champions the works he has created, but also those his master has, sometimes with astounding impudence, adapted. Such devotion is affecting, seeing that, under the actual conditions, it must be very strong indeed; and hence we are not disposed to harshly censure Mr. Bache for introducing Liszt's adaptation for piano and orchestra of Weber's Grand Polonaise Brillante. It may, nevertheless, be pertinently asked of Mr. Manns whether he thought "once, twice, and even thrice" before admitting such a thing into his programme. For what has Liszt done? He has not only garbled a perfect work of art by a master, but prefaced it with the largo from another work—Polonaise in E flat—by the same hand. In face of such an enormity, we do not care to inquire about the actual result, for that is a consideration by no means germane to the issue. Enough that violence, as unnecessary as, from every point of view, it is unlawful, has been done to an art-work which, though a trifle—a mere cabinet picture—is signed with a great name. We may be told that it is of no use to protest either against the doing of such a mischief, or the aiding and abetting of it by an unreflecting public. This is probably true, but we shall protest nevertheless, and continue to do so whenever like cause arises. (★) However little good may follow, it behooves all amateurs who witness the desecration of a master's artistic remains to show that they have neither part nor lot in the matter. . . . The music we hope never to hear again. It is not pleasant to see the "heavenly maid" dragged from her place to serve as a "dummy" for the display of modern fashions. [*The Daily Telegraph,* November 16, 1874]

To this reprint Bache added a series of footnotes, which must have created a tumult in the mind of the critic because it reminded everyone that Liszt was not alone in his "astounding impudence."

(★)The names of a few more "astoundingly impudent" musicians are here given, for future reprehension in the columns of the *Daily Telegraph*:

W. A. Mozart[d] had the astounding impudence to write accompaniments of an utterly un-Handelian character to "The people that walked in darkness" (Messiah)

F. Mendelssohn	had the astounding impudence				to provide with a pianoforte accomp. pieces which Bach had expressly intended for the violin solo.
Robert Schumann	"	"	"	"	
Johannes Brahms[b]	"	"	"	"	to paraphrase Weber's Rondo "Il moto continuo" and Chopin's Study in A flat, op. 25
Adolphe Henselt	"	"	"	"	etc. etc.
Hans von Bülow	"	"	"	"	
Joseph Joachim	"	"	"	"	
Stephen Heller	"	"	"	"	
Sir Julius Benedict[c]	"	"	"	"	to conduct Beethoven's C minor Symphony on an occasion when the original score was supplemented by a brass band.

FOOTNOTES to a, b, and c:

a. In palliation of their offences it might be urged that these unhappy men had to struggle through life without the guidance and counsel of the *Telegraph*.

b. *Anima durante, spes non dimmitenda est*. May they see the error of their ways.

c. Great excitement in the musical world! What will the *Telegraph* say? Must Sir Julius emigrate? Weeks elapse (Critic's wrath too great for utterance—Brother artists anxious and troubled—The thunderbolt must surely fall?)—*Benedict Testimonial*: "We have great pleasure in calling attention" &,&,—Verily thy ways, O *Telegraph*, are marvellous and strange: may we all live to comprehend them!

London had rarely before witnessed a full frontal assault on the critics. It was hardly surprising that Bache was shunned by the Philharmonic Society, which consistently refused to offer him a concerto engagement in its own London concert series, despite his growing reputation as a pianist. He was by now too tempting a target for his enemies.

In his zeal to protect the interests of modern music, as well as to encourage the audience to adopt a more respectful attitude toward it, Bache placed warning notices in his program booklets, which remind us of modern music's parlous state in England and the uphill task he faced in trying to improve matters. Consider the following:

N.B. The doors will be closed during the performance of each piece.

When translated into plain English this reads, "Abandon all hope of escape while the performance is in progress." And this, from the program of May 11, 1870:

The time-honoured custom of treating as an "out-voluntary" (a term familiar to church organists) whatever may have the misfortune to stand last on a concert programme, is most discouraging to those interested in its worthy performance. It is therefore respectfully suggested that those who do not remain until the end of the concert, should leave during any of the intervals which necessarily follow each piece.

When rendered into everyday language this means, "Do not use the music as background noise against which to mask your departure."

When Bache played Liszt's *Venezia e Napoli* Suite at one of these concerts, he felt it necessary to print beneath the titles a general alert:

N.B. This piece lasts seventeen minutes, and has no pause between the movements.

VI

As the year 1886 approached, and with it Liszt's seventy-fifth birthday, invitations poured in from many parts of Europe requesting his presence in celebration of the event—one of them from as far away as St. Petersburg. Liszt was by now quite frail, and the prospect of undertaking so much travel in his twilight years was daunting. One invitation he could not refuse, however, was the one extended to him by Bache, who had long cherished the notion of bringing his master back to London. Liszt wrote to him from Rome's Hotel Alibert on November 17, 1885: "Certainly your invitation takes precedence over all others. So choose the day that suits you, and I will appear. Without Walter Bache and his long years of self-sacrificing efforts in the propaganda of my works, my visit to London would be unthinkable."[25] Liszt had last visited England in 1841, forty-five years earlier, one year before Bache himself was born. That had been during his heyday as a virtuoso. How would he now be received?

VII

Liszt's London itinerary for April 1886 is very well documented and has attracted numerous studies. Rather than repeat everything here, we propose to mention in summary only those events involving Bache himself—a crowded itinerary to be sure.[26] The main ones were known by Liszt in advance of his trip, and undoubtedly contributed to his decision to visit England after such a long lapse of time. They were: (a) the establishment of a Liszt Scholarship in piano playing at the Royal Academy of Music; (b) a performance of his oratorio *Saint Elisabeth* in St. James's Hall; (c) an audience with Queen Victoria; and (d) a great public reception in his honor at the Grosvenor Gallery.

Liszt set out from Calais on April 3 and crossed the English Channel in the com-

---

25. LLB, vol. 2, p. 385.

26. My own account (in WFL, vol. 3, pp. 477–97) covers Liszt's London itinerary on an hour-by-hour basis.

ST. JAMES'S HALL.

REGENT STREET AND PICCADILLY.

MONDAY, 22nd OCTOBER, 1883,

At Half-past Three o'clock precisely.

MR. WALTER BACHE'S

Pianoforte Recital.

(FOURTEENTH SEASON.)

THE PROGRAMME WILL CONSIST OF ORIGINAL
COMPOSITIONS OF

FRANZ LISZT.

(Born October 22nd, 1811.)

Vocalist,

MISS AMBLER.

Stalls (*Numbered and Reserved*), **Five Shillings.**
Balcony, Three Shillings.   Admission, One Shilling.

Tickets may be obtained of
STANLEY LUCAS, WEBER & Co., 84, New Bond Street;
Cramer & Co., 201, Regent Street; Mitchell's Library, 33, Old Bond Street; Chappell
and Co., 50, New Bond Street and 15, Poultry; R. W. Ollivier, 36, Old Bond Street;
Keith, Prowse, and Co., 48, Cheapside, and 15, Grand Hotel Buildings, Charing Cross;
Barr, Queen Victoria Street; A. Hays, 4, Royal Exchange Buildings, and 26, Old Bond
Street; and at Austin's Ticket Office, St. James's Hall, Piccadilly.

[*For Programme see over.*

Printed by J. Miles & Co., 193, Wardour Street, Oxford Street, W.

Program of an all-Liszt recital by Walter Bache. St. James's Hall, London, October 22, 1883.

Liszt plays in the concert hall of the old Royal Academy of Music, Tenterden Street, London, April 6, 1886. (An illustration by Batt, based on eyewitness descriptions.)

pany of the conductor Alexander Mackenzie and Alfred Littleton of Novello & Co., who had traveled to France especially to meet the aging composer. The party was met at Dover by Walter Bache, and they all boarded the Continental Express train which normally traveled nonstop to Victoria Station. On this occasion, however, Bache had arranged for the train to be halted at Penge so that Liszt and his entourage could alight and then proceed by carriage to Westwood House, in Sydenham, the imposing mansion of Henry Littleton, the head of Novello, where Liszt was to stay as a guest for the duration of his visit to England.

Liszt's first public appearance was on Tuesday, April 6, at the Royal Academy of Music, to attend the inauguration of the Liszt Scholarship, founded with money raised largely through the efforts of Bache himself. As Liszt entered the concert hall on the arm of the Academy's principal, Sir George Macfarren, he was met with tumultuous applause from the students and faculty. There followed a concert of Liszt's music, and since the applause showed no signs of abating, Liszt walked to the platform and played one of his *Chants polonaises* and his "Cantique d'Amour."[27] A short presentation followed, during which Bache handed an envelope to Liszt (containing a check for eleven hundred pounds) who handed it in turn to Sir George. The first holder of the award, incidentally, was Grace Mary Henshaw, a pupil of Bache.[28] Liszt was then taken to Bache's apartment near Dorset Square in order to rest before his evening appearance. There they were joined by Bache's sister Constance, bearing a basket of roses tied together with the Hungarian colors, a symbolic allusion to the famous scene of the "Miracle of the Roses" from the oratorio *Saint Elisabeth,* a performance of which was mounted in Liszt's honor that same evening. Pinned to the roses was a poem by Constance (who had translated the text of *Saint Elisabeth* into English), which enshrined the point and purpose of Liszt's visit to England. Liszt had inspired many poems during his lifetime, written in German, French, Hungarian, and even in English, but few had touched him more than this one.

"To the Master Franz Liszt: A Welcome"

We welcome thee, from southern sunnier clime,
   To England's shore,
And stretch glad hands across the lapse of time
   To thee once more.
Full twice two decades swiftly have rolled by
   Since thou wast here;
A meteor flashing through our northern sky
   Thou didst appear.
Thy coming now we greet with pleasure keen
   And loyal heart,

---

27. No photograph was taken of this historic visit, which took place in the concert hall of the old Royal Academy of Music on Tenterden Street, just off Hanover Square. But some years later the artist Batt drew the scene from the memories of those present, and his drawing is reproduced on page 121.

Adding tradition of what thou hast been
    To what thou art.
No laurel can we weave into the crown
    Long years entwine
Nor add one honour unto the renown
    Already thine:
Yet might these roses waft to thee a breath
    Of memory,
Recalling thy fair Saint Elizabeth
    Of Hungary.
We welcome her, from out those days of old,
    In song divine,
But thee we greet a thousand thousand fold,
    The song is thine!

That same evening Liszt attended a performance of *Saint Elisabeth* at St. James's Hall, under the direction of Alexander Mackenzie, with Emma Albani in the title role. The performance was a triumph, and during the interval the Prince of Wales went round to Liszt's box in order to congratulate him. By popular demand *Saint Elisabeth* was repeated at the Crystal Palace, on April 17.

28. More details of the Liszt Scholarship are gleaned from an inspection of the minutes of the RAM Committee meeting held that same day (dated Wednesday, April 7, 1886): "A meeting for the reception of Dr. Franz Liszt took place on Tuesday, April 6. The Liszt Scholarship was formally handed to the principal of the Academy by Dr. Liszt.

"The Committee of Management acknowledge with much pride and pleasure the presentation of a scholarship to The Royal Academy of Music in honour of Dr. Franz Liszt, and the Committee will offer some comments upon the schedule of proposed rules at their next meeting.

"Dr. Franz Liszt was unanimously elected an Honorary Member."

The first competition was held on April 21, 1887. The jury consisted of Edward Dannreuther, Alexander Mackenzie, and Sir George Macfarren (chairman). The winner of this valuable scholarship was entitled to three years free tuition at the Royal Academy of Music, followed by two further years abroad. Thirty-nine competitors submitted their names; only twenty-four turned up for the theory portion of the examination, and two of these failed that test. As the *Musical Times* expressed it, "that such a prize . . . should not have brought forward a larger number of competitors seems surprising" (MT, May 1, 1887, p. 279).

The answer to this last question, even then, lay readily to hand. All candidates had to pass a preliminary examination in general knowledge before they were even allowed to demonstrate their skills at the piano itself. It consisted of English orthography and grammar, elementary arithmetic, the rudiments of geography and English history. This mindless ruling, typical of the English attitude toward music at that time, did not come from Bache but from the institution that imposed it. Clearly some of the best pianists may have been eliminated before they even reached a keyboard. Liszt himself might have failed a similar test.

In July 1887 Guiseppe Buonamici (a former Liszt pupil resident in London) gave a benefit recital in Princes' Hall, which raised a further sum of 50 pounds to be donated to the Liszt Scholarship (MT, October 1, 1887). After Bache's death the following year, a further sum of 500 pounds was collected in his memory and added to the parent fund. In July 1907 the scholarship was further enriched by the interesting addition of 960 pounds in Great Eastern Railway stocks, from an unknown source. The indenture, setting out the terms and conditions of the Liszt Scholarship, is preserved in the Scholarships and Prizes Archive of the Royal Academy of Music, London.

The following day, April 7, Liszt set out for Windsor Castle for an audience with Queen Victoria. The pair had last met more than forty years earlier, at the time of the unveiling of the Beethoven monument in Bonn. According to Queen Victoria's diary, the audience took place after luncheon in the Red Drawing-room, where "the benevolent looking old Priest, with long white hair, and scarcely any teeth . . . [played] a number of his own compositions."[29] Liszt improvised on themes from the ever topical *Saint Elisabeth,* and at the Queen's request played "The Miracle of the Roses" scene from the same work. He then launched into a Hungarian Rhapsody and concluded with Chopin's Nocturne in B-flat Minor, op. 9.

The phrase in Liszt's letter to Bache, "choose the day that suits you," was a reference to the great public reception that Bache had planned in Liszt's honor, and which was mounted in the Grosvenor Gallery on Thursday, April 8. Nearly four hundred guests were invited to his "Converzatione," as Bache called it, representing music, literature, art, medicine and the Church. A short concert of Liszt's music was given, including his "Angelus" arranged for strings, the "Chorus of Angels" (sung by female students from the Royal Academy of Music), some of Liszt's Schiller songs, and a concluding performance by Bache of the "Bénédiction de Dieu dans la solitude." Liszt himself then acknowledged the applause and played his arrangement of Schubert's "Divertissement hongroise" and a Hungarian Rhapsody. Sir George Grove was among the guests, and he later wrote:

> I went to Liszt's reception on Thursday and was delighted (1) by his playing, so calm, clear, correct, refined—so entirely unlike the style of the so-called "Liszt School," (2) by his face. Directly he sat down he dismissed that very artificial smile, which he always wears, and his face assumed the most beautiful serene look with enormous power and repose in it. It was quite a wonderful sight.[30]

The presence of another prominent guest should also be mentioned. The great violinist Joseph Joachim was in London giving concerts, and it was a stroke of diplomacy to invite him to be present. For many years Liszt and Joachim had been estranged because of artistic differences that went back to the Weimar years of the 1850s, at a time when Joachim was Liszt's orchestral leader. During the evening they came together and the *London Graphic* captured their friendly handshake for its readers in its issue of April 17, 1886.

During this visit to London, Liszt had an interesting altercation with Bache's old nemesis, the Philharmonic Society. He contacted the directors and asked them to consider giving Bache an engagement, having heard that in more than twenty years the society had never once offered him anything. Evidently he met with a refusal. For Liszt there was only one course of action: if the society was determined to shun Bache, Liszt would shun the society. We learn from the diary of Sir Arthur Sullivan that Liszt declined to attend one of the society's concerts because "the Directors

29. RA, unpublished diary entry for April 7, 1886.
30. GLL, pp. 311–12.

had taken no notice of his recommendation of Bache." Evidently Sullivan thought that he should try to patch up this difference with Liszt and invited him to dinner. But Liszt was not to be moved. Determined to register his disapproval in a more personal way, he went on to shun Sullivan himself. On April 14 Sullivan noted in his diary, "Received letter from Liszt—unable to dine with me, engaged every evening."[31]

Liszt's sojourn in Albion lasted for seventeen days, from April 3 to April 20. Suffice it to say that this London triumph did much to compensate for the many years of English neglect, and brought immense pleasure to Bache. On April 20 Liszt traveled back to the English Channel, boarded the boat at Dover and sailed for Calais. It was the last occasion on which that Bache saw Liszt alive.

VIII

Liszt's death in Bayreuth, on July 31, 1886, in the middle of the Wagner festival, caught Bache by surprise. The fact that he did not join Liszt's Weimar masterclass in May and June, according to his usual custom, is significant. The enormous expense of the Grosvenor Gallery reception had left him without funds, so he stayed in England. His sisters Constance and Margaret were already in Bayreuth, and it was Constance who sent him a telegram announcing the death of Liszt. Bache, Karl Klindworth, and Alfred Littleton set out for Bayreuth at once, arriving just in time to join the funeral party about to set out from Wahnfried, the Wagner family home. They were still in their dusty traveling clothes. As he marched with the other mourners down Maximilianstrasse, the funeral route to the Stadtfriedhof, Bache was pained to see Bayreuth filled with festival revelers, its streets decked out with bunting. Liszt's death had taken everyone by surprise, and the authorities could do little more than light the street lamps and drape them in black crepe as a mark of civic respect. After the graveside orations (given by Mayor Theodor Muncker and Liszt's old friend Dr. Carl Gille), various wreaths were laid, at which time Alfred Littleton advanced and placed one on Liszt's grave in the name of Queen Victoria. Bache, who had had no sleep for more than forty-eight hours, then returned to his lodgings exhausted.

He did not linger in Bayreuth. Within days he was already back in England, pondering what to do about his Liszt concerts. Could he afford to continue? If he harbored any doubts he appears quickly to have brushed them away. By February 1887 he had gathered enough money to pay for a recital in St. James's Hall containing, among other things, a group of the *Transcendental Studies* and the *Dante* Sonata. This recital was exceptionally well attended. Perhaps the memory of Liszt's triumphal visit to London still lingered in the mind of the public, or perhaps his recent death focused unusual attention on this concert. Whatever the reason, Bache actually managed to recoup his costs. The experience emboldened him to begin preparations for

---

31. From the unpublished diaries of Arthur Sullivan, April 10, 1886 (Beinecke Rare Book and Manuscript Library, Yale University).

a major memorial recital devoted in its entirety to Liszt, and he announced that it would take place in St. James's Hall on October 22, 1887, the day on which Liszt would have celebrated his seventy-sixth birthday.

ST. JAMES'S HALL
October 22, 1887

Hungarian Rhapsody no. 5, in E Minor ("Héroïde élégiaque")
Sposalizio
Il penseroso
Canzonetta del Salvator Rosa
Sonetto 123 del Petrarca
Après une lecture du Dante[32]
    (from the *Années de pèlerinage*, "Italie")

INTERVAL

Venezia e Napoli
    Gondoliera
    Canzone
    Tarantella

Although no one knew it, this was Walter Bache's swan song. He outlived Liszt by a mere eighteen months. He died after a brief illness at his home, 17, Eastbourne Terrace, Hyde Park, on March 26, 1888. According to his sister Constance he contracted a chill and developed an ulcerated throat but was otherwise not in poor health. He was actually teaching at the Academy on the 23rd, and gave private lessons at home on the 24th. Two days later he was dead. He was not yet forty-six years old. The funeral was delayed for five days and the cortege finally set out on the rather long journey from Eastbourne Terrace to Hampstead Cemetery (a traditional burial site for London-based Unitarians) on March 31. On March 28, the London *Times* had already carried an appreciative obituary notice of Bache. It paid tribute to the financial sacrifices he had made in support of Liszt across the years, and acknowledged his value as a teacher. But it offered faint praise for his career as a performer. "As a pianist," the obituary ran, "Mr. Bache represented the school to which he belonged, and although he did not play with the brilliancy of Sophie Menter, Stavenhagen, and other of Liszt's pupils, his earnestness of purpose, his energy and his unswerving study made up for the comparative want of what Liszt would have called the *feu sacré.*" The obituary was unsigned, but we suspect the hand of Francis Hueffer, who had succeeded J. W. Davison at the *Times* on the latter's retirement in 1879.

---

32. Since the critics had been nonplussed by the *Dante* Sonata in the earlier recital, one of them finding it "impossible to form any idea of the work at a first hearing," and complaining of "the constant progression of discords of which the piece is made up" (MT, March 1, 1887, p. 154), Bache had evidently decided to offer them a second helping on Liszt's birthday.

For Hueffer, a former pupil of Schopenhauer and an avid supporter of Wagner, Bache was a good soldier who lacked "the sacred fire."[33]

Five weeks after Bache's death, his sister Constance donated some memorabilia to the Royal Academy of Music from his estate. The materials included some music from his library and a photograph of Liszt which had hung for several years in his study at Eastbourne Terrace.[34] Constance was determined not to let the memory of her brother fade, and devoted herself to an English translation of the first two volumes of Liszt's collected correspondence, which included a number of important letters from Liszt to Bache.[35] She also wrote her affectionate memoir of Walter, in which the full extent of his many sacrifices for Liszt were made public for the first time.[36]

Bache was a saint. Without him Liszt's music would have gone under in Victorian England. All honor to his memory!

33. A somewhat more affectionate farewell than that proffered by the *Times* was given by Bache's fellow Unitarians, who attended his funeral in large numbers, together with some prominent members of the musical profession. The following obituary appeared in *The Christian Life: A Unitarian Journal* on April 7, 1888.

> The funeral of the late Mr. Walter Bache took place in the Hampstead Cemetery on Saturday [March 31] in the presence of a large gathering of professional and personal friends. The coffin was conveyed from the residence of the deceased at Eastbourne Terrace, Paddington, to the cemetery in a glass-panelled car, followed by several mourning and private carriages containing relatives and friends. The chief mourners were the two brothers and the two sisters of the deceased gentleman, together with Mrs. Alfred Bache, Mr. Russell Martineau, Mr. A. Higginson, Mrs. Edward Higginson, and Miss Martineau, relatives. The Royal Academy of Music, of which the deceased was a professor, was represented by Dr. A. C. Mackenzie, the new principal, and others. Mr. Stanley Lucas represented the Royal Society of Musicians. The Rev. Dr. Sadler, of Rosslyn Hill Unitarian Chapel, Hampstead, officiated, and delivered an appropriate address.

34. See the entry in the minutes of the RAM Committee, dated May 2, 1888. The legacy included a substantial amount of keyboard music ("miscellaneous piano studies and other works") some of which Bache had presumably studied with Liszt on his regular summer trips to Weimar. At that same meeting, the committee also considered an application from Martha Remmert, a distinguished pupil of Liszt, requesting a teaching appointment at the RAM. Perhaps she hoped to replace Bache, especially in the training of the Liszt scholarship holders. Her request was politely declined. The committee gave no indication of even knowing who she was.

35. LLB, vols. 1 and 2, which were published in London, in 1894. They are dedicated to the memory of Walter Bache and to A. J. Hipkins who, we recall, was one of the founding members of the pioneering Working Men's Society, which had done yeoman service for Liszt and modern music since the 1860s.

36. See BBM.

Liszt's Sonata in B Minor

The Sonata in B Minor is like a brilliant steam-driven mill which nearly always runs idle.
EDUARD HANSLICK[1]

I

No other work of Liszt has attracted anything like the amount of scholarly attention devoted to his Sonata in B Minor. Everybody appears to think that he is entitled to hold an opinion about it. And since many of those opinions are mutually exclusive, the literature has become a minefield through which both player and teacher proceed at their peril. Not the least of the sonata's many fascinations has to do with hidden programs, the pursuit of which has kept several generations of scholars busy despite Liszt's total silence on the matter; he simply called his work a "sonata," an inscrutable title which seems to close the door on all further speculation as to the work's extramusical meaning—or lack of it. For someone who attached titles and programmatic descriptions to possibly 90 percent of his output, his silence on the topic is eloquent. It has nonetheless been suggested that the sonata is a musical portrait of the Faust legend, complete with Faust, Gretchen, and Mephisto themes.[2] Others have seen in the work a depiction of the Garden of Eden, with themes symbolizing God, Lucifer, Adam and Eve, and the serpent.[3] Louis Köhler, the pianist, composer and influential critic for the Leipzig *Signale,* who was closely connected to Liszt and his circle, saw in the sonata a successful struggle of "an heroic spirit in a world full of strife."[4] From here it was but a short step to regard Liszt himself as the hero—a musical portrait whose strongly contrasted themes sprang from the contradictions within his own personality. One of the most recent among these "autobiographical" explanations tells us that Liszt encrypted his name, and that of Carolyne von Sayn-Wittgenstein, within the notes of the main themes.[5] The sonata is clearly intriguing enough to bear many interpretations, including that of an abstract instrumental composition.

1. RLS, p. 62.
2. OIL (JALS, vol. 10, pp. 30–38).
3. MRR, pp. 238–95.
4. Köhler's descriptive program was included in the annotations used for Walter Bache's London performance of the sonata on November 22, 1883 (Bodleian Library, shelf mark 7897.e.39).
5. MT, Spring 2003, pp. 6–14.

By common consent the sonata ranks among the crowning achievements of
Liszt's Weimar years. If he had composed nothing else, he would have to be regarded
as a major composer on the strength of this work alone. It represents one of the most
successful solutions to the problem of sonata form to come out of the nineteenth
century. The sonata unfolds nearly half an hour's unbroken music. Not only are its
four movements rolled into one, but they are themselves composed against a background of a full-scale sonata scheme—exposition, development, and recapitulation.
That is, Liszt has composed a sonata across a sonata, possibly the first time in musical history that such a thing had been attempted. Beethoven had occasionally linked
the movements of his sonatas and symphonies, of course; one thinks of the Fifth
Symphony and the *Appassionata* Sonata, whose respective finales emerge from the
previous movements without interruption. But the B Minor Sonata is different. Not
only are its four movements linked, but the material is constantly making contributions to two sonata forms simultaneously. This double-function structure was to
have no successor until Arnold Schoenberg did something similar in his First Chamber Symphony (1906) more than fifty years later. It may be expressed as follows:

	Exposition	Development and Leadback		Recapitulation	Coda
	I: Allegro	II: Andante	III: Fugato	IV: Allegro	Prestissimo
Intro.	B mi/D mj	F♯ mj	B♭ mi	B mi/B mj	
	m. 32	m. 331	m. 459	m. 533	m. 682

The devil lies in the details, and it is the details that continue to provoke dispute
among the analysts. Yet it is perfectly possible to accept the notion of two structures,
one resting on top of the other, so to speak, while acknowledging that these two
interconnecting sonata schemes may not always dovetail with that metrical precision so ardently desired by the scholars. Two men may argue about the position of
a wall separating their properties—an inch one way, a foot another. It is only when
you are standing next to the wall itself that the issue seems important; surveyed from
afar, such wrangles lose their meaning, as they always do when we hear this music
played.[6]

Even the B Minor Sonata did not come from nowhere. Unique as its structure
is, it had a model. During his years as a touring virtuoso Liszt had discovered Schubert's *Wanderer* Fantasie, becoming the first pianist to introduce the work to the general public. Its influence on Liszt's creative process cannot be overestimated. After he
had settled in Weimar, he returned to the *Wanderer,* making an arrangement for piano and orchestra and a second one for two pianos, symptoms of his boundless admiration for the work of the Viennese master. Later on he published his own edition

6. Incidentally, this view of the work as a "double structure" is not a modern interpretation. It was
taught by Ernst von Dohnányi to his pupils in Berlin before World War I, and later at the Liszt Academy
in Budapest. He appears to have acquired it from his teacher István Thomán, who was a pupil of Liszt.

of the *Wanderer,* which reveals an intimate knowledge of the original. On the structure of the B Minor Sonata, Schubert's Fantasie exerted a powerful spell. Not only
are the Fantasie's four movements linked, but they are unified by the use of the
"metamorphosis of themes" technique—in this case, the opening theme of Schubert's song "Der Wanderer," which re-appears in various guises throughout each of
the four movements and gives the Fantasie its name. The finale of the Fantasie is
even ushered in by a fugue, a landmark idea that is duly copied by Liszt. But there
the connections with the sonata end. It is Liszt's ability to make contributions to
two sonata forms simultaneously that sets his work apart.

In the beginning was the sound, not the symbol. Until it is played, music is void
and without form. It follows that any discussion of the piece should include the
player, whom we propose to address from time to time. It is the player, after all, who
must turn shadow into substance, silence into sound.

II

Much of the structure is generated from a small group of thematic "tags," metamorphosed throughout the sonata. They are first deployed in the introduction
(Lento assai / Allegro energico), but without reference to a definite key.[7]

Even seasoned players, and musicians familiar with every nook and cranny of the
sonata, are constantly surprised at the myriad ways in which these themes govern
the texture. Nor must we overlook the fact that the introduction is divided into two

7. Theme (a), the descending "gypsy" scale, is invariably reserved for marking off the important junctures of the structure; it occurs before the second subject and also before the development, and it sepa-
rates the slow movement from the Fugato. Its most notable appearances, of course, are at the very
beginning and the very end of the sonata. It has been likened to the descent of a curtain that serves to
separate the acts of a drama. For this reason it is sometimes called the "curtain theme."

parts, a Lento and an Allegro. Much mischief has been created by assuming that the Allegro marks the beginning of the sonata's exposition—as it would normally do in a classical sonata form. This assumption produces havoc later on and, as we shall see, obscures our understanding of where, exactly, the recapitulation begins.

In what key does the sonata commence? Most musicians would say G minor, but the A-flat at the end of the third measure of the "gypsy" scale forms no part of that key. Louis Kentner once put forward the interesting notion that the sonata actually begins in C minor, because in retrospect the descending scale takes on the trappings of a dominant preparation.[8] But since the tonic chord of C minor is nowhere to be found, we have to accept that the tonal ambiguity created by Liszt serves a special purpose. And when that moment comes, it enables him to assert the tonic key of B minor with the abruptness of someone switching on the light (m. 32).[9]

Liszt's metamorphosis technique is shown at its typical best in this first subject, which is derived from a combination of themes (b) and (c), now firmly established in the tonic key

Pianists: Although Liszt does not indicate it, a slight *ritardando* will underscore the arrival of the exposition in the tonic key (m. 32). It is the kind of thing that the veteran player will do instinctively, if left alone. Our chief tonal center of B minor, that all-important platform to which the sonata will return much later on, puts in its first unequivocal appearance here.[10]

Particularly rich in the deployment of contrasting themes is the second-subject

8. Letter to the author, dated August 30, 1969 (AWC, box 5, folder F 10[a]).

9. Liszt nowhere mentions the tonic key of B minor on the title page of the sonata. His holograph score bears the inscription "Grande Sonate pour la Pianoforte." By the time the piece was published, even the "Grande" had been dropped, and the score was identified simply as "Sonata für das Pianoforte." Since the tonic key of B minor plays such a crucial role in our understanding of the "double-function" structure indicated above, the question arises: did Liszt himself ever refer to the work with the title by which it is today universally acknowledged? The answer is that he did. In a letter to J.W. Wasielewski (January 1857), he specifically refers to it as "my Sonata in B minor" (LLB, vol. 1, p. 256).

10. Some analysts, for reasons that amount to a mystery wrapped inside an enigma, maintain that B minor was already established at the first appearance of theme (c). However, as Tovey long ago pointed out in his influential analyses of classical forms, there is a profound difference between being *on* a key and being *in* it. The former is like a journey in which we watch the scenery passing by without stopping. The latter is like a journey in which we arrive at our destination, alight, and put down roots. To put the matter technically: before we can say that we are in any key at all, we must prepare it via that key's dominant, here lacking.

stage of the structure, in the relative major, four of whose musical ideas are openly derived from the introductory material. The group begins with a theme marked "Grandioso," one of Liszt's noblest melodies, and a grand peak in the Romantic literature. Note the constant re-iteration of the accompaniment's eighth notes—derived from theme (c).

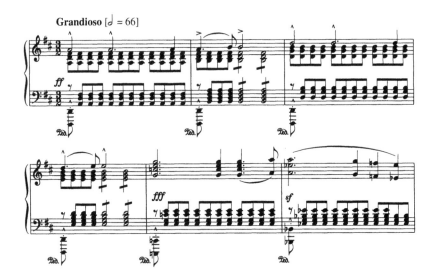

It has often been remarked that the outline of the Grandioso theme is that of the plainchant "Crux fidelis," which Liszt used in a number of other works—notably the symphonic poem *Hunnenschlacht* (1857), the oratorio *Saint Elisabeth* (1862), the *Gran* Mass (1855), and the late choral work *Via crucis* (1878). The "cross motif," as it is sometimes called, occupies a leading place in the theories of those who see the sonata as a depiction of the cosmic struggle between good and evil, between God and the Devil. Without question, a study of Liszt's life, especially that part of it devoted to religion, gives many of his works their oxygen. But when the sonata was composed, none of the other works whose verbal associations allow us to recognize this motif as having to do with the cross had as yet been written. The conclusion, in short, is drawn from evidence as yet uncreated. Aside from such considerations, the player can become so wrapped up in playing this most patrician of melodies that he may fail to ask an important question: What is it doing there? So extreme is its foreground contrast when set beside any of the sonata's preceding ideas, that some analysts claim it to be completely new. Is this what Hanslick had in mind when he referred to the sonata's "brazen juxtaposition of the most disparate elements"?[11] A careful inspection of the holograph yields an intriguing discovery. Liszt had originally intended to make the theme's connection to the rest of the sonata clear by combining it with the Allegro energico motif of the introduction (theme [b])—al-

11. RLS, p. 62.

beit in the recapitulation only—but he later dropped the idea. Here is his original notation.

Theme b

It reveals that our "new" Grandioso theme is a countermelody to theme (b), which remains unplayed. Liszt is pointing to a family connection; he is, so to speak, analyzing his music as he goes along. We can only suppose that the reason he abandoned this interesting revelation before it reached the printer is that it made the connection too obvious. Some truths become more eloquent if left unspoken.

There are three subsequent themes in this long and complex second subject group, which are likewise derived from (b) and (c) respectively. The gentle lyricism of the first of them, marked *dolce con grazia,* appears to place it a long way from anything previously heard in the sonata, but on closer scrutiny we recognize it as a metamorphosis of theme (b), in augmentation.

By way of extending this particular method of thematic evolution, Liszt creates yet another sharply defined contrast in the second group by treating theme (c) in augmentation as well, marking it *cantando espressivo.* Its connection to anything we have previously heard may seem remote. Cloaked within a melody of Chopinesque beauty, we nonetheless recognize the hammer blows of theme (c).[12]

---

12. For Liszt's own commentary on the connection see LLB, vol. 1, p. 157.

As for the last theme in the group, the melodic outline of theme (b) is clearly audible, enshrined as it is within the filigree-work of the right hand.

Pianists: There is a peripheral idea in the second group that contains much destructive power, a phrase we use advisedly. It is the recitative-like passage at measures 197–205, likewise derived from theme (b).

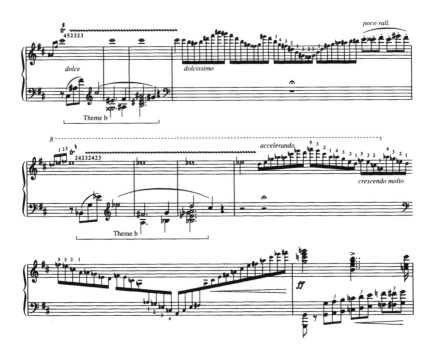

Here, if anywhere, the temptation to linger must be resisted; otherwise time will be lost that can never be made up. The resulting burden the player is forced to carry will exert a toxic influence on much that happens later, even though both player and listener may be unaware of the cause. In the B Minor Sonata nothing happens in isolation. Note, incidentally, Liszt's own fingerings, especially the right hand's three-finger trill at m. 201 [*2423/2423*] which ensures clearer articulation. Although somewhat unusual, it is symptomatic of Liszt's economical approach to technique: three fingers doing the work of two will do that work more effectively.[13]

Widely contrasting keyboard textures, like the ones we have seen displayed in the second group, open the door to a large topic. They represent a touchstone of what constitutes the expressive range of piano sound. And if we are fortunate, they allow us to greet the personality of the pianist himself—if he has one. Time was when one could recognize a pianist by the very sound that he produced. What for want of a better term we can call the "voice" of each player was unique and was what made him interesting. A Rachmaninoff could not be confused with a Rosenthal, a Horowitz with a Godowsky, a Schnabel with a Dohnányi. If the pianist does not posses that glowing palette of color, which alone will do justice to such a highly differentiated thematic group, he is wasting both his time and ours—a fairly common experience to be sure. Today we live in an age of anonymity. For the first time in musical history pianists seem willing to suppress their artistic personalities in order to model themselves on someone else's. The intelligentsia will still talk about the pianist's "fingerprints," of course, but the analogy quickly breaks down. Fingerprints are unique to their possessor, however mediocre the fingers. But what shall we say of all those pianists who share the same prints? They appear without trace, so to speak. They are to be heard in most of the large concert halls of the world every season, to say nothing of the teaming hundreds vacating the world's conservatories year after year, en route to oblivion.

The great Andante sostenuto (itself a compound ternary form) occupies that same world of blissful contemplation as some of the late Beethoven slow movements which Liszt knew and played so well. One of its contrasting themes offers a glimpse from afar of the second subject (*cantando espressivo*), which binds the movement to its surroundings. The Andante is set in Liszt's "beatific" key of F-sharp major, a wide topic that repays study. Liszt's choice of keys is frequently determined by a higher expressive purpose, and is rarely the result of random selection. The Paradiso section of the *Dante* Symphony, the "Bénédiction de Dieu" and "Les Jeux d'eaux à la Villa d'Este" (with its quotation from the Gospel according to St. John) have reli-

---

13. Liszt's fingerings always repay study. Of course, fingering represents such a personal aspect of piano playing that what suits one hand may not suit another. So why attach importance to Liszt's? Because he was familiar with the alternatives and had found them wanting. His unrivaled sense of the topography of the keyboard often leads him to the heart of the matter and provides the pianist with illuminating solutions to delicate problems. Rafael Joseffy, a pupil of Liszt who published one of the earliest and more consequential editions of the sonata, must have had this in mind when he said of the work that it was one of those compositions that plays itself, "it lies so beautifully under the hand" (HFL, p. 66).

gious connotations and are all cast in this remote key of F-sharp major—as if to
symbolize the unattainable.

Pianists: On no account must the minor ninth chord be spread (mm. 329–30). The
right hand must be struck cleanly, and if your hand is too small to accommodate a
tenth (a to c), it is better to compress the chord. We know that Liszt encouraged this
kind of thing for small hands, since he compressed many wide stretches in his edition of the Weber sonatas. In this connection it is worth recalling that Liszt himself,
contrary to mythology, did not have a particularly large hand. He found the stretch
of a tenth in the final chords of the Adagio of the *Hammerklavier* Sonata extreme.[14]

Liszt marks that minor ninth chord *una corda,* not so much to make it soft as to
introduce a new color. It is a striking effect and he obviously wishes to bathe the
Andante sostenuto in its subdued light, because seventeen measures later he reminds
the player, *sempre una corda.* It is the only time in the entire sonata that Liszt employs
a pedal marking of any kind. That is rather unusual when you compare the sonata
with other piano works of Liszt. One thinks of Funérailles, the *Transcendental Studies,* and above all the *Dante* Sonata, all of which are richly endowed with pedal markings that one ignores at one's peril. The rule in Liszt, however, is quite simple: pedal,
or the heart of the music will cease to beat. Pedal-less playing in Liszt is very rare,
and is reserved for special effects. Unless instructed otherwise, the pianist should allow the sustaining pedal to cast its radiating glow over the entire texture, adding
color and beauty to the very fabric of the music.

Rachmaninoff used to maintain that every piece of music has but one chief climax, and that it is the duty of the player to find it. This perceptive idea is open to
some objection, but it serves us well in the case of the B Minor Sonata. Measure
397 has some claim to be the crowning peak of the work. The player needs to ensure that none of the other climaxes takes away from the grandeur of this one. It is
one of the few places that Liszt marks *fff.* Although it may vie with the others in
sheer volume, the one under discussion has a greater claim on our emotions, and
that makes it decisive.

14. See LL, p. 165.

By incorporating a three-part Fugato into his sonata, Liszt once more reminds us of Beethoven. The telescoping of two forms that are basically incompatible always poses the same problem: where, exactly, to place the Fugato if both forms are to survive contact with one another. Liszt, true to the structure's "double function," turns his Fugato into both a third movement and an extended leadback into the recapitulation, a crowning moment which is still some distance away.

Bartók once reminded us that Liszt was the first composer in history to introduce irony into music.[15] He pointed to this Fugato as an early example of its type. What a later generation came to identify as the "Mephistophelian" strain in Liszt's personality (which reached its fullest expression in the diablerie of the *Mephisto* Waltzes) remains strikingly original even today. Wagner, Richard Strauss, and Mahler were all to do similar things, but their music came later. Irony they appeared to have learned from Liszt. How to present the ironic, the sardonic, the wry, the cynical even, in music? It is not an insuperable challenge. The passage must be drained of human feeling. It is the denial of self-expression, the suppression of "interpretation," that reveals the diabolical qualities lurking within. The colder and drier the performance, the more remorseless it will sound.[16]

The Fugato raises another problem, this one of a profoundly analytical kind. If we fail to understand its place within the structure as a whole, the "havoc" referred to earlier in this essay comes back to haunt us. By accepting the false notion that the exposition begins with the onset of the first Allegro (m. 8), it is but a short step to argue that the Fugato itself is the recapitulation, for no better reason than that its

15. "Liszt's Music and Today's Public," SBB, p. 452.

16. Side by side with this Fugato the player should study the Fugato from the finale of Liszt's *Faust Symphony*, with which it has much diablerie in common. Liszt has obligingly arranged the orchestral score for two pianos, making such a comparison quite practical.

thematic outline is identical to that of the Allegro, albeit a semitone lower in the remote key of B-flat minor. And there is indeed a school of thought that promotes
this proposition with vigor. That surely confuses sight with sound. Suppose that the
B Minor Sonata had never been printed, but had instead come down to us purely
as an aural tradition, without notation. We would have to rely on our ears and not
on our eyes. In these ideal circumstances, uncorrupted by a single glance at the
nonexistent printed page, we would never dream of calling the Fugato a recapitulation. We would hear it for what it is: simply another series of metamorphoses of
theme (b).[17] At one point the Fugato subject is turned upside down and presented
in counterpoint against itself.

Many a performance starts to flag at this stage, but the player must not allow energy
to be drained by these demanding textures. There must always be reserves of sta-
mina left over, otherwise the Fugato will communicate little more than the stress
and strain of playing it. One could adapt an observation Liszt once made about
Beethoven, and say that in order to play the B Minor Sonata well, somewhat more
technique is required than it actually demands.[18]

    As the Fugato nears the end of its tumultuous journey, its true destination comes
into view. It is actually possible to talk of the most crucial measure in the entire composition, measure 533, which heralds the beginning of the recapitulation and causes
the entire structure to snap to attention. If the function of that measure is misunderstood, then the structure of the sonata will be misunderstood too. Moreover, as

---

17. We are invited to compare other works of Liszt that are said to have recapitulations in the "wrong"
key, including some of the symphonic poems. With respect, this is to set a wrong standard that proves
nothing. We should instead take as our models the sonatas of Beethoven, Mozart, and Schubert. By calling his work "sonata" Liszt was inviting comparison not with himself but with them. And when we compare Liszt's sonata with the classical models with which he was so familiar, we find his recapitulation
normal in every respect.

18. FLL, p. 161.

if to emphasize the point, Liszt ushers in his first subject, in the tonic key, via a traditional leadback, which serves both as an exit from the Fugato and as an entrance
into the recapitulation. We reproduce the passage in full:

This is the only occasion in the entire sonata that the tonic key of B minor has returned (m. 533) since we moved away from it at the beginning of the exposition.
Looked at from afar, measures 32 and 533 are like the massive pillars of a bridge
spanning a huge divide. To be sure, that is how they must sound in performance,
too.

So far, so conventional. This is what classical composers have always done in their
sonata forms, above all Beethoven in the *Waldstein* and *Appassionata* sonatas, whose
leadbacks possess all the drama of drumrolls before the curtain rises on the final act
of the drama. But where have we heard this passage before? It is a recreation of measures 18–32 which prepared the way for the exposition's first subject, in the tonic.
We could well coin a new term and call it a "leadforward," because the function of
this passage remains the same—whether to lead forward or to lead back—but in
either case to lead ineluctably toward B minor. As if to signal this all-important return to the home key, Liszt himself changes the key signature to B minor (from the
B-flat minor/C major signatures through which the music had wandered) at mea-

sure 531. Some commentators not only gloss over this critical juncture but ignore it altogether.[19]

The recapitulation is a highly compressed re-creation of the exposition. Two of the latter's themes are omitted entirely, both from the second subject group (the one marked *dolce con grazia,* the other marked *vivamente*), together with certain recitatives and linking passages. This has the effect of reducing the length of the recapitulation by about 25 percent.[20] Throughout the remainder of the sonata, Liszt continues to ring the changes on his basic material. One of the many fascinations for the Liszt aficionado is to observe the myriad ways in which even the recitatives and ornaments owe their thematic integrity to the Ursätze first delineated in the introduction. Even the notorious octave passages in the coda turn out to be thematically determined—that is, they are yet another metamorphosis of theme (b):

Pianists: It has lately become fashionable to play the right-hand octaves too fast, presumably in the hope of obtaining some cheap applause. This yields a false victory. Nothing exposes the player to greater cruelty than the eight measures that follow, where the left hand is doomed to imitate what the right hand has so bravely pioneered. At this point, the player may learn with dismay that the left hand does not know what the right hand is doing. It is the thematic integrity of the passage, not the vanity of the player, that calls for expression. Liszt's sounding sense must not be turned into senseless sound.

The *tremolando* in measures 708–10 represents another great climax of the sonata. It will be all the more effective if the *fff* is simply released from the instrument, or-

19. Sharon Winklhofer is forced to gloss over it, because by denying that the sonata is a "double-function" structure (WLS, pp. 118–20) she must also repudiate the notion that the Fugato is a substitute third movement leading into a finale. She becomes entangled in a pointless argument with William S. Newman, to whom she wrongly attributes the discovery of the "double-function" structure in his influential book *The Sonata since Beethoven.* (In this connection see note 6 of the present essay.) Serge Gut, in his *Liszt* (Paris, 1989, pp. 323–27), does not mention this crucial return to the tonic key of B minor at all, because nowhere in his analysis does he cite a single one of the keys in which the thematic material unfolds, not even the tonic. For him, the sonata might as well not have a key scheme.

20. Such compressions were an essential part of the Romantic movement's contribution to the sonata form. See the first movement of Chopin's Sonata in B-flat Minor, for example; or better still, the first movement of Tchaikovsky's Symphony no. 4, in F Minor. In both compositions the recapitulation has been severely truncated.

ganlike, rather than forced from it. Note, too, that Liszt has written out his *tremolando* in full (eighteen divisions, no more, no less), implying that he wants each note to be accounted for.

The dramatic pause that follows must be long—long enough to wait until the tremendous volume of sound has vanished, to say nothing of the emotional tension associated with it. Once the storm and stress have melted away, the final calm of the ensuing Andante sostenuto will cast its benediction over the entire work.

Liszt originally intended the sonata to end with a loud flourish, in which form it has occasionally been performed, if only to satisfy the latent curiosity of those who like to wander through a composer's workshop. The holograph shows that the inspired quiet ending with which the work now concludes (a tranquil recollection of the Andante sostenuto) was an afterthought, for which all admirers of the sonata remain grateful.

This sovereign masterpiece comes to its close with a final appearance of the "curtain" theme, which descends on one of the great keyboard dramas of the Romantic era.

III

All of which raises the ticklish question: What sort of player does the B Minor Sonata require? First and foremost a strategist, not a tactician. The tactician may win battles, but of what use is that if he loses the war? Wars are won by field marshals who know how to direct the conflict from afar. Likewise this sonata, which requires the distant grasp. To continue the military analogy, the worst performances are given by players who are somewhat like foot soldiers, up to their knees in the mud and gore of trench warfare. Alas, the sonata continues to attract the foot soldier rather than the field marshal, and suffers accordingly. Dangers lurk in every corner of this complicated battlefield, and the unwary player can easily be ambushed. Indeed, admirers of the sonata know where the bodies are buried. It is the first half of the work that contains the graveyards. There is a temptation to linger over Liszt's filigree-work, to dwell lovingly on his decorations, even to stop and "polish the ornaments," like some house-proud spouse expecting a visitor. But one pays a high price for such self-esteem. It is by then difficult to redeem the second half of the sonata because the clock is already running out and one can never regain the lost time. I have long held the view that all the great performances of the sonata last less than 30 minutes, although there are some very good ones that may last longer.

There is more to this problem than a race against the clock. Throughout musical history, the great performers have given conclusive proof that tempo is a function of structure. Tempo, that is to say, arises from within, and is not imposed from without. It is a constant marvel to compare two performances of the same work, both of which unfold at exactly the same speed when checked against a stopwatch, *but which create the impression of moving at different tempi.* Dynamics, phrasing, rubato, agogic accents, pedaling—and all the other important ingredients of interpretation—contribute to the total impression of pace, which may well contradict the clock. Contrasts, in brief, are not what you express through time; time is what you express through contrasts. Mendelssohn used to maintain that even if you were to remove every tempo marking from a piece of music, together with all the other marks of expression, the true musician would be able to restore them, because they simply spring from the character of the work. After all, it is the character that forms the face; the face does not form the character.

With this in mind, the timings of some of the better-known pianists to have recorded the sonata are not without interest.

Daniel Barenboim	32:12
Alfred Brendel	28:34
Claudio Arrau	32:00
Vladimir Horowitz	
1932	26:30
1977	30:00
Maurizio Pollini	29:08
Simon Barere	27:04
Van Cliburn	29:22
Arthur Rubinstein	26:49
Sviatislav Richter	
1966	29:23

We use the phrase "better-known pianists" with caution, for it brings us to our second requirement. Like Flaubert, who once famously declared that a novelist "must be like God in the universe, present everywhere and visible nowhere," the best performer is the one you don't even notice. Not all the pianists just listed could be held to such a standard. The mere fact that the aficionado praises *x*'s powerful octaves, *y*'s fleet fingers, and *z*'s luminous tone already suggests that he has been diverted from the piece by the player's siren song. "The singer not the song" has become a mantra for our time; and whenever this dismaying trend manifests itself, it can easily result in the temporary loss of the sonata.

Our third requirement is best expressed as a paradox. If you wish to play Liszt well, it is better not to specialize in him. What do they know of Liszt who only Liszt know?[21] In order to become an insider you must first have been an outsider. To open yourself to the music of Bach, Beethoven, Schubert, Schumann, Chopin, and many other composers besides is a necessary preparation for Liszt. After all, that is simply to emulate the example of Liszt himself, who had studied all these composers before he penned a note of the B Minor Sonata. The result is an enrichment for the player that is both musical and spiritual. Have there been any great Liszt players whose careers were confined exclusively to his music? The answer is almost certainly no. On the other hand, plenty of careers have been sustained on an exclusive diet of Bach, Beethoven, and, above all, Chopin.

Finally, it goes without saying that the B Minor Sonata demands that elusive quality known as authority. Authority! The very word is one of the most abused in the critical lexicon. It cannot be taught, and yet we recognize it the moment we hear it. It is commonly confused with power, a concept with which it has nothing in common. By contrast, authority increases with the diminishing need to exert it. The greatest authority, then, must be that of which we remain unaware, even as it exerts its secret spell.

Many years ago, the interpretation of Liszt's piano music took a wrong turn. It fell into the hands of pianists who considered their duty done if they played his music fast and loud, without regard for its many finer points. Yet there is abundant evidence that in Liszt's own time it was those "finer points" that he himself cherished, and which he tried to cultivate in his students. His lessons (recorded in the diaries and memoirs of a number of his pupils) were filled with remarkable enjoinders: to adopt slower tempi, to sustain a bel canto line, to care for phrase endings, to clarify the pedaling, to let the music breathe, and above all to respect the text.[22] We call these things "remarkable" because they fly in the face of received opinion. The fact is that Liszt was never a member of the "blood and thunder" school of piano playing which took possession of his music after his death and frequently turned it into a vehicle of blatant physical display. What a fate for music that contains so many beauties! Unfortunately, the profession is still crowded with heavy-handed pianists who regard Liszt's piano music much as the rest of the world regards the Olympic Games. It arouses in them the competitive spirit and burdens the listener with performances whose chief purpose is to squash the opposition. There have always been

---

21. The paradox is as old as human experience itself. Rudyard Kipling enshrined it in some fine words when he wrote, "What should they know of England who only England know?" in his poem "The English Flag."

22. See the diaries of August Göllerich (GLK) and Carl Lachmund (LL), and the reminiscences of Frederic Lamond (LML) and Amy Fay (FMG), among others.

exceptions, of course. One treasures the aristocratic approach of Dinu Lipatti, of Grigor Ginsburg, of Emil von Sauer, and above all of Egon Petri, whose peerless Liszt interpretations remain the model for us all. These pianists had technique to burn, but it was never flaunted. With them it was woven into the very weft and weave of Liszt's music and became an essential part of its character. Not one of them recorded the Sonata in B Minor, incidentally. But their playing contains a cornucopia of clues as to how this music might be approached.

IV

The subsequent history of the sonata is worth relating. Not the least surprising thing about Liszt's masterpiece is that it had to wait nearly four years before receiving its first public performance. According to Liszt's own annotation on the manuscript's title page, he had completed the work on February 2, 1853. One or two modifications were made to the piece in the weeks following, but on May 12 he was able to tell Hans von Bülow, "As for music, I have finished my Sonata, and a Second Ballade."[23] The sonata was published in 1854 with a dedication to Robert Schumann, but it aroused hardly any interest in the wider world.[24] In brief, the sonata was born neglected.

Two private performances had already taken place, however, and they call for comment because they have entered the history books. The first was given by Liszt himself, in June 1853, before a small circle of friends and admirers at one of the regular musical matinees in the Altenburg. The previous day, the twenty-one-year-old Brahms had arrived in Weimar, in the company of the violinist Eduard Reményi. The pair were in the middle of a concert tour of Germany, and they turned up at the Altenburg bearing a letter of introduction from Joachim. Liszt at once issued an invitation to the concert the following day. Among those gathered were several of Liszt's pupils, including Karl Klindworth, Joachim Raff, Dionys Pruckner, and William Mason, who left an intriguing eyewitness account of the

23. LBLB, p. 21. Liszt's mention of the B Minor Ballade and the B Minor Sonata within one breath, so to speak, will surprise no one familiar with both compositions. Certain passages are virtually interchangeable with one another. Compare measures 82–85 of the ballade, for instance, with measures 40–45 of the sonata. Lining up the notes for an identity parade will not explain the phenomenon. In performance, we experience a déjà vu—a sudden shaft of recognition that we have been here before.

24. Within the inner circle of Liszt's own students, however, there were two who composed piano sonatas into which deep inroads were made by their study of Liszt's sonata. The Sonata in B-flat Minor (1857) by the twenty-three-year-old Julius Reubke would be unthinkable without Liszt's composition, for it actually quotes from it; and Reubke dedicated his sonata in tribute to Liszt. As for Rudolf Viole's sonata (1855) which remains almost totally unknown, it, too, is modeled on Liszt's and created a sensation when it appeared, drawing rave comments from Hans von Bülow (its dedicatee) who described it as "sweepingly innovatory, music of the future in the highest degree."

A response of a different kind came from Clara Schumann who was openly hostile to the sonata from the beginning. In her diary she records her distress (see p. 48, note 24 of the present volume). Schumann himself never heard the work.

event. Brahms had brought with him some of his own piano compositions, including the Scherzo in E-flat Minor which was still in manuscript. Liszt invited Brahms to play some of them, but Brahms was overcome with nervousness and declined. "Well, I shall have to play," remarked Liszt, and placed the manuscript of the Scherzo on the music desk. Mason tells us that he and Raff had already caught a glimpse of the untidy manuscript and, although Liszt had no peer as a sight reader, they still trembled for the result. But Liszt not only delivered a marvelous performance of the Scherzo; he also carried on a running commentary on the music as he played, much to Brahms's delight. Someone then asked Liszt to play his recently composed sonata, and he immediately returned to the piano and began playing. As the music progressed, he came to a particularly expressive moment and glanced around the room to observe the effect on his listeners. When he cast his eyes in Brahms's direction, however, he observed the young composer "dozing in his chair," as Mason later described it.[25] Liszt finished playing the sonata and then got up from the piano and left the room without saying a word. Mason tells us that although he knew that something untoward had happened, Brahms was hidden from his view so that he was at first unaware that the young composer had committed an indiscretion. It was Reményi who later explained to Mason what had happened.[26]

The second private performance, equally memorable, occurred nearly two years

---

25. MMML, p. 130.

26. We must not forget that Mason's memoirs were not published until 1901, many years after the events they purport to describe. In preparing his account, Mason took the precaution of asking Klindworth to corroborate his description, since Klindworth was by that time the only other person alive who had been present at Liszt's performance. Klindworth confirmed that something unusual had occurred to upset Liszt but was unable to lay the blame at Brahms's door. Reményi, however, who had been sitting next to Brahms throughout the performance, had already given an independent account of this episode in an interview with the *New York Herald* on January 18, 1879, the very first time that the story had found its way into print, and he asserted that "Brahms dozed" while Liszt played. The Reményi interview appeared under the title "A Twenty-five Years' Secret: Revelations That Will Stir the Musical World." According to Reményi, "while Liszt was playing most sublimely to his pupils, Brahms calmly slept in a fauteuil, or at least seemed to do so. It was an act that produced bad blood among those present, and everybody looked astonished and annoyed. I was thunderstruck. In going out I questioned Brahms concerning his behavior. His only excuse was: 'Well, I was overcome with fatigue; I could not help it.'" There are two things to note about this account. The first is that Reményi wrote it twenty-two years before Mason's better-known narrative. The second is that the interview appeared well within the lifetime of Brahms, from whom it provoked absolutely no response. Even had Brahms wished to reply, however, that would have been difficult for him because in this same interview Reményi discloses something that was not designed to make Brahms's day: he informs us that most of the melodies in Brahms's famous series of *Hungarian Dances*, were plagiarized, having been written by obscure Hungarian composers and simply published under Brahms's name. Hungarian Dance no. 7, in F minor, in fact, was actually composed by Reményi himself, and simply appropriated by Brahms. Brahms could hardly have addressed the one issue without addressing the other, and so remained silent on both. See also RKU, pp. 79–95.

Incidentally, only two other private performances by Liszt himself are mentioned in the literature. The first took place in Rome, possibly before a group of students, in March 1865 (BBM, p. 183). The second is not so well documented, but some sources mention a second performance four years later, in April 1869, in the Bösendorfer salon in Vienna.

later, when Karl Klindworth gave a private rendering for Wagner in London. Afterwards Wagner wrote to Liszt (in a letter headed "April 5, 1855, London 8:30 evening"):

> Klindworth has just played your great sonata to me. We passed the day alone together; he dined with me, and after dinner I made him play. Dearest Franz! You were with me, the sonata is beautiful beyond compare; great, sweet, deep and noble, sublime as you are yourself. It moved me most deeply, and the London misery was forgotten at once. More I cannot say, not just after having heard it, but of what I say I am as full as a man can be. Once more, you were with me! Ah, could you only be with me, body and soul, how beautiful we could make life!!
>
> Klindworth astonished me with his playing; no lesser man could have ventured to play your work to me for the first time. He is worthy of you. Assuredly, it was beautiful.[27]

The sonata languished in limbo for nearly four years, awaiting its first public performance. No one seemed in a hurry to present it to the wider world. But all that was about to change.

V

On January 22, 1857, a pale young man appeared at the unlikely venue of the Englischen Haus Hotel, in Berlin, glowered at the audience, as was his wont, and commenced to play this long and complex composition before a modest-sized audience. He had not proceeded very far before certain gentlemen of the press experienced signs of distress. The sonata appeared to them to be in no fixed key, with thematic contrasts that were so extreme they gave the impression of being non sequiturs. Two of these critics became stubborn opponents of the work, and were quick to denounce it. One was Otto Gumprecht of the *Nationale Zeitung,* and the other was Gustav Engel of the *Spener'sche Zeitung.* A few days after the performance Gumprecht wrote that the sonata was "an invitation to hissing and stamping,"[28] while Engel informed his readers that "not only had it nothing to do with beauty, but it conflicted with nature and logic."[29] It is tempting to adjust some words of Charles Ives, and say that "their ears were on wrong." But they expressed a majority opinion that was to prevail for a generation or more. The pianist was Hans von Bülow, and the sonata that he had just introduced to the Berlin public, and indeed to the world, had taken him more than two years to prepare, most recently under the guidance of Liszt himself.[30] The next morning, with all the enthusiasm of his twenty-

27. KWL, vol. 2, p. 65.
28. LLB, vol. 1, p. 323.
29. The full text is given in BB, vol. 3, pp. 65–66.
30. The background to Bülow's tussle with the press will be found in BB, vol. 3, pp. 63–68. Bülow

six years, Bülow wrote to Liszt, "I am writing to you the day after a great day. Yesterday evening I played your Sonata for the first time before the Berlin public, which applauded me heartily and called me back."[31] Then came the published reviews and the negative comments, which enraged Bülow, and marked the beginning of his toxic relations with the press. For the next several years, in fact, Bülow engaged in a bitter newspaper war with the Berlin critics, with Liszt's compositions at the center, until Liszt himself appealed to his old pupil to calm himself and desist from such a useless activity.

The date January 22, 1857, was important for another reason. That evening Bülow inaugurated the Bechstein grand piano, an instrument he eventually came to admire above all others.[32] Thereafter, he became a "Bechstein artist," and he and Carl Bechstein developed a close friendship. Their lively correspondence would last a lifetime.

VI

The sonata has a habit of yielding its secrets slowly, even to those who later became its most ardent champions. The case of Bartók is worth recalling. He tells us that he made a special study of the work while he was still a student, but abandoned it because he found the first half "cold and empty." Shortly afterwards he heard Dohnányi give a perfect performance of the sonata, but even then he was still far from understanding it. Some years later he returned to the sonata anew, because "its difficulties interested me." He gradually came to like it, though not yet uncondition-

---

had made his first acquaintance with the sonata in 1854, shortly after Liszt had sent him a newly printed copy of the work (LBLB, p. 75). The following year, on July 21, 1855, he had heard Liszt play it for a group of friends at the Altenburg, Liszt's house in Weimar, among whom were his thirteen-year-old-prodigy pupil Carl Tausig and the boy's father (HLSW, p. 68). It is evident that by then Bülow had already embarked on a serious conquest of the work, because the following month he gave it a preliminary run-through for Niels Gade in Berlin (LBLB, p. 141). On August 1, 1856, came the moment when Bülow was able to play it for his master for the first time. We know that Liszt was pleased with the performance, because the following day he wrote to his disciple Richard Pohl, "Bülow played several pieces for me quite wonderfully, among other things both my Polonaises and the Sonata" (WLP, p. 197).

31. LBLB, p. 188. Liszt himself was not present at the concert. He was ill in Weimar, hardly able to walk, and had been obliged to remain at home under medical care. For several weeks Liszt had been suffering from a form of blood poisoning. His feet were covered in abscesses, and whenever he left his bed he was forced to hobble around on crutches. His condition was made even more painful by the application of saltpeter, at the insistence of his Weimar physician Dr. Goullon. His letters to Wagner at this time hint at his health problems (KWL, vol. 2, pp. 130 and 155).

Incidentally, the concert was one of a series of so-called Trio-Soirées that Bülow arranged at his own expense during the winter months of the period 1856–58 and later moved to the Hôtel de Russie. These hotels contained assembly rooms large enough to mount chamber concerts. Later on Bülow moved them to the more imposing Singakademie (HMI, p. 66).

32. According to Bülow, this instrument had been specially built for him by Carl Bechstein, who had just opened his own factory, having earlier learned his craft at the Berlin firm of Perau, where he had been made foreman at the early age of twenty-one. It was Cosima who appears to have brought Bechstein and Bülow together (HMI, p. 66).

ally. When he spoke to Dohnányi about his conversion, he was astonished to discover that Dohnányi had undergone exactly the same sort of experience.[33] Busoni's transformation was even more striking. He started out actively disliking the composer who later became his idol and was only won over to the music slowly, eventually becoming one of the greatest Liszt interpreters of his age. All that was ninety years ago. Today we are no longer "astonished" at such things, to use Bartók's expression. It seems to be the fate of Liszt's music in general, and of this sonata in particular, to require much time for its manifold beauties to impress themselves on the listener. Liszt reception has always struck a mingled chime.

The history of first impressions is a notoriously dismal one, and the Sonata in B Minor has been accorded its fair share of incomprehension. As late as 1881 Hanslick was still huffing and puffing against the work, describing it as "a brilliant, steam-driven mill, which almost always runs idle"[34] and announcing "Whoever has heard *that,* and finds it beautiful is beyond help."[35] As Peter Raabe was later to observe, "such judgments make one ashamed for Liszt's contemporaries that they allowed themselves to be led for so long by a man who was both blind and deaf to the beauties of new music."[36] After such an uncertain beginning, pianists seemed afraid to touch it, although by 1861 Bülow had played it four more times in Berlin and Leipzig. Thereafter it fell silent for almost twenty years, until Saint-Saëns introduced it to Paris, in April 1880. Bülow then revived the work in Vienna, in 1881, provoking the aforementioned response of Hanslick.[37] Typical of the general neglect it endured was the fact that it had to wait more than twenty-three years before receiving its first public performance in England. That honor fell to Oscar Beringer, a pupil of Tausig, who gave the British premier in St. James's Hall on April 24, 1880.[38] It

---

33. SBB, pp. 453–54.

34. RLS, p. 62.

35. SLM, p. 116.

36. RLS, vol. 2, p. 62.

37. One little-known exception to this "silence" was the isolated public performance by Alida Topp (a Bülow pupil) at the Karlsruhe Festival in the summer of 1864. Liszt wrote of her, "She is quite simply a marvel. Yesterday she played for me by heart my Sonata and the *Mephisto* Waltz in a way that enchanted me" (LLB, vol. 6, p. 35). Liszt's Hungarian pupil Róbert Freund confirms the early neglect into which the sonata fell. In his unpublished memoirs Freund relates the story of his first encounter with Liszt in Pest, in 1871, when he was nineteen years old. "I requested permission to play something for him, and in reply to his question as to what I would play I said: 'the B minor Sonata'—a piece rather unknown at the time. He didn't even seem remotely to think of his own Sonata because he asked me again: 'What sonata?'" (FMML, p. 5)

38. *The Atheneum,* 1880, p. 546. This journal made the perspicacious observation, "Regarding this Sonata . . . opinions are not at all likely to be unanimous." The second British performance was given by Jessie Morrison, a pupil of Frits Hartvigson, just three weeks later, on May 12. When Walter Bache played the work more than two years later, on November 6, 1882, the Sonata received a drubbing from the English critics that matched the one that it had provoked when Bülow had played it in Vienna the previous year. *The Musical Times* wrote, "the elaboration of this rhapsody, mis-named a sonata, is to our thinking positively ugly" (MT, December 1, 1882, p. 664). Bache, with that dogged determination so characteristic of his promotion of Liszt's music in England, gave the critics a second helping by including it in his next annual all-Liszt recital on October 22, 1883, in the same hall, with equally lamentable results, the critic of the *Musical Times* declaring on that occasion that the work had no right to the title "sonata," unless the works of the classical masters be renamed (issue of November 1, 1883, p. 606).

took even longer for its American premier to take place. Liszt's pupil Karl Klindworth played the Sonata in New York's Steinway Hall on January 31, 1888. Another Liszt pupil, Arthur Friedheim, then took up the work and played it in the same city, first in 1892 and again in 1901. Until the end of the nineteenth century its reputation was by no means secure, although it was already in Busoni's repertoire by the early years of the twentieth century. It was only with the wholesale revival of the music of the Romantic era, after World War II, that the sonata finally came into its own. It is now universally regarded as Liszt's greatest composition for solo piano and has entered the musical pantheon. The statistics are impressive. To identify more than a dozen or so performances anywhere in the world before the early 1900s is difficult. A century later, the sonata has become the most frequently played piano composition in the Greater New York area alone, with twenty or more performances each season—season after season.

Liszt and the Lied

If a few singers could be found . . . who would boldly venture to sing songs
by the notorious noncomposer Franz Liszt, they would probably find a public for them.

FRANZ LISZT[1]

I

In 1847, when he was thirty-five years old, Franz Liszt abandoned his career as a
traveling virtuoso and settled in Weimar in order to devote himself more fully to
musical composition. The thirteen years he spent in the city were among the most
productive of his life. It was there that he composed twelve of his symphonic poems, the *Faust* and the *Dante* symphonies, the two piano concertos, and the B Minor Piano Sonata. At the same time he revised many of his earlier compositions,
such as the *Transcendental* and the "Paganini" studies, bringing them to their definitive form.

Liszt also came to maturity as a Lieder composer during his Weimar years. He
had already begun to write songs ten years earlier, while he was resident in Italy (the
three *Petrarch Sonnets* were first sketched there), and by the time he got to Weimar
he had a dozen or more Lieder in his portfolio. He now added to them and eventually produced an impressive collection of more than seventy pieces in this genre.

The songs are strangely neglected today. They rarely turn up in the modern
Lieder recital, and some of them are unknown even to specialists. This is surprising,
for a closer acquaintance with the best of them suggests that they represent a "missing link" between Schumann and Mahler. In fact, the history of the German Lied
is incomplete without taking Liszt into account.

Such a view may seem difficult to sustain. After all, Liszt was born in Hungary,
spent his formative years in France, and then traveled through so many different
countries that he is often described as "cosmopolitan." Yet the evidence is there.
Liszt's first language was German;[2] and the years that he lived and worked in

---

1. LLB, vol. 1, pp. 343–44.
2. Until he was eleven years old he would have spoken German in the Austrian dialect prevalent in
western Hungary at that time. After he settled in Paris in December 1823, he quickly mastered French,
which became his language of preference. For about twenty years thereafter he was removed from the
everyday use of German. Already in 1840 we find him complaining to his friend Franz von Schober,
"Excuse the writing and spelling of these lines. You know that I never write German" (LLB, vol. 1, p. 41).

Weimar—the city of Goethe and Schiller—brought him into daily contact with German poets, painters, playwrights, and musicians. Some of his best settings are of such poets as Heinrich Heine, Friedrich Rückert, Hoffmann von Fallersleben, Ludwig Uhland, Ludwig Rellstab, and of course Goethe and Schiller themselves. This distinguished roll call indicates that Liszt wanted to be associated only with the greatest wordsmiths. He was aware of Voltaire's sarcastic dismissal of many songs of the day—"The words that are sung are those that are not fit to be spoken"—and he went out of his way to rise above it. And Liszt had other credentials, too. During his virtuoso years he had transcribed for solo piano more than fifty Schubert songs, and twenty more by Schumann, Mendelssohn, and, later on, by Eduard Lassen and Robert Franz as well—transcriptions that reveal an insider's knowledge of the originals. And after he had settled in Weimar and taken up his duties as an opera conductor, he had worked with some of the finest singers in Germany. In short, he was very well equipped to write Lieder, for he understood the human voice as well as anybody in the nineteenth century.

II

It is no accident that Liszt was beguiled by the Lied during his Weimar years. He had at his disposal a number of gifted singers attached to the Court Opera, who were ready and able to do these pieces justice. Rosa Agthe was only twenty-one years old when Liszt engaged her for the Weimar Theater. This gifted soprano, the daughter of a local orchestral player, created the role of Elsa in Wagner's *Lohengrin* and Liszt chose her to be one of the Aachen Festival soloists in 1857. She married the Russian baritone Feodor von Milde, whom Liszt had invited to Weimar as a guest singer in Donizetti's *Lucia di Lammermoor.* He was so warmly received that he made Weimar his home. The von Mildes could have made more lucrative careers elsewhere; but when they were asked about that Feodor gave the unanswerable reply that they stayed in Weimar simply because Liszt was there.[3]

Among the other singers who worked with Liszt were the tenor Franz Götze and the contralto Emilie Genast. Liszt himself recognized in Franz Götze a leading exponent of his songs. This singer was one of the best lyric tenors of the day, and he eventually became a teacher of singing in Leipzig, where he communicated his enthusiasm for Liszt's songs to his many pupils. This was not so easy in the 1850s and 1860s, for it was a time when Liszt's music was embroiled in controversy. The so-called War of the Romantics was at its height, and conservative Leipzig was generally hostile to the works of progressive Weimar. When the *Collected Edition* of the

---

Even as late as 1854, we find him complaining to his fellow Hungarian Joseph Joachim, "What do you say to my German scribbling? . . . It feels to me all the time . . . like finger exercises in syntax." (MBJ, vol. 1, p. 179). After he had put down roots in Weimar, however, he began to regain fluency in the language.

3. The von Mildes asked Liszt to be the godfather of their son, who was born in 1855, and was baptized Franz (SNW, vol. 2, p. 39).

songs appeared in 1860, Liszt asked his publisher to be sure to send a copy to Götze because his pioneering work gave him a special claim to them. Götze's talented daughter, the soprano Augusta Götze, was equally devoted to the songs. When Liszt first heard her he begged Götze to allow her to become a professional singer, an idea that Götze at first resisted. "The artistic gifts of your daughter are as rare as they are pronounced," wrote Liszt, and he proceeded to get concert engagements for her.[4] Augusta repaid Liszt in a most unusual way. So convinced was she of the worth of the songs that she carried out a hoax on the Leipzig public, passing off certain songs by Liszt as posthumous ones by Schubert—and she was encored. Liszt was delighted when he heard what had happened and hoped that the joke might be continued, because, as he put it, it took place "in salons that are very much set against me."[5]

The contralto Emilie Genast likewise aroused Liszt's admiration for the way in which she handled his songs—particularly "Mignons Lied" and "Die Lorelei." She was the daughter of the Weimar stage manager, Eduard Genast, and Liszt first engaged her for a performance of Beethoven's Ninth Symphony which he conducted in Weimar in the early 1850s. He was so impressed with her voice that he regularly entrusted her with recitals of his songs, particularly after he had become involved with the Lower Rhine Music Festivals at such places as Aachen, Karlsruhe, and Cologne during the 1850s. All these singers had the supreme advantage of being coached by Liszt himself, and may therefore be said to have sung his songs with authority. The Sunday afternoon "matinees" held in the large music room of the Altenburg provided a perfect setting for the performance of these pieces within the charmed circle of Liszt's own admirers, often with Liszt himself presiding at the keyboard. Historically, these matinees may be regarded as the natural successors to the "Schubertiads" that had taken place in Vienna some thirty years earlier.

III

We previously described Liszt's songs as a "missing link" between Schumann and Mahler. This notion is borne out the moment we consider his setting of Goethe's "Freudvoll und leidvoll" (Joyful and Sorrowful). The switch from major to minor (from "Freudvoll" to "leidvoll," as it were), and the subtle enharmonic changes Liszt employs to paint these words, are typical Mahlerian devices (see ★ below; measures 2 to 4 and measures 6–8 are virtually identical in pitch, but their notation is different). They tell of a composer who was not only sensitive to the meaning of words, but was moving toward the language of high romanticism.

---

4. LLB, vol. 1, p. 374.

5. LLB, vol. 1, p. 344. Liszt does not mention Augusta Götze by name in connection with this story. But since the enterprising *Sängerin* to whom he refers was the only female singer in Leipzig publicly promoting his songs, it is nowadays accepted that it was she who perpetrated the hoax. It was for Augusta, incidentally, that Liszt composed his recitation "Leonore," which she performed in Jena in November 1860.

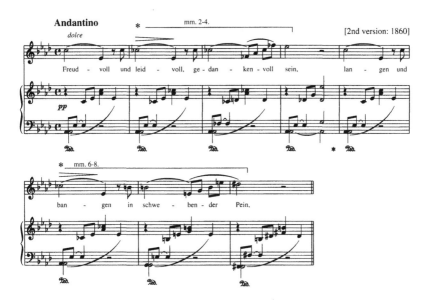

One of Liszt's truly great songs, and one which carries the Mahler connection still further, is his setting of Georg Herwegh's "Ich möchte hingehn wie das Abendroth." It is a song of farewell, and it is deeply autobiographical. In 1844 Liszt was giving concerts in the small town of Pau in southern France, near the Spanish border, and he was there reunited with Caroline d'Artigaux (*née* Saint-Cricq), his first love, whom he had last seen in 1828 when he was only seventeen years old. The young couple had been separated by a disapproving father who had forced Caroline into an unwelcome marriage with a stranger. This early episode had thrown the young Liszt into despair and precipitated a nervous breakdown. At Pau, Caroline and Liszt reminisced about their early love. As he left the city his emotions welled up and he composed "Ich möchte hingehn" in memory of the reunion. "Would that I might pass away like the sunset's glow," longs the poet. It is a foretaste of the nostalgic world of Mahler's *Das Lied von der Erde,* and especially of its last movement "Der Abschied" (Farewell). But there is an even deeper affinity with Mahler's song "Ich bin der Welt abhanden gekommen" (I have grown apart from the world). Did Mahler know Liszt's setting? It seems inconceivable that he could have composed his own commentary on mankind's weariness with the things of this world without some knowledge of Liszt's interpretation of this same experience. Everything is here—the world-weariness; the sunset glow; the longing to pass away gently like a flower's scent, like the dew in the valley, like a fleeting note. Yet the poet goes on to remind us that this is not the lot of mankind. Only in nature does death come gently. "You will indeed pass away, leaving no trace." But "misery will first sap our strength, then break our hearts."

The song begins with a yearning, Tristanesque motif on the piano, which starts in the "wrong" key and ascends ever higher as if in search of its goal. The singer then takes over and the music emerges tentatively in the tonic key of A major.

We call this visit to the tonic key "tentative" because of the tonal ambiguities that immediately pervade the rest of the song and which are clearly meant to depict the poet's search for the meaning of life and death.[6]

6. The second of Mahler's *Kindertotenlieder* "Nun seh' ich wohl, warum so dunkle Flammern," especially in its lesser-known setting for voice and piano (as opposed to the widely admired orchestral setting), presents another startling connection with this song. Both songs begin in a parallel manner, with nearly identical melodic motifs. Rückert's words in the Mahler run: "Now I understand why such dark flames / Were strewn on me when you looked at me. / O eyes!" Herwegh's words in the Liszt run: "Would that I might pass away like the sunset's glow." Beneath the loving surface of both texts, in fact, lie thoughts of death.

Moving restlessly back and forth between major and minor the song leads quickly to one of those wonderful enharmonic changes so typical of Liszt (F♮ becomes E♯; see ★ below). As the music is about to enter the remote world of C-sharp major, it pauses abruptly and returns, as if in resignation, to the Tristanesque motif of the beginning.

At the end of the fifth verse, and the words "You will not slip away silently like the stars," Liszt presents us with a major surprise. The Tristanesque mood which has hovered over the song now flowers into a direct quotation from the opening of *Tristan* itself.

We use the term *quotation* with some caution. Liszt saw the manuscript of Act One of *Tristan* for the first time on December 26, 1858. "Ich möchte hingehn" was first composed in 1844, ten years before Wagner penned a note of *Tristan*. That led Peter Raabe to suppose that Wagner might have acquired the opening of his masterpiece from Liszt, and there has been much talk along those lines ever since.[7] But Liszt revised the song in 1856, and an inspection of the manuscript reveals these measures to have been an even later "paste-over," clearly implying a last-minute modification.

7. RLS, vol. 2, p. 127.

These measures have meanwhile become a locus classicus for Liszt scholars who like to point to Wagner's indebtedness to Liszt for a number of his leading ideas. The search is well worthwhile, but on this occasion they may have to look elsewhere.[8]

At the close of this long, involved song, the poet imparts a bleak message: for mankind there are no fading sunset glows, no drifting away on perfumed air, no sounds that vanish into the distance. We are first broken by misery and despair, and then our hearts are shattered. Liszt portrays life's brutal conclusion through a harsh and unexpected ending to the song. There is a violent outburst from the singer and some chilling chords from the pianist which end the piece in the wintry key of the tonic minor. Note the hollow, final chord held by the right hand alone—and the emptiness below it.

On a manuscript copy of this composition, which he revised several times before its publication in 1859, Liszt wrote, "This song is a testament of my youth—therefore no better, but also no worse."[9]

IV

With his setting of "Mignons Lied" ("Kennst du das Land"), Liszt reached the height of his powers as a song composer. He was well aware that other composers before him had set this celebrated text from Goethe's *Wilhelm Meister,* including Beethoven, Schubert, and Schumann; and after Liszt would come Hugo Wolf. But Liszt's setting can stand comparison with all of them and it brings out new beauties enshrined in Goethe's words.

The poem tells of an Italian girl, Mignon, who has been abducted by vagabonds, abused, and brought to Germany, where she is forced to dance and sing in a troupe of entertainers. In her sad condition she remembers the beauties of her southern homeland, its lush foliage, the splendid house in which she once lived, and the

---

8. Rena Charnin Mueller has pointed out that the manuscript paper employed by Liszt for this paste-over was not used by him before 1856. This still leaves a small window of opportunity for Liszt himself to have originated these measures before the Prelude to *Tristan* came into his possession toward the end of 1858, but the possibility is not great. For those who continue to look for a "Tristan connection" with Liszt, the opening of "Die Lorelei" would be a better place to start (see pp. 160–61).

9. "Dieses Lied ist mein jugendliches Testament—deswegen aber nicht besser—und auch nicht schlechter" (GSA 60/D37).

mountain gorges through which she was brought by her captors. Each of the three verses poses a searching question, pierced with nostalgia. "Do you know the land where the lemon trees bloom?" "Do you know the house?" "Do you know the mountains?" And to each of these questions, Mignon provides the same refrain: "There, there would I go with you!"

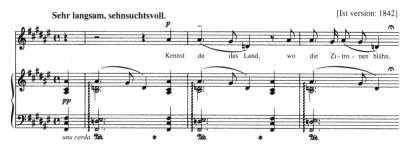

Liszt chooses the remote key of F-sharp major for his setting, as if to symbolize the faraway memories evoked by Mignon's questions. And he pursues this idea of a distant world by setting her eager refrain "Dahin! Dahin!" (There, there!) to rising intervals—the better to view Mignon's lost land from afar, so to speak. It will not escape attention that having allowed Mignon to reach her highest pinnacle of hope on a top F♯, Liszt dashes her aspirations by abruptly pivoting to the key of G major, which has the effect of transforming the F♯ from a tonic into an unresolved leading-note. It is a cruel view to nowhere; the phrase collapses back into F-sharp major, hope unfulfilled.

Incidentally, in order to emphasize Mignon's mounting aspirations, Liszt has added one more "Dahin!" to Goethe's text. This simple repetition of a single word by Germany's greatest poet opens the door to a large topic. When Peter Raabe once talked of Liszt "doing violence to words," he unwittingly set in motion a school of Liszt criticism that still lingers. Of the several examples he gives of Liszt's "short-comings" in this area, not one of them makes sense to a musician.[10] As Suzanne Langer pointed out long ago, there is no such thing as a successful marriage in the arts, only rape. Music is by far the most dominant art form, and will always subject words to its will. That is why every poet, from Goethe down, has feared being set to music, has feared keeping the company of composers, lest he become the recipient of "violence." To speak plainly, the moment that music takes possession of words, it distorts them. Every Lied and every opera ever written involves by definition a distortion of words; otherwise, those words would simply remain spoken. And yet worse is to come. When inferior poetry is set to superior music, the result remains superior. When superior poetry is set to inferior music, the result remains inferior. Music, in brief, casts its defining mantle over everything it touches. That is why we must judge Liszt, as we would judge any other lieder composer, on the quality of his musical material.

It so happens that Liszt himself is his own best witness to the truth of this last statement. In his first setting of Goethe's "Mignons Lied" (1842) the famous opening lines

> Kennst Du das Land
>   wo die Zitronen blühn?
> [Do you know the land
>   where the lemon trees blossom?]

receive some unnatural emphases. In spoken German the words *Du* and *Die* would receive no stress, as Raabe is quick to point out. Liszt has mistakenly emphasized them by placing them on the first beat of the bar:

When he came to revise the song, eighteen years later, Liszt changed the time signature, as well as the note lengths of the musical phrases, in order to conform with the natural flow of the spoken words. His years of residency in Germany had doubtless refined his ear for the language. These same words *Du* and *Die* are now relegated to unstressed parts of the bar:

---

10. RLS, vol. 2, pp. 112–31. See also Raabe's preface to his edition of the songs in the Breitkopf *Collected Edition* (section 7, vol. 1).

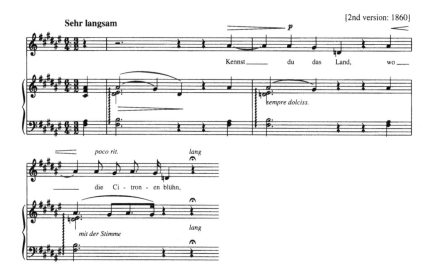

A comparison between the two versions brings us to the nub of the matter. The revision may be more respectful of Goethe's verbal rhythms, but it is by no means superior, musically speaking, to the first version. It is now the words which are bending music to their will. There are in any case far worse transgressions in Schumann and Schubert than the false verbal emphases of which Liszt stands accused. In his well-known song "Widmung," Schumann recapitulates the first six lines of Rückert's verse in their entirety, and we happily sit through the repetition as the song draws to a close. Schubert is even more disrespectful. In his setting of Goethe's "Gretchen am Spinnrade," he not only subjects the entire last verse to a repeat—"Und küssen ihn so wie ich wollt" (And kiss him just as I liked)—but at the point of repetition he actually changes Goethe's words to "O könnt ich ihn küssen so wie ich wollt" (O could I but kiss him just as I liked!). The case against Liszt starts to collapse by virtue of the distinguished company he keeps.

For the rest, words and music have always made strange bedfellows. In the entire history of music, few more contentious issues have ever been aired than how to persuade the lion to lay down with the lamb. It went to the heart of the Council of Trent's resolution to reform church music and render vocal polyphony more intelligible.[11] It is what Johann Scheibe complained of in Bach. It is what Goethe complained of in Beethoven. Oil and water would stand a better chance of blending than such minds. The issue was especially familiar to Schopenhauer, for whom mu-

---

11. Hans Pfitzner's opera *Palestrina* takes the subject of the Council of Trent and raises it to high historical drama. Palestrina's alleged response to the constraints of the council, whose zealotry would have suppressed the beauties of vocal polyphony, was to compose his divinely inspired *Missa Papae Marcelli*, thus rendering further discussion mute. And Wagner's opera *Die Meistersinger von Nürnberg* is absorbed with a similar problem, the relationship between words and music. Beckmesser, it will be recalled, writes his inferior songs by way of the stereotyped rules of word-setting. Walther's "Prize Song," on the other hand, comes to him in a dream.

sic, too, was the most powerful of the arts. He once famously observed the physical accident that makes the human voice serve both the faculty of speech and the faculty of song. If mankind had been equipped with two separate sets of vocal organs, he argued, one for speech and one for song, the peculiar idea of emitting words and music simultaneously might never have arisen. And during a passage on jokes, he cited an amusing non sequitur: "You like to walk alone; I like to walk alone. Let us therefore walk together." How often have solitary speech and solitary song been obliged to walk together! In any case, the pedantically correct fitting of words to their proper articulation in music has never been of overriding concern to the vast majority of composers, as the study of any strophic song (where different verses are set to identical music) would reveal.

So what conclusions can be drawn? We should not press the case too hard, otherwise we will surely fall into a reductio ad absurdum: the only texts that could be set with absolute authority would be by composers working in their mother tongue. This would exclude the English-speaking Benjamin Britten (*Les Illuminations*), the Russian-speaking Stravinsky (*The Rake's Progress*), and above all the German-speaking Handel, the text settings of whose oratorios have so often been faulted by the English-speaking Beckmessers of music criticism that it is perplexing to observe how these same oratorios have found the strength to become part of the glory of Britannia's church music. Franz Liszt set texts in no fewer than six languages—German (59), French (12), Italian (4), English (1), Russian (1), and Hungarian (1). The essential point, for him, was always to get to the heart of the meaning of a poem and to illuminate that meaning in music. For the rest, Peter Pears was surely right when he observed that "the more realistic the setting of the words becomes, the less interesting does its music tend to be."[12]

V

One of Liszt's best-known songs is his setting of Heine's "Die Lorelei." The Lorelei is a steep rock that rises perpendicularly on the right bank of the Rhine. Legend has it that a beautiful siren sits on the rock and with her enchanted song lures mariners to a watery death.[13] Liszt had sailed past the Lorelei many times during his heyday as a touring virtuoso, and he found the legend impossible to resist. The introduction contains a striking allusion to the opening bars of *Tristan*, not the first time that Liszt had stolen from the future of music.[14]

---

12. MKB, pp. 62–63.

13. This legend was actually the invention of the poet Clemens Brentano who introduced it in 1802.

14. This is the second version of "Die Lorelei," composed in 1856, three years before the appearance of *Tristan*. The first version, composed in 1841, does not possess this introduction.

The poet is reflecting on the old legend, which haunts his mind. The setting sun is making the mountaintop radiant with light. A beautiful woman sits there, combing her golden hair with a golden comb, singing her siren song. The Rhine flows ever swifter. The sailor hears the song of the enchantress and is enraptured by its beauty. In Heine's words:

> The mariner in his little ship
> is seized with wild anguish.
> He does not see the reefs,
> he looks only upward to the heights.
> I think that in the end the waves
> engulf the boatman and his boat;
> and the Lorelei did that
> with her singing.

> [Den Schiffer im kleinen Schiffe
> ergreift es mit wildem weh,
> Er schaut nicht die Felsenriffe
> Er schaut nur hinauf die Höh.
> [Ich glaube, die wellen verschlingen
> Am Ende Schiffen und Kahn;
> Und das hat mit ihrem Singen
> Die Lorelei getan.]

Liszt portrays this dramatic scene with music of great power. The storm he draws from the piano is a high point of the song, and it is clearly meant to depict the turbulence of the water as the mariner and his frail barque are engulfed and sink into the depths.

Such passages have led a number of critics, the editor of the *Penguin Book of Lieder* among them, to observe that Liszt's settings are frequently too elaborate for their text.[15] These complaints are advanced from the usual standpoint of literary bias, and they are essentially motivated by that same mistaken notion of "violence to words" against which Raabe spoke. The setting prevails, as usual, because the music itself is of superior quality.

It was for Emilie Genast that Liszt provided an orchestral accompaniment for "Die Lorelei"—one of several similar settings that he made during his Weimar years.[16] When Fräulein Genast sang it in Berlin, in 1860 (together with the orchestral setting of "Mignons Lied"), the genre was new. The idea of a Lieder singer being accompanied by a full orchestra was still a novelty in 1860, and in Berlin it was probably without precedent. The chief precursor had been Berlioz's song cycle *Les Nuits d'été*, published four years earlier, in 1856. Did Liszt know the Berlioz songs? It is entirely possible, but we cannot be sure. That Genast had a runaway success on her hands is borne out by Liszt's correspondence. All the more surprising, then, that these orchestral settings, too, have since languished. Here, if anywhere, we can talk of a conspiracy of silence. Yet these pieces would make a ravishing adornment to any orchestral concert today.

VI

To the telling example of "word-painting" in "Die Lorelei" could be added many others. It would be surprising if the inventor of the symphonic poem, the leading advocate of program music, the composer who had always tried to bring words and music into closer alliance, had not left us numerous illustrations of music's power to enhance the texts of his songs. In fact, the Lieder provide a rich treasury of programmatic effects. In his setting of another of Heine's poems, "Im Rhein, im schönen Strome," Liszt's rippling accompaniment in the right hand suggests a flowing river. The key is E major, a sure sign that Liszt is in his religious mode.

---

15. PPL, p. 86.

16. The others include Goethe's "Mignons Lied" (1860); Lenau's "Die Drei Zigeuner" (1860), Hugo's "Jeanne d'Arc au bûcher" (1858, revised 1874); and three songs from Schiller's "Wilhelm Tell" (1855, revised 1872).

As we move down the Rhine, we understand why. The poet tells of seeing Cologne
Cathedral mirrored in the water. He is reminded that within this mighty structure
one can view a picture of Our Lady, painted on gilded leather, with "flowers and
angels floating around"—an image that draws from Liszt a fluttering of angels' wings
in the upper register of the piano.

Then comes the climax of the poem—and of Liszt's setting. The poet confides that
this painting of Our Lady, which has "cast such rays of light on the wilderness of his
life," reminds him of his beloved—"her eyes, her lips, her cheeks." This blasphemous
parallel between the purity of the Virgin Mary and the poet's own loved one with
its carnal connections, is typical of the agnostic Heine, and it gives Liszt pause. The
beating of the angels' wings ceases, and before the sacrilegious words are uttered he
ushers in two measures of erotic music, pianissimo, which move to opposite ends of
the keyboard, abruptly switching from G major to D minor. We call the effect
"erotic" because it is like the drawing aside of a veil, to disclose the poet's sensual
secret.

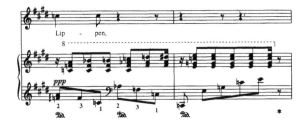

Incidentally, the first line of Heine's poem runs "Im Rhein, im heiligen Strome," a reference to "the holy river." Liszt changed that all-important phrase to, "Im Rhein, im schönen Strome," which refers to "the beautiful river." Was this deliberate, or did Liszt's memory play him false? It is almost as if the Catholic Liszt had decided to secularize the poem before allowing Heine to draw his profane connection.

In the spring of 1854 Liszt's Weimar circle was enlivened by the arrival of Heinrich Hoffmann von Fallersleben. A professor of philology at the University of Breslau, and a poet of standing, Fallersleben had been exiled from that city because of his revolutionary activities during the central European uprisings of 1849, and by the time he got to the city of Goethe and Schiller he was still being pursued by the police. Weimar offered him a hearth and a home, and the grand duke of Weimar granted him the protection of his realm, at the same time appointing him editor of the *Weimarisches Jahrbuch,* the official record of the cultural life of Weimar. But nowhere was he made more welcome than by Liszt at the Altenburg. He became an unofficial "poet in residence" there, writing plays and sketches for various celebrations (including some verses in celebration of Liszt's birthdays); he even wrote a poem in praise of The Altenburg itself. Liszt acted as godfather to Fallersleben's first child, who bore the name Franz in his honor. Four of Liszt's most attractive settings are of poems by Fallersleben: "Wie singt die Lerche schön," "In Liebeslust," "Lasst mich ruhen," and "Ich scheide."

It is not hard to hear the ascending lark in the left-hand accompaniment of Hoffman von Fallersleben's "Wie singt die Lerche schön," while the right hand provides the fluttering wings—an up-and-down motion characteristic of the lark's hovering in flight.

In "Lasst mich ruhen" the poet contemplates the joys and sorrows of bygone days, and seeks to assuage the pain of recollection by mingling them with memories of soft evening breezes, rustling leaves, the silver moon reflected in the brook's dark water, and the sound of the nightingale.

> Let me rest, let me dream
> Where the evening winds gently
> Rustle in the blossoming trees,
> Where the nightingale's song
> Pours out in leafy twilight.

At the fourth line we hear the nightingale come to life on the words *Nachtigallen Lieder,* starting with the slowly repeated G♯s in the right hand before developing into a full-fledged warble:

This fairly literal piece of word-painting is not obtrusive. Moreover, it contains a touch of autobiography. There were nightingales in Weimar's Grand Ducal Park, and Liszt sometimes went out of his way to listen to them. On one occasion he and a party of students ventured into the park well after midnight and listened in silent rapture to the songs of this nocturnal creature. As far as we know, the number of times that Liszt invites the nightingale into his music has not been catalogued. But it would certainly include the songs "Schwebe, schwebe, blaues Auge," "Die tote Nachtigall," the final page of the First *Mephisto* Waltz, his transcription of Alexander Alabieff's "The Nightingale," and the duet "O night of love, O starlit sky!" in the central episode of his paraphrase of Gounod's *Faust*.[17]

Far more subtle than this evocation of birdsong is Liszt's setting of the last stanza of Hoffmann von Fallersleben's poem, where the poet not only longs to rest, to dream and to listen to the nightingale, but to do so for evermore. On the word "Evermore!" which Liszt repeats no fewer than four times, his harmonies slowly drift away from the tonic key of E major, and within four measure they are dwelling in the remote world of G-sharp major, in which unusual key the song comes to rest. Is there a better way to depict eternity than to leave the listener suspended there?

A more profound example of word-painting occurs in his setting of Goethe's "Über allen Gipfeln," in which the poet begins by contemplating the peace that prevails over the mountain peaks. (Like "Lasst mich ruhen," it is set in Liszt's "religious" key of E major.) The poet goes on to remind us that one day soon we will likewise be at peace. As Liszt's final chords ascend slowly toward the rarified atmosphere of the mountain peaks, as it were, there is a brief shaft of sadness, on the entirely unexpected chord of G major (see ★ below), as if to afford a final glimpse of times now past, before everything finds repose on the home chord of E major.

17. The ornithological effect is not in Gounod's score; it is Liszt's idea. Liszt has moreover transposed the entire episode into A-flat major, his "key of love." Gounod's own keys for this music are G major and D-flat major, respectively.

Beguiled by Liszt and his Berlin recitals during the winter of 1841/42, the beautiful Bavarian actress Charlotte von Hagn on one occasion scribbled a poem, "Was Liebe sei," on the back of her fan, and handed it to Liszt.

> Poet! Do not hide from me what love might be!
> Love is the breath of the soul.
> Poet! Reveal what a kiss might be!
> The shorter it is, the greater the sin!"

These coquettish lines drew an appropriate response from Liszt in his playful accompaniment. We can hear the graceful swish of Charlotte's fan in the brief introduction, as she prepares to address the poet.

And at the conclusion of this brief song (at a mere twenty-five bars, it is one of the shortest compositions Liszt ever wrote[18]) there is a gentle outbreak of mirth at the keyboard, provoked by the chimerical thought that "the shorter the kiss, the greater the sin":

Long after Liszt had said goodbye to Charlotte, and after she herself was married, she paid him the best compliment he could receive about their brief encounter: "You have spoiled all other men for me. Nobody can stand the comparison."[19]

At the opening of Liszt's terse song "Und wir dachten der Toten" (a setting of words by Ferdinand Freiligrath) the piano slowly descends into the lower regions of

18. But not the shortest. The song "Einst" contains a mere 14 bars; another song "Und wir dachten der Toten," contains 23. "Preludio," the first of the *Transcendental Studies,* also contains 23. These and other examples prove that Liszt's reputation for long-windedness is not always deserved.

19. LLF, p. 113.

the keyboard in order to depict the singer's dark opening line, "And then came the
night," leading to the words that give the piece its title: "And we thought of the dead."

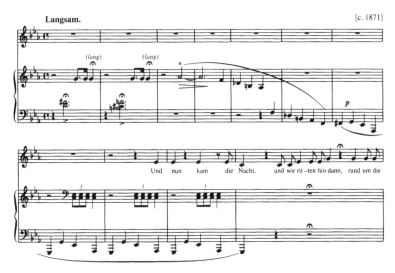

Liszt's setting of "Die Macht der Musik" (1848) would grace any lieder recital, but
it is hardly performed today. It was composed shortly after Liszt had settled in
Weimar to assume his full-time duties as its royal kapellmeister. Like so much of
Liszt's other music, it contains autobiographical allusions. The text is by Duchess Helene of Orléans, a relative of Grand Duke Carl Friedrich of Weimar. In 1848, after
the failed revolution in France, Helene, widow of Louis-Philippe's heir and mother
of the pretender to the French throne, had become an exile, and she now lived under Carl Friedrich's protection in Eisenach Castle. Appropriately, Liszt dedicated the
song to Carl Friedrich's wife, the Grand Duchess Maria Pawlowna, his greatest supporter in Weimar and the person in whom he had invested most of his hopes for
the development of music in that city. Such a gift, with such a title, would surely
have appealed to the music-loving Maria Pawlowna. The subject is one to delight
the heart of any composer, since it apotheosizes the art of music itself. At the climax of the song, where the words "Music, Thou Mighty Music" put in an appearance, Liszt moves back and forth between G major and E-flat major, as if rejoicing
in music's majesty and its power to transfigure humanity:

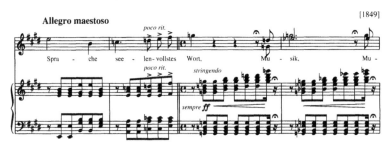

VII

Because Liszt had handpicked his Weimar singers for their musical intelligence, he felt free to make unusual demands on them. In general the songs are characterized by an unparalleled freedom of the vocal line, which often unfolds across an advanced harmonic texture on the piano. Moreover, Liszt's penchant for plunging back and forth from one extreme key to another means that his melodies are often fraught with enharmonic subtleties. It is one thing to employ the technique on the piano, where the player simply manipulates a keyboard; it is quite another to employ it through the human voice, where those same pitches have to be created by throat and larynx. A good example occurs in the setting of Heine's "Vergiftet sind meine Lieder" (My songs are poisoned), where the singer is asked to approach a high F♮ and quit it as an E♯.

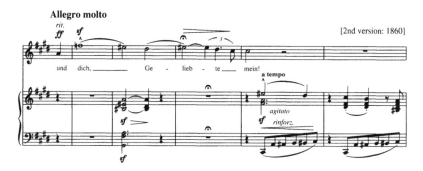

Liszt often asked his singers to "color" their voices where the poem required it. Scattered throughout his manuscripts are such unusual imperatives as *fast gesprochen* (almost spoken), *mit halber Stimme* (with a half voice), *geheimnisvoll* (mysterious), *phlegmatisch* (dull or heavy), and *hinträumend* (daydreaming).

And he could also be demanding in the use of the full range of the voice. In his setting of "Der alte Vagabund" Liszt calls for a bass singer with this wide compass:

This taxing song concludes with an almost impossible instruction for a low E♮, sung *fortìssimo,* with a crescendo at the end.

In the hands of Liszt, the use of the piano in the Lied underwent a profound transformation. It is perfectly natural that from time to time the "King of Pianists" would want to cast off the subservient role of mere provider of "sounding wallpaper," and indulge in an occasional outbreak of virtuosity. The accompaniment to "Die Drei Zigeuner," for example, requires a pianist who has a more than passing acquaintance with the *Hungarian Rhapsodies.* As for Liszt's setting of Schiller's "Der Fischerknabe," it could well be described as a piano concerto with vocal obbligato. Perhaps one reason why this fine song is neglected is that accompanists of transcendent power are still in short supply.

VIII

There are two other qualities connected to Liszt's songs worth mentioning here. Not the least remarkable thing about them is the speed with which some of them were composed—often within the space of two or three hours. Thus the first version of "Freudvoll und leidvoll" bears the inscription "composed June 25, 1844"; "Kling leise, mein Lied"—"composed March 30, 1848"; and "Es muss ein Wunderbares sein"—"composed July 13, 1852." Liszt tended to work quickly as a matter of course. But there are few better examples of his moving with somnambulistic certainty toward his goal.[20] The other quality is brevity. Liszt's reputation for long-windedness—especially in some of the orchestral works—has already been remarked. But the songs show that he could be direct, concise, and economical. All these points are nicely illustrated in his setting of Heine's "Vergiftet sind meine Lieder," which lasts about one and a half minutes, and comes across with the force of an aphorism.

By the end of the 1850s Liszt had accumulated a large portfolio of songs. Some were revisions from earlier years; others were new and had never been published before. All had been tested in performance, however. His correspondence makes clear that he now began to harbor the desire to publish them in a "Collected Edition," but he also expressed some anxiety in this regard. He wrote to his disciple Franz Brendel, who was now the editor of Schumann's old magazine the *Neue Zeitschrift für Musik,* asking for advice about possible publishers: "It is of great consequence to me not to delay any longer the publication of my 'Gesammelte Lieder.' Forgive me, therefore, if today I am somewhat troublesome to your friendship." To which he added these defensive lines: "The songs can hold their ground in their present form (regardless of the inevitable criticism of our obstinate and biting opponents!); and if a few singers could be found, not of the *raw* and *superficial* kind, who would boldly venture to sing songs by the notorious *noncomposer* Franz Liszt, they would probably find a public for them."[21]

Liszt's nervousness about how the songs might be received can only be understood within the wider context of the "War of the Romantics," a struggle which had been raging throughout the 1850s, with Liszt at its centre. On one side were the forces of conservatism based in Leipzig and Vienna, represented by the music of Mendelssohn, Schumann, and later of Brahms. Their spokesman was the powerful critic Eduard Hanslick, who dealt out death and destruction in the columns of the *Neue Freie Presse* in Vienna. Ranged against them was the music of Liszt and Wagner, and of their various disciples, representing the avant-garde. Their spokesman was Franz Brendel, who had turned the *Neue Zeitschrift für Musik* into a mouthpiece for

---

20. On the day he composed his setting of Hoffmann von Fallersleben's "Ich Scheide" (May 27, 1860) he tore up several versions in the search for the one that eluded him. He told Princess Carolyne, "I did three or four different versions, torn up one after the other—and, tired out with the struggle, I finished it last night" (LLB, vol. 5, p. 8).

21. LLB, vol. 1, pp. 343–44.

the New German school, centered in Weimar. By 1859 the "War" had assumed European dimensions, and Liszt was mired in controversy.

Brendel suggested that C. F. Kahnt would be the best publisher for the songs, and Liszt was delighted at the prospect.[22] Kahnt himself traveled to Weimar in the early part of 1860 in order to resolve some contractual problems (which included acquiring the rights to some of the earlier songs from the publisher Schlesinger). Later that year the *Gesammelte Lieder* appeared; Liszt's letters reflected the uneasiness he felt for their well-being, letters that contain his tongue-in-cheek references to "that notorious *noncomposer* Franz Liszt"—a phrase so frequently thrown at him by his critics that he now wore it as a badge of pride.

IX

The songs were now published. But another anxiety returned to haunt Liszt. He became concerned lest they fall into the hands of inexperienced arrangers, the sort of people commissioned by publishers to churn out instant piano reductions, whose sole purpose was to make the songs themselves popular and turn a profit—a common enough practice at that time. Since Liszt could not bear the thought of being confronted with inferior versions of music to which he was deeply attached ("it would not be pleasant to me if any really too-stupid arrangements should come out"[23]) he begged to be allowed to re-issue some of his own earlier concert arrangements and also to undertake some new ones. That is how we come to have two volumes of piano pieces entitled *Buch der Lieder für Piano allein,* although only the first one was published during Liszt's lifetime, in 1843; it was reissued in 1862. Its contents are as follows:

"Die Lorelei"

"Am Rhein im schönen Strome"

"Mignons Lied"

"Der König von Thule"

"Der du von dem Himmel bist"

"Angiolin del biondo crin"[24]

Ever since their first appearance, these six arrangements have created a paradox. Instead of popularizing the songs, they themselves have endured almost constant ne-

22. Kahnt was Brendel's employer. Since 1854 he had been the publisher of the *Neue Zeitschrift für Musik,* so it made perfect sense for Brendel to recommend that Kahnt become the publisher of Liszt's songs.

23. LLB, vol. 1, p. 350.

24. These six transcriptions "for piano alone" follow the running order given in Liszt's *Buch der Lieder,* the songs originally published in Berlin by Schlesinger, in 1843.

glect. That fact is almost more difficult to explain than the cloud of obscurity that had descended on the songs themselves, a cloud these arrangements were meant to dispel. For there are some stunning solo piano pieces here, worthy of a place in any modern piano recital. The arrangements of "Die Lorelei," "Mignons Lied," and "Am Rhein" reveal Liszt at the peak of his form in a genre he had long since made his own. Rather like the piano arrangements of the three *Sonetti del Petrarca,* or the three *Liebesträume,* which also started out as songs, their craftsmanship is so superior that the ear is deluded into believing them to be original compositions, born at the piano keyboard.

As for the recently published second *Buch der Lieder für Piano allein,* the contents are:

"Oh, quand je dors"

"Comment disaient-ils"

"Enfant, si j'étais roi"

"S'il est un charmant gazon

"La tombe et la Rose"

"Gastibelza"

The generally accepted view today is that Liszt worked on the manuscripts of this second set of transcriptions during his three-month sojourn in Woronince, in the winter of 1847–48. Everything was finished save the directions for performance and the insertion of marks of expression. Liszt then took the manuscripts to Weimar with him, but further work was shelved. They were not published until 1985.

X

Liszt put the best of himself into his songs. That they failed to make their way into the standard repertoire during his lifetime was among his major disappointments. It would cause him no surprise to learn that they are still underrated today—although there are signs that this is about to change. Liszt used to hide his frustration behind a shield of irony and wry humor, a usual defense with him. In May 1877, for example, the annual festival of the Tonkünstler-Versammlung was held in Hanover, and a number of Liszt's compositions were played, including a rare recital of his songs—"Die Lorelei" and "Es muss ein Wunderbares sein" among them. The event was an unexpected success and Liszt, tongue in cheek, indulged in some wordplay in a letter to Princess Carolyne: "*Die Lorelei*'s little triumph has been surpassed by that of the song: *Es muss ein Wunderbares sein* [It must be a miracle] . . . Since then, fashion has had a hand in it—and crowds of singers imagine *dass es ein Wunderbares sein müsste* [that it must have been a miracle] because of their talents and personalities!"[25]

Liszt's ironic allusion to himself as "that notorious *noncomposer* Franz Liszt" reminds us that he was well aware that his contemporaries never quite forgave him for giving up the concert platform in favor of composing. Saint-Saëns, an early admirer, put it best of all when he declared, "The world persisted to the end in calling him the greatest pianist in order to avoid the trouble of considering his claims as one of the most remarkable of composers."[26] Posterity has slowly come to agree with that verdict, for the songs add luster to Liszt's reputation whenever they are sung.

25. LLB, vol. 7, p. 191.
26. SHM, p. 155.

Liszt as Editor

The Urtext? Yes, it is very important. But the "Urspirit"
is still more important for a true interpretation.
DINU LIPATTI[1]

I

We do not readily think of Liszt as an editor. Yet during the course of his long life
he brought out editions of Beethoven, Bach, Chopin, Weber, Schubert, John Field,
and others. They are rarely remembered today, not even by specialists, in part because they preceded the early music movement with its insistence on urtexts. The
romantic excess that often attached itself to this kind of work aroused suspicion. Yet
Liszt's editions are models of their kind. His fingerings and pedalings should not be
beneath any pianist's while to consider. As to what he sometimes charmingly called
his "variants," they offer a treasure trove of insights, not only into the compositions
themselves, but also into the topography of the keyboard and Liszt's mastery of it.
Ultimately, the chief value of these editions may be what they have to tell us about
the way in which Liszt himself played this repertory. In brief, they offer that most
instructive of opportunities: a glimpse of one great musical mind coming to terms
with another.

Liszt did not have the luxury of consulting autographs. He worked mainly from
first editions. Both Sigmund Lebert and Breitkopf (two of the publishers for whom
he undertook editorial work) sent him printed scores, on which he made his editorial emendations. The impulse to make them sprang from two sources: first, from
the experience of having played this music across a period of many years, often under the stress of concert conditions; secondly, from the requirements of the modern
piano, which was, after the 1850s, an altogether different instrument from the one
used by Weber, Beethoven, and Schubert, and even by Liszt himself during his hey
day as a performer.

"Performance practice" is a relatively new discipline—so new, in fact, that at present it means only one thing: the reproduction of music's sonic surface in accordance with conditions that prevailed at the time of its composition. But with the

---

1. BTDL, p. 147.

Romantic revival, we are already witnessing the first quibbles over this constricting definition. How did the nineteenth century itself play the music of the eighteenth? Indeed, how did it play its own music? These, too, are valid questions for the twenty-first century to consider.

II

Liszt's celebrated edition of Beethoven's thirty-two piano sonatas first appeared in 1857. It was commissioned by the publisher Ludwig Holle, of Wolfenbüttel, who wrote a fulsome introduction in praise of Liszt's interpretations of these works. Liszt's lifelong championship of Beethoven was by then well known. During his years as a touring virtuoso he had often included the composer's sonatas, and some of the sets of variations, in his recital programs. He had championed the *Hammerklavier* Sonata at a time when the work was regarded as "difficult," even "unplayable." He himself tells us that he had played this Olympian composition from the age of ten, "doubtless very badly, but with passion—without anyone being able to guide me in it. My father lacked the experience to do it, and Czerny feared confronting me with such a challenge."[2] In 1845, as we have seen, Liszt was the central figure in the Beethoven celebrations in the city of Bonn that marked the seventy-fifth anniversary of the composer's birth.[3] Even before his permanent arrival in Weimar, in 1848, Liszt had begun to conduct Beethoven symphonies in public, and within weeks of picking up the baton as a part of his professional duties there, he had mounted a production of Beethoven's opera *Fidelio* at the Weimar Court Opera (March 21, 1848), to coincide with the revolutionary fervor and the struggles for individual freedom that were sweeping across Germany at that time. Liszt had a special affinity with the Ninth (*Chorale*) Symphony, and insisted on conducting it at some of the great German festivals at a time when the works of Beethoven's last period were generally regarded as incomprehensible. Later on, he would bring to completion his remarkable series of piano transcriptions of the nine symphonies, begun as early as 1837. In his music room in Weimar stood Beethoven's Broadwood grand piano and Beethoven's death mask, sacred relics which he had acquired during his concert tours and which he would eventually donate to the Hungarian nation.[4] It was in Weimar, too, that he began his famous masterclasses, in which Klindworth, Tausig, and above all Bülow were introduced to the Beethoven sonatas, and became the

2. LLB, vol. 7, p. 164.

3. See the essay "Liszt and the Beethoven Symphonies," pp. 14–15.

4. Beethoven's Broadwood grand piano, which dates from 1817, was presented to Liszt by the Viennese publisher Anton Spina, during a series of ten recitals Liszt gave in Vienna in 1846, as a mark of appreciation for all that Liszt had done in Beethoven's behalf. The Broadwood was the instrument on which Beethoven had composed his later keyboard music, including the last three sonatas. It has six octaves, running from ⸜⸜⸜c to c‴, and was within arm's reach, so to speak, as Liszt worked on his Beethoven edition. The instrument is today on display at the Hungarian National Museum, Budapest. As for the death mask, that had been given to Liszt as early as 1840 by the painter Joseph Danhauser, who had himself taken the impression of Beethoven's features at the master's deathbed.

beneficiaries of Liszt's interpretations. Enshrined within Bülow's own edition of the sonatas are many of Liszt's ideas, and it remains one of the best sources for knowing how he may have played these pieces. Liszt's credentials as a Beethoven specialist, then, were beyond reproach.

Time and again Liszt's pupils observed the special regard he had for Beethoven's music. He was always more exacting with Beethoven than he was with the music of other composers, including his own. He attached particular importance to the correct tempo and frowned on any interpretation that sacrificed detail on the altar of speed. In May 1882 his Dutch student Henryk van Zeyl brought the *Waldstein* Sonata to the Weimar masterclass and was reprimanded for starting the Finale too fast.[5] Liszt's chief concern with this movement was to moderate the tempo so that later on, when the player arrived at the fast left-hand scales against the right-hand trills, they could be played with clarity (mm. 337–44). When Liszt himself sat down to play the opening, he "took the time quite measured," in Lachmund's telling phrase.[6]

The first thing we notice about Liszt's edition of the Beethoven sonatas is his reluctance to touch anything. This sets it apart from much of his other editorial work, and reflects the respect he felt whenever he was in Beethoven's presence, as it were. His suggested fingerings and pedalings are kept to a minimum; and the "variants," which are quite prodigal in the Schubert and Weber editions, are here almost non existent.

Almost but not quite. The ones that do exist are therefore bound to command attention. In the Largo of the Sonata in A Major, op. 2, no. 2, all the early editions notate measure 29 with the D-sharp on the first beat, whereas Liszt delays it until the second.

Largo

Was this a lapse on Liszt's part? His version is quite beautiful, and his interior voice-leading is logical because it anticipates what follows in the next measure. He may well have adopted this practice from his teacher Czerny, Beethoven's best-known pupil. The autograph manuscript is lost, so the question cannot be resolved with fi-

---

5. His fellow student Carl Lachmund, doubtless in consideration of such things, had nicknamed van Zeyl "the Flying Dutchman."

6. LL, p. 35. It is worth recalling that when Liszt conducted the Beethoven symphonies it was his leisurely tempi that attracted attention. The critic of the *Allgemeine Musikalische Zeitung*, J. C. Lobe, heard Liszt conduct three of the symphonies and wrote, "Liszt took the Beethoven symphonies mostly in a slower tempo than we heard them previously, and with surprising profit for their realization" (issue of March 6, 1844). The three symphonies in question appear to have been no. 3, in E-flat major (*Eroica*); no. 5, in C minor; and no. 6, in F major (*Pastorale*).

nality. Meanwhile, Liszt's reading has been copied by various subsequent editions, notably that of Paul Dukas.

In the first movement of the *Appassionata* Sonata, Liszt divides the tremolo figure at measure 202 into six quadruplets of sixteenth notes, something that runs contrary to Beethoven's autograph. Our informant is Bülow, who in his own edition refers with approval to Liszt's practice and offers it as an alternative to the urtext.

In the Finale of the E Major Sonata, op. 109, Liszt continues the pattern abandoned by Beethoven in measure 187, by taking the syncopated arpeggio all the way down to the reprise of the main theme. Without mentioning Liszt, Donald Tovey voices a mild reproach against this practice which, he says, denies to the note A "the opportunity of sharing with the trill the function of leading to the first note of the theme instead of completing the [arpeggio]."[7] This is an unusually esoteric observation from one of the twentieth century's Analysts-in-Chief, who has wisely instructed us elsewhere that what one cannot hear ought not to be admitted into evidence. It is the trill, in fulfillment of its long journey as it comes to rest on the G♯, that captures the ear's attention:

7. BCPS, vol. 3, p. 194.

The presence of Beethoven's Broadwood piano in his studio would have been a daily reminder to Liszt of its limited compass, and there are times when Liszt knowingly includes notes beyond the range of the instrument, implying that the composer himself would certainly have used them had they been available. In the first movement of the Sonata in D Major, op. 10, no. 3, at measure 103, Liszt continues the upward sequence that Beethoven was obliged to abandon because he had run out of notes. No one can call the results anachronistic, because they fit in perfectly with the musical context.

Another small, yet revealing, departure from the standard text occurs in the Finale of the D Major Sonata (*Pastorale*), at measure 71:

Liszt's version makes absolute melodic sense, because once again it preserves the voice-leading, unaccountably lost in Beethoven's text—indicated in small notes. In the Scherzo of this same sonata, incidentally, Liszt provides a metronome marking of ♩. = 92, one more proof that he favored somewhat slower tempi in Beethoven's faster movements than is usual today; while in the Finale itself he recommends ♩. = 84. This raises a large topic, as the following table shows.

Pastorale Sonata, op. 28

	Scherzo	Finale
Liszt	♩. = 92	♩. = 84
Brendel	♩. = 96	♩. = 76
Barenboim	♩. = 92	♩. = 84
Kempff	♩. = 100	♩. = 84
Schnabel	♩. = 100	♩. = 88

SONATEN

für das

PIANOFORTE SOLO

von

LUDWIG van BEETHOVEN.

Erste vollständige Gesammtausgabe

unter Revision

von

FRANZ LISZT.

I. Band,

enthaltend

die ersten 18 Sonaten, Oeuvre 2 bis 31.

Preis 2 Thlr. 28 Sgr.

Mit Beethoven's Portrait in Stahlstich.

WOLFENBÜTTEL,

Druck und Verlag von L. Holle.

The title page of Franz Liszt's edition of the Beethoven sonatas, 1857.

Among latter-day interpreters, Daniel Barenboim adheres exactly to Liszt's tempi—whether by accident or design. Schnabel is much faster; he takes the Scherzo at ♩. = 100 and the Finale at ♩. = 88. Brendel has it both ways, taking the Scherzo at a brisk ♩. = 96 and the Finale at a leisurely ♩. = 76. Kempff's performance of the Scherzo is as fast as Schnabel's, but his Finale is as moderate as Liszt's.

"The letter killeth, but the spirit giveth life." Liszt often fell back on this Biblical saying in the course of his teaching. It assumes peculiar force within the context of his Beethoven editions. After all, anyone who takes on the responsibility of examining Beethoven's texts, bar by bar, lives for extended periods in a world of minutiae where the Spirit stands in constant danger of being overshadowed by the Letter. During his lifetime Liszt saw the emergence of the "classical" pianist who played as if he had just entered the witness box to give evidence at trial, having first sworn to play "the text, the whole text, and nothing but the text." Liszt had no quarrel with the first two promises. It was the third one that gave him pause. He called such playing the "Pontius Pilate offense," where the artist metaphorically washes his hands in public of the music's interpretation, so to speak. He had no time for the denial of artistic individuality, which, as a matter of historical record, led straight to the Age of Anonymity which is everywhere upon us. On the other hand, he was equally aware of the dangers of self-indulgence, and upbraided his students if he detected it in them. He would surely have approved of Schnabel's celebrated dictum that "musical interpretation is a free walk across firm ground."

Perhaps the only thing worse than that free walk without the firm ground beneath it is the firm ground without the free walk above it. Finding a balance goes to the heart of musical interpretation. It lies at the center of all our disaffection with performers great and small. The notes are important, but they are not the piece—a paradox that is not sufficiently valued. How often have we witnessed performances in which the notes are all there but the piece is missing! And by the same token, we have all attended those miracles of interpretation where the piece comes vividly before us, despite the missing notes. There is a ghost in the machine, which it is the primary task of the interpreter to release.

There is some anecdotal evidence to inform us of the unique way in which Liszt executed certain passages when performing Beethoven. Bülow tells us that in the *Hammerklavier* Sonata, for example, it was Liszt's practice to play the climactic ending to the fugue in the following manner:

This is a spectacular departure from Beethoven's text (and from Liszt's, too, for that matter, because it nowhere appears in his edition), but before dismissing it the pianist should try it. It not only draws more power from the instrument at the very point where power is needed, but it also bestows clarity on the trills.

Liszt's affinity with the *Hammerklavier* Sonata, and especially with its great Adagio, has passed into legend. Those who witnessed his performance are agreed on one thing: he seemed to make the Adagio float above the keyboard, as if the music had become detached from the instrument and was no longer of this earth.[8] One of the best ear-witness descriptions comes from Count Albert Apponyi, who was present when Liszt played the work while on a visit to Wahnfried and the Bayreuth Festival, in 1876, a performance that overwhelmed Richard Wagner.

> "When the last bars of that mysterious work had died away, we stood silent and motionless. Suddenly, from the gallery on the first floor, there came a tremendous uproar, and Richard Wagner in his nightshirt came thundering, rather than running, down the stairs. He flung his arms round Liszt's neck and, sobbing with emotion, thanked him in broken phrases for the wonderful gift he had received. His bedroom led onto the inner gallery, and he had apparently crept out in silence on hearing the first notes and remained there without giving a sign of his presence. Once more, I witnessed the meeting of these three—Beethoven, the great deceased master, and the two best qualified of all living men to guard his tradition. This experience still lives within me, and has confirmed and deepened my innermost conviction that those three great men belonged to one another."[9]

Liszt's metronome marking of the Adagio, incidentally, is $\eighth = 84$. Schnabel's edition, on the other hand, recommends $\eighth = 92$. That is a vast difference for music of such gravity, which can add several minutes to the total length. (In his recording of this movement, Schnabel does not follow his own advice but opts for Liszt's slower tempo.) Felix Weingartner, in his notable arrangement of this sonata for string orchestra, gives a metronome marking of $\eighth = 80$. At this pace the movement lasts for twenty minutes or more (it is one of the longest slow movements in the classical repertory, unfolding a full-fledged sonata form), and there is no doubt that Weingartner's and Liszt's preference for a slower tempo carries with it some real dangers. Tovey even suggests that Weingartner's tempo is about as fast as the movement can

8. "How it hovers! How detached it is from the world!" (LL, p. 164.)
9. AAM, p. 101.

bear without losing detail, and he too opts for ♪ = 80 in his own edition. (Evidently he remained unaware of Liszt's and Bülow's faster tempi.) We recall that Weingartner, like Bülow, was a pupil of Liszt and had heard the master play this movement. By an interesting coincidence, Schnabel's much faster tempo of ♪ = 92 agrees exactly with Bülow's edition. In a footnote, however, Bülow makes the intriguing point that the tempo may be taken slower "on very sonorous pianos." Was he recollecting a comment of Liszt's? In any case his remark opens up a neglected topic. How many pianists have the courage to let their piano determine the tempo of their piece? For the rest, "the greater the sonority the slower the tempo" is a maxim that has much to commend it.

The following table summarizes the wide variety of tempi that has emerged since Liszt's day. It is instructive to compare his recommended metronome marking of ♪ = 84 with that of some of his distinguished successors—both editors and performers.

Franz Liszt ♪ = 84

Hans von Bülow ♪ = 92

Artur Schnabel ♪ = 92

Felix Weingartner ♪ = 80

Donald Tovey ♪ = 80

Wilhelm Kempff ♪ = 70

Solomon ♪ = 60

Sviatislav Richter ♪ = 60

One noteworthy feature in Liszt's edition is his attempt to identify all the major themes by attaching rehearsal letters to them. The practice may be one of the first attempts to provide some insight into the structure of these sonatas, many of which (especially the later ones) were regarded as problematic in Liszt's time. His method is primitive by modern standards, but it helps us to know what Liszt regarded as the main junctures of the form.

At Ludwig Holle's further invitation, Liszt went on to edit nine volumes of *Selected Works* by Beethoven. Although his name appears on every volume, the extent of his personal involvement is presently under review. We know, however, that he was directly responsible for the piano quartets, and most likely for the sonatas for violin and piano as well. As usual, his insights into this music came from playing it, particularly during his Weimar years at the matinees held in the Altenburg—with Joachim, Eduard Reményi, and members of the Weimar String Quartet often taking part.[10] Later on, he was also to arrange the last three piano concertos for two

---

10. The diary of Liszt's American pupil, William Mason, informs us about these Altenburg matinees. On May 1, 1853, for instance, Liszt played Beethoven's A Major Sonata (the *Kreutzer*) with Henryk Wieniawski, and on May 20 Liszt attended the performance of one of the Beethoven quartets, with Joachim playing first violin (MMML, pp. 122–25).

pianos, and provide cadenzas for them. They were published by the firm of J. W. Cotta in 1879.

III

In 1868 Liszt was approached by Sigmund Lebert[11] to take on the task of editing a selection of piano pieces by Weber and Schubert for inclusion in a so-called Instructive Edition of classical composers. Lebert was a cofounder of the Stuttgart Conservatory and well known for his *Grosse Klavierschule,* published in collaboration with his colleague Ludwig Stark. The proposed Instructive Edition, like the *Klavierschule* itself, was to be published by J. W. Cotta of Stuttgart, and was intended for the use of students enrolled at the conservatories of Vienna and Stuttgart, and the Neue Akademie der Tonkunst in Berlin.[12] Liszt was more than ready to accept this assignment, not for the money and certainly not for recognition, but rather because he had played the piano music of Schubert and Weber since his youth and was deeply attached to it. Among Liszt's first recommendations for works to be included in the Instructive Edition were Weber's "Concertstück," the ever-popular "Invitation to the Dance," the "Momento capriccioso," the four sonatas, and two polonaises. For the Schubert selections he recommended the impromptus, the C Major Fantasie, the Moments musicaux, a selection of the sonatas, and a volume of waltzes and Ländler.

In a letter to Lebert,[13] Liszt made his editorial principles clear:

1. "fully and carefully to retain the original text together with tentative indications of *my* way of rendering it, by means of *distinguishing* letters, notes and signs;

2. "the *variant readings* to be printed in small notes throughout the whole edition."

These two principles immediately set Liszt apart from the vast majority of his contemporaries. The respect with which he approached the printed text, and his insistence that his own performing directions be set in relief, in a different typeface, are twin ideals still followed by scholars today.

By early January 1870, Liszt had dispatched to Lebert the proofs of his edition of

---

In later years Liszt often played with violinists Eduard Reményi and Heinrich Ernst. And in the last couple of years of his life he several times played Beethoven's Sonata in F Major (the *Spring*) with his young American follower Arma Senkrah.

11. Lebert (1822–1884) was a well-known pianist and a co-founder of the Stuttgart Conservatory of Music.

12. The other editors of the Instructive Edition were Immanuel Faisst, Ignaz Lachner, and Hans von Bülow, who was offered the task of editing the Beethoven sonatas, an edition to which we have already alluded.

13. LLB, vol. 2, p. 129–30; dated "Rome, October 19, 1868."

the Weber and Schubert sonatas. His covering letter makes clear the care with which he had approached his labor of love:

> My endeavor with this work is to avoid all quibbling and pretentiousness, and to make the edition a practical one for teachers and players. And for this reason at the very least I added a goodly amount of fingering and pedal marks; kindly get the printers to excuse this, and I trust that the trouble it causes will not prove unnecessary. With regard to the deceptive *Tempo rubato,* I have settled the matter provisionally in a brief note (in the finale of Weber's A-flat Major Sonata);[14] other occurrences of *rubato* may be left to the taste and spontaneous feeling of gifted players. A metronomical performance is certainly tiresome and nonsensical; time and rhythm must be adapted to and identified with the melody, the harmony, the accent and the poetry. . . . But how to indicate all this? I shudder at the thought of it.[15]

When the Schubert edition finally appeared, later that year, it contained an "Editorial Preface" which set forth the main principles that Liszt had earlier outlined in his letter to Lebert, and from which we have already quoted (see page 184). Liszt's personal tribute to Schubert, written at this time, must also be mentioned. It was not seen by the world until after Liszt's death, but explains his willingness to become involved in the sort of work that others might regard as humdrum. Liszt's powerful attachment to Schubert stands revealed in such lyrical thoughts as:

> Our pianists scarcely realize what a glorious treasure they have in Schubert's piano compositions. Most pianists play them over *en passant,* notice here and there repetitions, lengthiness, apparent carelessness . . . and then lay them aside. It is true that Schubert himself is somewhat to blame for the very unsatisfactory manner in which his admirable pianoforte pieces are treated. He was too immoderately productive, wrote incessantly, mixing insignificant with important things, grand things with mediocre work, paid no heed to criticism, and always soared on his wings. Like a bird in the air, he lived in music and sang in angelic fashion.
> O never-resting, ever-welling genius, full of tenderness!
> O my cherished Hero of the Heaven of Youth! Harmony, freshness, power, grace, dreamings, passion, soothings, tears and flames pour forth from the depths and heights of thy soul, and thou makest us almost forget the greatness of thine excellence in the fascination of thy spirit![16]

---

14. Liszt's note runs: "Die Bezeichnung '*Tempo rubato*' welche vor Chopin nicht gebräuchlich war, würde bei dieser und andren Stellen Weber's passen. Es bleibe dem Geschmeck und Affekt des Spielers überlassen das verführerische Tempo rubato richtig vorzutragen." (The indication "*Tempo rubato,*" which was not used before Chopin, would be suitable at these and other places. It is left to the taste and emotion of the player to deliver the seductive Tempo rubato correctly.)

15. LLB, vol. 2, p. 156; dated "Villa d'Este, January 10, 1870."

16. LLB, vol. 2, pp. 132–133; dated "Villa d'Este, December 2, 1868."

As scrupulous as the public preface is, with its respect for scholarly exactitude, and as moving as the private comments are, with their unabashed declarations of love for Schubert (addressed to him directly in the intimate form of speech), one still wonders, Where is the pianist today who would venture to play Liszt's bold rewriting of the recapitulation of Schubert's Impromptu in G-flat Major, op. 90? Liszt appears to have temporarily abandoned his role as editor and adopted the mantle of arranger. No pianist should dismiss the following passage without first considering it, however. It is quintessential Liszt. The relief it affords from Schubert's literal repetition of the main theme, however magical that theme may be, is wonderful; and it makes one almost regret that Schubert himself had not thought of it—the only condition on which our puritanical age would tolerate it.[17] As everyone knows, Schubert's publisher issued a transposed version of this impromptu in the simpler key of G major, which Liszt adopts for Lebert's Instructive Edition

17. Liszt's rewriting of the ending of the Finale of Chopin's Piano Sonata in B Minor falls into a somewhat similar category, although it was intended for purely private use. In all probability it was undertaken in 1868–69 for his Polish pupil Olga Janina, who owned this particular manuscript for a time. Robert Bory reproduced it in his "Chopin par l'image," p. 166 (Geneva, 1936). Doubtless it was such things that prompted Bartók to observe that "[Liszt] corrected and transcribed with brilliant additions masterpieces that not even a Liszt had any right to touch." Bartók intended the remark as a reprimand, but it is the phrase "brilliant additions" that lingers in the mind (SBB, p. 451).

The title page of Franz Liszt's edition of Schubert's Impromptus, op. 90, 1870.

The protest that this goes too far, that it harms the original, that it is akin to putting a mustache on the Mona Lisa, rests on a fallacy. If you place a moustache on the Mona Lisa something has indeed been permanently harmed. But if you re-arrange Schubert, nothing has been harmed at all. The original is still there, waiting to be played. And Liszt displays his alternative version quite openly.

A modification of a more modest kind occurs in the middle episode of the Impromptu in E-flat Major, op. 90. Again Liszt prints his alternative in smaller type above the Schubert original, so that the player may choose. On this occasion he has filled in with chords what he considers to be a "hole" of three octaves between the hands in measures 1 and 2:

As in his edition of the Weber sonatas, which we shall come to presently, Liszt's fingerings are engrossing. The following example of "finger substitution" looks provocative, but it is necessary if Schubert's legato line is to be preserved. Many pianists, fearing some permanent digital entanglements, would rely on "pedal down Schubert" at such places. But a study of Liszt's piano playing teaches us that he rarely called on the pedal to do the work of the fingers, but rather used it to color the work that the fingers do.

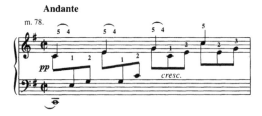

It was through Liszt's performances of Schubert's great Fantasie in C Major (the *Wanderer*) that the work was first brought to public attention. Few pianists before Liszt were even aware of its existence. During his halcyon years as a touring virtuoso, in the 1830s and 1840s, the work turns up frequently in his recital programs. Its unusual structure evidently made a deep impact on him. Schubert rolls the four contrasting movements of a complete sonata into one, and unifies the whole through the technique of "metamorphosis of themes." These are the very procedures that Liszt himself put to such effective use in his symphonic poems, and above all in his Sonata in B Minor, a connection to which we alluded previously (pp. 129–30). The *Wanderer Fantasie* can thus be said to be a model for much of his later work. After he had settled in Weimar he returned to Schubert's masterpiece and produced two highly individual arrangements, one for piano and orchestra and another for two pianos (both after 1851). The two-piano arrangement was often played with success by his pupils Tausig, Bülow, Hans von Bronsart, and Dionys Pruckner. Today it is all but forgotten.

This much background is necessary to explain the unusually large number of "variants" that Liszt proposes along the way. He was clearly in his element in this piece, and by the year 1870 he doubtless wanted to use his authority to remind young pianists of some of the startling things that he had done with it, thirty years earlier—among them the following, a way of producing a greater volume of sound at the climactic return of the main theme, bars 68–69:

It is our contention that not one in a hundred listeners would know that Schubert's texture had been modified at such points. They would know only that the player had succeeded in releasing more volume from the instrument at the very moment it is required.

At the beginning of the Adagio, Liszt addresses the player: "Meines Erachtens nach sollte dieser Satz sehr langsam, pathetisch, *ab imo pectore vorgetragen* werden." (In my opinion this movement should be delivered very slowly, with elevation, *and from the depths of the heart*.) Liszt writes these last words in Latin, as if to emphasize the dignity of their meaning.

For the Finale Liszt offers a completely reworked alternative. That is to say, his version is a bold metamorphosis of the entire last movement of the Fantasie. It is the only time as an editor that he allows himself to do such a thing. His rewriting takes the form largely of revised textures to secure greater "playability" from the instrument.

IV

We know that Liszt first came into contact with Weber's piano music as a child. According to contemporary reports, the ten-year-old boy actually gave a public performance of Weber's "Momento Capriccioso" at a concert in Pest on May 19, 1823, the details of which have been preserved in the Hungarian press.[18] This allows us to clear up a piece of misinformation still current in the literature. Liszt could not have been introduced to the piano music of Weber by Wilhelm von Lenz, as the latter claimed in his celebrated book *Die grossen Pianoforte-Virtuosen unserer Zeit*. Still, there is no reason to doubt Liszt's enthusiastic response to such pieces as the sonatas and the "Invitation to the Dance" when, in December 1828, Lenz showed them to the young virtuoso who was then in his eighteenth year. Lenz has told us how it came about.[19] He was on a visit to Paris from Russia in pursuit of higher piano studies with Kalkbrenner, when he abruptly took it into his head to visit Liszt, who lived at that time in an apartment he shared with his mother on the rue Montholon in the district of Montmartre. After some preliminary conversation with Anna Liszt, who told him that "her Franz was always in church and busied himself no more with music," Liszt himself entered the room. He was "a pale and haggard young man," Lenz tells us, with a smile "like the glitter of a dagger in the sunlight," who reclined on a sofa and smoked a long Turkish pipe. When he invited Lenz to play something, the latter took out of his briefcase the famous "Invitation to the Dance." (In those days, Lenz informs us slyly, all that the Parisians knew of Weber was the opera *Der Freischütz*, which they insisted on calling "Robin des Bois"!) Liszt was so delighted with the "Invitation" that he undertook to give lessons to Lenz for having introduced it to him. At the first lesson, a few days later, Liszt could not tear himself away from the piece. He repeated certain passages over and over, trying them out in a variety of different ways. This encounter with Weber's piano music was a revelation to him. "He was inexhaustible in his praise of Weber," wrote Lenz. Years later, as Lenz was reflecting on this early meeting with Liszt, he observed, "Imagine a genius like Liszt, not yet twenty years old, coming into contact for the first time with such a magnificent composition, with that apparition of this Knight in Golden Armor.[20] . . . How Liszt glorified Weber on the piano! How like an Alexander he marched in triumphant procession with Weber (especially in the "Concertstück") through Europe, and future times will speak of it."[21] And it was because those "future times" had already turned his performances into legend that Liszt in the 1870s found himself assuming the role of Weber's editor.

In the Sonata no. 1, in C Major, op. 24, there are some excellent examples of Liszt's "goodly amount of fingering and pedal marks." Especially absorbing are his fingerings of certain passages in the Adagio. Consider the care Liszt takes to secure a legato line in the right-hand octaves at measure 51:

18. *Tudományos Gyüjtemény*, vol. 7, 1823, pp. 122–23.
19. See LGPZ which contains a memoir by von Lenz of Liszt published forty-three years after the encounter took place.
20. LGPZ, p. 13.
21. LGPZ, p. 16.

The use of 5-4-3 as successive fingers on the black keys results in a perfectly natural hand position, and even though an octave stretch between first and third fingers is called for, it is not uncomfortable.

In this same sonata Liszt recommends altering the title of the Menuetto to what he calls a "better name," namely a Scherzo, which, as he points out in an editorial footnote, is not only in keeping with Weber's tempo marking of Allegro, but actually becomes mandatory if Liszt's own recommended tempo of Presto agitato be adopted.

The famous Presto Finale is a *perpetuum mobile,* which the composer himself nicknamed "L'infatigable." Weber, who was an outstanding pianist, often played the movement in C-sharp major as a warm-up exercise, a fact well known to Liszt and his contemporaries. Weber was, however, spared all knowledge of Brahms's difficult arrangement for the left hand, to say nothing of Henselt's still more formidable version, which is so overloaded with additional technical difficulties that it amounts to a pact with the Devil:

Incidentally, Liszt offers the following alternative to measures 115–18—

—not only because it is physically more secure, but because it sounds yet more powerful and brilliant than the original. We have to stress that Liszt is simply offering options, which are there to be rejected if the player does not wish to accept them. His many "variants," which were intended primarily for teachers and students in this Instructive Edition, are readily identifiable, and are invariably illuminating. He once explained such matters like this: "It seems to me that what may be more *literally* accurate ought often to give way to what sounds better and even to what is more convenient for the players at the piano."[22] Unlike many editors who came after him, Liszt did not make changes of the surreptitious kind for which the nineteenth century acquired such a bad reputation.[23]

Liszt's earlier question to Lebert, "But how to indicate all this?" comes vividly to mind in the sonata's Finale. In order to avoid a purely mechanical rendering of the *moto perpetuoso* he brings out the correct phrasing by the use of some nimble agogic accents. But because there is no recognized notation for an agogic accent, Liszt introduces the comma ('), knowing that because its meaning in literature is clear, its meaning in music will be clear as well:[24]

The player will not fail to note the special use of the pedal, which unexpectedly begins on the upbeat to bars 2 and 4, and not on the downbeat. The effect is subtle, its purpose being to help the right hand to pick up harmonic resonances it might otherwise lose.

Two other examples of Liszt's fingering call for comment. In the aforementioned Scherzo of the C Major Sonata, Liszt treats the player to a startlingly obvious solution to the following passage:

22. LLB, vol. 2, p. 302.

23. This practice reached a climax, of sorts, in the editorial work of Harold Bauer, who, to give a random example, cheerfully omitted entire sections of the Schubert Sonata in B-flat Major (op. posth.) without telling anyone.

24. Liszt's editorial note runs: "NB. Die Punkt (staccato) sind von Weber nicht bezeichnet; jedenfalls aber soll die Stelle scharf syncopirt und markirt werden, was nur durch Abstossung der letzten Noten der Figur und Aufhebung der Hand effectuiren" (The staccatos are not indicated by Weber. In any case, these places should be sharply syncopated and marked, something that can only be effected through the recoil of the last notes of the figure and the lifting of the hand).

"Obvious," that is, once it has been pointed out. And in the Rondo finale of the Sonata in D Minor, Liszt establishes a sequence of fingerings that is so fluent and natural that it gives the player the impression that it was always there, merely waiting for Weber to provide some notation to bring it into existence:

The first time that Liszt ever heard the great Sonata no. 2, in A-flat Major, op. 39 (which was regarded as Weber's pianistic masterwork during his lifetime) he was captivated by the originality of the opening.[25] No sonata had ever begun like this, with a tremolo in the bass, and the theme rising above it "like the sunrise over an enchanted forest." Liszt became restless and finally pushed von Lenz aside with the words, "Wait! Wait! What is that? I must try that for myself!"

As in the case of the "Invitation to the Dance," Liszt immediately began experimenting with different effects as the movement unfolded, and at the close of the exposition he observed, "It is marked *legato*. Yet would not one do it better *pp* and *staccato*? Now there is a *leggieramente* as well." [26] The A-flat Major Sonata demands fleet fingers and, in places, a wide stretch. Weber shows no mercy to pianists with small hands, to which the following passage bears witness. To help these unfortunates who might otherwise be discouraged from playing the sonata in public, Liszt puts his authority behind some eminently sensible alternatives, and rewrites the left hand thus:

25. During the second lesson he gave to von Lenz, in 1828.
26. LGPZ, pp. 13–14.

Likewise, in the Finale, Liszt recommends the following transformation of Weber's difficult left-hand texture:

No one can reasonably complain of such changes. It is very difficult to hear the difference in performance, and the feeling of physical security that Liszt once more gives the player, who might otherwise have to decline to play the piece, is a handsome bonus.

V

In 1879, the firm of Breitkopf and Härtel began publishing its *Complete Edition* of Chopin's works in fourteen volumes. Its distinguished editorial team consisted of the following musicians: Woldemar Bargiel, Johannes Brahms, Auguste Franchomme, Franz Liszt, Carl Reinecke, and Ernst Rudorff. The project was not brought to completion until 1902, by which time most of the editors were dead. It is unfortunate that Breitkopf did not see fit to disclose how the fourteen volumes had been distributed among these distinguished musicians. That simple oversight led to much speculation and, in the case of Liszt, some false deductions. Peter Raabe concluded that Liszt had edited the *Twenty-four Studies*, and he based that determination on a published letter of Liszt, dated September 26, 1877, in which the composer told Breitkopf that, given a choice, he would have liked to edit those pieces.[27] We now know that Liszt was not given a choice. The archival correspondence between Liszt and Breitkopf reveals that Breitkopf had already allocated the *Studies* to

27. LLB, vol. 2, p. 258.

Ernst Rudorff, so Liszt graciously yielded. He was allowed instead to fall back on the *Twenty-four Preludes,* op. 28. The full story is contained in a series of little-known letters from the Breitkopf archives kept in the Hochschulbibliothek in Darmstadt, and published for the first time in 1997.[28]

The inclusion of Rudorff on the editorial team was especially perverse, but for reasons that have nothing to do with his displacement of Liszt as the editor of the *Studies.* According to Leopold Godowsky, who worked with him briefly, Rudorff had a low opinion of Chopin generally, and dismissed him as a drawing-room composer—a type of Chaminade. "Think of it!" Godowsky burst out in exasperation, as he contemplated such a comparison. As a youth Godowsky had prepared the Scherzo in B-flat Minor for Rudorff, but the latter had refused to hear it, dismissing the work as salon music ("Have you nothing else to play?"), a view that was widespread in Germany at the turn of the century.[29] How Liszt would have reveled in Godowsky's *Fifty-three Studies on Chopin's Etudes,* which takes piano technique to a new level, just as Liszt's own *Transcendental Studies* had taken it a century earlier.

Liszt had never really wanted to be on the editorial team of a Chopin project, and he accepted Breitkopf's invitation with reluctance. He had already refused a similar invitation from Schlesinger in 1875, and he now expressed some reservations to Breitkopf as well. There were two reasons for his disinclination. First, he told Breitkopf that the ongoing complete edition of Chopin's music by his former pupil Karl Klindworth (begun in 1873, in Moscow) rendered a second attempt superfluous. Liszt had a high opinion of this edition. He kept a copy in his Budapest library, and his annotations show that he had studied it with care. He even urged Breitkopf to include Klindworth on the editorial team, in view of the latter's vast experience, but the request fell upon deaf ears. The second reason was still more relevant. In a further letter to Breitkopf, Liszt made the interesting point that "little really remains

---

28. See Mária Eckhardt's groundbreaking essay, "Liszt's Contributions to the Breitkopf Chopin Edition," in SDNL, pp. 167–80.

29. NG, p. 16. Ernst Rudorff, a former student of Ignaz Moscheles at the Leipzig Conservatory of Music, was at the time of the Breitkopf enterprise a well-known professor at the Berlin Hochschule für Musik, and personally opposed to Liszt. It will not have escaped attention that most of the other musicians on the editorial team were opposed to Liszt as well, together with his championship of modern music. They tended to be associated with the conservative movement, centered around the Leipzig Conservatory, which for years had stood in opposition to radical Weimar and Liszt. Brahms's antagonism toward Liszt was by now well established. As for Woldemar Bargiel, he was a product of the conservatory, the son of Friedrich Wieck's ex-wife Marianne Tromlitz, and the stepbrother of Clara Schumann, all of whom (whatever they thought of one another) were solidly united in their dislike of Liszt. But this was especially the case with Rudorff, who now made a profession in Berlin of instructing his students in the ways of the traditional masters, strongly advising them against playing the music of Liszt and his followers whom he regarded as "poseurs." (See the article on Rudorff by Imogen Fellinger, in MGG, vol. 11, p. 1063.) The Berlin Hochschule für Musik eventually imposed a ban on the performance of Liszt's works by its students. As for the city of Leipzig, the home of Breitkopf and Härtel, it happened to be the place that had handed Liszt several defeats in the course of his musical career. We assume that Liszt's name on the title page was required by Breitkopf more for purposes of window dressing than anything else. Brahms and Rudorff did the lion's share of the work. For a complete distribution of the editing, see Margit L. McCorkle, *Johannes Brahms: Thematisch-Bibliographisches Werkverzeichnis,* Munich, 1984, p. 750.

to be done to Chopin's compositions, as he himself, with praiseworthy and exceptional accuracy, added every possible instruction to the performer—even to the
pedal indications, which in no other composer appear so frequently."[30]

Liszt's desire to edit the *Studies* was an obvious one, and it still causes surprise that
Breitkopf would have frustrated him. After all, the first book of *Twelve Studies,* op.
10, was dedicated to Liszt; while the second book of *Twelve Studies,* op. 25, was dedicated to Countess Marie d'Agoult, his longtime companion and mother of his three
children. We also know that Liszt's performances of these difficult pieces had aroused
Chopin's admiration in the earlier years of their friendship, and that Chopin had
once famously written, "I should like to rob [Liszt] of the way to play my own studies."[31] We earlier observed that Liszt was unable to consult autographs. Breitkopf
well understood their value, however, and the firm made a valiant attempt to re-
trieve as many of the holographs as possible from Chopin's sister Izabela Barcińska
in Warsaw, including the Preludes for Liszt.[32] The correspondence shows that he
was unsuccessful, and Liszt's own efforts to procure a manuscript source through the
good offices of the Polish composer Józef Wieniawski (who was the brother of the
famous violinist Henryk, and had been a pupil of Liszt in the 1850s in Weimar) also
failed;[33] so Liszt worked from various published scores, including Klindworth's.[34]
Liszt's offer to edit the *Preludes* was made on September 6, 1877, while he was staying at the Villa d'Este, in Tivoli, and that is where he began work on them, later taking them to Rome and to Budapest as he pursued his busy itinerary. It is a quixotic
thought, but at this very period he was also bringing simultaneously to fruition some
of his Villa d'Este pieces, including "Aux Cyprès de la Villa d'Este" and "Les Jeux
d'eaux à la Villa d'Este," which are far removed in spirit from anything that Chopin
composed.[35] On December 20, 1877, Liszt was able to inform Breitkopf that he had
already finished his task. It had taken him three and half months. Breitkopf later sent

---

30. LLB, vol. 2, p. 258.

31. Letter to Ferdinand Hiller; dated Paris, June 20, 1833 (HSC, p. 117). In explaining why he had
wanted to edit the *Studies,* Liszt told Breitkopf, "I chose the Etudes because the first volume was dedicated to me," and then he added the revealing comment, "and the second one too for that matter (at that
time)" (LLB, vol. 2, p. 258). This chance remark helps to clear up a small mystery. It has long been ru-
mored that Marie d'Agoult was not Chopin's first choice of dedicatee for op. 25, but that he had placed
her name on the title page after having had a tiff with Liszt. Liszt and Marie d'Agoult were at that time
(1837) languishing with George Sand at Sand's country house at Nohant, and Sand herself was about to
embark on her much-publicized affair with Chopin. The complex relations among this quartet of lovers,
marked as they were by much turbulence, are of small concern and Liszt does not mention them. What
matters is that Liszt here provides us with documentary evidence of something long suspected: namely,
that Chopin had originally intended to dedicate the entire set of *Twenty-four Studies* to his great contemporary, and had then changed his mind.

32. The letter is dated February 1, 1878. See SDNL, p. 172.

33. SDNL, pp. 173–74.

34. The editions that Liszt had at his disposal in 1878 were: the first French edition of Adolphe Catelin,
Paris 1839; the first German edition of Breitkopf and Härtel, Leipzig, 1839; the first English edition of
Christian Wessel, London 1840; and of course Klindworth's edition of 1873, the most recent to appear.

35. Although it is a commonplace of music criticism to read that Chopin's influence on Liszt's piano
writing was fundamental, it is nowhere to be found in these pieces.

him his editor's honorarium. It was entirely typical of Liszt that he returned it, with good wishes for the future of the Chopin project.[36]

What youthful memories would have stirred in Liszt as he turned the pages of these pieces! He had often played Chopin's music during his heyday as a touring virtuoso. And although he had long since retired from the concert platform, his pupils continued to bring a lot of Chopin to the masterclasses in Weimar, Rome, and Budapest. Carl Lachmund reports that in the summer of 1883, when Liszt was in his seventy-second year, a young female pupil (whom he fails to identify) brought some of the *Preludes* to the Weimar masterclass. When she arrived at the one in G major she played it like a Czerny etude.

Liszt gently pushed her from the chair and played it himself:

> Charmingly he subdued the murmuring runs in the left hand—and how beautifully the melody sang out in the right! The pupil's face brightened; she had learned. But Liszt, with a roguish look in his eyes, now played part of it again, mimicking the way she had played it. All laughed and learned yet more. Not yet satisfied with his object lesson, he played parts of several other of the preludes, and played them as only Liszt could play them. Arising from the chair he said: "There are more musical thoughts in these preludes than in many symphonies of the present-day kapellmeister composers."[37]

We do not know which edition the pupil brought to the class. But unlike some of the editions of the day, Liszt calls for alla breve time, and it unwittingly restores Chopin's own direction in the autograph that Liszt never saw. This particular prelude is treacherous enough, but the Alla breve requirement makes it more hazardous still.

Liszt liked the F-sharp Minor Prelude (marked Molto agitato) to move slowly

36. SDNL, p. 175. Liszt's generosity, as Eckhardt points out, placed Barcińska in an unfortunate light. She had done nothing for the project, and for several months had not answered a single letter sent to her by Breitkopf. Then suddenly she inquired about her own honorarium. Breitkopf informed her that she was not entitled to anything (SDNL, p. 175).

37. LL, pp. 211–12.

enough to make audible the myriad details of the right hand. When his pupil Elsa Sonntag played it for him (on June 13, 1884) she took it so fast that he told her that the resulting swirl sounded like rinsing out the mouth and brushing the teeth. He also insisted that the accompanying left-hand triplets ought likewise to be audible.[38]

A particular favorite of Liszt's was the Prelude in E Major, which, according to Lachmund, "touched deep chords in his heart." Arthur Friedheim once brought some of the *Preludes* to the masterclass, and when he came to this one Liszt stopped him and said, "I will play this."

> As he came to the last measure [Lachmund wrote] he looked away from the music and began to improvise, enlarging on the grand theme in the form of a transcription to the extent of three times its length, or more. This time it was serious; he soared like an eagle; it was glorious! With it all, there was no effort, no hesitation; sometimes he looked about the room or at us. Once more . . . we could rejoice in saying; "I have heard Liszt improvise!"[39]

The thought of Liszt improvising on a Chopin prelude may not win him many friends as an editor of that music. Yet an inspection of Liszt's edition, as in the case of the Beethoven sonatas, reveals scarcely any departures from Chopin's text. For that very reason the ones that remain arouse our curiosity. Only in the C Major Pre-

38. GLK, June 13, 1884.
39. LL, pp. 147–48.

lude do we find ourselves in rare disagreement with Liszt for having corrected Chopin's highly individual, seemingly "inconsistent" notation. Liszt prefers to continue the metrical pattern of right-hand triplets established by Chopin in the very first bar, and he relegates to an *ossia* Chopin's abrupt switch to quintuplets, which he prints in small notes above the main text (see m. 18 and elsewhere).

But Chopin's quintuplets serve a highly expressive purpose: they are the only measures in which both hands strike the main beat simultaneously. In all the others the right hand begins with a sixteenth-note rest, "an intake of breath" so to say. That rest was, perhaps, Chopin's attempt to notate an agogic accent, and the expressive contrast with his quintuplets is striking. Chopin's autograph is beautifully clear on this point, and leaves no doubt as to his intentions. As a matter of fact, it shows that the quintuplets were an afterthought on Chopin's part, an integral part of his creative intentions: the sixteenth-note rests that were originally in place have been vigorously struck out by him. If Liszt had been able to consult the autograph, he would surely have retained Chopin's notation intact, to say nothing of his opening dynamic marking of *mezzo forte,* for which Liszt has substituted *forte.*

Among Liszt's other rare changes to Chopin's notation, the solitary one that he introduces into the F-sharp Major Prelude also calls for comment. All the editions that Liszt had at his disposal give a B♮ in the right hand at measure 32 —all save Klindworth's, which gives an A♯ (★). Liszt follows Klindworth, because the inner logic of the melodic line seems to demand an A♯.[40] Moreover, this change brings the music into line with its model, first heard at measure 16.

---

40. Perhaps it would be equally correct to say that Klindworth was following Liszt, since Klindworth had doubtless heard Liszt himself play the *Preludes* in earlier years.

Nonetheless, an inspection of Chopin's manuscript shows quite clearly that he wrote a dissonant B♮ at measure 32. Autographs do not always represent Holy Writ, of course, and it is possible that Chopin himself made an error. What is certain is that Liszt here rejected the first editions, which had been proofread by Chopin himself.

VI

The temptation to dismiss Liszt's editions as historical curiosities, condemned to perpetual imprisonment in time and place, is a powerful one. After all, this is the Age of the Urtext, and authenticity is the thing. Paradoxically, the first casualty of this constraining view is the player, who is discouraged from mounting the concert platform with Liszt's editions of Beethoven, Schubert, and Weber in his fingers. The second casualty is the listener, who never gets to hear them. The question inevitably arises: Why should he? Is not the only text worth having the one bequeathed by the composer himself? History, versus historiography, is a relatively new discipline in music, and the ramifications are endless. Such performances as Liszt himself gave would have every claim to the title "historic," unlocking a door on history, and some of them might even beguile the listener with their old-world charm.

It would be highly stimulating to one's sense of history to hear an entire recital of music in Liszt's editions, complete with all his "variants." The originals are in any case so very well known that they are secure from harm—both real and imagined. Thomas Edison invented the first recording machine in 1877, too late to be of practical use in deciding the question, How did Liszt interpret the music of times past?[41]

41. Liszt never made a gramophone record, despite many rumors to the contrary. Although he was to live for another nine years after Edison gave his epoch-making invention to an unsuspecting world, and although Edison sent out emissaries across Europe to record everyone of stature (including Alfred Lord Tennyson, Brahms, and even Allessandro Moreschi—"the last castrato"—in the choir of the Sistine Chapel, Rome), they never approached Liszt. They did, however, approach his pupil Bülow (see pp. 101–2).

Liszt's editions do not provide a complete answer, but they open a window on an obscure corner of the Romantic period and reveal some intriguing vistas along the way.[42]

42. A complete catalog of Liszt's editions may be found in *The New Grove Dictionary of Music and Musicians* (2nd ed.), vol. 14, London, 2001, pp. 867–68. The catalog is larger than might generally be supposed and contains music by composers not mentioned in this essay, including Bach, Handel, Scarlatti, Muzio Clementi, John Field, and Johann Nepomuk Hummel.

Liszt's Technical Studies

Some Thoughts and Afterthoughts

*It is useful to exercise the fingers, the ears, and the mind simultaneously; and,
together with the mechanics, to study the dynamics and rhythm inherent in music as well.
Consequently, these first exercises should be practiced with all degrees of intensity: crescendo,
from pianìssimo to fortìssimo; diminuendo, from* fortìssimo *to* pianìssimo.

FROM LISZT'S INTRODUCTION TO THE *TECHNICAL STUDIES*

I

In early July 1868 the Abbé Liszt set out from Rome in the company of his theology tutor Father Antonio Solfanelli for a brief holiday in Grottamare, on the Adriatic coast. The impulse for such an unusual excursion had come from Solfanelli, who was recovering from a serious illness and needed the benefits of sea air and warm sunshine to aid in his convalescence. The pair followed the ancient route of the pilgrims—Spoleto, Cascia (where they paid their respects before the preserved remains of Saint Rita), Assisi, Fabriani and Loreto. Along the way Solfanelli continued to offer Liszt instruction in the Breviary, lessons they had begun in Rome shortly after Liszt had been inducted into the four minor orders of the church, in order to prepare him for the order of subdeacon.[1] Arrived in Grottamare, the pair were guests of Solfanelli's uncle, Count Carlo Fenili, whose home overlooked the Adriatic Sea. Liszt's apartment afforded splendid views of the beach and the ocean and he went sea bathing every day, an unusual experience for him.

In Grottamare he read the Breviary daily, with Solfanelli as his guide. It was in Grottamare, too, that he began work on his three volumes of *Technical Studies* for the piano. The scene is intriguing. For a part of the day Liszt is a pupil, sitting at the feet of his religious mentor, learning the basic Latin texts. For the rest of the day, however, he becomes the master addressing his acolytes, albeit imaginary ones, teaching

---

1. Liszt had received the tonsure on April 25, 1865, and had been admitted into the four minor orders on July 30 of that same year. Although he was in the meantime contemplating the idea, Liszt never sought admission to the order of subdeacon, the first of the three sacramental orders of the priesthood. He stood by an earlier decision: "It is enough for me to belong to the hierarchy of the Church to such a degree as the minor orders allow me to do" (LLB, vol. 2, p. 81).

them in turn the basic keyboard configurations. The psychological compensation is obvious, and helps to explain the unusual origins of this unique work. The *Technical Studies* are a "breviary" of piano playing, an "order of service," so to speak, for all those novices who desire advancement at the keyboard. Liszt had no piano at his disposal at Grottamare, an extraordinary fact when we consider the specialized nature of this pedagogical work. He told his colleague Carl Gille, "To be sure, they kindly offered to order an instrument and have it placed in my sitting room, but I raised the most decided protest."[2] He described his time at Grottamare as "two months of tranquillity and simple contentment. . . . Such an occupation is enough to live and die well."[3] Although Liszt only managed to write down about twenty pages of the *Studies* at Grottamare, he had certainly finished the rest in his head by the time he left the Adriatic resort.[4] It took him at least two more years to bring the *Studies* to completion, however. During this time he added some fingerings, grouped the *Studies* according to genre (scales, octaves, thirds, chords, etc.), and gave written indications that each study was to be played in all the major and minor keys.

II

At first glance, these studies appear to be little more than endurance exercises of the old-fashioned kind, made familiar by Hanon, Philipp, Brahms, Tausig, Dohnányi, and a host of others which cast a blight on the happiness of students everywhere. If you can work your way through the myriad difficulties that Liszt places in your path, you certainly possess an above-average command of the keyboard. But there is more to it than that, as a closer inspection of the text reveals. Aside from the obvious configurations, Liszt also provides some uncommon twists which give the player pause for thought.

Consider the first of his so-called Scales with Alternating Hands. It is to be played with the alternating *second finger* of each hand, through all the major and minor keys:

This is audacious. The problem is mental, not physical. And halfway through the study, Liszt varies the challenge by confronting the player with an intriguing paradox: "Arpeggios," he seems to say, "can also become scales, once you have grasped the connection." He then telescopes the hands to reveal a hidden possibility:

2. SLG, p. 33.
3. LLB, vol. 6, p. 186.
4. LLB, vol. 2, p. 125.

This highly creative approach to scale building carries the idea of finger equalization to its limit; one might as well number the fingers from one to ten and have done with it. One way to practice this study, in fact, is to take each hand separately. Once the arpeggios have been identified, they are easily dovetailed into one another, with the left hand over the right. The "scale" will emerge as an unexpected bonus. At such places the links between these studies and Liszt's piano compositions stand revealed. You need go no further than the opening cadenza of *Totentanz* to observe a similar configuration. Once the basic pattern of interlocked hands is in place, the rest is simply a matter of velocity—which, to be sure, can be a problem in itself:

These echoes of Liszt's own music within the *Technical Studies* raise the general question, how widespread are the connections between them? Liszt himself was absolutely silent on the matter. There is no suggestion that he ever regarded these studies as a preparation for the performance of his own compositions; nor did he recommend their use to his students. Yet the fact remains that the *Technical Studies* were formed in the same mind and flowed from the same pen as the great cycles of piano pieces known as the *Années de pèlerinage,* the "Paganini" Studies, the *Transcendental Studies,* the *Harmonies poétiques et religieuses,* and a host of other compositions. It would be unreasonable to suppose that the *Technical Studies* were somehow created in a vacuum, isolated from all the rest of his music. Here is a task worthy of Liszt scholarship: a collected edition of his keyboard music with each piece linked to the technical study that best embodies the physical challenge within it. In the absence of such a collection, however, the following examples will serve as a first, pioneering effort.

  In the climactic, final page of his "Scales with Alternating Hands," Liszt takes a long, backward glance at the odyssey he has traversed, pulls everything together, and presents the player with a closing cascade of chromatic scales played in turn with one, two, three, four, and then all five fingers in alternation with one another. That is to say, he accumulates more and more fingers in the service of the scale.

Behind this seemingly dry and anonymous display of mechanics shimmers some of Liszt's best-known piano music. Consider these examples drawn at random from his oeuvre:

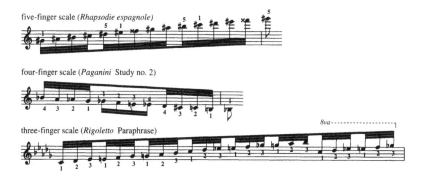

five-finger scale (*Rhapsodie espagnole*)

four-finger scale (*Paganini* Study no. 2)

three-finger scale (*Rigoletto* Paraphrase)

They suggest that the *Technical Studies* represent a wonderful portal through which the player passes en route to Parnassus.

In his youth Liszt sometimes practiced for ten or twelve hours a day, and much of this labor was expended on technical exercises—scales, arpeggios, trills, tremolos, and repeated notes.[5] He set great store by the absolute independence of each finger. Every scale was practiced with the fingering of every other scale (using, say, C-major fingering for F-sharp major, and D-flat-major fingering for C major). Liszt's fingering is both imaginative and original and often looks far into the future of the keyboard. We know that in order to secure a perfectly independent technique, one that would function in any emergency, the young Liszt devised some practice methods which in later life he shunned. Chief among them was his recommendation to read a book while sitting at the keyboard and have the fingers go through their daily drill unsupervised, as it were.[6] That level of automation is difficult to achieve. Another recommendation was to practice "on the brace," an invention made famous by Kalkbrenner, which was fixed to the keyboard and meant to ensure the correct position of hand and fingers. Later on he shunned that, too.

The device of alternating chromatic octaves, with interlocked thumbs, was one of Liszt's most famous keyboard discoveries, and it still bears his name: "Liszt octaves." It is a spectacular advance over ordinary double octaves (whose effect it imitates and was intended to replace) because it enables the player to move at twice the speed with half the effort. Its basic form in the *Technical Studies* runs:

Liszt could work up some dramatic storms with the device, one of the best known occurring in his "St. Francis Walking on the Waters." Another rousing application occurs in the leadback section of the *Rákóczy* March, where we hear the roll of thunder reverberating like cannon fire across a distant battlefield. One of its most

5. He spent four to five hours daily on technique alone (LLB, vol. 1, p. 7).

6. BLP, Lesson 21. That was in 1832. Many years later, as the "Abbé" Liszt living in Rome, he told Wolfgang Helbig that he had kept an encyclopedia on the piano which he read diligently while playing (HLR, p. 77).

telling appearances may be found in his Spanish Rhapsody, made all the more palpable because it is used thematically to reinforce the melodic outline of the *Jota aragonesa:*

Close descendants of "interlocked octaves" are "interlocked thirds." The hands form themselves into forks, so to speak, with the second and third fingers serving as the prongs. Once they have been fitted inside one another, the left hand on top of the right, the alternating fingers may unfold the scale at speed. Like so much else in Liszt's keyboard writing, it is a test of mind over matter. The basic pattern shown in one of the *Technical Studies,*

Technical Study

emerges in all its diamond brilliance in "La campanella."

"La campanella"

In his childhood, we recall, Liszt had been a pupil of Carl Czerny, the leading representative of the "finger equalization school," and with whose own *School of Velocity* the eleven-year-old boy had enjoyed daily encounters. Because the fingers possess different characteristics, so the theory goes, it must be a function of the teacher to equalize them away. Something of this notion lingers in Liszt's own approach to the keyboard, though it would be a mistake to pursue the connection too closely. Look at the very first study, called "Exercises in Strengthening the Fingers and Making Them Independent, with the Hand in a Quiet Position." It could have come straight from Czerny, or better still from Clementi's *Gradus ad Parnassum* (a work that Liszt had also studied with Czerny). The opening configuration is not difficult:

* The whole notes to be silently depressed.

but this long and increasingly complex study becomes problematic when Liszt calls for a show of independence from the fourth fingers:

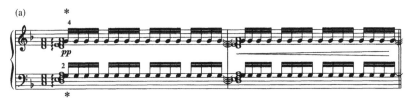

* The whole notes to be silently depressed.

* The whole notes to be silently depressed.

This same exercise flows into the measured trill, from whose rigors the weak fingers are once more not spared. In fact, Liszt goes out of his way to call first for a legato trill and then for a staccato one. That requires enormous control:

Of course, total independence of the fingers is one of the primary goals of the player. Until it is achieved, one's activity at the keyboard is constrained. In the nineteenth century many exercises were invented to secure the liberty of the fourth finger especially, whose freedom is hard to obtain. So elusive is the solution to this particular problem that pianists were even known to submit their hands to surgery, having the webbing between the fingers cut to increase their stretch. As interest in the pianist's problems grew, the medical profession even developed an operation to sever the tendons that bind the fourth finger to its fellows.[7] How many promising careers were destroyed in this way we shall never know. We have already observed the abhorrence with which Liszt regarded all such unnatural interventions, and the unequivocal advice that he had given to his pupil Johanna Wenzel after learning of her desire to gain the independence of her fingers by means of surgery.[8]

Leaps are another feature of Liszt's *Technical Studies* which were often neglected in the old-fashioned collections of endurance exercises. The study in the category called "Leaps in Contrary Motion" would be a wonderful preparation for the closing pages of the First *Mephisto* Waltz:

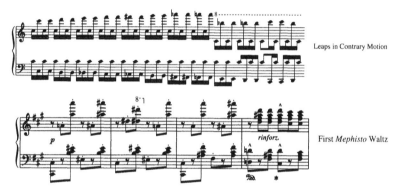

Leaps in Contrary Motion

First *Mephisto* Waltz

And where Liszt, in the continuation of this particular pattern, produces one of those unexpected twists we mentioned earlier (in which the left hand leaps, while the right hand plays repeated chords interlocked within the interval), the results can be positively nostalgic. It is as if he were quoting from one of his own youthful *Hungarian Rhapsodies,* for which this study could become a useful warm-up exercise.

Technical Study
for Interlocked Leaps

7. In August 1885 the *Musical Times* reported on the work of a surgeon Mr. Noble Smith, who had written in the *British Medical Journal* about the operation as follows: "I have just succeeded in freeing the ring finger of the right hand of an accomplished lady pianist, without causing her much more pain than is felt from the prick of a needle. Before the operation she was able to raise the finger only five-eighths of an inch beyond the others. Directly after the operation she could raise the finger easily to one-and-a-half inches, without the least feeling of loss of control over its action. The division was, of course, made subcutaneously, so that only a minute wound was left in the skin, one-eighth of an inch in length."

8. See p. 57, n. 11, and LLB, vol. 2, p. 174.

Hungarian Rhapsody no. 10

In 1823 the Paris-based firm of Sébastien Erard unveiled its newly patented "double escapement" action. Overnight this invention transformed the piano into an instrument of dazzling virtuosity. Briefly, the double escapement allowed the player to produce a seemingly endless stream of rapid-fire note repetitions, deluding the listener into thinking that the piano had been turned into a sustaining instrument of infinite duration—as opposed to the percussion instrument that it really is, whose sounds begin to die the moment they are born. The revolutionary feature of the double escapement was that the hammers did not fall back to their starting points after striking the strings, but came temporarily to rest at the halfway point. The flight of the hammer was now reduced, enabling the player rapidly to repeat single notes from a point midway in the key's descent—literally bouncing the hammers off the strings at speed. Hitherto, the player could only depress the key again after it had fully returned to the surface—a major disadvantage for the virtuoso. In fact, when faced with rapid-fire note repetition (a rare occurrence before late Beethoven) the earlier instruments often behaved as if they had feet of clay.

A few weeks after Erard's new instrument had been launched, the twelve-year-old Liszt arrived in the French capital and acquired one for himself.[9] He became one of the first virtuosos to exploit the new possibilities that it offered him, and he seized upon them even in his juvenile works.[10] It is hardly surprising, then, that Liszt provides an entire smorgasbord of note repetitions in his Technical Exercises, regarding them as a fundamental requirement for the modern performer. Here are just a few samples, with Liszt's endlessly varied fingerings:

9. Erard actually made a gift of one of his latest instruments to the young Liszt. In return Liszt promoted the firm of Erard wherever he could. During his tour of Great Britain in the summer of 1824, for instance, the billboards outside the Theatre-Royal, Manchester, proclaimed that "Master Liszt" would perform on "Erard's New Patent Grand Piano-Forte of Seven Octaves" (see WFL, vol. 1, p. 108).

10. See, for example, his *Eight Variations in A-flat Major* (1824), written within weeks of his acquiring Erard's new instrument, and which abound in note repetitions of various kinds. The work is appropriately dedicated to Sébastien Erard.

These patterns open the door to such gossamer textures as the central episode of the Tarantella movement from Liszt's *Venezia e Napoli*. The fingering is Liszt's.

Liszt ends his *Technical Studies* with a reference to the tremolando, a device that can sound cheap and tawdry in the wrong hands. It so rarely turns up in the music of Chopin, Schumann, Mendelssohn, and Brahms that it can be said hardly to exist for them. But tremolandos abound in Liszt; indeed, many of his works are absolutely dependent upon them. Compositions such as "Les Jeux d'eaux à la Villa d'Este" and his transcription of the "Liebestod" from Wagner's *Tristan* fall lifeless to the ground if the player cannot sustain a convincing tremolando from beginning to end. How often do we hear it said that it is a purely orchestral device (granted, it is absolutely indigenous to the strings) and out of place on a piano keyboard. But when properly played, the tremolando becomes an indispensable part of the pianist's armory. It can release tremendous volumes of sound akin to those of the orchestra; at the opposite end of the spectrum it can bewitch us with the soft magic of its veiled colors. Everything depends on the player. Liszt himself liked the tremolando to be played as quickly as possible, with a scarcely visible *trembling* of the hand, and with the keys already halfway depressed—as if the fingers themselves were thrumming against the strings. To those of his students who used too much forearm rotation he would make the predictable comment, "Do not make omelets!" Many omelets were

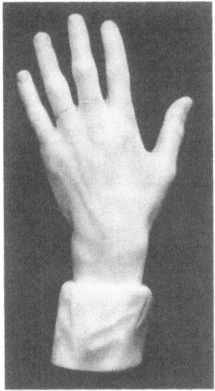

Cast of Liszt's left hand. (A photograph.)

made in Liszt's masterclasses, and even today his culinary analogy springs to mind as the modern virtuoso tries to subdue the keyboard, with varying degrees of failure, at the opening of the "Liebestod":

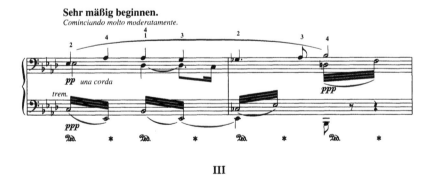

III

The fact that Liszt composed a set of technical studies at all gives us pause. During his later years he showed a near-total disregard of technique and actively discouraged his students from flaunting it. Frederic Lamond has told us that, "The mere mechanical attainments of pianoforte technique meant very little to him. Speed, pure and simple, of which so much is made by many pianists of the present day, he held in contempt."[11] That was in 1885. The comment was especially true of Liszt's own music. He frequently told his students that they played it too fast. When Liszt himself played it, it was apparent to all that he placed more value on clarity, nuance, and "breathing" than on speed and volume.

Liszt was nonetheless aware of the central role of virtuosity in musical performance and would surely have approved Saint-Saëns's aphorism: "In art, a difficulty overcome is a thing of beauty."[12] This telling idea is well illustrated by an incident from Liszt's later life. He was once approached by Henri Maréchal, the French composer and winner of the Prix de Rome, who informed him of the contempt he felt toward "an imbecile pianist" whom he had just witnessed playing Liszt's *Rigoletto* Paraphrase in a difficult arrangement for the left hand alone. Halfway through the performance, Maréchal continued, this charlatan had had the nerve to pull out a silk handkerchief with his right hand and had proceeded to blow his nose with it in order to prove that only the left hand was working. As Maréchal was telling Liszt that such things were fit only for the fairground, Liszt gently squeezed his arm, saying, "*Mon cher enfant,* for a virtuoso, that is necessary! It is absolutely indispensable."[13]

Although Liszt was proud to declare, "I am no piano professor!", stayed aloof from methods and systems, and was the sworn enemy of conservatories, it is clear that he often meditated privately about the physical requirements of piano playing. His Italian student Giuseppe Ferrata once engaged Liszt in conversation about piano technique, and later wrote:

> "More than once I accompanied him to the Church of S. Carlo al Corso, Rome, to hear Mass. We would often walk from the Hotel in Via Aliberti to the Church, a little distance off, arm in arm, and once he said to me, "Many students of piano run up and down scales for hours every day, thinking they will reach the heaven of technical attainments, but athletes develop their muscles and get resistance and control of them by exercises that are based on sudden contraction and expansion. These principles should apply also to students of piano, who should formulate exercises for sudden expansion and contraction of the muscles of their arms and hands."[14]

With such intriguing ideas before us, it is a matter of regret that Liszt never attempted the "Piano Method" that he was commissioned to write by the directors of the Geneva Conservatoire, in the mid-1830s, when he briefly headed the Piano Department there. Rumors of a "missing" method have dogged the literature for years, but we know that Liszt never wrote it. We have his own word for that. When

11. LML, p. 68.
12. MT, September 1921, p. 623.
13. MRS, pp. 111–12.
14. LL, p. 362; letter from Giuseppe Ferrata to Carl Lachmund, dated December 5, 1917.

Lina Ramann inquired about it, many years later, he assured her, "I have never written such a work and will never think of writing one. . . . The only methodical work I have written down is a series of *technical* [his italics] studies which will perhaps promote the present stage of the mechanics of piano playing."[15] Nonetheless, it is perfectly clear from the literature that Liszt was known to have practiced technical exercises in his youth and to have prescribed them to his students. Is it unreasonable to assume that the *Technical Studies* he actually began to write down, in that Italian summer of 1868, were retrieved from buried memories of long-ago work routines?

IV

The subsequent history of the *Technical Studies* is worth relating. In 1871 Liszt concluded an agreement with the New York publisher Julius Schuberth, whereby he was to receive one thousand dollars on delivery of all three volumes. Liszt had meanwhile entrusted the task of making a fair copy of his untidy manuscript to his eccentric pupil Olga Janina. The self-styled "Cossack Countess" had joined Liszt's circle in the summer of 1869. From the start she stood out from the other students because of her many idiosyncracies. She dressed like a man, smoked cigars, and proclaimed the virtues of free love. She also wore a Circassian belt and dagger which, according to her own account, carried a poisoned tip. In addition to these charming accoutrements she also sported a revolver, much to the consternation of the other students, who regarded her as unstable. Olga also took drugs, mainly laudanum, with which to color her perception of the world. Soon this dangerous young woman had fallen violently in love with Liszt who, because he failed to return her feelings, became the recipient of some difficult "scenes" and recriminating language. Although Liszt was embarrassed by her behavior, both in public and in private, he kept her on as a student because of her undeniable talent as a pianist and her skills as a copyist. After two years of her company, however, it was clear to Liszt that she would have to be detached from his circle, and he actively encouraged her to seek her fame and fortune in the New World. In the summer of 1871 Olga set out for New York with a letter of recommendation from Liszt and the manuscript copies of the *Technical Studies.* Her search for a new career quickly foundered. Olga not only pocketed the one thousand dollars from Julius Schuberth but absconded with the manuscript of the third volume as well, which she may well have sold to eke out her flagging finances.[16] When Liszt discovered what had happened, he found the prospect of making yet another fair copy of the *Studies* so irksome that publication of the project was postponed. In the event, he never lived to see the *Studies* in print. In 1886, shortly after Liszt's death, his pupil Alexander Winterberger came out with a truncated version, re-arranged in twelve slim volumes, a scheme never envisaged by Liszt.

15. RL, p. 39.
16. The story of Olga's subsequent return to Europe, and of her failed attempt to shoot Liszt in his Budapest apartment and then commit suicide by swallowing poison, has been reviewed in depth in my biography of Liszt (WFL, vol. 3, pp. 171–90).

And what of the missing third part? In due time it came into the possession of another of Liszt's students, Karl Goepfart, and was acquired by the Weimar Archive in 1975. It was eventually published for the first time in 1983, together with the earlier volumes. Liszt had already given this third part the intriguing title *12 Grosse Etuden,* a piece of information that is disclosed in the memoirs of Alexander Gott-schalg,[17] leading some observers who had never seen the score to conclude that these were concert pieces. In fact, they continue the style of the preceding exercises, although they are somewhat more difficult, and they feature aspects of piano playing not encountered in the earlier volumes, including octave leaps, extended chords, and protracted tremolandos.

Until the "lost" third volume was re-united with its companions, the overall plan of the *Technical Studies* remained obscure. But now that everything has come together, we can stand back and view the work whole. The *Technical Studies* are constructed as an entity, not unlike an entire musical composition. This is proven by the elaborate key schemes, which unfold three quite distinct systems:

1. Exercises that progress through the cycle of fifths:
   a. majors and their relative minors, descending in the subdominant direction;
   b. majors and their tonic minors, ascending in the dominant direction.
2. Exercises that progress chromatically, through all twelve levels of the chromatic scale.
3. Exercises that progress through cycles of thirds, major and minor.

Such a plan suggests that the *Studies* were meant to be performed in a continuous progression. It not only relieves the ear of the monotony that would otherwise arise from playing these exercises in the same key, but the challenge of progressing through all the tonalities also means that the physical "imprinting" of the keyboard on hands and fingers as they wend their way through all the possible geometrical permutations is made more secure. Incidentally, once mastered, the entire set of studies would take at least forty-five minutes to perform, an excellent warm-up period for pianists at any level. And the notion that they are really a kind of musical composition, albeit one to be played in private, is borne out at the very end of the third volume, where Liszt closes down his stint of labor with a series of triumphant, vale-dictory chords, as if to achieve both physical and emotional release.

Pianists who like to wander through Liszt's workshop would do well to make themselves acquainted with the diaries of his pupils Carl Lachmund[18] and August Göllerich,[19] since the advice he gave to the members of his masterclasses is enshrined there in his own words and helps to round out our impressions of him as a

17. GLW, p. 117.
18. LL.
19. GLK.

teacher. Equally indispensable is Lina Ramann's *Liszt Pädagogium.*[20] This compilation of observations on piano interpretation, supported by commentaries from Liszt's own lips, and illustrated by Ramann with judiciously chosen examples from Liszt's own music, offers some further insights into his approach to the keyboard. Ramann was closely acquainted with Liszt during the last years of his life, after she had been appointed his official biographer. She was, moreover, an experienced piano teacher with a flourishing music school in Nuremberg, and had a natural curiosity about piano pedagogy. She used her connections to Liszt wisely, and her *Pädagogium,* published long after Liszt had died, reminded posterity of Liszt's special relationship to the keyboard and of his important place in the history of piano playing. When these three sources are consulted in conjunction with the *Technical Studies,* we have as complete a picture of Liszt's relationship to the keyboard as most of us are likely to require.

Ramann once asked Liszt to comment on his technical achievements which, even in old age, and long after he had ceased to practice, ranked so much higher than the ordinary. His reply is worth pondering, even though we have considered it elsewhere in this volume. "Technique should create itself from spirit, not from mechanics," he told her.[21] Liszt often touched on this concept, which has a biblical aspect to it. He told his American pupil Carl Lachmund, "When I have the will to do, I can do. But when that will is lacking, I can do no more than the ordinary." Because Lachmund was aware of Liszt's strong religious beliefs, he immediately saw the connection, and thought, "Yes, it is the spirit that quickeneth." Many years later, when Lachmund told Rafael Joseffy of Liszt's remarkable playing, notwithstanding that "three score years and ten" had bowed his shoulders at the time he heard him, Joseffy (who was himself a Liszt pupil) remarked, "I have always held that great technique does not come from the fingers; it is the *intellectual spirit* that gives the power for the technique."[22] This observation could only have originated with Liszt himself, since it is so much in tune with his own thinking on the topic. Liszt knew that although his *Technical Studies* might offer the player a glimpse of Parnassus, they could never of themselves guarantee a conquest of the peak. In order to make so formidable a journey, to say nothing of achieving so spectacular a victory, the player would need the spirit, too. For if my earlier analogy with the Breviary is to remain meaningful, it would be absolutely necessary for the player to commune with his god as well.

20. See RL-P.
21. "Aus dem Geist schaffe sich die Technik, nicht aus der Mechanik!" (RL-P, p. 6).
22. LL, p. 33.

Liszt the Writer

On Music and Musicians

I have an immense need . . . to learn, to know, to deepen myself.
FRANZ LISZT[1]

The dispute over the exact authorship of Liszt's literary works is likely to remain alive for some time to come. His books, brochures, and many articles, written across a period of nearly forty years, have been subjected to much scrutiny and endless debate. It is a considerable legacy of six volumes of prose, comparable in size and scope to the literary works of Robert Schumann, Hector Berlioz, and Richard Wagner.[2] The old, unthinking view used to be that Liszt had no literary talents whatsoever. Emile Haraszti once famously declared that "Liszt wrote nothing but his personal correspondence,"[3] and he mischievously advised his fellow Liszt scholars to "cherchez la femme." What he meant by that was that all Liszt's early articles, including the Bachelor of Music essays published in the 1830s and early 1840s, were the work of Liszt's first mistress, Countess Marie d'Agoult; while the later articles and books published during the Weimar years, including *Frédéric Chopin* and *Des Bohémiens et de leur musique en Hongrie,* were the work of his second, Princess Carolyne von Sayn-Wittgenstein. Both ladies had literary pretensions, and after their encounter with Liszt they went on to publish a considerable amount of prose under their own names (or, in the case of Marie d'Agoult, under her pseudonym "Daniel Stern"), some of it important. In brief, Liszt's literary legacy, to quote Haraszti once more, was a hoax.

Such a view is no longer possible to sustain. More than 230 pages of Liszt's holographs have come to light since Haraszti's day, proving yet again that nothing should be taken for granted with Liszt. For as Francis Bacon has reminded us, truth is the daughter of time, not of authority.

The main documents are:

---

1. ACLA, vol. 1, p. 82.

2. Edited by Lina Ramann, this edition has done yeoman service for more than a century. Liszt's prose works are currently being revised and re-issued in a new edition by Detlef Altenburg, and published by Breitkopf and Härtel. It will contain much that is new, and will eventually run to nine volumes.

3. HPL, p. 130.

1. A 143-page holograph of the brochure *De la fondation- Goethe à Weimar,* with corrections and emendations in Princess Carolyne's hand. It bears the date 1850.[4]

2. A 28-page holograph sketch, dated September 1849, which forms the preliminary draft of the above brochure.[5]

3. A 3-page holograph of the introduction to Liszt's symphonic poems, signed by him and dated Weimar, March 1856.[6]

4. A comprehensive 12-page holograph draft of part of Liszt's early article "On the Position of Artists" (1835), signed by him.[7]

5. A 3-page holograph of part of Liszt's obituary notice of Paganini (1840).[8]

6. A 23-page holograph of the second chapter of Liszt's book on Chopin, with emendations in the hand of Princess Carolyne.[9]

7. A holograph page of the article "Criticism of Criticism."[10]

8. A 7-page manuscript entitled "Publications pour le piano (Kroll, Reinecke)," in the hand of Princess Carolyne but with corrections by Liszt. The document, dated Weimar, June 10, 1849, is signed by Liszt.[11]

9. A 2-page holograph of the preface to the piano transcriptions of the Beethoven symphonies, signed by Liszt.[12]

10. An 8-page holograph of the "Letter on Conducting: A Defense," signed by Liszt.[13]

Today we also know much more about Liszt's working methods.[14] During the Weimar years, especially, Liszt employed a small army of researchers, translators, and proofreaders to help him prepare his articles for the press, including his pupils Hans von Bülow and Peter Cornelius, as well as Princess Carolyne herself. He may have

---

4. GSA 3/1; RGS, vol. 5, pp. 1–109.

5. GSA 3/1; RGS, vol. 5, pp. 1–109.

6. GSA 5/1; CE, vol. I.

7. Brit. Lib. add. ms. 33965. Fol. 237–42.

8. GSA 1/1; RGS, vol. 2, pp. 108–12.

9. RGS, vol. 1, pp. 20–40. The manuscript was sold at auction in Tutzing in 1976 and is now in the hands of a private collector in Germany.

10. Liszt Museum, Sopron.

11. BN NAF, Doc. R. 607.

12. BN NAF 25180, f. 17. The holograph bears no date, but the format of the pale blue-green paper is identical to that Liszt used in Milan around February 1838.

13. Library of Congress, Music Division, Rosenthal Liszt Collection. Letters of Liszt to Richard Pohl, no. 6.

14. I devoted an entire chapter in the second volume of my Liszt biography to clearing up the question of authorship, and do not propose to go over that ground again here. See the chapter entitled "The Scribe of Weimar" in WFL, vol. 2, pp. 368–96.

relied on others to polish his prose, but he held himself entirely responsible for the content, and frequently referred to these works as "mine." But there is more to it than that. There is a golden thread running through Liszt's literary works that links them to his private correspondence (the authorship of which no one denies): a harmony of ideas, an identity of opinions about music and musicians, and a consistently unfolding philosophy of Art. In fact, a comparison of Liszt's prose works with his thousands of letters leaves no doubt that with few exceptions everything came from one mind and one pen, Liszt's own.[15] Open these volumes at random, and the composer's humor, generosity, and insights into music and musicians come tumbling from the pages.

It has often been said that a well-stocked library indicates a well-stocked mind. Liszt collected books all his life; his personal library, or that part of it that survived his itinerant lifestyle, is now housed at the Liszt Research Centre in Budapest. Many items in this collection contain his underlinings and marginal comments, from which we infer that the passages in question made an impact and elicited a response. But Liszt possessed a far larger collection than the four hundred items catalogued in this particular depository would suggest.[16] After his death in July 1886, another large collection that had been housed in Germany since his Weimar years came on the market, and in 1887 it was put up for auction by an antiquarian book dealer in Erfurt.[17] This collection consisted of 1298 items, including volumes of philosophy by Leibniz, David Hume, Plato and Schopenhauer; poetry by Lamartine, Petrarch, and Milton; novels by Musset, Eugène Sue, and Edgar Quinet; biographies of Mary Stuart, Beaumarchais; and the standard literary works of Homer, Goethe, Schiller, Shakespeare, Dante, Byron, Voltaire, Balzac and Victor Hugo. There was also a large collection of modern English authors, represented by Dickens, Macaulay, Trollope, and Disraeli. It would have been an impressive enough library for a professional man of letters; but to find it in the possession of a Franz Liszt comes as a welcome surprise. There is much more here than the "French veneer covering the Hungarian peasant," the withering description of Liszt provided by Marie d'Agoult at the height of their estrangement. He had an easy familiarity with many of these sources and he quoted from them constantly throughout his life.

Liszt's prose is often laced with Latin quotations and references to the works of the political and social thinkers of the day; it also shows more than a passing acquaintance with the classics. His quicksilver wit, expressed through a sharp pen, and a propensity for subtle punning, suggests a man of superior education, one perhaps trained in the humanities. Nothing could be further from the truth. None of Liszt's

---

15. The exceptions are rare. When the literary works express opinions that are flatly contradicted by signed letters, it is to the signed letters that we owe our allegiance. A good example would be the anti-Semitic material found in the second edition of *Des Bohémiens et de leur musique en Hongrie* (1881), which led to accusations that he was racist. Liszt's letter to the Hungarian press (LLB, vol. 2, pp. 345–46) is a powerful rebuttal of such an idea. We now know these problematic passages to have been the work of Princess Carolyne, although Liszt never exposed her. It is one of those times when Haraszti's phrase "cherchez la femme" holds true.

16. EFL, vol. 1.

17. E-LWB, pp. 21–56.

later sophistication was granted to him as a birthright. He had to work for it, and he often lamented the fact that his early general education was badly neglected. In his childhood and youth much time was deliberately sacrificed to his development as a musician, under the rigorous guidance of his authoritarian father, Adam Liszt. He once told Lina Ramann that in his childhood he had no idea of history, of geography, or of the natural sciences.[18] And in a letter to Princess Carolyne von Sayn-Wittgenstein, he confessed that his poor primary education had always been a handicap to him, and that he felt he had never been able to remedy this capital defect.[19] He was at that time fifty-seven years old. Music aside, he learned in childhood only what he was able to glean from the humble classes he attended at the village school in his native Raiding, before his father uprooted him and took him to Vienna for piano study with Carl Czerny, and then, when he was only eleven years of age, on the European tours that were to make him famous. Of all the great composers, in fact, Liszt started life with some of the fewest advantages. It was only when he was in his early twenties, had settled in Paris, and had begun to mix in French high society that he started to make good on his missed education. He became an avaricious reader. "Homer, the Bible, Plato, Locke, Byron, Hugo, Lamartine, Chateaubriand, Beethoven, Bach, Hummel, Mozart, Weber, are all around me," he wrote when he was not yet twenty-one years old. "I study them, meditate on them, devour them, with fury."[20] In later life, books remained his constant companions. As the Liszt scholar Ben Arnold has reminded us, he read them on trains, on cabs, out of doors, and even in bed. And then, when his eyesight began to fail in old age, his friends and his students took turns in reading his favorite authors aloud to him.[21] His pupil August Stradal has told us that whenever Liszt traveled he invariably took with him Goethe's *Faust* and Dante's *Divine Comedy,* masterworks that he read over and over again.[22]

This, then, was the rich backdrop against which Liszt unfolded his work as a writer. Today we are in a far better position to know what Liszt "devoured with fury." He was at least as well read as his great contemporaries Berlioz, Wagner, and Schumann, all three of whom are respected for their insights into music and musicians, and for their published prose. Do Liszt's letters, books, articles, and even his spoken word, stand on an equal footing with theirs? Let his vast legacy speak for itself. The first prerequisite, however, is to become aware of it. Here, to begin, are some of the more memorable of his observations on life and death, genius and talent, music and musicians.

18. RLKM, vol. 1, p. 152.
19. LLB, vol. 6, p. 184.
20. LLB, vol. 1, p. 7.
21. SDNL, p. 47.
22. SE, p. 72.

APHORISMS, MAXIMS, AND QUOTATIONS

On Genius and Talent

"Genius has obligations!"[23]

"Genius does nothing without a reason. Every artist of genius breathes into his work an unexpressed idea which speaks to our feelings even before it can be defined."[24]

"Genius is the agency through which the supernatural is revealed to man."[25]

"What are the dying bouquets of an hour to those whose brows claim the laurel of immortality?"[26]

On Art and Artists

"For the formation of the artist, the first prerequisite is the improvement of the human being."[27]

"The artist's destiny is a sad and great one. A sacred predestination marks him at birth. It is not he who chooses his profession—it is his profession that chooses him."[28]

"Art must remind the people of the beautiful self-sacrifice, the heroic determination, the fortitude, and the humanity of their peers."[29]

"The artist—in our sense—should be neither the servant nor the master of the public. He remains the bearer of the *Beautiful* in the inexhaustible variety that is appointed to human thought and perception—and this inviolable consciousness alone assures his authority."[30]

"Art is a heaven on earth, to which one never appeals in vain when faced with the oppressions of this world."[31]

"One cannot speak only of secular or religious art—one must always speak of divine art. And when man is taught from his early days that God has given him reason and free will and a conscience, he should always add: 'And Art!' For art is truly divine."[32]

---

23. RGS, vol. 2, p. 112.
24. RGS, vol. 3, p. 42.
25. RGS, vol. 2, p. 109.
26. LFC, p. 86.
27. RGS, vol. 5, p. 195.
28. RGS, vol. 2, p. 135.
29. RGS, vol. 2, pp. 157–58.
30. LLB, vol. 1, p. 263.
31. From an entry in the autograph book of Varnhagen von Ense, Weimar, May 1858.
32. RGS, vol. 5, 1855.

"May we never forget that Art and Science—Poetry and Thought, Beauty and Truth—are the two archangels who open the golden gates of the Temple of Humanity."[33]

"Music could be called the universal language of humanity."[34]

"As an artist, you must not [be allowed to] rake in a million marks without making some sacrifice on the altar of Art."[35]

"The Word of God reveals itself in the creations of genius."[36]

"There is nothing better than to respect, admire, and study the illustrious dead; but why not also sometimes live with the living?"[37]

"Unless they appear over a well-known name, the finest works risk passing unnoticed or unappreciated by the public."[38]

"There is in Art a pernicious offense, of which most of us are guilty through carelessness and fickleness; I would like to call it the [Pontius] Pilate offense. The Classical way of doing and playing things, which have become the fashion in recent years, and which on the whole may be regarded as an improvement in our musical state of things, hide in many a one this fault, without eradicating it. More could be said on this point, but it would lead me too far."[39]

On Critics and Criticism

"No one has the right to teach and take on the public profession of a music critic before he has passed a test and received a certificate."[40]

"The field of musical literature is far too little cultivated by practicing artists. If they continue to neglect it they will have to bear the consequences and pay their damages."[41]

"Either the critic is unintelligent, insolent, absurd—or he is biased, filled with rancor and envy. . . . Would it not be wiser and more profitable to remain silent?"[42]

"Critics! If one wants to be a critic, one begins with self-criticism!"[43]

33. LS, p. 1.
34. RGS, vol. 4, 1855.
35. RL, p. 298.
36. BWL, vol. 1, p. 204.
37. LLB, vol. 1, p. 199.
38. WLLM, p. 488.
39. LLB, vol. 1, p. 258.
40. RGS, vol. 2, p. 47.
41. LLB, vol. 1, pp. 196–97.
42. RGS, vol. 2, p. 234.
43. WEG, pp. 119–20.

"Critics—the men of the 'yet' and the 'but,' who would crush to death every living endeavor."[44]

"Nowadays people hear and judge [music] only by reading the newspapers. . . . What is the good of *performances* to people who only want to read newspapers?"[45]

"Taste is a negative thing. Genius affirms and always affirms."[46]

"The critics are puffed up with their own importance, very real in the outside world, often venial and concerned with quite different questions than those of art and artists. Musicians and musical people, editors, stockbrokers, antique dealers, etc. are full of impertinence, jealousy, and stupidity. That is the picture offered to impartial judgment, more or less the same everywhere with mild variations. How can one create art in this wasteland? Yet it must be done, and we shall create it for them willy-nilly."[47]

"To surpass in the Arts means to equal."[48]

"I hear from Paris that at all the street corners they are selling a little pamphlet for a sou entitled 'Le seul moyen de ne pas mourir le 13 Juin à l'apparition de la Comète' [The only way to avoid dying at the appearance of the comet on June 13]. The only way is to drown oneself on June 12. Much of the good advice that is given to me by the critics is very like this 'only way.' Yet we will not drown ourselves—not even in the lukewarm waters of criticism—and we will also for the future stand firm on our own legs with a good conscience."[49]

"Beethoven's symphonies were not applauded in Paris until after Beethoven's death. *A Midsummer Night's Dream* Overture was a fiasco at the Paris Conservatory (I was there) some twenty-five years ago, and during Mendelssohn's lifetime they did not play a single note he had composed. Examples of this kind abound and prove unquestionably two things at once: that the public is only infallible at the last appeal, and that every composer with a failure on his hands has not for that reason the right to consider himself a Beethoven or a Mendelssohn!"[50]

"If the critic is not also an artist, if he is unable to practice what he professes to preach, one mistrusts his expert judgment (and one is probably right to do so), and one denies that he is competent to understand and criticize the results. If as a critic he is solemn and severe, people will laugh at him for

44. LLB, vol. 1, p. 245.
45. LLB, vol. 2, p. 220.
46. LLB, vol. 4, p. 7.
47. LLB, vol. 4, p. 425.
48. RGS, vol. 4, pp. 268–69.
49. LLB, vol. 1, pp. 275–76.
50. LLB, vol. 3, p. 110.

failing to understand the inner processes at work and will regard his severity as rage and impotence. Artists will spurn him, and whatever he may do
he will suffer not only the hatred but also the contempt of those on whom
he lavishes the most extravagant praise.

"The position of the artist-critic is ten times worse. If he dares to pass con-
scientious judgment on what he finds unsatisfactory in the works of great
masters, his temerity is intolerable; if he criticizes his colleagues and contemporaries, he is said to be driven by "pure envy." Those composers with
whom he is on terms of personal friendship accuse him of "ingratitude,"
while those who have never met him wonder what they have done to deserve such treatment. Although he believes he has raised only questions of
art, it transpires that he has raised personal questions affecting hundreds,
and that he has attracted as many enemies as the people he criticized have
spouses, brothers, cousins, patrons, and sometimes even fellow countrymen!"[51]

"A critique that dwells only on the defects of a work of art is itself open to
criticism; it should discover and bring out also its redeeming features. An
absence of defects does not make a work of art, but an absence of beauty
condemns it."[52]

"Would not the best result of criticism be for it to inspire the artist to renewed creativity?"[53]

"An original thinker said: 'As our emblem and coat of arms, I suggest a tree
swaying violently in the storm, which reveals the ripe fruit on every branch
withal. Underneath, the inscription: "*Dum convellor mitescunt*" (While I am
uprooted the fruit ripens) or else: "*Conquassatus sed ferax*" (Shaken but
fruitful).'"[54]

On Composition

"New wine demands new bottles."[55]

"My one remaining ambition . . . is to hurl my lance into the boundless
realms of the future. So long as this lance is of good quality and does not
fall back to earth, the rest is of no importance to me whatsoever!"[56]

"One could say that in order to counterbalance the works of genius, a
wicked fairy sometimes gives a magical success to the most vulgar com-

51. RGS, vol. 2, pp. 233–34.
52. RGS, vol. 3, p. 115.
53. LLB, vol. 1, p. 73.
54. LLB, vol. 1, p. 272.
55. SE, p. 76.
56. LLB, vol. 7, p. 58.

positions and presides over their propagation, seeming to favor those whom inspiration has passed by, in order to push its elect into the shadows. That is no reason for discouragement, however; for what does it matter, the *sooner* or the *later*?"[57]

[To a young composer who had brought him some rather empty compositions:] "My friend, if one invites guests to the table, one does not set before them cigar ash and sawdust."[58]

"In everything I create, I think I have something quite new to say. It is therefore essential that my thought and feeling be assimilated [by the performer], so that they are not betrayed by a ruinous performance. . . . The Spirit must blow on these sonorous waves as on the waters of Creation."[59]

"The day has not yet dawned when composers will consider it beneath their dignity to write music to words of which Voltaire, with biting sarcasm, made the remark so often repeated since: 'The words that are sung are those which are not fit to be spoken.'"[60]

"The history of music teaches us that every school perishes through the principle that gave it birth. It flourishes until that principle has been carried to its last consequences; thereupon new ideas bud forth, taking up the thread of progress, like a new generation, and developing until the ideas of the preceding school have been supplemented."[61]

"Music is never stationary; successive forms and styles are only like so many resting places—like tents pitched and taken down again on the road to the Ideal."

"The lied is, from both a poetical and a musical point of view, strictly a specialty of German music, and, again, the terms *Sehnsucht* and *Gemuth* (yearning and sentiment) which mark its sphere, and are its lifeblood, are untranslatable, and are peculiar to the German language. Assuredly, other nations, too, have their songs, but in nature and character those songs have nothing in common with the lied."[62]

On Program Music

"It is obvious that things that can appear only objectively to perception can in no way furnish connecting points to music; the poorest of apprentice landscape painters could give with a few chalk strokes a much more faith-

57. LLB, vol. 1, p. 70.
58. WEG, p. 118.
59. LLB, vol. 4, p. 235.
60. RGS, vol. 3, p. 87.
61. RGS, vol. 3, p. 62.
62. RGS, vol. 4, p. 212.

ful picture than a musician operating with all the resources of the best orchestras. But if these same things are subjected to dreaming, to contemplation, to emotional uplift, have they not a kinship with music, and should not music be able to translate them into its mysterious language?"[63]

"I have latterly traveled through many new countries, have seen many different places, and visited many a spot hallowed by history and poetry; I have felt that the varied aspects of nature, and the different incidents associated with them, did not pass before my eyes like meaningless pictures, but that they evoked profound emotions within my soul; that a vague but direct affinity was established between them and myself, a real though indefinable, a sure but inexplicable means of communication, and I have tried to give musical utterance to some of my strongest sensations, some of my liveliest impressions."[64]

"Abuse, bad taste, blunders, and failures, have made program music so ridiculous, that its adversaries may well propose its total abolition. But if it be right to condemn wholesale whatever is liable to abuse, it is assuredly the entire art of music that should be so condemned, seeing that the works offered to the public are in great part worthless rather than valuable, absurd rather than intellectual, devoid of taste rather than full of new material!"[65]

"A Slavic poet once proclaimed: 'The word lies to the thought; / The deed lies to the word.' But music does not lie to the feelings."[66]

On the Piano

"You do not know that to speak of giving up my piano would be to me a day of gloom, robbing me of the light that illuminated all my early life, and has grown to be inseparable from it.

"My piano is to me what his vessel is to the sailor, his horse to the Arab, nay even more, till now it has been myself, my speech, my life. It is the repository of all that stirred my nature in the passionate days of my youth. I confided to it all my desires, my dreams, my joys, and my sorrows. Its strings vibrated to my emotions, and its keys obeyed my every caprice. Would you have me abandon it and strive for the more brilliant and resounding triumphs of the theater or orchestra? Oh, no! Even were I competent for music of that kind, my resolution would be firm not to abandon the study and development of piano playing, until I had accomplished whatever is practicable, whatever it is possible to attain nowadays.

---

63. From the general preface to the Symphonic Poems.
64. From the preface to *Album d'un voyageur*, and later the Swiss volume of the *Années de pèlerinage*.
65. RGS, vol. 4, p. 177.
66. RGS, vol. 4, pp. 31–32.

"Perhaps the mysterious influence that binds me to it so strongly prejudices me, but I consider the piano to be of great importance. In my estimation it holds the first place in the hierarchy of instruments. . . . In the compass of its seven octaves it includes the entire scope of the orchestra, and the ten fingers suffice for the harmony that is produced by an ensemble of a hundred players."[67]

"The piano is the microcosm of music. . . . Singers, flautists and bassoonists, even cornettists and kettledrummers, have to learn the piano if they want to find their bearings intelligently in their own field."[68]

"Even if one accepts that the player uses the pedal correctly, because of various unpleasant assaults on my ears, I have returned to the practice of notating exact pedal indications with utmost care."[69]

"I do not play according to measure. One must not imprint on music a balanced uniformity, but kindle it, or slow it down, according to its meaning."[70]

"Bad singers are able to find good engagements, since theatres are everywhere necessary. It's another thing for pianists of both sexes. Ninety-nine out of a hundred are at least superfluous, if not downright pests. One of their wittiest rivals said to me yesterday: 'We are decidedly far too many: there ought to be a St. Bartholomew's Massacre among pianists. Without one we shall all perish."[71]

On Piano Technique

"Technique should create itself out of spirit, not out of mechanics."[72]

"I don't want to listen to how fast you can play octaves. What I wish to hear is the canter of the horses of the Polish cavalry before they gather force and destroy the enemy."[73]

"For your glissando exercises I once again advise you to use only the nail, either of your thumb or of your index or third finger, *without even the tiniest area of flesh.*"[74]

67. RGS, vol. 2, p. 151.
68. LLB, vol. 7, p. 208.
69. LLB, vol. 2, p. 48, n. 1.
70. BLP, p. 35.
71. HLSW, pp. 221 and 227.
72. RL-P, p. 6.
73. LML, p. 68.
74. WLLM, p. 390.

On Virtuosity

"What makes the virtuoso? Is he really a mere spiritless machine? Do his hands only attend to the office of a double winch on a street organ? Has he to supply the ear only with a photograph of the object before him?

"... The virtuoso is not a mason, who, with the chisel in his hand, faithfully and conscientiously cuts his stone after the design of the architect. He is not a passive tool who reproduces feeling and thought without adding any himself. He is not the more or less experienced reader of works that have no margin for his notes, and which make no insertions necessary between the lines.... He creates just like the composer himself, for he must embrace in himself those passions which he has to bring to light in their complete brilliance. He breathes life into the lethargic body, infuses it with fire, and enlivens it with the pulse of gracefulness and charm. He changes the clay-like form into a living being, penetrating it with the spark which Prometheus snatched from the fire of Jupiter. He must make this form move through transparent ether; he must arm it with a thousand wings; he must unfold scent and blossom and breathe into it the breath of life. Of all artists the virtuoso reveals perhaps most immediately the overpowering force of the god who, in the glowing embrace of his proud muse, lures every hidden secret from her."[75]

"During that time [ca. 1830], both at public concerts and in private salons (where people never failed to observe that I selected my pieces very badly), I often performed the works of Beethoven, Weber, and Hummel, and let me confess to my shame that in order to wring bravos from a public that, in its awesome simplicity, is always slow to comprehend beautiful things, I had no qualms about changing the tempos of the pieces or the composers' intentions. In my arrogance I even went so far as to add a host of rapid runs and cadenzas, which, by securing ignorant applause for me, sent me off in the wrong direction—one that I fortunately knew enough to abandon quickly. You cannot believe, dear friend, how I deplore these concessions to bad taste, those sacrilegious violations of the *Spirit* and the *Letter,* because the most profound respect for the masterpieces of great composers has, for me, replaced the need that a young man barely out of childhood once felt for novelty and individuality."[76]

"However so-called sober-minded musicians may disparage consummate brilliancy, it is nonetheless true that every genuine artist has an instinctive desire for it."[77]

75. RGS, vol. 4, pp. 194–96.
76. CPR, p. 104.
77. RGS, vol. 4, p. 207.

"The end of mastery of style is to enable an artist to execute the most intricate and difficult compositions, indeed, so indispensable is it, that no artist can cultivate it enough."[78]

On Musical Education: A Manifesto

"In the name of all musicians, of art, and of social progress, we require:

(a) The foundation of an assembly to be held every five years for religious, dramatic, and symphonic music, by which the works that are considered best in these three categories shall be ceremonially performed every day for a whole month in the Louvre, being afterwards purchased by the government, and published at their expense. In other words, we require the foundation of a musical museum.

(b) The introduction of musical instruction into the primary schools, its extension into other kinds of schools, and, at that point, the calling into existence of a new church music.

(c) The re-organization of choral singing and the reformation of plainchant in all the churches of both Paris and the provinces.

(d) General assemblies of Philharmonic Societies in the manner of the great musical festivals of England and Germany.

(e) Opera productions, concert and chamber music performances, organized after the plan sketched in our previous article on the conservatoire.

(f) A school of advanced musical studies, established quite separately from the conservatoire by the most eminent artists—a school whose branches shall extend to all the provincial towns having a chair in the history and philosophy of music.

(g) A cheap edition of the most important works of old and new composers, from the musical Renaissance to the present time. It will embrace the development of the art in its entirety, from folk song to Beethoven's *Chorale* Symphony. This publication as a whole might be called the 'Pantheon of Music.' The biographies, treatises, commentaries, and glossaries that would have to accompany it would form a true 'Encyclopedia of Music.'"[79]

On Infant Prodigies

"Artists who *are* to be!"[80]

"Nowadays we all too often see parents who, alas, pointing to certain shining examples [in history], and prompted by motives that have nothing to do with the love of the beautiful, wear out their children and exhaust them

78. RGS, vol. 3, p. 129.
79. RGS, vol. 2, pp. 53–54.
80. FMG, p. 251.

on mechanical studies whenever they show the slightest spark of talent and the smallest hope of material gain. They waste all on the attainment of a fruitless virtuosity ... on a soulless, senseless delivery of masterworks, which for sheer thumping and thrashing cannot be comprehended. The fledglings remain strangers to all other intellectual development and are in danger (unless they are outstandingly gifted) of running wild into a purely material sleight-of-hand."[81]

On Concerts and Concertizing

"Le concert, c'est moi!"[82]

"Always concerts! Always to be a valet of the public! What a trade!"[83]

"A major blemish on the performances of opera in Italy is the great and all-too-evident lack of balance between the brass and the string sections of the orchestra. The trombones and trumpets (with or without valves, which are much abused today) are not played softly or gently enough to match the violins and basses, and the result is a terrible racket—music, one might say, that is capable of arousing elephants or rhinoceroses. Only by shouting coarsely can the singers make themselves heard above the din. I doubt that the walls of Jericho were ever subjected to such a merciless assault."[84]

"True art deals only with the educated and select few, and would perish without their support."[85]

"It is unfortunately true that, in our day, neither opera managers, nor celebrated singers, nor conductors, consider it their duty to offer to the public really valuable works, and much less to enable the public to become better acquainted with works that do not earn immediate applause. In thus pandering to the most unreasonable caprices of the public, they are like the tutors of princes, who indulge their pupils in their whims without bridling them."[86]

Maxims of Life

"Create memories!"[87]

"To become noble is better than to be born noble."[88]

81. RGS, vol. 4, pp. 197–98.
82. LLB, vol. 1, p. 25.
83. PBUS, p. 50.
84. L'Artiste, August 1839, p. 257.
85. RGS, vol. 3, part 1, p. 100.
86. RGS, vol. 3, part 1, pp. 119–20.
87. LL, p. 331.
88. KL-B, p. 92.

"In life one must decide whether to conjugate the verb 'to have' or the verb 'to be.'"[89]

"To bear and forbear is ever our life's task."[90]

"The times do not concern themselves with me, so I do not concern myself with the times."[91]

"Nowadays, in our artistic world, character is still rarer than talent."[92]

"Wasting time is one of the worst faults in the world. Life is so short, every moment is so precious; yet we live as if life will never end."[93]

"There are few things that are impossible in themselves. We lack merely the application, not the means, to make them succeed."[94]

"The world is so formed that the practice of the Good and the search for the Better are not made agreeable to anyone; not in the things of Art, which appear the most inoffensive, any more than in others. In order to deserve well, one must learn to endure well."[95]

"Courage is the vital nerve of our best qualities; they fade away when it is wanting, and unless one is courageous one is not even sufficiently prudent."[96]

Maxims of Death

"[The death penalty is an] abominable social crime. It is obvious that we are all more or less guilty, deranged, or crazy, but it does not follow that we ought to be guillotined, hanged, or, as an act of mercy, shot."[97]

"Ever since the days of my youth I have considered dying much simpler than living. Even if there is often fearful and protracted suffering before death, yet death is nonetheless the deliverance from our involuntary yoke of existence."[98]

"I am extremely tired of living; but as I believe that God's Fifth Commandment "thou shalt not kill" also applies to suicide, I go on existing."[99]

89. WEG, p. 117.
90. LLB, vol. 2, p. 364.
91. HLR, p. 177.
92. LLB, vol. 2, p. 190.
93. From the diary of the fifteen-year-old Liszt, April–June, 1827. FLT, p. 21.
94. From the diary of the fifteen-year-old Liszt, FLT, p. 5.
95. LLB, vol. 2, p. 113.
96. LLB, vol. 2, p. 130.
97. WLLM, p. 418.
98. LLB, vol. 2, p. 348.
99. WLLM, p. 299.

"Suffering, pain, and sorrow are the lot of mankind. . . . Since we must all live and die, let us know how to do so in noble simplicity."[100]

"*Il mondo va da sè* [The world keeps going]—one lives one's life, occupies oneself, grieves, suffers, makes mistakes, changes one's mind, and dies as best one can! The sacrament most to be desired, it seems to me, is that of extreme unction!"[101]

"My sole claim on this earth, while I am on it, is to *impersonality.*"[102]

"Last Friday I entered my seventieth year. It might be time to end things well . . . all the more since I have never wished to live long. In my early youth I often went to sleep hoping not to awake again here below."[103]

"Let my body be buried, not in a church, but in some cemetery, and let it not be removed from that grave to any other. I will not have any other place for my body than the cemetery in use in the place where I die. . . . The inscription on my tomb might be: *Et habitabunt recti cum vulto tuo"* [The upright shall dwell in Thy presence; Psalm 140:13]."[104]

On Other Composers

J. S. BACH
"Bach . . . might well be called the Saint Thomas Aquinas of music."[105]

LUDWIG VAN BEETHOVEN
"For us musicians, Beethoven's work is like the pillar of cloud and fire that guided the Israelites through the desert—a pillar of cloud to guide us by day, a pillar of fire to guide us by night—'so that we may progress both day and night.'"[106]

HECTOR BERLIOZ
"With or without the magisterial permission of the titulary (or non titulary) professors—and even without that of the illustrious director of the Paris Conservatoire, who visited Berlioz's concerts quite regularly in order, as he put it, 'to learn how not to do it'—everybody who wants to keep up with contemporary art must study the scores of this master . . . precisely in order 'to learn how to do it.'"[107]

100. WLLM, p. 395.
101. LLB, vol. 7, p. 131.
102. WLLM, p. 313.
103. WLLM, p. 384.
104. LLB, vol. 2, p. 152.
105. LLB, vol. 2, p. 153.
106. LLB, vol. 1, p. 123.
107. RGS, vol. 4, p. 60.

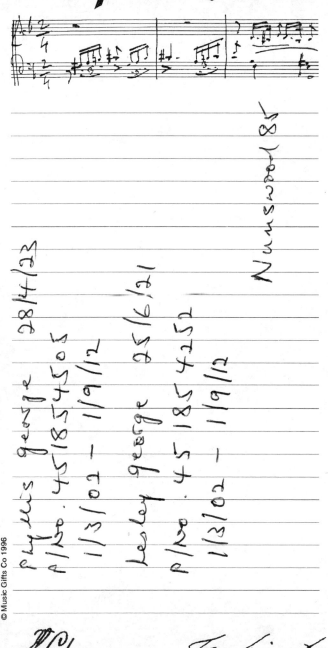

"The hypocrisy of his envious opponents consists in refusing to pay him the tuition they owe, and which they have on their conscience, while they publicly tread into the mire everything of his which they are not and never will be capable of imitating. They privately pull out all his feathers and use them as ornaments for themselves."[108]

ALEXANDER BORODIN

"Unquestionably Borodin is a great figure. The instrumentation of his symphony [no. 1, in E-flat major] is completely successful."[109]

FRYDERYCK CHOPIN

"Chopin never performed anything requiring bravura or endurance; he was too weak for it. His Study in C Minor [op. 25, no. 12] he never played."[110]

"In confining himself exclusively to the piano, Chopin has, in our opinion, given proof of one of the most essential qualities of a composer—a just appreciation of the form in which he possessed the power to excel. . . . Far from being ambitious of the uproar of an orchestra, Chopin was satisfied to see his thought integrally produced upon the ivory of a keyboard."[111]

"The *Preludes* of Chopin are quite special compositions. They are not merely pieces, as the title might suggest, intended to be played as an introduction to other pieces. Rather, they are poetic preludes, like those of a great contemporary poet, which lull the soul in golden dreams and raise it to ideal realms. Admirable in their variety, they contain a skill and substance that are appreciated only after careful study. The music is spontaneous, brilliant and fresh. They have the freedom and spaciousness characteristic of works of genius."[112]

CARL CZERNY

"Of all living composers who specialize in playing and writing for the piano, I know of none whose views and opinions coincide so exactly with what has actually been achieved. In the 'twenties, when for most musicians the greater number of Beethoven's creations were a kind of sphinx, Czerny played Beethoven *exclusively*, with an understanding that matched his technique. Nor did he close his mind to the progress that was made in technique later on, and in his teaching and his compositions he actually made a substantial contribution to it. One's only regret is that through an abundance of productivity he actually weakened himself and proceeded no farther along the path of his first sonata [op. 6, in A-flat major] and some

108. Ibid.
109. To follow.
110. RGD, p. 738.
111. LFC, pp. 17–19.
112. *Revue et Gazette musicale de Paris,* May 2, 1841.

other works of that period—works of which I think very highly and place in the noblest rank as important and beautifully constructed compositions. Alas, the social and publishing influences in Vienna at that time were detrimental to art, and Czerny did not possess the requisite dose of toughness to avoid them and uphold his *better self.* This latter task is generally very hard to achieve, the solution of which brings in its train much inconvenience, even for the ablest and highest-minded."[113]

JOHN FIELD

Field's *Nocturnes* have preserved their youth, unlike so many works grown old before their time. After more than thirty-six years they still retain a balmy freshness, and seem to exhale copious perfumes. Where else shall we meet such perfection of incomparable naïveté? No one since then has been able to reproduce the charms of his speech, caressing as a moist and tender gaze; soothing as the slow, measured rocking of a boat or the swinging of a hammock, amid whose smoothly placid oscillations we seem to hear the dying murmur of melting caresses. No one has revived these vague Aeolian tones, these half-sighs of the breezes, plaintive wails, ecstatic moans. No one has dared attempt them; no one, especially one who has heard Field himself play, or rather dream his pieces, wrapt in inspiration, not limiting himself to the written notes, but incessantly inventing new groups with which to garland his melodies; at each repetition he would adorn them diversely with a flowery rain, yet they never wholly disappeared beneath an ornamentation that veiled, without hiding, their languishing undulations and ravishing outlines. What an inexhaustible wealth of variations he lavished on the embellishment of his thought! With what rare taste would he intertwine around it, without smothering it, the most subtle weft of arabesques!"[114]

ROBERT FRANZ

"Franz writes songs as Schubert did; but he differs from him so essentially that under his pen the lied has entered upon a new stadium. He will build up a school and find imitators, if he has not already found them, just as Franz Schubert did." (1855)

"I wrote that 16 years ago. . . . I have scarcely thought it worthwhile to change a sentence, or retract a single word. . . . Franz long ago assumed the position that belongs to him, among the best German names, where his songs are now in the standard repertoire of the concert hall and the parlor." (1871)[115]

---

113. LLB, vol. 1, p. 219.
114. RGS, vol. 4, pp. 263–64.
115. RGS, vol. 4, p. 242.

FERDINAND HILLER

"Hiller's conducting is like his whole personality: accommodating, rounded, correct, even distinguished, but without tension and energy, and consequently without authority or communicative electricity. He might well be reproached with having no faults, and thus with giving criticism no foothold."[116]

FELIX MENDELSSOHN

"He is a man of remarkable talent and very cultivated intelligence. He draws marvelously, plays the violin and viola, is currently reading Homer in Greek, and speaks four or five languages fluently."[117]

MIHÁLY MOSONYI

"The death of Mosonyi places the heart in mourning. It makes us grieve as well for music in Hungary, of which Mosonyi was one of the noblest, most valiant and praiseworthy representatives. . . . Let us honor his memory by resolving to make his examples and teaching bear further fruit!"[118]

NICCOLÒ PAGANINI

"His god was never any other than his own gloomy, sad 'I.' "

"May the artist of the future gladly and readily decline to play the conceited and egotistical role which we hope has had in Paganini its last brilliant representative. May he set his goal within, and not outside himself, and be the means of virtuosity, and not its end. May he constantly keep in mind that, though the saying is *Noblesse oblige!* in a far higher degree than nobility—*Génie oblige!*"[119]

ANTON RUBINSTEIN

"As usual [Rubinstein] is spending his time composing a mass of works. I regret that the two most recent pieces he played for me show no advance on their predecessors. Still, he is young and robust. If only he could succeed in curbing his productive incontinence, he would reach loftier regions. . . . His character is a nobly proud one. I am afraid, however, that the strings of love and sorrow do not vibrate with enough energy in his soul!"[120]

FRANZ SCHUBERT

"Our pianists scarcely realize what a glorious treasure they have in Schubert's piano compositions. Most pianists skim over them *en passant,* notice

---

116. LLB, vol. 4, p. 217.
117. ACLA, vol. 1, p. 416.
118. LLB, vol. 2, p. 164.
119. *Revue et Gazette musicale,* August 23, 1840.
120. LLB, vol. 5, p. 229.

here and there repetitions, lengthiness, apparent carelessness . . . and then lay them aside. It is true that Schubert himself is somewhat to blame for the very unsatisfactory manner in which his admirable pianoforte pieces are treated. He was too immoderately productive, wrote incessantly, mixing insignificant with important things, grand things with mediocre work, paid no heed to criticism, and always soared on his wings. Like a bird in the air, he lived in music and sang in angelic fashion.

"O never-resting, ever-welling genius, full of tenderness! O my cherished Hero of the Heaven of Youth! Harmony, freshness, power, grace, dreamings, passion, soothings, tears and flames pour forth from the depths and heights of thy soul, and thou makest us almost forget the greatness of thine excellence in the fascination of thy spirit!"[121]

CLARA SCHUMANN

"For a number of years Madame Schumann has played only now and then in public. Fate has led her recently to make new concert tours, and to turn her special attention once more to virtuosity. As Weimar was one of the first cities included in her plan, we had an opportunity over several days to measure the significant development that her talent had meanwhile undergone. The lovely companion of the Muses has meanwhile turned into a consecrated, devoted, severe Priestess. To the moist, youthful luster of her eyes has succeeded a fixed and anxious look. The garland of flowers, once so loosely woven into her hair, now barely hides the vivid scars that the crown of thorns has impressed so deeply on her brow. . . . An unimpeachable perfection characterizes every tone of this soft, suffering Sibyl, who, breathing heaven's air, remains connected only by her tears with earth."[122]

ROBERT SCHUMANN

"He is a musician who must be rated highly and studied closely if one wants to be well informed about the most polished and best compositions of the last dozen years."[123]

"For my part, I need not in the least reproach myself with ever having denied my sympathy and reverence for Schumann; and a hundred younger artistic contemporaries in every country could testify that I have always expressly directed them to a thorough study of his works, and have strengthened and refreshed myself through them."[124]

---

121. LLB, vol. 2, pp. 132–33.

122. RGS, vol. 4, p. 203. This essay was written a year after Robert Schumann had tried to commit suicide. He was now a patient at the asylum in Endenich.

123. LLB, vol. 3, p. 6.

124. LLB, vol. 1, p. 258.

"He began as a genius, and ended as a talent."[125]

Bedřich Smetana
"Smetana's death has moved me deeply. He was a genius."[126]

Ludwig Spohr
"Spohr is a fine and worthy man, decent and diligent. He must be about seventy-five now, and of all the musicians of his generation I regard him as the most competent and best by far. His twin career as composer and virtuoso is likewise honorable. But in both the one and the other the element of the extraordinary is missing, which quite simply is what is meant by genius. . . . He is a patriarch of Art, but he is neither a prophet nor an apostle."[127]

Camille Saint-Saëns
"For many years I have made much of his talent, as everybody knows. To define him for you in one word, I shall say that he is the French Rubinstein—therefore at one and the same time he is an eminent virtuoso and a very productive composer, widely gifted, having a claim to excel in all the genres: symphony, oratorio, chamber and salon music, and opera. He is, besides, an admirable organist."[128]

"I know of no one among contemporary artists who, all things considered, is his equal in talent, knowledge, and variety of skills—except Rubinstein. However, the latter does not have the advantage of being an organist, in which capacity Saint-Saëns is not merely in the first rank but incomparable, as is Sebastian Bach as a master of counterpoint."[129]

Sigismond Thalberg
"Thalberg was much more a favorite of the Parisians than I, who reached deeper in piano performance. Everything with him was refined, finished, whereas I was such a medley of temperaments."[130]

Richard Wagner
"Of Wagner I will only say to you that my deep and lovingly passionate admiration for his genius continues to increase. I leave it to others to criticize and haggle. To me he is the equal of Dante. King Ludwig of Bavaria

---

125. GSA, Kasten 29.
126. LLB, vol. 2, p. 362.
127. LLB, vol. 3, p. 22.
128. LLB, vol. 7, p. 133.
129. WLLM, pp. 300–01.
130. RGD, p. 738.

and my daughter have the right perspective—adoration. To pass judgment often amounts to misinterpreting."[131]

"In the world of contemporary art there is one name that has already become glorious, and which will become ever more so—Richard Wagner. His genius has been to me a flaming torch; I have followed it, and my friendship for Wagner has always been of the character of a noble passion."[132]

"Neither Schumann nor Berlioz could remain content at seeing the steady advance of Wagner's works. Both of them suffered from a suppressed enthusiasm for the *Music of the Future.*"[133]

"What am I to say to you of Wagner? . . . It is a pity that we cannot procure a stream of gold for him, or have some palaces of gold built for him! What can he do with admiration, enthusiasm, devotion, and all such nonessential things?"[134]

"To Bayreuth I am not a composer, but a publicity agent."[135]

131. WMML, pp. 345–46.
132. LLB, vol. 5, p. 56.
133. LLB, vol. 2, p. 121.
134. LLB, vol. 2, p. 29.
135. PEMH, p. 535.

Epilogue

An Open Letter to Franz Liszt

Concerning great men everything may be said, for it does not injure them.
FERDINAND RIES ON BEETHOVEN[1]

Dear and highly esteemed Master!

I have long cherished the notion of writing to you, and I am grateful beyond measure that I now have an opportunity to do so. To many people it may seem strange that I would want to communicate with you at all, you who have been dead for more than a century. If so, that can only be because they lack imagination and are incapable of understanding how important your life and work have become to me. Suffice it to say that during the twenty-five years I worked on your biography, which surely gives me some claim to your attention, there were times when I longed to set aside my work in order to consult you directly about the problems before me. On these occasions I became envious of your first official biographer, Lina Ramann, who had ready access to you while you were still alive. You not only granted her the inestimable privilege of holding personal interviews, but you replied promptly and conscientiously to the many handwritten questionnaires she sent you in the 1870s. I found it inexplicable that she failed to use so much of this irreplaceable material in her narrative, and even more so that it remained in the Weimar Archives until 1983, hardly consulted by others. You yourself had some reservations about Ramann. "Do not entangle yourself in so many details,"[2] you told her after the interviews had got underway. And to your longtime companion Princess Carolyne von Sayn-Wittgenstein, you observed, "I fear that [Ramann] will be unable to see the wood for the trees"[3]—a sure sign that you lacked confidence in her.

Do not chastise me for these words, revered Master, at least not until you have read everything that I have to say. If I am critical about certain aspects of your life and work, that in no way diminishes my respect and admiration for the way you lived out your allotted span. In so many ways, yours was the life of a hero. Those of

1. SB, p. 26.
2. RL, p. 407.
3. LLB, vol. 7, p. 181.

us who are familiar with the minutiae of your daily toil still marvel at your grace
under pressure. I will, in any case, work hard to see things from your point of view.

I

What better place to start than at the beginning? Your early education was neglected, a situation you strove to overcome in later years. I recall reading somewhere
that you attended school in your natal village of Raiding from your sixth year and
received some basic tuition in reading and writing from the village schoolmaster Johann Rohrer. The most telling image I retained when considering your rustic education was that the schoolroom in which you and your fellow pupils were prepared
for the outside world by Rohrer was a mere twenty feet in length and fourteen feet
in width. From this early constriction, you widened your boundaries to a point
where you were able to embrace the whole world.

You remained in Rohrer's charge for a mere two years, after which your father
took you away to Vienna for piano studies with Czerny. Until then, your father
Adam, an amateur musician, had been your only piano teacher. Music took up all
your time until your late teens, at which point you were a prodigy of European
fame. Somehow you discovered the joy of books and gradually turned yourself into
a voracious reader. Your bookshelves included both the sacred and the secular; your
readings ranged from the "Defense of Catholicism" by the Abbé Lamennais to the
skeptical writings of Montaigne, from the religious poetry of Lamartine to the agnostic prose of Voltaire. You often stayed up half the night with such literature in
search of some key with which to unlock the riddles of this world. Your soul, in Ramann's telling words, was full of presage. Are there not echoes of these belated struggles to acquire an education in your admonitions to your son Daniel to do better
than you did, and profit from the material advantages you were making available to
him? You drove him hard, but he rewarded you by winning the national Prix d'hon-
neur in classical studies when he was only seventeen years old; he was awarded this
coveted prize by Marshal Pélissier on behalf of the Emperor Napoleon III himself.

Despite the neglect of your primary education, which you yourself described to
Princess Carolyne as a "capital defect" which you had never been able to remedy,
you later became the one great composer with the most advanced social ideas, particularly with regard to education and the fairer distribution of wealth. You wrote
about these topics at length in your early articles. What I found impressive was that
you were no armchair philosopher but were committed to putting your ideals into
practice. Even as a young man you visited hospitals, insane asylums, and those condemned to die. You brought music to society's outcasts, and gave these unfortunates
a degree of comfort in their hour of distress. The accounts of your visits to the
Salpêtrière Hospital in Paris, in 1833, and to the insane asylum in Cork, Ireland, in
1841 make haunting reading still. When you entered the asylum in Cork, it was with
the intent of playing the piano for the inmates. But you were so overcome at the
horrors you witnessed in the so-called unclean women's room that you were obliged

to withdraw. About thirty females were confined to one area, some howling, some bent up like animals, some scraping the walls, others rolling on the stone floor. To this menagerie of depraved human beings you offered the balm of music. We cannot begin to imagine what your distinguished contemporaries Chopin, Brahms, Wagner, or Mendelssohn would have made of your attitude. Without exception, they would not have gone near the building.

I have always respected your stand against the death penalty, which must have been formed early, and which was likewise advanced for its time. Already you perceived it to be state-sponsored murder. In later life you wrote to your friend Baroness Meyendorff, "[The death penalty is an] abominable social crime. It is obvious that we are all more or less guilty, deranged, or crazy, but it does not follow that we ought to be guillotined, hanged, or, as an act of mercy, shot."[4] That phrase "an act of mercy" reveals a streak of irony, an essential part of your character. How kind of the state, you seemed to say, to put on display for the benefit of those condemned to die the varied forms this final solution might take—and then deny them any choice in the matter.

Your general opposition to suicide sprang from the same source: your abhorrence of all killing. The German noun *Selbstmord* (literally "self-murder") puts it with brutal frankness. (The English prefer to borrow the elegant French term *suicide*. Even though they possess the richest language in the world, they have no word to describe this ultimate act of violence against oneself.) You knew that the Roman Catholic Church forbade suicide, of course, and as a minor cleric you understood better than most that those people who discarded their lives in this way would not be buried in consecrated ground but would be excommunicated, their souls sent to purgatory. But even on this issue you were ahead of the Church and foresaw a time when all that would change, as it has. In a dark hour you yourself once contemplated suicide, but were prevented from carrying out this act by your strong Catholic faith.[5]

II

It was the same with your notion of the musician and his place in society, which was revolutionary for its time and placed the profession of music on a completely new plane. It still arouses my admiration whenever I think about what you achieved. Even as a young man you articulated a vivid idea when you said that "the Artist is the bearer of the Beautiful," and you likened the vocation of music to that of the priesthood. You talked of a sacred predestination that marks the artist at birth. "It is not he who chooses his profession—it is his profession that chooses him."[6] The idea that one has as little choice in the decision to become a musician as one has in de-

4. WLLM, p. 418.
5. WLLM, p. 299.
6. RGS, vol. 2, p. 135.

termining the color of one's eyes is arresting. It suggests that the musician is in the grip of forces he cannot understand but has no alternative but to obey. I cannot help observing the similarity with Freud's famous aphorism "We are lived"—which yours predates by eighty years. To probe this idea still further: you are reminding us that the vocation of music cannot be confused with a mere trade. The butcher, the baker, and the candlestick-maker can all change places with one another. But not one of them can change places with a musician. Nobody is called upon to be a candlestick-maker. You did not stop there, however. You already knew that there had to be consequences. If Art was God given, something had to be given back. Your motto "Génie oblige!"[7] was a rallying cry that contained within it an ethical imperative: music forces mankind to confront its nobility. This most wondrous of the arts, you maintained, ought not to be sacrificed on the altar of Mammon but should be used to benefit the whole of humanity. And you lived out the precept. You made a fortune during your years of vagabondage, but you exhausted your wealth by giving most of it away to the huddled masses, much of it anonymously. Your Hungarian pupil Janka Wohl recalled that whenever you visited Budapest in later years, you would spend time filling envelopes with banknotes and address them to the needy, anonymously. It is a compelling image.

Nobody should have been surprised at your anger when the German newspapers published the will of Theodor Kullak, which revealed that he had amassed a personal fortune of several million marks from teaching. His Neue Akademie der Tonkunst in Berlin was the largest private piano school in Germany, with over a hundred teachers and eleven hundred students. You told your pupils that it was "a burning shame" that Kullak had left nothing for needy musicians.[8] To Lina Ramann you were more forthright still. "As an artist, you must not rake in a million marks without performing some sacrifice on the altar of art."[9] Most of us would have left it there. But you wrote an open letter to the editor of the *Allgemeine Musikalische Zeitung*,[10] suggesting that Kullak's sons should use their inheritance to establish some scholarships for musicians in need. Many people must have thought that such a public interference on your part was unwarranted. Should not one be allowed to leave one's hard-earned money to whomsoever one chooses? Kullak's sons certainly thought so, for nothing happened. Still, if anyone had a right to voice a protest it was you, who had given so much back to the profession during your lifetime.

Here, as elsewhere, you possessed the vice of your virtues. Consider the disastrous performance of your *Gran* Mass in the St. Eustache Church in Paris, in 1866. The conditions were appalling, and you knew in advance that they would be. Your mass was preceded by a series of polkas played by a military band. A detachment of soldiers, responding to the barked commands of their officers, created a counterpoint to your "Kyrie Eleison." In the middle of the "Sanctus" a drummer performed

---

7. RGS, vol. 2, p. 112.
8. LL, p. 226.
9. RL, p. 298.
10. Issue of September 5, 1885.

an obbligato! No wonder that the gentlemen of the press tore you to pieces the next day. And your response? "The mistake I made," you later wrote, "was not to have forbidden a performance given under such deplorable conditions." So why did you permit it? "I did not wish to deprive the fund for the poor of the guaranteed receipts of more than 40,000 francs."[11] You yourself described it as a philanthropic gesture, without value in matters of Art. So be it.

III

Your critics have argued that your philanthropy, especially when it was expressed in so public a fashion, was simply an expression of personal aggrandizement. I do not know, honored master, whether you are familiar with the Yiddish proverb, "If you want to beat a dog, you are sure to find a stick," but it is one that springs constantly to mind whenever I contemplate the ingratitude your generosity encountered. Perhaps the most striking examples have to do with your unflinching support of Richard Wagner and Hector Berlioz. You championed their music at a time of its most serious neglect. The great Wagner and Berlioz festivals you mounted in Weimar during the 1850s remain largely unsung by posterity, but they brought your two great contemporaries into prominence at the very moment when they were about to go under. Wagner, especially, owed you a special debt since he was at that time condemned to a Swiss exile for his revolutionary activities, his music banned from every German state—including yours. You took exceptional political risks in mounting *Tannhäuser, The Flying Dutchman,* and *Lohengrin* in such an incendiary atmosphere, which put a strain on your personal friendship with the grand duke of Weimar. Nor were these the humdrum performances one might have expected from Weimar's tiny opera house. The world still does not know enough about your exceptional efforts, so let it be said that for the world premier of *Lohengrin* (August 28, 1850) you were obliged to conduct forty-six rehearsals before everything came together. Wagner dedicated the opera to you in gratitude. It was one of the few such acknowledgments you ever received from him. How fortuitous of you to have kept all his letters to you! After his death in 1883 your daughter Cosima wanted them returned to her; as Wagner's widow she doubtless felt that she had some rights in their ownership; but you refused to give them up. Within two years of your own death they had been published, and the world was at last able to appreciate what a one-sided friendship your relationship with Wagner had been. You gave him everything; he gave back nothing. He was the first Wagnerian.

But there was much more to your support of new music than these highly visible efforts, important though they were. It was the daily grind of shoring up the untried and the untested, sometimes in the face of impossible odds, that was so impressive. When you settled in Weimar, in 1848, the reactionaries were everywhere in control. I have somewhere called the opposition aroused by your evangelical work

11. WPL, p. 409.

on behalf of modern music as the "War of the Romantics." Vienna, which had dominated the European scene for sixty years, had lapsed into sterile academicism since the death of Beethoven. The position in Leipzig was worse; Mendelssohn had been cut off in his prime and the schoolmen had taken over, the "posthumous party" as you so contemptuously called them, because of their interest in dead forms—Moritz Hauptmann, Julius Rietz, and Ferdinand David—and who had placed modern music in a straitjacket. As for Paris, it was dominated by the Opera House, and it was virtually impossible for an unknown composer to gain a foothold there. The younger generation of composers now looked to Weimar and to you for leadership. With characteristic generosity you placed yourself and your resources wholeheartedly at the service of all who sought your help. What battles were fought at that time! No cause, however modest, was turned away if you thought it had merit, even when your own preferences failed to correspond to it. Overnight you turned Weimar into a mecca of modern music and became a champion of the new. Raff, Cornelius, Reubke, Bronsart, Johann van Hoven, Lortzing, Heinrich Dorn, Draeseke, Sobelewski, Lassen, and a host of aspiring young composers grouped themselves around you. To put the matter simply, you defended the defenseless; you gave a voice to the voiceless.

IV

But all this benefaction to others stood in stark contrast to the austere treatment you meted out to your three children. How can we reconcile your generosity to the world at large with your severity as a father? I do not wish to provoke your anger, but this paradox has always caused me bewilderment. After your rupture with Countess Marie d'Agoult, the mother of these children, which was admittedly a difficult episode in both your lives and one that was filled with verbal abuse on both sides, you removed them from her by force of law, and arranged for Blandine, Cosima, and Daniel to be brought up by your own mother, Anna Liszt, in Paris. It was a wonderful solution to a difficult problem, for your mother loved them as if they were her own, and she was loved by them in turn. But why did you then behave as if you yourself were absolved from all further participation in their upbringing, and virtually withdraw from their lives? You did not see them again for eight years.

Eight years! That reflects badly on you. You will say that you legitimized them, that you gave them a family name of which they could be proud, that you transferred substantial sums of money to your mother in order to purchase their material comforts, that you conducted a long correspondence with them, that you settled large dowries on your two daughters to secure good marriages. All that is true. But these children missed you, longed for a visit from you, and grew up barely knowing you. They were obliged to do what everybody else in Europe was doing: follow your meteoric career from afar. Indeed, you once advised Blandine to look you up on the map; you were in Gibraltar at the time.[12] No cruelty was intended on your part, but cruelty was what the children sometimes perceived, and after them certain biographers. Did it never occur to you that Cosima's ambivalence toward you in her maturity was a direct consequence of your neglect of her during her childhood? It comes out forcefully in her diaries, the reading of which you were spared, since they were published long after both you and she had gone to meet your Maker. All your children, but especially Cosima, missed you at that crucial time of transition from childhood to adolescence, so that in later life you were a stranger to them, whatever impressions of amity you and they worked so hard to present to the outside world.[13] You paid a terrible price for neglecting Cosima. She was the only one of your children to survive into old age. But she carried the poisoned brew of her early years into maturity, and with it she contaminated your old age. You virtually spent your dying days as her victim in alien Bayreuth, where you were subjected to indignity and subordinated to the memory of her late husband Richard Wagner. Of course, she did her duty as your daughter and tended you in your final hours. But that duty was as cold as charity. What was it that your much-admired Goethe used to say? "Säen ist nicht so beschwerlich als ernten" (Sowing is not as difficult as reaping). And you did indeed reap a bitter harvest.

V

I must also tell you that as your biographer I see an affinity between your almost reckless generosity to others and your almost reckless creativity. Both are manifestations of an unbridled personality. Your catalog of works tells us that you composed more than fourteen hundred pieces of music. That is an astounding number. The combined catalogues of Chopin, Schumann, and Brahms do not equal it. It contains sovereign masterpieces such as the Sonata in B Minor, the *Faust* Symphony, and the Thirteenth Psalm, mixed in with compositions of lesser worth. The time-worn question remains: would it not have been better to have composed fewer works and to have held back the ones of dubious value? Perhaps the question itself is a rather foolish one. Art is long; criticism is short. In a hundred years, who knows whether time itself will not have revealed mediocrities to be masterpieces? I am mindful of your much-maligned *Hungarian Rhapsodies*. They are today enjoying an unprecedented renaissance—the critical cant and hypocrisy once surrounding them, together with the "Hungarian question," having evaporated. For the rest, it has been well said that a true composer can no more "hold back" a composition, of whatever worth, than an apple tree can hold back certain apples; the whole tree needs must come to fruition, whatever the condition of the fruit. A Romantic notion? Perhaps. But you were a child of your time, and it holds true for you.

12. WFL, vol. 1, p. 413.
13. WEG.

Revered master, I must prevail upon your good nature still further and raise with you a related question: that of your transcriptions and paraphrases. An inspection of your catalog of works tells us that nearly half that bountiful figure of fourteen hundred items consists of arrangements, either of your own music or of the music of others. This represented an enormous expenditure of time and effort in pursuit of a genre that by its nature is usually prevented from rising to the level of original creation. Your detractors have often asked the question, Why spend so much effort on the humdrum task of adapting the music of others for your own hands to play? Would it not have been better to reserve your creative energy for original things? After all, your great contemporaries Chopin, Schumann, and Mendelssohn showed so little interest in arrangements that for them the genre could hardly be said to exist. Your answer, of course, has to do with your unique historical position and even more with your sense of mission. You saw yourself and your piano as vessels through which the whole of music might pass—operas, symphonies, lieder, and so forth. It was another aspect of "Génie oblige!" You then presented this music to those many thousands of people who never had the chance to go to concerts and operas. Your audiences in the European hinterland, in the towns and villages of central and eastern Europe, heard this music for the first time when your matchless fingers brought it to life. Self-effacement is the correct term to attach to such things as your superb transcriptions of the Beethoven symphonies and the Bach organ preludes and fugues, which are as rigorous as a prison sentence (you yourself once described the activity as "the ball and chain of transcription"). To survey this branch of your work in all its glorious entirety is to wander through the halls of history—for to the names of Bach and Beethoven we must add every composer of note from Palestrina to Berlioz. These works have been called "the gramophone records of the nineteenth-century." But the gramophone record has meanwhile been invented, and your arrangements are so compelling that they themselves have been recorded—a sure sign that they are valued as independent creations. That is the true measure of your success in this field. Nevertheless, in one unexpected and entirely unpredictable sense your critics were right to chastise you. To hyphenate your name with those of other composers turned you into a victim of history. You could not have foreseen the rise of musicology, with its insistence on urtexts. This development had the dramatic effect of seeming to turn the arrangement itself into second-class music (by definition the genre can only exist by defiling the urtext, a concept of which you were mercifully spared) and helped to keep your name off the concert programs of Europe and North America for many years when arrangements fell out of fashion.

For all that, it still arouses astonishment that you were able to achieve so many new things in art. Pianist, composer, teacher, conductor, author, administrator, and cofounder of the Romantic movement in music, you left your mark on everything that you touched. But you suffered for pursuing such diversity. You demonstrated the old truth that it is possible to have so many gifts that they turn into liabilities, so many talents that clamor for attention that they cancel one another out. The multigifted artist ought to be a cause for general rejoicing. Yet all too often we place him in limbo, unable to cope with his versatility. And limbo was your lot until recent times. You introduced the symphonic poem (your reply to the classical symphony); you constructed strange new forms and made them coherent through your cultivation of the technique of "metamorphosis of themes"; and you advanced the language of harmony more rapidly than any composer of your time, pushing it to the borders of atonality. Your work as a mentor calls for special mention. More than four hundred pupils passed through your hands and some of them—Tausig, Bülow, Rosenthal, Sauer, Siloti, among others—became eminent. For this priceless instruction you charged nothing. You were also the first modern conductor, an achievement that has gone largely unrecognized because your tenure at Weimar was cut short before the full impact of your reforms on the podium could be felt; it was left to your pupil Hans von Bülow to continue your tradition through his sterling work as conductor of the Meiningen Court Orchestra. In the aiding and abetting of Bülow's career, incidentally, you did much good by stealth. A book could be written on the topic.

The price you paid for being in the vanguard was severe. Your profile was the highest, so it presented the most obvious target for conservative critics to attack. It still stretches incredulity that your music was banned by a number of music conservatories, including the Berlin Hochschule für Musik, whose director was Joseph Joachim (your erstwhile friend), and the Royal Academy of Music in Britain. As Sir George Macfarren (the principal of the academy) piously expressed it, "Liszt is working a great evil on music." Not content to regard you as an instrument of Mephistopheles, Sir George went on to turn you into a musical bartender, arguing that "were you to preach temperance at a gin-shop door, and let your congregation taste the poison sold therein, that they might know its vileness, they would come out drunkards."[14] At the time of your death Clara Schumann wrote in her diary that you were "a dangerous example for the young" and that "as a composer he was terrible."[15] Madame Schumann doubtless drew comfort from the fact that the really nice thing about speaking ill of the dead is that they cannot answer back. But posterity has answered for you. Clara Schumann, Joseph Joachim, Sir George Macfarren, and the comedy of errors they created around you have been overtaken by history. The future was always on your side.

VI

Your relations with the critics were never easy. You will not like it when I tell you that your dealings with these gentlemen were frequently reckless and did you little good. You wrote far too many letters to the press. You were too tightly sprung, too ready to enter the rough-and-tumble of debate. You always seemed to be defending

14. BGM, p. 296.
15. LCS, vol. 3, p. 479.

something—presumably because you thought it vulnerable and needed protection—new music, your pupils, the place of the musician in society, even yourself. Some of the issues were important; others were trivial. But you were ever ready to put yourself in harm's way. What matter that some of Europe's leading critics did not like your music? Silence would have been a stronger response than a letter of protest. You should have let your music speak for itself, the most eloquent reply of all. Instead, your letters to the editors of sundry newspapers showed that you had been stung, and some of them served only to bring yet more attention to your opponents, especially to your nemesis Eduard Hanslick. In the 1850s, especially, you were so concerned about the promotion of new music, not just your own but that of the younger generation as a whole, that your polemical instincts got the better of you and your rancor sometimes showed. The words of Dr. Samuel Johnson were as true in your day as in his: "Why, Sir, a fly may sting a stately horse and make him wince. But the one is still a horse, while the other remains a fly."

VII

I have left until last the tangled topic of your relations with women. You will rebuke me for raising the subject at all, but of all the issues in your long and productive life, this one creates the worst impression to the world at large. You have been variously depicted as a Don Juan, a philanderer, even a sexual predator, activities (so we are told) that were in no wise diminished even after you had donned the cassock. In truth you were none of these things. The popular biographies have nonetheless painted a picture of you as a tabloid character, a pop star of the nineteenth century with screaming fans in your wake, an image that has survived to our own time.

On his deathbed, your father showed much prescience when he told you that although you were not lacking in intelligence, he feared that women would trouble your existence and dominate your life. You were only fifteen at the time of his death, but he had already perceived your preference for female company, a preference that grew with the passing years. Caroline Saint Cricq, Countess Marie d'Agoult, Charlotte von Hagn, Marie Duplessis (the inspiration for Hugo's *La dame aux camélias*), Lola Montez, Princess Carolyne von Sayn-Wittgenstein, Agnes Street-Klindworth, Baroness Olga von Meyendorff, and Olga Janina are but a few of the names that spring to mind. Women seemed to throw themselves in your path, and you made few attempts to prevent them from doing so. I somewhere likened the reckless behavior of certain of these ladies to the potential suicides who annually make their way to the brink of Niagara Falls. Some of them even throw themselves over the brink and into the churning depths below. No one blames the Falls.

There were only two occasions on which you were known to have contemplated matrimony. The first was an inexplicable offer of marriage to Countess Valentine de Cessiat, the twenty-four-year-old niece of Lamartine, in 1845. I call it "inexplicable" because you had seen her but once, and her nunlike devotion to her famous uncle, from whom she resolutely refused to be parted, would have meant your absorption into the Lamartine household. There is a tantalizing dearth of documentation on this strange encounter. It was impulsive behavior, doubtless prompted by the permanent rupture of your relationship with Marie d'Agoult a few months earlier. Nietzsche famously diagnosed your personality as "Dionysiac." This god of fertility, this god of wine, this son of Zeus ruled your passions, or so he thought. You were not displeased with Nietzsche's observation, but your rebuttal was beautifully dismissive: "I do not have the advantage of knowing him."[16] The other marriage proposal I will come to presently. It was one of the central episodes of your life.

It would have been to your long-term advantage if you had been less tolerant of some of these women, especially the fortune seekers among them. Your widely reported liaison with Lola Montez and (when you were approaching your twilight years) Olga Janina, resulted in scandals of your own making. The case of La Janina, sometimes called the "Cossack Countess," was especially galling, and ineptly handled by you. If you had not been so accepting of this emotional cripple, you would have been rid of her much sooner. The world would then have been spared her "autobiographical" novels, in which you were caricatured, and which were written in a spirit of revenge after you had finally ended all contact with her. Had those novels never existed, her links with you would have been so tenuous as to have rendered preposterous her claim to a sexual encounter with you. And in the absence of the novels, your English character-assassin Ernest Newman would never have been able to use this spurious material against you. In your defense it ought to be said that you were almost certainly being blackmailed by La Janina, a fact of which the world knows too little, and Newman knew nothing. Your Catholic religion had given you a horror of suicide, and once Janina had grasped that fact all she had to do was to threaten to take her own life in order to exact from you whatever she wished—from concerts to caresses. And she had weapons enough at her disposal to emphasize the point—including knives, a revolver, and a pharmacy of toxic drugs.

The two women who were central to your life—Countess Marie d'Agoult and Princess Carolyne von Sayn-Wittgenstein—fall into a very different category, and it would be derelict to mix their names with those of Janina and Montez. These long liaisons (twelve years in the case of the former, and nearly thirty years in the case of the latter) were more durable than many a modern marriage and generally more productive. Yet you made a fatal error in allowing these women into your workshop and assigning them a role in the writing of your prose works. Both of them had literary pretensions, and they went to work with a will. In consequence, a long shadow was cast across your prose, and the authenticity of your collected literary works is still disputed. Beyond question, Princess Carolyne prepared the second edition of your book on the Gypsies without consulting you, expanding the anti-Semitic passages that she herself had smuggled into the pages of the first edition. This unleashed a firestorm in the press, and you were accused of being anti-Semitic. "Really—your father, a Jew-baiter!" exclaimed Wagner to Cosima in a fit

16. WLLM, pp. 38–39.

of glee after reading the reviews.[17] It was a calumny, of course; there is not a scintilla of evidence that you were racially prejudiced, against Jews or any other group, and much evidence that you were not. It was the cruel exploitation of your name by Princess Carolyne, in pursuit of her own ends, that placed you in this false position. Why did you not tell her to concentrate on writing her own books, and leave yours to be written by you? We know the answer, of course, and it takes us to the heart of a chief criticism against you: misplaced chivalry. Chivalry is a noble quality when placed in the service of noble things. But Princess Carolyne's anti-Semitism was not noble. Your silence served to protect her, and you received abuse that ought more properly to have been directed against her. Once again it was left to Wagner, alas, to sum up your plight. "Your father," he told Cosima, "goes to his ruin out of pure chivalry!"[18]

When the dust has finally settled on the long-running dispute over the exact authorship of your prose works, one legitimate complaint remains. Why did you not spend more time writing about your own music, instead of that of others? Major essays flowed from your pen on the music of Berlioz, Wagner, Schumann, Chopin, Beethoven, Franz, and Field. But hardly a word about your own! We have to go to your personal correspondence in order to gather what few scraps of information you offer about your compositions. On rare occasions you actually favor your correspondent with music examples, the better to explain the inner workings of your creative process. The letter you wrote to your uncle Eduard Liszt, giving details about certain thematic connections within your E-flat Major Piano Concerto, is the sort of thing of which we possess too little.[19] Instead of working these ideas into a major essay, which pianists the world over would have found so useful, you spent your substance writing publicity puffs for Sobelewski's *Vinvela* and Boieldieu's *Weisse Dame*. Inevitably the gap has been filled by others, with mixed results. We marvel at the range of interpretations our musicological age continues to attach to your pianistic masterpiece, the Sonata in B Minor, and we would give much to observe your reactions to them. If only you yourself had written as many words about this sonata as you wrote (say) about the nocturnes of John Field, a number of experts would have been rendered silent. But since you didn't, they continue to pile speculation upon conjecture. Meanwhile, you are probably consoling yourself with the German proverb, "Even a blind hen will sometimes pick up a grain."

VIII

Forgive me, dear master, for remembering that second marriage proposal, the one that you offered to Princess Carolyne von Sayn-Wittgenstein. That it was made at all used to be disputed by your biographers, especially the ones who disliked her.

17. WT, vol. 2, p. 756.
18. WT, vol. 2, p. 756.
19. LLB, vol. 1, pp. 270–76.

They were fond of quoting Cosima, who once observed that you looked forward to a marriage with Carolyne as to a burial service. Yet they should examine your will, in which you wrote that you "dearly wished to call [Carolyne] by the sweet name of wife."[20] The marriage documents, to which both you and Carolyne attached your signatures, in October 1861, are also there to be inspected.[21] I do not want to incur your wrath by reviewing in detail the thirteen-year struggle that Carolyne mounted against those high-ranking Roman Catholic clerics who wanted to block the annulment of her first marriage in order to prevent a union with you. Blackmail, bribery, perjury, and prevarication were all part of the ungodly mixture. The trail of mendacity led right into the heart of the Vatican, with filthy lucre as its goal. You were still in Weimar at that time, awaiting the outcome of this Byzantine process, while Carolyne drummed up support in Rome. After Carolyne's appeal to Pius IX, her case prevailed. Pius himself approved the decree of annulment on January 8, 1861.[22] It was a sweet victory, which both you and Carolyne savored to the full. But you made a fatal blunder, which I have never properly understood. You prevaricated. Had you and Carolyne sought out any village priest, in any part of Catholic Europe, he would, on the authority of this annulment document alone, have joined you in holy matrimony. It was probably vanity in victory that led Carolyne to insist on a highly public wedding in Rome, months later, on your fiftieth birthday, October 22, 1861, under the noses of the very cardinals who had blocked her. By taunting them in this fashion, she gave them time to regroup, and they found enough evidence in the mountain of paper that she had accumulated in pursuit of her annulment, to bring charges of perjury against her. When you finally arrived in Rome, two days before the ceremony, your wedding plans were in disarray. No Hollywood scriptwriter could have improved on the tale. It has, in fact, been projected more than once onto the silver screen, with a leading role for the woman who had placed you in such a predicament. "I fear that women will trouble your existence": your father's deathbed prophecy frequently came back to haunt you.

There is one question that has always intrigued me about your thwarted marriage to Carolyne. Three years after the debacle, her husband Prince Nicholas died. No impediment now stood in the way of your marriage. Yet it never took place. Why not? The grand duke of Weimar made the same point. In reply you quoted Pascal: "The heart has its reasons of which reason knows nothing."[23] I have never considered that to be a satisfactory explanation. But it is the only one you ever offered.

IX

A still more painful episode awaited you in 1868 when Cosima deserted her first husband Hans von Bülow, your favorite pupil, and eloped with Richard Wagner,

---

20. WFL, vol. 2, p. 556.
21. WELC.
22. It is reproduced in WFL, vol. 2, p. 573.
23. LLCA, p. 128.

your best musical friend. After years of deceit, and after giving birth to Wagner's children, Isolde and Eva, Cosima fled Munich and joined Wagner in Switzerland. Your blistering letter of condemnation deserves to be better known.[24] It suggests that the sacrament of marriage was of such importance to you that you would sooner keep Cosima and Hans shackled in their misery than break their vows. Conjugal bliss, or lack of it, was not a consideration with you. A strange contradiction from one who had lived with his paramour for so many years without benefit of clergy. You removed your blessing from Cosima; you even went to Switzerland to accost Wagner. You likened that meeting to confronting Napoleon on St. Helena. Cosima then renounced her Catholic faith and embraced Protestantism in order to marry Wagner. That was the hardest blow of all. The reason is not hard to find.

Three years earlier, in 1865, you had received the tonsure, had taken Holy Orders, and had donned the cassock. You were now known as "Abbé" Liszt. The man who had provoked such "Lisztolatrie" in earlier years had bowed his head to the tonsure! Your critics, unable to grasp the volte-face, had had a field day, accusing you of insincerity. These men of the "yes" and the "but," as you dubbed them, recalling your clanking medals, your sword of honor, and Lola Montez, took it to be a superb coup de théâtre by a master showman. They even accused you of entering the priesthood in order to avoid marriage. This showed scant knowledge of your life, and scant knowledge of the church. The minor orders you embraced—reader, acolyte, doorkeeper, exorcist—left you free to marry and even free to leave the clerical life; you were bound by no sacraments. At the time of these criticisms you had offered the only reply possible when you said that the decision to take Holy Orders allowed you to fulfill all the antecedents of your youth. "When the monk is already formed within, why not appropriate the outer garment of one?"[25] The child had become father to the man.

This was the position you found yourself in at the time of Cosima's public betrayal, first of her marriage to Bülow and then of a religion you held dear, and it devastated you. Carolyne later observed, "I went through the death of his son with him, as well of those of his daughter Blandine and of his mother—but nothing that can be compared with this despair."[26] You broke off relations with Richard and Cosima Wagner, a rupture that lasted nearly five years. But Wagner needed a rapprochement, and the laying of the foundation stone for his Bayreuth Theater in 1872 created the pretext. Better by far never to have seen the precious pair again. But you proceeded to make one major blunder after another with regard to Wagner and Cosima. Beguiled by the man and his music, you became Wagner's leading ambassador and a major fund-raiser. You should have given Bayreuth a wide berth. Instead you became "Bayreuth's poodle," to use your own self-disparaging phrase. What a role, illustrious master, for you so willingly to assign yourself. By now you had made a bonfire of your vanities. Self-abnegation prevailed to such a degree that nothing less than a full-scale psychological study could do it justice.

24. WFL, vol. 3, pp. 135–36.
25. LLB, vol. 2, p. 81.
26. RL, p. 76.

X

Then came the ultimate catastrophe. I am referring to your unexpected death in Bayreuth, and Cosima's attempts to keep your remains in that city, where they still rest beneath Wagner's shadow. "If only I do not die here," was your constant refrain, as if in premonition of what might happen after your decision to attend the Bayreuth Festival during that fatal summer of 1886. But you did die there. And for the confusion and ill will that surrounded the ensuing struggle for your remains, you yourself must bear a portion of responsibility. The drama that unfolded in the weeks and months following your demise matched anything that happened to you during your long and checkered life. Why did you leave no provision in your will for the disposition of your body? It would have been a simple enough matter to add such a clause to your testament of 1860. That omission gave an impression of indifference. In the event, Cosima, in her determined attempts to exert authority over your posthumous fate, rested her decision on a letter in which you had once declared that you "wanted to be buried where you fell."[27] Too late to protest that this letter did not have the force of a will, that it was written in haste before Richard and Cosima Wagner were married, before they had even settled in Bayreuth (a city you had never been known to frequent until they lived there), and before the Bayreuth Festival itself existed. All this was true. But it was also true that you never clarified your wishes; rather, you made them impossible for others to understand and therefore act in your best posthumous interests. You once told Cardinal Hohenlohe that you wanted to be buried in Tivoli. To the Franciscan fathers in Pest you expressed the desire to be buried in their monastery. To your son-in-law Emile Ollivier you casually vouchsafed the thought that the south of France, near the grave of your daughter Blandine, would be a peaceful resting place. Your Hungarian colleagues Kornél Abrányi and Ödön Mihalovich insisted that they had heard you say many times that you wanted to be buried in Hungary. Random contenders came forward suggesting that Rome, Eisenach (with its frescoes of Elisabeth of Hungary hanging in the Wartburg Gallery), and your natal village of Raiding would all be better places for your grave than Bayreuth. The grand duke of Weimar even offered to have you buried with full honors in Weimar, where you had spent your most productive years, and he sent Cosima a special invitation to that effect. In the face of such a clamor, Cosima played her hand with skill, particularly in the case of the grand duke. She told him that it was honor enough to have received his invitation, so the honor of *actually* transferring your body to Weimar was unnecessary. Small wonder that confusion reigned among your friends and supporters even as your coffin was being lowered into what they hoped would be a temporary grave in Bayreuth's Stadtfriedhof. As the weeks and then the months rolled by, Cosima saw to it that your temporary grave became permanent. It still suits the Bayreuth publicity machine to have you there as a tourist attraction.

---

27. LLB, vol. 6, pp. 228–29.

XI

It will hardly surprise you to learn that you have not yet been accorded your proper place in history. Even during your lifetime you knew that there might be problems in that regard. Too few of your works have entered the standard repertoire. It is true that such pieces as the Piano Sonata in B Minor, the *Weinen, Klagen* Variations, the *Faust* Symphony, and the *Totentanz* are widely regarded as leading works of the Romantic movement in music. And many others are played with frequency, above all *Les Préludes* and the two piano concertos. As for the cornucopia of shorter piano pieces, a great many of them are performed as often as similar pieces by Chopin, Schumann, and Brahms. They certainly include "Funérailles," "Bénédiction de Dieu," "La campanella," the three *Petrarch Sonnets,* the Concert Study in D-flat Major (*Un Sospiro*), "La Leggierezza," and the ever-popular *Liebestraum* no. 3. These pieces have not so far been consumed through use—a sure symptom of their value. As for the rest of your vast output, too much of it is presently performed as a result of fervent proselytizing by the evangels who have always been a part of your retinue. At some point, it must be detached from their missionary zeal and be allowed to speak for itself. Whenever the long-term fate of your music was raised, you used to say, "Ich kann warten" (I can wait). More than 120 years have passed since you last uttered those words. It is an unusually generous measure of time for posterity to get to know such compositions as your oratorios *Christus* and *Saint Elisabeth,* to say nothing of your seventy songs—music that has still to find a proper audience.

On the other hand, whatever fate posterity ultimately assigns to your compositions, you have become an undisputed historical force, and that cannot change. In a celebrated aphorism, Voltaire once observed that if God had not existed it would be necessary to invent Him, otherwise so much that goes on in the world would lack a rational explanation. To adapt Voltaire's words, "If Liszt had never existed it would be necessary to invent him." You will not approve of that parallel, dear Master—you might even be offended by it—but others before me have made it, so let it stand. Your removal from nineteenth-century music history would create some baffling anomalies. Return you to your rightful place, however, and everything once more makes sense. It is an honorable position to be in. It is one that you did not deliberately seek, but one with which you are probably content. The notion sounds prosaic, but has been rendered poetic in words that make a better epitaph for such a life as yours than many that were provided at the moment of your death.

> Lives of great men all remind us
> We can make our lives sublime,
> And, departing, leave behind us
> Footprints on the sands of time.
> Footprints, that perhaps another,
> Sailing o'er life's solemn main,
> A forlorn and shipwrecked brother,
> Seeing, shall take heart again.[28]

28. "A Psalm of Life," by Henry Wadsworth Longfellow, whom Liszt met in Rome in 1868 and came to esteem.

Having observed your footprints on the sands of time, far more people than you could ever imagine have seen them, have been inspired by them, and have taken heart again. That includes your biographer, who was honored to chronicle your life. In the deepest sense the best biography is motivated by admiration. And along the way it may even reveal some autobiography trying to get out.

Sources

AAM   Apponyi, Count Albert. *Memoirs.* London, 1935.

ACLA   d'Agoult, Marie. *Correspondance de Liszt et de la Comtesse d'Agoult.* Edited by Daniel Ollivier. 2 vols. Paris 1933–34.

AWC   Alan Walker Collection. Division of Archives and Research Collections, Mills Memorial Library, McMaster University, Hamilton, Ontario.

BB   Bülow, Hans von. *Briefe und Schriften.* Herausgegeben von Marie von Bülow. 8 vols. Leipzig, 1899–1908.

BBLW   Bülow, Marie von. *Hans von Bülow in Leben und Wort.* Stuttgart, 1925.

BBM   Bache, Constance. *Brother Musicians: Reminiscences of Edward and Walter Bache.* London, 1901.

BCPS   *Beethoven: Complete Piano Sonatas.* Edited by Harold Craxton. Annotated by Donald Francis Tovey. Associated Board of the Royal Schools of Music. London, 1931.

BFA   Bowen, Catherine Drinker. *"Free Artist": The Story of Anton and Nicholas Rubinstein.* New York, 1939.

BGM   Banister, Henry C. *George Alexander Macfarren: His Life, Works, and Influence.* London, 1892.

BK   *Ludwig van Beethovens Konversationshefte.* Herausgegeben im Auftrag der Deutschen Staatsbibliothek Berlin von Karl-Heinz Köhler und Dagmar Beck unter Mitwirkung von Gunter Brosche. Leipzig, 1983 – .

B-KMCE Beatty-Kingston, William. *Men, Cities and Events.* London, 1895.

BL   British Library, London.

BLP   Boissier, Mme Auguste. *Liszt Pedagogue: Leçons de piano données par Liszt à Mlle Valérie Boissier en 1832.* Paris, 1927.

BN   Bibliothèque nationale, Paris.

BNB   Bülow, Hans von. *Neue Briefe.* Herausgegeben und eingeleitet von Richard Graf du Moulin Eckart. Munich, 1927. Translated by Hannah Waller as *Letters of Hans von Bülow.* New York, 1931.

BRS   Boetticher, Wolfgang. *Robert Schumann: Einführung in Personlichkeit und Werk.* Berlin, 1941.

BTDL   Bargauanu, Grigore, and Dragos Tanaescu. *Dinu Lipatti.* Lausanne, 1991.

BWL   *Briefwechseln zwischen Wagner und Liszt.* 2 vols. Leipzig, 1900.

CFL   Corder, Frederick. *Ferencz Liszt.* London, 1925.

CLBA   Csapó, Wilhelm von, ed. *Franz Liszts Briefe an Baron Antal Augusz, 1846–78.* Budapest, 1911.

CLC   Carl Lachmund Collection. Special Collections Department of the Performing Arts Division of the New York Public Library. Call no. JPB 92–1.

CLW   Cornelius, Peter. *Literarische Werke.* 4 vols. Leipzig, 1904–5.

CPR   Chantovoine, Jean, ed. *Franz Liszt: Pages Romantiques.* Paris, 1912.

DFB   Dent, Edward. *Ferruccio Busoni.* London, 1933.

DRK   Dubal, David. *Reflections from the Keyboard: The World of the Concert Pianist.* 2nd ed. New York, 1997.

DRS   Davario, John. *Robert Schumann, Herald of a "New Poetic Age."* New York, 1997.

DSM   Deutsch, Otto Erich. *Schubert: Memoirs by His Friends.* Translated by Rosamond Ley and John Newell. London, 1958.

EFL   Eckhardt, Mária. *Franz Liszt's Estate at the Budapest Academy of Music.* Vol. 1: *Books.* Translated by Erzsébet Meszáros, Budapest 1986. See also "Liszt's Weimar Library: The Hungarica." *New Hungarian Quarterly* (Summer 1991): 156–64.

E-LWB   Eckhardt, Mária, and Evelyn Liepsch. *Franz Liszts Weimarer Bibliothek.* Laaber, 1999.

FBLM   Frimmel, Theodor von. *Beethoven Studien.* Vol. 2: *Bausteine zu einer Lebensgeschichte des Meisters.* Munich, 1906.

FLL   Friedheim, Arthur. *Life and Liszt: The Recollections of a Concert Pianist.* Edited by Theodore L. Bullock. New York, 1961.

FLT   *Franz Liszt Tagebuch, 1827.* Im Auftrag der Stadt Bayreuth herausgegeben von Detlef Altenburg und Rainer Kleinertz. Vienna 1986. Facsimile volume.

FMG   Fay, Amy. *Music Study in Germany: From the Home Correspondence of Amy Fay.* Edited by Mrs. Fay Pierce. New York, 1880.

FMML   Freund, Róbert. *Musical Memories and Letters.* Unpublished typescript in the Alan Walker Collection, McMaster University, Hamilton, Ontario. Series III, Box 20.

GLK   Göllerich, August. *Franz Liszts Klavierunterricht von 1884–1886: Dargestellt an den Tagebuchaufzeichnungen von August Göllerich.* Edited by Wilhelm Jerger. Regensburg, 1975.

GLL   Graves, Charles L. *The Life and Letters of Sir Charles Groves, C.B.* London, 1903.

GLW   Gottschalg, Alexander. *Franz Liszt in Weimar, und seine letzten Lebensjahre: Erinnerungen und Tagebuch notizen.* Berlin, 1910.

GSA   Goethe- und Schiller-Archiv, Liszt Collection held by the Nationale Forschungs- und Gedenkstätten der klassischen deutschen Literatur, Weimar.

HAG   Hecker, Jutta. *Die Altenburg: Geschichte eines Hauses.* Berlin 1983.

HFL   Huneker, James. *Franz Liszt.* New York, 1911.

HGC   Hanslick, Eduard. *Geschichte des Concertwesens in Wien.* 2 vols. Vienna, 1869, 1870.

HLR   Helbig, Nadine. "Franz Liszt in Rom." *Deutsche Revue* 32 (January–March 1907) and 33 (April–June 1907). An expanded English version appears in certain editions of Raphaël Ledos de Beaufort's *The Abbé Liszt,* London, 1886.

HLSW   Hugo, Howard, ed. and trans. *The Letters of Franz Liszt to Marie zu Sayn-Wittgenstein.* Cambridge, Mass., 1953.

HMML   Haweis, H. R. *My Musical Life.* London, 1886.

HMI Hinrichsen, Hans-Joachim. *Musikalische Interpretation: Hans von Bülow.* Stuttgart, 1999.

HMR Hoffmann, Richard. "Some Musical Recollections of Fifty Years." *Scribner's Magazine* 47 (March–April 1910).

HPL Haraszti, Emile. "Le Problème Liszt." *Acta Musicologica* (December 1937).

HSC Hedley, Arthur, ed. and trans. *Selected Correspondence of Fryderyk Chopin.* London, 1962.

JSB Jansen, F. Gustav. *Robert Schumann's Briefe.* Neue Folge, 2nd ed. Leipzig, 1904.

JSF Jones, Ernest. *Sigmund Freud: Life and Work.* 3 vols. London, 1956–58.

Jugendbriefe von Robert Schumann. Edited by Clara Schumann. 3rd edition. Leipzig, 1898.

KE Kellermann, Berthold. *Erinnerungen: Ein Künstlerleben.* Herausgegeben von Sebastian Hausmann und Helmut Kellermann. Zürich, 1932.

KFLB Kalischer, Alfred. "Der Knabe Franz Liszt und Beethoven." *Neue Zeitschrift für Musik* 42–43 (October 1891). And Lina Ramann's response: "Lisztiana." *Neue Zeitschrift für Musik* 47 (1891): 503.

KJB Kalbeck, Max. *Johannes Brahms.* 4 vols. Berlin, 1904–14.

KL-B Kapp, Julius. *Liszt-Brevier.* Leipzig, 1910.

KWL Kloss, Erich, ed. *Briefwechsel zwischen Wagner und Liszt.* 2 vols. Leipzig, 1910.

LBLB La Mara, ed. *Correspondance entre Franz Liszt et Hans von Bülow.* Leipzig, 1899.

LBLCA La Mara, ed. *Briefwechsel zwischen Franz Liszt und Carl Alexander, Grossherzog von Sachsen.* Leipzig, 1909.

LBW La Mara. "Beethoven's Weihekuss." *Allgemeine Musikzeitung* 17 (1913).

LCS Litzman, Berthold. *Clara Schumann: Ein Künstlerleben.* 3 vols. Leipzig, 1902–8.

LDML La Mara. *Durch Musik und Leben im Dienste des Ideals.* 2 vols. Leipzig, 1917.

LFC Liszt, F. *Frédéric Chopin: A Biographical Sketch and Study of His Work.* Translated from the French by Martha Walker Cook. Boston, 1863. Fourth edition revised.

LFP Lott, R. Allen. *From Paris to Peoria: How European Piano Virtuosos Brought Classical Music to the American Heartland.* New York, 2003.

LGPZ Lenz, Wilhelm von. *Die grossen Pianoforte-Virtuosen unserer Zeit.* Berlin, 1872.

LL *Living with Liszt: The Diary of Carl Lachmund, an American Pupil of Liszt, 1882–1884.* Edited, annotated, and introduced by Alan Walker. Stuyvesant, N.Y., 1995.

LLB La Mara, ed. *Franz Liszts Briefe.* 8 vols. Leipzig 1893–1905. Vol. 1: *Von Paris bis Rom.* Vol. 2: *Von Rom bis ans Ende.* Vol. 3: *Briefe an eine Freundin.* Vols. 4–7: *Briefe an die Fürstin Sayn-Wittgenstein.* Vol. 8: *Neue Folge zu Band I und II.*

LLF La Mara, ed. *Liszt und die Frauen.* Leipzig, 1911.

LLM-K La Mara, ed. *Marie von Mouchanoff-Kalergis (geb. Gräfin Nesselrode) in Briefen an ihre Tochter.* Leipzig, 1911.

LML Lamond, Frederic. *The Memoirs of Frederic Lamond.* Glasgow, 1949.

LS *Liszt Saeculum,* vol. 33, London 1984.

LSS Legouvé, Ernest. *Soixante Ans de souvenirs.* 4 vols. Paris, 1887.

MAML Moscheles, Ignaz. *Aus Moscheles' Leben, nach Briefen und Tagebüchern herausgegeben von seiner Frau.* 2 vols. Leipzig, 1872–73.

M-JEG Monrad-Johansen, David. *Edvard Grieg.* Oslo, 1934.

MBJ Moser, Andreas, ed. *Briefe an und von Joseph Joachim.* 3 vols. Berlin, 1911–13.

MKB Mitchell, Donald, and Hans Keller, eds. *Benjamin Britten: A Commentary on His Works from a Group of Specialists.* London, 1962.

MMML Mason, William. *Memories of a Musical Life.* New York, 1901.

MRR   Merrick, Paul. *Revolution and Religion in the Music of Liszt.* Cambridge, 1987.

MRS   Maréchal, Henri. *Rome: Souvenirs d'un musicien.* Paris, 1904.

MST-B   McCorkle, Margit L. *Robert Schumann. Thematisch-Bibliographisches Werkverzeich-*
           nis. Unter Mitwirkung von Akio Mayeda und der Robert-Schumann Forschungsstelle.
           Düsseldorf and Munich, 2003.

MT   *The Musical Times.* London. Cited by issue.

NCC   Nevinson, H. W. *Changes and Chances.* New York, 1923.

NG   Nicholas, Jeremy. *Godowsky: The Pianists' Pianist.* Hexham, England, 1989.

NL   Nohl, Ludwig. *Franz Liszt.* Leipzig, 1882.

NLB   Nohl, Walther. "Der elfjährige Liszt und Beethoven." *Neue Musik-Zeitung*
           (Stuttgart) 9 (1927): 307–9.

NZfM   *Neue Zeitschrift für Musik.* Leipzig. Cited by issue.

OIL   Ott, Bertrand. "An Interpretation of Liszt's Sonata in B minor." *Journal of the*
           American Liszt Society 10 (December 1981): 30–38.

PBUS   Prahács, Margit, ed. *Franz Liszt. Briefe aus ungarischen Sammlungen, 1835-86.* Bu-
           dapest-Kassel, 1966.

PEMH   *Pléiade Encyclopedia of Music History.* Paris, 1963. Vol. 2, article on Liszt by Emile
           Haraszti.

PPL   Prawer, Siegbert. *The Penguin Book of Lieder.* London, 1964.

PWC   Pretzsch, Paul, ed. *Cosima Wagner und Houston Stewart Chamberlain im Briefwech-*
           sel, 1888–1908. Leipzig, 1934.

RA   Royal Archives, Windsor Castle, England.

RGD   Riesberg, Frederick W. "Gala Days with Liszt at Weimar." *Etude* (November
           1936).

RGS   Ramann, Lina, ed. and trans. *Franz Liszts Gesammelte Schriften.* 6 vols. Leipzig,
           1880–83.

RKU   *Edouard Reményi, Musician, Litterateur, and Man: An Appreciation, with Sketches of*
           His Life and Artistic Career by Friends and Contemporaries. Compiled by Gwen-
           dolyn Dunlevy Kelly and George P. Upton. Chicago, 1906.

RL   Ramann, Lina. *Lisztiana: Erinnerungen an Franz Liszt in Tagebuchblättern, Briefen*
           und Dokumenten aus den Jahren 1873–1886/87. Herausgegeben von Arthur Seidl.
           Textrevision von Friedrich Schnapp. Mainz, 1983.

RLKM   Ramann, Lina. *Franz Liszt als Künstler und Mensch.* 3 vols. Leipzig, 1880–94.

RL-P   Ramann, Lina. *Liszt-Pädagogium: Klavier-Kompositionen Franz Liszt's nebst noch*
           unedirten veränderungen, zusätzen und Kadenzen nach des Meisters Lehren päda-
           gogisch glossirt. Leipzig, 1901.

RLS   Raabe, Peter. *Franz Liszt: Leben und Schaffen.* 2 vols. Stuttgart, 1931; revised
           1968.

RMM   Reid, Charles. *The Music Monster: A Biography of James William Davison, Music*
           Critic of The Times of London, 1846–78. London, 1984.

RWGS   *Richard Wagner's Gesammelte Schriften und Dichtungen.* 10 vols. 3rd ed. Leipzig,
           1897–98.

SB   Schindler, Anton. *Biographie von Ludwig van Beethoven.* 3rd edition. Münster,
           1860. Translated as *Beethoven as I Knew Him,* ed. Donald W. MacArdle. Trans-
           lated by Constance S. Jolly. London, 1966.

SBB   Suchoff, Benjamin, ed. *Béla Bartók Essays.* London, 1976.

SCW   Susskind, Pamela. "Clara Wieck Schumann as Pianist and Composer." Ph.D. diss., University of California, Berkeley, 1971. p. 232.

SDNL   Saffle, Michael, and James Deaville, eds. *New Light on Liszt and His Music: Essays in Honor of Alan Walker's 65th Birthday.* Stuyvesant, N.Y., 1997.

SE   Stradal, August. *Erinnerungen an Franz Liszt.* Berne, 1929.

SHM   Saint-Saëns, Camille. *Harmonie et Mélodie.* Paris, 1885.

SLE   Schorn, Karl von. *Lebenserrinerungen: Ein Beitrag zur Geschichte des Rheinlands im neunzehnten Jahrhundert.* 2 vols. Bonn, 1898.

SLG   Stern, Adolf. *Franz Liszts Briefe an Carl Gille.* Leipzig, 1903.

SLM   Slonimsky, Nicolas. *Lexicon of Musical Invective: Critical Assaults on Composers since Beethoven's Time.* New York, 1952.

SLRW   *Selected Letters of Richard Wagner.* Translated and edited by Stewart Spencer and Barry Millington. London, 1987.

SNW   Schorn, Adelheid von. *Das Nachklassische Weimar.* 2 vols. Weimar, 1911–12. Vol. 1: *Unter der Regierungszeit Karl Friedrichs und Maria Paulownas.* Vol. 2: *Unter der Regierungszeit von Karl Alexander und Sophie.*

SPRL   Strelezki, Anton. *Personal Recollections of Chats with Liszt.* London, 1893.

SRR   Strauss, Richard. *Recollections and Reflections.* Edited by Willi Schuh. Translated by L. J. Lawrence. London, 1953.

TBL   Thayer, Alexander Wheelock. *Ludwig van Beethovens Leben.* 5 vols. Edited by Hermann Deiters. Revised and completed by Hugo Riemann. Leipzig, 1907–17.

VFL   Vier, Jacques. *Franz Liszt: L'Artiste, le clerc; Documents inédits.* Paris, 1951.

WBR   Weingartner, Felix. *Buffets and Rewards: A Musician's Reminiscences.* Translated by Marguerite Wolff. London, 1937.

WEG   Wagner, Cosima. *Franz Liszt: Ein Gedenkblatt von seiner Tochter.* Munich, 1911.

WELC   Walker, Alan, and Gabriele Erasmi. *Liszt, Carolyne, and the Vatican: The Story of a Thwarted Marriage.* Stuyvesant, N.Y., 1991.

WFL   Walker, Alan. *Franz Liszt.* 3 vols. New York. Vol. 1: *The Virtuoso Years, 1811–47.* 1983; revised 1987 and 1990. Vol. 2: *The Weimar Years, 1848–61.* 1989; revised 1993. Vol. 3: *The Final Years, 1861–86.* 1996.

WLCC   Walter, Teréz. *Liszt Ferenc árvizi hangversenyei Bécsben, 1838–39* [Liszt's Charity Concerts in Vienna, 1838–39, after the Flood in Hungary]. Translated and annotated from the German diary of Theresa Walter by Béla Csuka. Budapest, 1941.

WLLM   Waters, Edward N., ed. *The Letters of Franz Liszt to Olga von Meyendorff, 1871–1886.* Translated by William R. Tyler. Dumbarton Oaks, 1979.

WLP   Waters, Edward N. "Franz Liszt to Richard Pohl." *Studies in Romanticism* (Boston) 6, no. 4 (Summer 1967).

WLS   Winklhofer, Sharon. *Liszt's Sonata in B Minor: A Study of Autograph Sources and Documents.* Ann Arbor, 1980.

WMC   Weingartner, Felix. *Weingartner on Music and Conducting.* New York, 1969.

WML   Wagner, Richard. *Mein Leben.* Munich, 1911. Authorized English translation, London, 1912.

WMME Walker, Bettina. *My Musical Experiences.* London, 1890.

WPL   Williams, Adrian. *Portrait of Liszt, by Himself and His Contemporaries.* Oxford, 1990.

WT   Wagner, Cosima. *Die Tagebücher,* 2 vols. Ediert und kommentiert von Martin
         Gregor-Dellin und Dietrich Mack. Munich 1976 and 1977. Translated as *Cosima
         Wagner's Diaries,* by Geoffrey Skelton. London and New York, 1978 and 1980.
WTV   Walter, Bruno. *Theme and Variations: An Autobiography.* Translated by James A.
         Galston. New York, 1946.

Index

[main entries in bold type]

Aachen (Germany), 152
Abert, Hermann (1871–1927), 40
Ábrányi, Kornél (1822–1903), 253
Agoult, Countess Marie Catherine Sophie d'
    (1805–1876), xiv, 5, 27, 83, 196, 217, 219,
    249
Alabieff, Alexander (1787–1851), 166
Albani, Emma (1847–1930), 123
Albert, Eugène d' (1864–1932), xiv, 28
Alexandre et fils (Paris), 53
Allegri, Gregorio (1582–1652), 9
    "Miserere," 9
Allgemeine Musikalische Zeitung (Leipzig), 177, 242
Altenburg, Detlef, 217
Amadé, Count Thadé (1782–1845), 27
America (steamship), 96
American Art Journal (New York), 102
Andersen, Hans Christian (1805–1875), 53
Apel, Pauline (1838–1926), 55
Arnold, Ben, 220
Arrau, Claudio (1903–1991), 142
Artigaux, Caroline d' (*née* Saint-Cricq) (c. 1811–
    1872), 153, 248
Assisi (Italy), 202
Atheneum, The (London), 148
Auden, W. H. (1907–1973), xvi
Augusz, Baron Antal (1807–1878), 1

Bach, Johann Sebastian (1685–1750), 7, 12, 39,
    68, 113, 143, 159
    Chaconne in D Minor, 112
    Chromatic Fantasy and Fugue, 63, 108
    "Forty-eight," 7, 71, 85
    Suite in E-flat Major, 77

Bache, Walter (1842–1888), 51, 90, **106–27**, 128,
    148
    Alfred (brother), 109
    Constance (sister) (1846–1903), 108, 111, 125,
      126
      Liszt's translator, 122
      "Ode to Liszt," 122–23
    Emily (mother, *née* Higginson), 107
    Francis Edward (brother) (1833–1858), 107
    Margaret (sister), 125
    Samuel (father), 107
    Annual Concerts of, **112–15**
    bequests of, 127
    critics and, 111, **116–19**
    death of, 126
    funeral of, 127
    Liszt's funeral and, 125
    "Liszt Scholarship" and, 119, **123**
    meets Liszt (1862), 107–8
    obituary notice of, 126
    program notes of, 115
    Working Men's Society and, 115, 127
Bad Eilsen (Germany), 81
Bad Ischl (Austria), 67
Balakirev, Mily (1837–1910), 63
    Islamey, 63
Baltimore (America), 95, 97
    Peabody Institute, 97
Balzac, Honoré de (1799–1850), 219
Barenboim, Daniel (b. 1942), 142, 179, 181
Barere, Simon (1896–1951), 142
Bargiel, Woldemar (1828–1897), 194, 195
Bartók, Béla (1881–1945), 28
    on Liszt, 137, 147–48, 186

Bartolini, Lorenzo (1777–1850), 13, 14
Bauer, Harold (1873–1951), 192
Bayreuth (Germany), 245, 252
  Festival, 253
  Landesgericht, 84
  Maximilianstrasse, 125
  Stadtfriedhof, 125, 253
  Theater, 84, 116
  Wahnfried, 125
Beatty-Kingston, William (1837–1900), 67
Beaumarchais, Pierre-Augustin (1732–1799), 219
Bechstein, Carl (1826–1900), 83, 84–85, 98, 147
Bechstein pianos (Berlin), 53, 83, 147
Beethoven, Ludwig van (1770–1827), xiii, xv, 7,
    8, 27, 39, 58, 79, 129, 138
  Karl (nephew) (1806–1858), 4–5
  Broadwood piano, 176, 179
  Conversation Books, **3–5**, 8
  death mask of, 176
  Festival in Bonn (1845), **14–15**, 40
  Festival in Weimar (1870), **73–74**
  Liszt and, **1–10, 11–26**
  Liszt's comments on, 232
  Memorial Committee, 13, 40, 46
  Memorial Statue (1845), **13–15**, 40–41
  WORKS
  An die ferne Geliebte, 41, 42
  Choral Music:
    Missa Solemnis, 74
  "Diabelli" Variations, op. 120, 49
  Opera:
    Fidelio, 176
  Piano concertos:
    in C Minor, 14
    in E-flat Major (*Emperor*), 12, 73, 74, 90, 93
  Piano sonatas, 85, 87:
    in A Major, op. 2, no. 2, 177
    in D Major, op. 10, no. 3, 179
    in C-sharp Minor, op. 27 (*Moonlight*), 9, 86
    in D Major, op. 28 (*Pastorale*), 14, **179–81**
    in G Major, op. 31, no. 3, 86
    in D Minor, op. 31, no. 2 (*Tempest*), 86
    in C Major, op. 53 (*Waldstein*), 138, 177
    in F Minor, op. 57 (*Appassionata*), 14, 79,
      129, 138
    in F-sharp Major, op. 78, 86
    in B-flat Major, op. 106 (*Hammerklavier*), 13,
      101, 136, 176, **181–83**
    in E Major, op. 109, 63, 101, 178
    in A-flat Major, op. 110, 86, 101
    in C Minor, op. 111, 101
  Ruins of Athens, 83

String quartets, 26, 183
String trio in D Major, op. 9, no. 2, 48
Symphonies:
  no. 3, in E-flat Major (*Eroica*), 9, 14, 20,
    22–23
  no. 5, in C Minor, 11, 14, 19, 30, 129
  no. 6, in F Major (*Pastorale*), 14, 30
  no. 7, in A Major, 9, 14, 30
  no. 8, in F Major, 21
  no. 9, in D Minor (*Chorale*), 24–26, 74, 86,
    95, 176
Bendel, Franz (1833–1874), 68
Benedict, Sir Julius (1804–1885), 91
Bennett, Sir William Sterndale (1816–1875), 91,
  106
Bergman, Carl (1821–1876), 93–94
Beringer, Oscar (1844–1922), 68, 148
Berlin (Germany), 33, 47, 64, 148, 162
  Belle Alliance Cemetery, 75
  Englischen Haus Hotel, 146
  Hedwigskirche, 83
  Hochschule für Musik, 92, 247
  Hôtel de Russie, 147
  Neue Akademie der Tonkunst, 184, 242
  Pankow clinic, 103
  Philharmonic Orchestra, 100, 102–3
  Singakademie, 147
  Wilhelmstrasse, 83
Berlioz, Hector (1803–1869), xiii, xiv, 14, 39, 101,
  217, 243
  Les Nuits d'été, 162
  Liszt's comments on, 232
Bilse, Benjamin (1816–1902), 102
Birmingham (England), 107, 108
  Church of the Messiah, 108
Blöchlinger Institute (Vienna), 5
Böhme, Ferdinand (1815–1883), 49
Böhner, Ludwig (1787–1860), 12
Boieldieu, François-Adrien (1775–1834), 250
  Weisse Dame, 250
Bonn (Germany), 6, 98
  Domplatz, 14
  Festhalle, 14
Borodin, Alexander Porfir'yevich (1833–1887), 233
  Liszt's comments on, 233
Bösendorfer pianos (Vienna), 52, 66, 145
Boston (America), 92–93, 97, 101
  Beacon Street, 93
  Music Hall, 93
Brahms, Johannes (1833–1897), xvi, 85, 99, 105,
  194, 200, 211, 241, 245
  friendship with Tausig, **65–66**

hostility toward Liszt, 171
opinion of Liszt's B Minor Sonata, 145
Weber's music and, 191
WORKS
Fifty-one Exercises, 70–71
Hungarian Dances, 145
"Paganini" Studies, op. 35, 65, 70
Piano Quintet in F Minor, op. 34, 66
Scherzo in E-flat Minor, op. 4, 145
Breitkopf & Härtel (Leipzig), 16, 17, 24, 26, 175
Beethoven *Collected Edition*, 19
Chopin *Complete Edition*, 92, 194–95
Liszt *Collected Edition*, 19, 28, 158
Brendel, Alfred (b. 1931), 142
Brendel, Franz (1811–1868), 171, 179, 181
Brentano, Clemens (1778–1842), 160
British Medical Journal (London), 209
Britten, Lord Benjamin (1913–1976), 160
Les *Illuminations*, 160
Broadwood pianos (London), 52, 111, 176, 179
Bronsart von Schellendorf, Hans (1830–1913),
53, 61, 98, 189
Bruch, Max (1838–1920), 92
Budapest (Hungary), 1, 33
flood of 1838, 27
Hungarian legislature, 27
Hungarian National Museum, 176
National Széchényi Library, 41
National Theatre, 83
Royal Academy of Music, 1, 54–55, 87, 113, 129
Bülow, Baron Hans Guido von (1830–1894), xiv,
15, 17, 51, 63, 77, 78, 107, 112, 113, 144, 183,
184, 247, 251–52
Blandine Elisabeth (daughter) (1863–1941),
77, 83
Cosima Francesca Gaetana (first wife, *née*
Liszt) (1837–1930), 98, 99; elopement
with Wagner, 252; marriage to Bülow
Daniela Senta (daughter) (1860–1940), 83
Eduard (father) (1803–1853), 80
Franziska Elisabeth von (mother) (1800–
1888), 80, 81, 82, 83
Marie (second wife, *née* Schanzer) (1857–
1941), 101
ambivalence toward Liszt, 87–88
American tours of, 92; (1875–76), **92–98**;
(1889), 101; (1890), 101
anti-Semitism of, 88
conducting of, **99–100**
criticism of England, 90–91
critics and, 146–47
death of, **103–5**

descriptions of his playing, **85–87**, 102
divorce of, **84–85**, 87, 90, 251–52
edition of the Beethoven sonatas, 88, 184
eulogy for Tausig (1871), 77
Gold Medal of the Philharmonic Society, 90
illnesses of, 79, 90, 97–98, 103-4
infatuation with Baroness Romaine Overbeck, **95–97**
Liszt and, **79–105**, 89
Liszt's high opinion of (1881), 88
marriage to Cosima Liszt (1857), 83–84
marriage to Marie Schanzer (1882), 101
Meiningen Court Orchestra and, 99, 102
Philharmonic Society and, 90
photographic memory of, 79
suicide attempt of, 84–85, 98
wax cylinders of, **101-2**
WORKS
Ballade, op. 11, 63
Julius Caesar, op. 10, 101
Nirvana, op. 20, 101
Buonamici, Guiseppe (1846–1914), 123
Busoni, Ferruccio Dante Michelangiolo Ben-
venuto (1866–1924), 11, 12, 50, 148, 149
Byron, Lord George Gordon Noel (1788–1824),
219

Cairo (Egypt), 104
Calais (France), 125
Carl Alexander (1818–1901), Grand Duke of
Weimar (1853–1901), 8
Carl Friedrich (1783–1853), Grand Duke of
Weimar (1828–1853), 168
Cascia (Italy), 202
Cato the Elder (234–149 b.c.), 105
Cessiat, Countess Valentine de (1820–1894),
248–49
Chaminade, Cécile (1857–1944), 195
Chappell & Co., (London), 11
Charnin Mueller, Rena, 156
Chateaubriand, Viscount François-René (1768–
1848), 220
Chélard, Hippolyte André Jean Baptiste (1789–
1861), 14
Chickering, Frank (1827–1891), 94
Chickering Hall (New York), 94
Chickering pianos (Boston), 94–95
Chopin, Fryderyk Franciszek (1810–1849), xiii,
xvi, 30, 78, 82, 143, 241, 246
Izabela (sister), 196
Klindworth's edition of, 195, 196, 199
Liszt's comments on, 233

Chopin, Fryderyk Franciszek (1810–1849) (*cont.*)
Liszt's edition of, 92, **194–200**
WORKS
Nocturne in B-flat Minor, op. 9, 124
Polonaises:
in C-sharp Minor, op. 26, no. 1, 108
in A-flat Major, op. 53, 56, 61
Preludes, op. 28, 195, 196:
in C Major, 199
in G Major, 197
in F-sharp Minor, 197–98
in E Major, 198
in F-sharp Major, 199–200
Scherzo no. 2, in B-flat Minor, op. 31, 195
Sonata in B-flat Minor (*Funeral March*), op. 35,
76, 140
Sonata in B Minor, op. 58, 186
Studies, opp. 10 and 25, 194, 196
Winter Wind Study, op. 25, 69
Clementi, Muzio (1752–1832), 111, 201
Gradus ad Parnassum, 71, 208
Cleveland (America), 97
Cliburn, Van (b. 1934), 142
Cohen, Hermann ("Puzzi") (1821–1871), 47
Cologne (Germany), 163
Cathedral, 163
Constantinople (Turkey), 52
Corder, Frederick (1852–1932), 5, 6
Cork (Ireland), 240
Cornelius, Karl August Peter (1824–1874), 8, 53,
61, 66, 67, 218, 244
"zu Beethoven's Geburtsfeier," 8–9
Cossmann, Bernhard (1822–1910), 81
Cotta, J. W. (Stuttgart), 88, 184, 184
Council of Trent (1545–1563), 159
Courrier de Lyon, 35
Cramer, Johann Baptist (1771–1858), 29
Studies, 79
Cummings, William Hayman (1831–1915), 113
Cusins, Sir William (1833–1893), 90
Czerny, Carl (1791–1857), 3, 7, 12, 13, 27, 88, 177,
220, 240
Liszt's comments on, 233–34
School of Velocity, 82, 207

Dahlgren, Rear Admiral John Adolphus Bernard
(1809–1870), 96
Daily Telegraph, The (London), 117
Damrosch, Leopold (1832–1885), 74, 94
Danhauser, Joseph (1805–1845), 176
Dannreuther, Edward (1844–1905), 34, 67, 69,
86, 115, 123

Dante Alighieri (1265–1321), 219
Divine Comedy, 220
Darmstadt (Germany), 195
David, Ferdinand (1810–1873), 74, 244
Davison, James William (1815–1885), 111, 115, 127
Debussy, Achille-Claude (1862–1918), xiv, 78
Deppe, Ludwig (1828–1890), 56
Diabelli, Anton (1781–1858), 28, 29
Dickens, Charles (1812–1870), 219
Disraeli, Benjamin (1804–1881), 219
Dohnányi, Ernst von (1877–1960), 135, 203
Liszt Sonata and, 129, 147–48
Donizetti, Gaetano (1797–1848), 99, 151
La fille du regiment, 99
Lucia di Lammermoor, 151
Dorn, Heinrich Ludwig Egmont (1804–1892),
244
Dover (England), 111, 122, 125
Dresden (Germany), 35, 38, 47, 64, 79, 82
Uprising (1849)
Dubal, David (b. 1940), 46
Dukas, Paul (1865–1935), 178
Du Moulin Eckart, Count Richard (1864–1938),
80
Duplessis, Marie (1824–1847), 248
Düsseldorf (Germany), 115
Dwight's Journal of Music (Boston), 77

Eckhardt, Mária (b. 1943), 195, 197
Edinburgh (Scotland), 115
University of, 115
Edison, Thomas Alva (1847–1931), 101, 200
Edward, Prince of Wales (1841–1910), 123
Ehlert, Ludwig (1825–1884), 73
Ehrlich, Heinrich (1822–1899), 69–70
Eisenach Castle (Germany), 168, 253
Eismann, Georg (1899–1968), 41
Eliot, George (pseud. for Marian Evans) (1819–
1880), 53
Endenich (Germany), 48, 57, 98, 236
Engel, Gustav (critic), 146
Epstein family (Berlin), 68
Erard pianos (Paris), 64, 210
"double-escapement," 210
Erfurt (Germany), 55
Erkel, Ferenc (1810–1893), 83
Ernst, Heinrich Wilhelm (1814–1865), 184
Esztergom (Hungary), 1, 2
Etude, The (New York), 85

Fabriani (Italy), 202
Faisst, Immanuel (1823–1894), 184

Fay, Amy (1844–1928), 68–69, 143
  description of Tausig, 69
Fenili, Count Carlo (1799–1874), 202
Ferrata, Guiseppe (1865–1928), 213
  description of Liszt, 213
Field, John (1782–1837), 175, 201, 250
  Liszt's comments on, 234
Flaubert, Gustave (1821–1880), 142
Fleischhauer, Friedhold (1834–1896), 74
Fliess, Wilhelm (1858–1928), 103
  Neue Beitrage und Therapie der nasaelen Re-
    flexneurose, 103
Florence (Italy), 13, 85, 107
Franchomme, Auguste (1808–1884), 194
Frankfurt (Germany), 56
Franz, Robert (1815–1892), 151, 250
  Liszt's comments on, 234
Freiligrath, Ferdinand (1810–1876), 167
Freud, Sigmund (1856–1939), 103, 242
Freund, Róbert (1852–1936), 71, 148
Friedheim, Arthur (1859–1932), 53, 56, 149,
  198
Friedman, Ignaz (1882–1948), 78, 87
Frimmel, Theodor von (1853–1928), 9
Furtwängler, Wilhelm (1886–1954), 103

Gade, Niels Vilhelm (1817–1890), 147
Gazette de Hongrie (Budapest), 88
Genast, Eduard (1797–1866), 152
Genast-Merian, Emilie (1833–1905), 151,
  152, 162
Geneva Conservatoire (Switzerland), 213
Gibralter, 245
Gilbert, Mrs. Eliza ("Lola Montez") (1818–
  1861), 15, 248, 249, 252
Gilels, Emil (1916–1985), 71
Gille, Carl (1813–1899), 55, 125, 203
Ginsburg, Grigor (1904–1961), 144
Glasgow (Scotland), 90
Gobbi, Henrik (1842–1920), 1
Goddard, Arabella (1836–1922), 111
Godowsky, Leopold (1870–1938), 78, 135
  Fifty-three Studies on Chopin's Etudes, 195
Goepfart, Karl (1859–1942), 215
  Liszt's Technical Studies and, 215
Goethe, Johann Wolfgang von (1749–1832), 158,
  245
  Gretchen am Spinnrade, 35–36
  Erlkönig, 33
  Faust, 33, 220
  Wilhelm Meister, 156
Goethe-Schiller Archive (Weimar), 29

Göllerich, August (1859–1923), 49, 143, 215
Gorissen-Mutzenbecher, Cécile (1849–1907),
  101, 102
Gospel According to St. John, 135
Gottschalg, Alexander Wilhelm (1827–1908), 62,
  215
Gottschalk, Louis Moreau (1829–1869), 87
Götze, Franz Carl (1814–1888), 151–52
  Augusta (daughter), 152
Gounod, Charles François (1818–1893), 166
  Faust, 166
Grant, President Ulysses Simpson (1822–1885),
  97
Grieg, Edvard Hagerup (1843–1907), 12
  Piano Concerto in A Minor, op. 16, 12
  Sonata in G Major, for violin and piano, op.
    13, 12
Grosskurth, Emma, 50, 89
Groth, Klaus (1819–1899), 105
Grottamare (Italy), 202-3
Grove, Sir George (1820–1900), 124
  description of Liszt (1886), 124
Gumprecht, Otto (1823–1900), 146
Gut, Serge (b. 1927), 140

Hagn, Charlotte von (1809–1891), 167, 248
  "Was Liebe sei," 167
Hähnel, Ernst-Julius (1811–1891), 14
Halász, István, 2, 5, 10
Hallé, Sir Charles (1819–1895), 14, 91
Hambourg, Mark (1879–1960), 87
Hamburg (Germany), 49, 100
  Michaeliskirche, 104
  Ohlsdorf crematorium, 104
  Opera, 104
  Philharmonic Orchestra, 100
  subscription concerts, 103
Handel, George Frideric (1685–1759)
Hanon, Charles-Louis (1819–1900), 203
Hanover (Germany), 98, 99, 173
Hanslick, Eduard (1825–1904), 65, 76, 171
  Liszt and, 128, 132, 148, 248
  Tausig and, 65
Haraszti, Emile (1885–1958), 217
  Liszt, xiv, n. 2
Harper's Weekly (New York), 94
Hartvigson, Frits (1841–1919), 115, 148
Haslinger, Tobias (1787–1842), 14, 28, 37, 38
Hauptmann, Moritz (1792–1868), 107, 244
Hegel, Georg Wilhelm Friedrich (1770–1831),
  65
Heine, Heinrich (1797–1856), 151, 162, 169

Helbig, Wolfgang, 206
Helene of Orléans, Princess of Mecklenburg-
    Schwerin (1814–1858), 168
Hellmesberger, Joseph (1828–1893), 74
Henselt, Adolf (1814–1889), 82
Henselt (cellist), 79
Henshaw, Grace Mary, 122
Herwegh, Georg (1817–1875), 153
Herz, Henri (1803–1888), 92
Hildebrand, Adolf von (1847–1921), 104
Hiller, Ferdinand (1811–1885), 92
    Liszt's comments on, 235
Hipkins, Alfred James (1826–1903), 115, 127
Hippe pianos (Weimar), 82
Hoffman, Richard (1831–1909), 101
Hoffmann von Fallersleben, August Heinrich
    (1798–1874), 151, 164, 171
    Franz (son) (b. 1855), 164
Hohenlohe-Schillingsfürst, Cardinal Gustav
    Adolf von (1823–1896), 253
Höhne pianos (Weimar), 53
Holle, Ludwig (publisher), 176, 183
Homer (9th–8th c. b.c.), 220
Horowitz, Vladimir (1903–1989), 135, 142
Horowitz-Barnay, Ilka, 7, 8, 10, 135
    Berühmte Musiker, 7
Hoven, Johann van (pseud. for Baron Vesque von
    Püttlingen (1803–1883), 244
Hueffer, Francis (1845–1889), 111, 126–27
Hugo, Victor Marie (1802–1885), 162
Hume, David (1711–1776), 219
Hummel, Johann Nepomuk (1778–1837), 11, 23,
    63, 201
Hüttenbrenner, Anselm (1794–1868), 30

Ibach pianos (Barmen/Cologne), 53
Ives, Charles (1874–1954), 146

Janina, Olga (the "Cossack Countess"). See
    Zielinska-Piasecka, Olga
Jansen, Gustav (1831–1910), 48
Jena (Germany), 55, 74
Jensen, Adolf (1837–1879), 68
Joachim, Joseph (1831–1907), 53, 81, 92, 105, 124,
    144, 183, 247
Johnson, Dr. Samuel (1709–1784), 248
Joseffy, Rafael (1853–1915), 68, 135, 216
    on piano technique, 216
Jota aragónese, 207

Kahnt, Christian Friedrich (1823–1897), 172
Kalbeck, Max (1850–1921), 65

Kalkbrenner, Friedrich (1785–1849), 11, 20, 23,
    25, 190
    "hand-rail," 57, 206
Kant, Immanuel (1724–1804), 65
Karlsruhe Festival (1864), 148, 152
Kellermann, Berthold (1853–1926), xv, 49
Kempff, Wilhelm (1895–1991), 179, 181
Kentner, Louis (1905–1987), 87, 131
Kipling, Rudyard (1865–1936), 143
Klindworth, Karl (1830–1916), 61, 115, 125, 145,
    146, 176
    Chopin edition, 195, 196, 199
    Wagner transcriptions, 116
    Working Men's Society and, **115–16,** 127
Köhler, Louis (1820–1886), 128
Kömpel, August (1831–1891), 74
Krockow, Countess Elizabeth (1820–1882), 75,
    77
Kugler, Pál (1836–1875), 1
Kullak, Theodor (1818–1882), 56, 83, 242

Lachmund, Carl Valentine (1853–1928), 6, 49,
    143, 177, 197, 198, 215
Lachner, Ignaz (1807–1895), 184
La Mara (pseud. for Marie Lipsius) (1837–
    1927), 9
Lamartine, Alphonse Marie Louis de Prat de
    (1790–1869), 219, 248
Lamennais, Abbé Felicité-Robert de (1782–
    1854), 240
Lamond, Frederic Archibald (1868–1948), xvii,
    53, 56, 100, 143, 212–13
Langer, Susanne (1895–1985), 158
Lassen, Eduard (1830–1904), 76, 151, 244
Laub, Ferdinand (1832–1875), 63
Laussot, Jessie (*née* Taylor) (1827–1905), 107
    Eugène (first husband), 107
    Karl Hillebrand (second husband) (1829–
        1884), 107
    Società Cherubini, 107
Lebert, Sigmund (1821–1884), 175, 184, 192
    Grosse Klavierschule, 184
Legouvé, Ernest (1807–1903), 30
Lehmann, Lilli (1848–1929), 101
Leibniz, Gottfried Wilhelm (1646–1716), 219
Leipzig (Germany), 33, 47, 82, 148
    Conservatory of Music, 108, 195
    Gewandhaus, 47
    St. Jacob Hospital, 75
Leipzig *Signale,* 77, 90
Lenau, Nikolaus (1802–1850), 162
Lenbach, Franz von (1836–1904), 105

Lenz, Wilhelm von (1809–1883), 72–73
description of Liszt (1828), **190**
Die grossen Piano Virtuosen unserer Zeit, 190
Leschetizky, Theodor (1830–1915), 56
Lessmann, Otto (1844–1918), 75
obituary of Tausig, 75–76
Lipatti, Dinu (1917–1950), 144
Lisbon (Portugal), 52
Liszt, Franz (1811–1886)
Adam (father) (1776–1827), xvi, 3, 220
Blandine-Rachel (daughter) (1835–1862), 15,
83, 108, 244
Cosima Francesca Gaetana (daughter) (1837–
1930). See Bülow
Daniel Heinrich Franciscus Joseph (son)
(1839–1859), 15, 240, 244
Eduard (uncle-cousin) (1817–1879), 66, 82,
250
Maria Anna (mother) (1788–1866), 244
aphorisms and maxims of, **221–38**
"autobiography" of, xv
Bach and, 232
Beethoven and, xiii, xiv, xvii
edition of the sonatas (1857), **176–84**
Festival in Bonn (1845), 6, **14–15**, 124
"kiss of consecration" (1823), **1–10**
letter to the Memorial Committee (1839), 13
Preface to the symphony transcriptions
(1865), 16–17
conducting of, 15
correspondence of, xiv–xv
creative process of, xv–xvi
critics and, 146–47, 247–48
death of, 125, 253
descriptions of
(1828), 190
(1876), 182
(1883), 197, 198
early education of, 240
editions of
Beethoven 32 Sonatas, xiii, **176–84**, 200
Chopin Preludes, op. 28, xiii, **196–200**
Schubert Collected Keyboard music, xiii,
30, **185–89**
Weber Collected Keyboard music, xiii, 36,
189–94, 200
editorial principles of, **184–85**
"farewell" Vienna concert (1823), 3
"Génie oblige!" 246
Grieg and, 12
hands, description of, 33–34
holy orders and, 95, 202, 252

infant prodigies and, 229–30
library of, 219
Lisztomania, 47
"missing method" of, 213–14
musical education and, 240
Philharmonic Society and, 124
program music and, **225–26**
pupils and, **51–59**
Schubert and, xvii, **29–30, 185**
Schumann and, **40–50**, 211
"Society of Murls," 115
Sword of honour, 52
Tausig and, 61–64
teaching and, **52–59**
virtuosity and, 213
LISZT AT THE PIANO:
fingerings, 19, 33, 135, 188, 190–91, 193,
203–6
finger injury, 12
leaps, 209
notation, 35
note-reiteration, 210–11
octaves, 206–7
pedaling, 26, 136, 188
scales, 203–6
sight-reading, 12
tempo rubato and, 185
tremolandos, 140, 211–12
trills, 208
COMPOSING TECHNIQUES:
"Cross" motif, 132
key-characteristics, 135–36, 162–63, 166
metamorphosis of themes, 130–35, 188
word-painting, **162–69**
word-setting, **157–60**
LISZT THE WRITER, **217–38**
catalogue of holographs, 218
Des Bohémiens et de leur musique en Hongrie,
217, 219
Frédéric Chopin, 217
Maxims and Aphorisms, **221–38**
WORKS
choral compositions:
Christus Oratorio, xvi, 2, 254
Gran Mass, 2, 132, 242–43
Saint Elisabeth Oratorio, 116, 132, 116, 119,
122, 124, 254; "Miracle of the Roses,"
122, 124
Thirteenth Psalm, 112, 113, 245
Via crucis, 132
ORCHESTRAL COMPOSITIONS:
Dante Symphony, 62, 135, 150

Liszt, Franz (1811–1886) (*cont.*)
  Faust Symphony, xvi, 53, 62, 99–100, 112,
    137, 150, 245, 254
  Symphonic Poems:
    Ce qu'on entend sur la Montagne, 62
    Festklänge, 112, 113
    Hamlet, 62
    Hunnenschlacht, 132
    Les Préludes, 62, 63, 254
    Orpheus, 62, 112
    Prometheus, 62
    Tasso, 112
  PIANO AND ORCHESTRA:
    Concerto no. 1, in E-flat Major, 113, 250
    Concerto no. 2, in A Major, 112
    Fantasia on Hungarian Folk-themes, 93
    Fantasia on Themes from Beethoven's *Ruins
      of Athens*, 83
    Totentanz, 204, 254
  SOLO PIANO:
    Cyclical Compositions:
      Années de pèlerinage:
        Volume I ("Suisse"): Au bord d'une
          source, 113; Eglogue, 113
        Volume II ("Italie"): *Dante* Sonata, 125,
          126, 136
        Volume II (Supplement): Venezia e
          Napoli, 119, 126, 211; Tarantella, 211
        Volume III: Les Jeux d'eaux à la Villa
          d'Este, 135, 196, 211; Aux Cyprès de
          la Villa d'Este, 196
      Harmonies poétiques et religieuses, 204:
        Bénédiction de Dieu dans la soli-
        tude, 124, 135, 254; Cantique
        d'Amour, 122; Funérailles (October
        1849), 136, 254
      Hungarian Rhapsodies: no. 4, in E-flat Ma-
        jor, 113; no. 5, in E Minor (Héroïde
        élégiaque"), 126; no. 6, in D-flat
        Major, 70; no. 10, in A Minor, 210;
        no. 15, in A Minor ("Rákóczy
        March"), 206
    Studies:
      6 "Paganini" Studies, 30, 46, 65; no. 2, in E-
        flat Major, 116; no. 3, in G-sharp Mi-
        nor ("La Campanella"), 30, 106, 207,
        254; no. 6, in A Minor, 65
      12 Transcendental Studies, 35, 61, 125, 136, 150,
        167, 195, 204; No. 1, in C Major (*Prelu-
        dio*), 167; no. 3, in F Major (*Paysage*),
        92, 113; no. 4, in D Minor (*Mazeppa*),
        62, 89; no. 7, in E-flat Major (*Eroica*),

    62; No. 8, in C Minor (*Wilde Jagd*),
      113; no. 11, in D-flat Major *(Harmonies
      du soir)*, 56
    Concert Studies: "Gnomenreigen," 56; "La
      leggierezza," 113, 254
    Technical Studies (3 vols.), **202–16;** history
      of, 214–15; scheme of, 215
  Miscellaneous:
    Ballade no. 1, in D-flat Major, 114
    Ballade no. 2, in B Minor, 144
    Fantasie and Fugue on "B.A.C.H.," 75
    Franciscan Legends: No. 1. "St. Francis
      Preaching to the Birds," 114; No. 2. "St.
      Francis Walking on the Waters," 206
    "Marche funèbre" (1827), xvi, 6
    Mephisto Waltz, no. 1, 137, 148, 166, 209
    Petrarch Sonnets, 173
    Polonaises, 114
    Sonata in B Minor, 48, **128–49,** 189, 245,
      250, 254; "double function" structure
      of, 129; duration of, 142; first perfor-
      mance of (1857), 83, **146–47;** Brahms's
      opinion of (1853), 48, 144–45; Han-
      slick's opinion of (1881), 148; Wagner's
      opinion of (1855), 146; interpretations
      of, **141–44;** programmatic content of,
      128; reception of, **146–49**
    "Spanish Rhapsody," 207
    "Weinen, Klagen" Variations, 254
  OPERATIC PARAPHRASES:
    Don Juan Fantasy (Mozart), 63
    "Liebestod" from *Tristan* (Wagner), 211–12
    Rigoletto (Verdi), 213
    Tannhäuser Overture (Wagner), 81
  TRANSCRIPTIONS:
    Beethoven symphonies, **11–26:**
      no. 3, in E-flat Major (*Eroica*), 20, 22–24,
        177
      no. 5, in C Minor, 19–20, 177
      no. 6, in F Major (*Pastorale*), 177
      no. 8, in F Major, 21
      no. 9, in D Minor (*Chorale*), 24–26
    Buch der Lieder für Piano allein (Liszt):
    Volume I
      "Die Lorelei," 152, 172, 173
      "Am Rhein, im schönen Strome," 172
      "Mignons Lied," 152, 172
      "Der König von Thule," 172
      "Der du von dem Himmel bist," 172
      "Angiolin del biondo crin," 172
    Volume II
      "Oh, quand je dors," 173

"Comment disaient-ils," 173
"Enfant, si j'étais rois," 173
"S'il est un charmant gazon," 173
"La tombe et la rose," 173
"Gastibelza," 173
Schubert songs, **27–39**
  "Auf dem Wasser zu singen," 31
  "Ave Maria," 34
  "Die Rose," 28
  "Erlkönig," 29, **31–33**, 35
  "Frühlingssehnsucht," 38
  Geistliche Lieder, 28
  "Gretchen am Spinnrade," **35–36**
  "Ihr Bild," 37
  Müllerlieder, 28
  Sechs Melodien, 28
  Schwanengesang, **37–38**
  "Ständchen," 36–37
  "Ungeduld," 37
  Winterreise, 37
Miscellaneous:
  Chorus of Reapers," from Herder's
    "Prometheus," 113
  "Spinning Song" (Wagner), 95, 115
  "Les Patineurs" (Meyerbeer), 108
  "Soldatenlied," from Goethe's *Faust*,
    113
ORGAN:
Evocation à la Chapelle Sixtine, 9
SONGS:
"Der alte Vagabund," 169
"Der Fischerknabe," 170
"Die drei Zigeuner," 162, 170
"Die Lorelei," **160–62**
"Die Macht der Musik," **168–69**
"Du bist wie eine Blume, 113
"Einst," 167
"Es muss ein Wunderbares sein," 113, 171,
  173
"Freudvoll und leidvoll," 152–53, 171
"Ich möchte hingehn," **153–56**
"Ich scheide," 164, 171
"Im Rhein," **162–64**
"In Liebeslust," 113, 164
"Jeanne d'Arc au bûcher," 162
"Kling leise, mein lied," 171
"Lasst mich ruhen," 164, **165,** 166
"Mignons Lied," **156–59**, 162
"Oh! Quand je dors," 113
"Schwebe, schwebe, blaues Auge," 166
"Was Liebe sei," **167**
"Wie singt die Lerche schön," **164**

"Über allen Gipfeln," 166
"Und wir dachten der Toten," **167–68**
"Vergiftet sind meine Lieder," 169, 171
Littleton, Alfred (1845–1914), 122, 125
Littleton, Henry (1823–1888), 122
Liverpool (England), 90
Lobe, Johann Christian (1797–1881), 177
Loën, Baron August von (1827–1887), 77
Logier, Johann Bernhard (1777–1846), 57
  "Chiroplast," 57
London (England), 33
  Beethoven Rooms, 111
  Chappell building, 111
  Collard's Rooms, 111
  Crystal Palace Concerts, 112, 117, 123
  Grosvenor Gallery, 119, 124, 125
  Hampstead Cemetery, 127
  Queen's Concert Rooms, 111
  Rosslyn Hill Unitarian Chapel, 127
  Royal Academy of Music, 113, 119, 124, 127,
    247
  St. James's Hall, 90, 111, 113, 119, 126, 148
  Victoria Station, 122, 124
London Graphic, 124
Longfellow, Henry Wadsworth (1807–1882), 254
  "A Psalm of Life," 254
Lortzing, Albert (1801–1851), 244
  (France), 35

Macaulay, Baron Thomas Babbington (1800–
  1859), 219
Macfarren, Sir George Alexander (1813–1887),
  107, 122, 123, 247
Mackenzie, Sir Alexander Campbell (1847–
  1935), 122, 123
Madrid (Spain), 52
Mahler, Gustav (1860–1911), 78, 100, 104, 105,
  137, 150
  Das Lied von der Erde, 153
  "Der Abschied," 153
  "Ich bin der Welt abhanden gekommen," 153
  Kindertotenlieder, 154
Manchester (England), 90
  Hallé Orchestra, 91
  Theatre Royal, 210
Manns, Sir August (1825–1907), 91, 112, 117
Maréchal, Henri (1842–1924), 213
Maria Pawlowna (1786–1859), Grand Duchess of
  Weimar (1828–1853), 51, 168
Martineau, Russell, 127
Mason, William (1829–1908), 53, 145, 183
Mayer, Leopold de (1816–1883), 87

Mehlig, Anna (1843–1928), 116
Meiningen Court Orchestra (Germany), 87, 99–100, 247
Mendelssohn-Bartholdy, Felix (1809–1847), 21, 30, 39, 48, 142, 106, 151, 171, 211, 241, 244, 246
   Liszt's comments on, 235
   WORKS
   Fantasie in F-sharp Minor, 108
   Piano Concerto in D Minor, op. 40, 47
   St. Paul (Oratorio), 108
Menter, Sophie (1846–1918), 53, 126
Menzel, Adolf (1815–1905), 105
Merseburg (Germany), 109
   Cathedral organ, 109
Meyendorff (*née* Princess Gortchakova), Baroness Olga (1838–1926), 241, 248
Meyerbeer, Giacomo (pseud. for Jakob Liebmann Beer) (1791–1864), 14, 29, 48
Michelangelo, Buonarotti (1475–1564), 16
   Judgement Day, 9
Mihalovich, Ödön (1842–1929), 253
Milan (Italy), 107
Milde, Hans Feodor von (1821–1899), 8, 151
   Rosa (wife, *née* Agthe) (1827–1906), 151
Milton, John (1608–1674), 219
"Mona Lisa" painting, 188
Montaigne, Michel de (1533–1592), 240
Montez, Lola. *See* Gilbert, Mrs. Eliza
Monthly Musical Record (London), 77, 186
Moreschi, Allessandro (1858–1922), 200
Morrison, Jessie, 148
Moscheles, Ignaz (1794–1870), 14, 15, 29, 107, 195
Mosonyi, Mihály (pseud. for Michael Brandt) (1815–1870), 235
   Liszt's comments on, 235
Mottl, Felix (1856–1911), 105
Mouchanoff-Kalergis, Countess Marie von (1822–1874), 75, 76
Mozart, Wolfgang Amadeus (1756–1791), 29, 39, 52, 138
   Symphony in G Minor, K. 550, 21
Mrazeck, Anna, 84
Muncker, Dr. Theodor von (1823–1900), 125
Munich (Germany), 84, 90, 99
   Royal Opera House, 84, 116
Musical Times, The (London), 90, 91, 102, 127, 148, 209
Musical Trade Review, The (New York), 86
Musset, Alfred de (1810–1857), 219

Napoleon III (1808–1873), Emperor of the French (1852–1870), 240

Nationale Zeitung (Berlin), 146
Nero (a.d. 37–68), Emperor of Rome (a.d. 54–68), 58
Neue Berliner Musikzeitung, 75
Neue Freie Presse (Vienna), 7, 171
Neue Zeitschrift für Musik (Leipzig), 1, 7, 46, 47, 67, 171, 172
Neuhaus, Heinrich (1888–1964), 71
New German School, 100
Newman, Ernest (pseud. for William Roberts) (1868–1959), 249
   The Man Liszt, xiv, 249
Newman, William Stern (1912–2000), 140
New York (America), 149, 214
   Broadway Theatre, 101
   Carnegie Hall, 46
   Chickering Hall, 94
   Steinway Hall, 94
New York Herald (New York), 94
New York Sun (New York), 94
New York World (New York), 86, 97
Niecks, Frederick (1845–1924), 115
Nikisch, Arthur (1855–1922), 100, 103
Nohant (France), 27, 196
Nohl, Ludwig (1831–1885), 9
Nohl, Walther, 1
Nourrit, Adolphe (1802–1839), 35
Novello publishers (London), 122
Nuremburg (Germany), 216

Ortigue, Joseph Louis d' (1802–1866), 5
Overbeck, Baroness Romaine von, *née* Goddard, **95–97**
   Daniel Goddard (father) (b. 1829), 96
   Gustav, Baron von Overbeck (husband), 95, 96
   Madeleine (mother), 96
   Bülow's infatuation with, **95–97**

Pachmann, Vladimir de (1848–1933), 87
Paganini, Niccoló (1782–1840), 30, 235
   Liszt's comments on, 235
Paris (France), 29, 148, 244
   Opera Orchestra, 29, 244
   Salpêtrière Hospital, 240
   St. Eustache Church, 242
Parthia (steamship), 92
Pau (France), 153
Pears, Sir Peter (1910–1986), 160
Pélissier, Marshal Aimable Jean-Jacques (1794–1864), 240
Penguin Book of Lieder, 162
Perau pianos (Berlin), 147
Petersen, Dori (1860–1902), 89

Petri, Egon (1881–1962), 144
Pfitzner, Hans (1869–1949), 159
  Palestrina, 159
Pflughaupt, Robert (1833–1871), 53
Philharmonic Society (London), 52, 106, 118
  Gold Medal of, 90
Philipp, Isidor (1863–1958), 203
Pinelli, Ettore (1843–1915), 109
Pisa (Italy), 13
Pius IX, Pope (Mastai-Ferretti, Giovanni Maria)
  (1792–1878), 251
Plaidy, Louis (1810–1874), 79
Plato (c. b.c. 428–347), 219
Pohl, Richard (1826–1896), 147
Pollini, Maurizio (b. 1942), 142
Ponte a Seraglio (Italy), 77
Pozsony/Pressburg (now Bratislava, Slovakia), 2,
  27, 67
Prague (Czech Republic), 38, 47
Prout, Ebenezer (1835–1909), 115
Pruckner, Dionys (1834–1896), 61, 144, 189
Prussian State Library (Berlin), 5, 8

Quinet, Edgar (1803–1875), 219

Raabe, Felix, 8
Raabe, Peter Carl Ludwig Hermann (1872–
  1945), 28, 148, 155, 158, 162
Rachmaninoff, Sergei (1873–1943), 78, 135, 136
Raff, Joseph Joachim (1822–1882), 81, 145, 244
  Piano trio, 81
Raiding/Doborjan (Hungary), 220, 240, 253
Ramacciotti, Tullio (1819–1910), 108
  Ramacciotti chamber concerts (Rome), 108
Ramann, Lina (1833–1912), 1, 6, 7, 12, 214, 217,
  220
  Liszt biography and, xiv, 5, 29, 48, 239
  Lisztiana, xiv, n. 2
  Liszt Pädagogium, 216
Randhartinger, Benedict (1802–1893), 27, 35
Redoutensaal (Vienna), 1, 3, 7, 9
Reichstag (steamship), 104
Reinecke, Carl (1824–1910), 194
Reisenauer, Alfred (1863–1907), 53
Rellstab, Ludwig (1799–1860), 37, 151
Reményi, Ede (Eduard Hoffmann) (1828–1898),
  144, 183
Remmert, Martha (1854–1941), 127
Reubke, Julius (1834–1858), 144, 244
  Sonata in B-flat Minor, 144
Revue et Gazette musicale, La (Paris), 5, 46
Richarz, Dr. Franz, 48, 57
Richter, Hans (1843–1916), 2, 92, 100

Richter, Sviatislav (1915–1997), 71, 142, 183
Riedel Verein (Leipzig), 74
Riemann, Hugo (1849–1919), 9
Ries, Ferdinand (1784–1838), 7
Riesberg, Frederick W.(1863–1950)
Rietz, Julius (1812–1877), 244
Rohrer, Johann (1783–1868), 240
Rome (Italy), 1, 106, 253
  Aliberti Hotel, 119
  English church, 109
  Madonna del Rosario, xv, 15, 17, 24, 108, 109
  Monte Mario, 17
  San Carlo al Corso, 213
  Santa Francesca Romana, 12
  Sistine Chapel, 9
  Vatican, 16, 109, 251
  Via Aliberti, 213
  Via della Frezza, 108
  Via Felice, 17
Rosen, Charles (b. 1927), 46
Rosenthal, Moriz (1862–1946), xiv, 53, 135, 247
Rousseau, Jean Jacques (1712–1778), 57
Rubinstein, Anton Grigorovich (1829–1894), 33,
  74, 76, 78, 85, 93
  Nicholas (brother) (1835–1881), 93
  Liszt's comments on, 235
  Piano Concerto no. 3, in G Major, 90
Rubinstein, Arthur (1887–1982), 142
Rückert, Johann Michael Friedrich (1788–1866),
  151, 154, 159
Rudorff, Ernst (1840–1916), 92, 194, 195

Saint-Saëns, Charles-Camille (1835–1921), 74,
  148, 213
  description of Liszt, 174
  Liszt's comments on, 237
  virtuosity and, 213
Salieri, Antonio (1750–1825), 27, 29, 30
Sams, Eric (b. 1926), 40
Sand, George (pseud. for Aurore Dupin, Baroness
  Dudevant) (1804–1876), 27, 196
Sauer, Emil von (1862–1942), 28, 53, 144, 247
Sayn-Wittgenstein, Carolyne Jeanne Elisabeth
  von (1819–1887), 15, 62, 66, 81, 98, 128,
  171, 173, 217, 220, 239, 239, 248, 249, 250–
  51
Scarlatti, Domenico (1685–1757), 71, 201
Schauffler, Robert Haven (1879–1964), 40
Scheibe, Johann (1708–1776), 159
Schiller, Johann Christoph Friedrich von (1759–
  1805), 24, 162, 170
Schilling, Gustav (1805–1880), 5
  Encyclopedia, 6

Schindler, Anton Felix (1795–1864)
 Beethoven's *Conversation Books* and, **3–6**, 8
 Biography of Beethoven, 6
Schlegel, Friedrich von (1772–1829), 42
Schlesinger, Maurice (1797–1871), 172, 195
Schlözer, Kurd von (1822–1894), 95, 96
Schmalhausen, Lina (1864–1928), 89
Schnabel, Artur (1882–1951), 78, 135, 179,
 181
Schoenberg, Arnold (1874–1951), 129
 First Chamber Symphony, 129
Schopenhauer, Arthur (1788–1860), 58, 65, 127,
 159–60, 219
Schorn, Adelheid von (1841–1916), 76, 89
Schorn, Karl von (b. 1818), 15
Schott, Anton (1846–1913), 99
Schröder-Devrient, Wilhelmine (1804–1860), 35
Schubert, Franz Peter (1797–1828), 27, 37, 138,
 143
 Ferdinand (brother) (1794–1859), 37
 Liszt's comments on, 235–36
 Liszt's devotion to, 185
 Liszt's edition of, **185–89**
 WORKS
 Opera:
 Alfonso und Estrella, 30
 Piano:
 Divertissement hongroise, 124
 Impromptus:
 in E-flat Major, op. 90, no. 2, 188
 in G-flat Major, op. 90, no. 3, 186
 Ländler, 184
 Moments musicaux, 184
 Sonata in A Major, 69
 Wanderer Fantasie, 30, 129–30, **188–89**
 Songs:
 "Auf dem Wasser zu singen," 28
 "Ave Maria," 28
 "Der Wanderer," 130
 "Die Rose," 28
 "Erlkönig," 28
 "Gretchen am Spinnrade," 159
 "Hörch, hörch, die Lerch!," 28
 Müllerlieder, 28, 37
 Sechs Melodien, 28
 Schwanengesang, **37–38**
 "Ständchen," 36–37
 Winterreise, 28, 37
Schuberth, Julius (1804–1875), 214
Schumann, Robert Alexander (1810–1856), xiv,
 30, 39, 159, **217**, **40–50**, 82, 98, 143, 144,
 246

Clara (wife) (1819–1896), 40–41, 42, 79, 86;
 attitude toward Liszt, 46, 47, 48, **144**, 247
 Liszt's comments on, 236–37
 criticisms of Liszt, **47–48**
 finger injury, 57
 metronome of, 49
 suicide attempt of, 48
 WORKS
 Piano:
 Carnaval, op. 9, 49
 Fantasie in C Major, op. 17, **40–50**
 Humoreske, op. 20, 46
 Kinderszenen, op. 15, 46
 Kreisleriana, op. 16, 46
 Toccata, op. 7, 77
 Chamber music:
 Piano Quintet in E-flat Major, op. 44, 48
 Songs:
 "Widmung" (Myrthen), op. 25, 159
 Orchestral:
 Manfred, op. 115, 48
 Scenes from 'Faust', 48
 Opera:
 Genoveva, op. 81, 48
Seidl, Johann Gabriel (1804–1875), 37
Seneca, Lucius Annaeus (c. 4 b.c.–a.d. 65), 58
Senff, Barthol Wilhelm (1815–1900), 91
Senkrah, Arma (anagram for Mary Harkness)
 (1864–1900), 184
Sgambati, Giovanni (1841–1914), 109
Shakespeare, William (1564–1616), 16
Sheffield (England), 90
Siegel, Jeffrey (b. 1942), 46
Siloti, Alexander (1863–1945), 53, 247
Simson, Herr (attorney), 85
Singer, Otto (1833–1894), 19, 21–22
Smart, Sir George Thomas (1776–1867), 14
Smetana, Bedřich (1824–1884), 237
 Liszt's comments on, 237
Smith, Mr. Noble, 209
 finger operation of, 209
Sobelewski, Friedrich (1808–1872), 244
 Vinvela, 250
Solfanelli, Father Antonio (Liszt's theology tutor),
 202
Solomon, Cutner (1902–1988), 183
Sonntag, Elsa, 198
Sothebys (London), 40, 41
Spener'sche Zeitung (Berlin), 146
Spielhagen, Friedrich (1829–1911), 105
Spina, Anton (1790–1857), 176
Spitzweg, Eugen (1840–1914), 98

Spohr, Ludwig (1784–1859), 14, 106
  Liszt's comments on, 237
Spoleto (Italy), 202
Stark, Ludwig (1831–1884), 184
Steinway Hall (New York), 94
Steinway pianos (New York), 94–95
Stern Conservatory (Berlin), 83
Steubenville (America), 95
Stimpson, James (1820–1886), 107
St. Gallen (Switzerland), 99
St. Louis (America), 97
St. Petersburg (Russia), 33, 119
  Hall of the Nobles, 72–73
Strachwitz, Count Moritz (1822–1847), 71
  Out of the Northlands, 71
Stradal, August (1860–1930), 220
Strauss, Johann (1825–1899), 71
Strauss, Richard (1865–1949), 78, 87, 104, 137
  description of Bülow, 87
  Macbeth, 100
  Serenade for Thirteen Wind Instruments, 100
  Symphony in F Minor, 100
Stravinsky, Igor (1882–1971), 160
  The Rake's Progress, 160
Street-Klindworth, Agnes (1825–1906), 248
Streicher pianos (Vienna), 52
Strelezki, Anton (pseud. for Theophilus Burnand)
  (1859–1907), 33
Stuttgart Conservatory (Germany), 184
Sue, Eugéne (1804–1857), 219
Sullivan, Sir Arthur Seymour (1842–1900), 106
  Liszt and, 124–25
Suttoni, Charles, xiv
  Liszt Correspondence in Print, xiv

Tartini, Guiseppe (1692–1770), 109
  Devil's Trill Sonata, 109
Tausig, Carl (1841–1871), xiv, 26, 51, **60–78**, 147,
  176, 189, 203
  Aloys (father) (1820–1885), 60–61, 147
  Brahms and, **65–66**, 70
  Chopin interpretations of, 67, 76, 78
  descriptions of his playing, 60, 63, 65, **67–68**,
    73, **78**
  funeral of, 75, 76
  ill-health of, 66–67
  insolvency of, 66
  Liszt and, **60–63**, 73–74
  marriage and divorce of, 67
  obituary of, 75–76
  School for Advanced Piano Playing, 68–69,
    73

Wagner committee chairman, 64, 77
Wagner and, **64**
  WORKS
  Original:
    Das Geisterschiff, **71–72**
    Le Ruisseau, 71
    L'Espérance, 71
    Rêverie, 71
    Tägliche Studien, 69, 70
    "Ten Preludes," 70
  Transcriptions:
    Beethoven quartet transcriptions, 26
    Die Meistersinger, 62, 159
    "Liebestod" from *Tristan* (Wagner), 64
    "Ride of the Valkyrie" (Wagner), 64
Tchaikovsky, Peter (1840–1893), 93
  Piano Concerto no. 1, in B-flat Minor, op. 23,
    93
  Symphony no. 4, in F Minor, op. 36, 140
Tennyson, Lord Alfred (1809–1892), 200
Thalberg, Sigismond (1812–1871), 60
  Liszt's comments on, 237
Thayer, Alexander Wheelock (1817–1897), 9
Thomán, István (1862–1940), 129
Thomas, Theodore (1836–1905), 101
Tiefurt (Germany), 55
Timanova, Vera Victorovna (1855–1942), 69
Times, The (London), 111
Tivoli (Italy), 196, 253
  Villa d'Este, 56, 196
Tonkünstler-Versammlung, 173
Topp, Alida, 148
  Liszt's opinion of, 148
Toscanini, Arturo (1867–1957)
Tovey, Sir Donald Francis (1875–1940), 11, 20,
  178, 183
  Essays in Musical Analysis, 11
Triebschen (Switzerland), 77
Trieste (Italy), 104
Trollope, Anthony (1815–1882), 219
Tromlitz, Marianne (1797–1872), 195

Uhland, Ludwig (1787–1862), 151
Uhlrich, Karl Wilhelm (1815–1874), 74
Ullman, Bernard, 92, 93, 94, 98
Unitarian Church, 126
Unitarian Journal (London), 127
  obituary of Bache, 126
Urhan, Chrétien (1790–1845), **29–30**
  String Quintets based on Schubert, 30
  Piano Studies based on Schubert songs,
    30

Vác (Hungary), 1

Verdi, Guiseppe (1813–1901), 29, 39

Viardot-Garcia, Michelle Ferdinande Pauline
(1821–1910), 74

Victoria (1819–1901), Queen of England (1837–
1901), 14, 119, 125
description of Liszt, 124

Vienna (Austria), 46, 66, 82, 148
Kunsthistorisches Museum, 53
Opera House, 66
Redoutensaal, 1
Schwarzspanier House, 7, 8
University, 65

Vinton, Samuel Finlay (1792–1862), 96

Viole, Rudolf (1825–1867), 144
Piano Sonata, 144

Voltaire (pseud. for François Marie Arouet)
(1694–1778), xiii, 219, 240, 254

Vrabély, Szerafina von (1841–1931), 67, 75
Stephanie (sister), 67

Wagner, Richard Wilhelm (1813–1883), xv, 39,
88, 94, 100, 101, 137, 243, 245
Eva (daughter) (1867–1942), 84
Isolde Ludowika Josepha (daughter) (1865–
1919), 84
Siegfried (son) (1869–1930), 84
Bayreuth Festival, 64, 84
Erard piano of, 64
Liszt's comments on, 237–38
marriage to Cosima, 84
Mein Leben, xiii, 64, 66, 75
opinion of Liszt's B Minor Sonata, **146**
Patron's Voucher Committee, 64, 77
Tausig and, **64**; epitaph for, 77
WORKS
Fliegende Holländer, Der, 115, 243
Götterdämmerung, 104
Lohengrin, 81, 94, 99, 243
Meistersinger, Die, 66, 84, 92, 99
Rheingold, Das, 116
Tannhäuser, 243
Tristan und Isolde, 66, 84, 90, 99, 155, 160
Walküre, Die, 101, 116

Walker, Bettina (d. 1893), 68

Walter, Bruno (1876–1962), 102–3

Walter, Theresa (1819–1866), 28

Wangemann, Theodore, 101–2

"War of the Romantics," 82, 151–52, 171–72,
244

Warsaw (Poland), 60, 61, 196

Washington, D.C. (America), 95, 97
German embassy, 95
Library of Congress, 98, 218

Wasielewski, Wilhelm Joseph von (1822–1896),
49, 131

Weber, Carl Maria von (1786–1826), xiii, 71,
99, 136
"Concertstück," 184
Der Freischütz, 99, 190
"Invitation to the Dance," 190
Liszt's edition of, **189–94**
Momento Capriccioso, 184, 189
Polonaise Brillante, op. 72, 117
Sonatas:
no. 1, in C Major, op. 24, **190–93**
no. 2, in A-flat Major, op. 39, 185
no. 2, in D Minor, op. 49, 193

Weimar (Germany)
Altenburg, description of, **51–53**, 61, 81–82,
144, 147, 164, 183
Belvedere Allee, 53
Court Theatre, 77, 176
Erbprinz Hotel, 55, 81
Grand Ducal Park, 165
Herder Festival, 81
Hofgärtnerei, description of, **53–54**, 59
Marienstrasse, 53
String Quartet, 183

Weimarisches Jahrbuch, 164

Weingartner, Felix (1863–1942), 15, 55, 56, 100,
105
Beethoven interpretations of, 15, 183
description of Liszt, 55
On Conducting, 100

Weissheimer, Wendelin (1838–1910), 66

Weitzmann, Carl Friedrich (1808–1880), 68,
114

Wenzel, Johanna (d. 1928), 57

Wessel, Christian Rudolph (1797–1885), 196

Westwood House (Sydenham), 122

Wieck, Friedrich (1785–1873), 47, 79–80, 195
Clara (daughter). *See* Schumann, Clara
Clavier und Gesang, 57
on Liszt, 47
teacher of Bülow, 79–80

Wiener Allgemeine Zeitung (Vienna), 4

Wieniawski, Henryk (1835–1880), 183, 197

Wieniawski, Józef (1837–1912), 197

Wild, Dr. (physician), 104

Wilhelm Friedrich (1795–1861), King of Prussia
(1840–1861), 14

Wilhelmj, August (1845–1908), 112
Willheim, Etelka, 55
Windsor Castle (England), 124
Winklhofer, Sharon, 140
Winterberger, Alexander (1834–1914), 109, 214
Wohl, Janka (1846–1901), 242
Wolfenbüttel (Germany), 176
Wolff, Dr. O. L. B. (1799–1851), 14, 15
Wolff, Hermann (1845–1902), 102

Wolfrum, Philip (1854–1919), 28
Woronince (Ukraine), 173

Yale University Library, 125

Zeyl, Henryk van, 177
Zielinska-Piasecka, Olga ("Olga Janina") (b. 1845), xiv, 186
   Liszt and, 214, 249
Zurich (Switzerland), 64, 99

Lightning Source UK Ltd.
Milton Keynes UK
UKHW02f1244200518

322825UK00006B/333/P